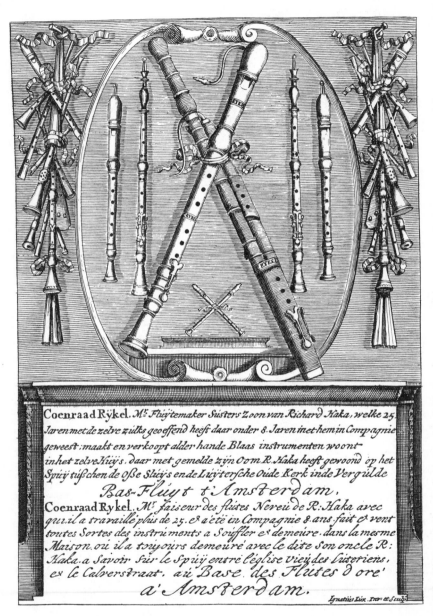

AN 18TH-CENTURY WIND INSTRUMENT MAKER'S TRADE CARD

Musical Wind Instruments

Adam Carse

Dover Publications, Inc.
Mineola, New York

Bibliographical Note

This Dover edition, first published in 2002, is an unabridged republication of the
work originally published by Macmillan and Co., Limited, London, 1939.

Library of Congress Cataloging-in-Publication Data

Carse, Adam von Ahn, 1878–1958.
    Musical wind instruments / Adam Carse.
       p. cm.
    An unabridged republication of the work originally published by Macmillan,
London, 1939.
    Includes bibliographical references (p.) and index.
    ISBN 0-486-42422-7 (pbk.)
       1. Wind instruments. I. Title.

ML930.C38 M9 2002
788'.19—dc21

                                                                2002067319

Manufactured in the United States of America
Dover Publications, Inc., 31 East 2nd Street, Mineola, N.Y. 11501

PREFACE

The following pages are concerned mainly with the wind instruments which have been used for cultured music in European orchestras, military and other wind-bands during the last four centuries ; these are, the various types and sizes of the flute, oboe, clarinet and bassoon families, popularly classed as " woodwind ", and those usually described as " brass " instruments, comprising trumpets, cornets, horns, trombones, bugles and kindred types. With the former are associated a few all-metal instruments which employ similar methods of sound-production, such as saxophones and sarrusophones, and with the latter a number of obsolete instruments sounded by means of cupped mouthpieces, such as serpents, keyed bugles and ophicleides. The above limitations, therefore, exclude wind instruments of the organ, harmonium, accordion and bagpipes families, also some of low musical status and a number of primitive or pastoral instruments used for giving sound-signals or for the untutored music-making of peasant folk.

The sources of information on which an historical survey of the development of wind instruments must depend are : (a) a large number of old instruments now preserved in public and private collections, together with descriptive catalogues and photographs of the same ; (b) written descriptions, instructions for playing on them, fingering charts and illustrations of old instruments from contemporary sources ; (c) contemporary music specifically written for the instruments. Hardly any wind instruments made earlier than the 16th century have survived the passage of over 400 years ; the first books to yield technical information on musical instruments and on how to play them are those by Virdung (1511) and his adaptors Agricola (1528) and Luscinius (1536) ; little or no music for wind instruments earlier than the 17th century is available ; such information as

v

may be gathered from all sources previous to the 16th century is therefore scanty, speculative and non-technical. The occurrence of the names of wind instruments in the records and literature of the Middle Ages, or contemporary pictorial or carved representations of such, do little more than establish the existence of certain types at more or less vague periods, but even when these can be identified with certainty, more precise details as to measurements, pitch, scale, compass, mechanical equipment and technical capabilities are not forthcoming till the 16th century yields its actual instruments and contemporary written information concerning them ; it is only then that the historian can begin to get into close touch with his material. In these pages no attempt is made to penetrate the darkness which obscures the development of wind instruments in the dim prehistoric past or in the musically remote Middle Ages ; the story begins with the oldest surviving 16th-century instruments and the homely words of Sebastian Virdung.

Undoubtedly the most satisfying historical evidence is that which is provided by actual instruments, tangible objects that can be seen, handled, examined, photographed, or which may perhaps even be made to sound. The value of the evidence they supply may depend to some extent on how accurately they can be dated. Brass instruments of all periods very generally bear the names of the maker and the town where he worked, and the inscriptions on those made from early in the 16th up to about the end of the 18th century frequently include the year of manufacture ; these dated instruments tell their story and announce their period with welcome precision. On the other hand, it was only towards the close of the 17th century that makers began to inscribe their names on wood-wind instruments, and even after that time they were rarely dated ; thus, estimates of the period of the earlier wooden instruments must allow room for a considerable margin of error, but the inscribed instruments of the 18th century can generally be placed with fair certainty within a period of about twenty or twenty-five years. The more precise records of 19th-century makers which are available make it possible to date their instruments of both classes with a still smaller margin of error. Whatever their age, the detail on old wind instruments demands close scrutiny, and the investigator must always be on the alert to detect signs of alterations or additions made at some later period.

Some of the particulars which cannot be gleaned from surviving specimens may be supplied by the 16th- and 17th-century treatises on musical instruments. If Virdung and his immediate followers were much too reticent about the brass instruments of their day, they were the first to give the compass and fingering for such flutes and double-reed instruments as they knew. The famous works of Praetorius (1619) and Mersenne (1636) are important and much more comprehensive and specific ; it is true, both authors sometimes withhold the very information for which the enquirer is most anxiously searching, and if they are all too sparing with names and dates, and are not very sure of their ground when dealing with acoustical matters, what they contributed to a knowledge of wind instruments in the first half of the 17th century is much too valuable to be ignored ; rather than dwell on their shortcomings, the historian might well wish there had been a Praetorius or a Mersenne to cover the same ground in the second half of the same century.

Speer's book of 1687, Mattheson's of 1713 and Walther's Lexikon of 1732 are useful sources from which many later 18th-century writers derived their information. A large number of 18th-century dictionaries, encyclopedias, histories, essays and periodicals, both musical and general, provide ample and widely scattered material for research. It is true that much of the matter concerning wind instruments in this comprehensive field can be recognised as having been derived from earlier sources, and although statements handed on from one book to another are only too often blindly accepted without question, and much out-of-date or unauthenticated matter is repeated with wearying persistence, the investigator cannot afford to ignore any possible source of enlightenment even if the yield be small in comparison with the labour expended in research.

The instruction books or tutors for wind instruments, which began to appear towards the close of the 17th century and increased considerably in number during the course of the 18th century, are of value mainly on account of the technical information they impart ; even if the instructions contained in most of these are often ridiculously concise, much that is indispensable and which cannot be found elsewhere may be learned from the fingering charts which are usually provided in these contemporary tutors.

Illustrations of wind instruments, usually woodcuts, are to be found in many of the old musical treatises and instruction books, and they occur occasionally in paintings, engravings and etchings by reputable artists of all periods.   The latter may provide good evidence of how an instrument was held when it was being played, and from such sources we may learn for what purpose an instrument was used, on what occasions it might be played and with what other instruments it was customarily combined.   It would be unwise, however, to accept implicitly everything that contemporary pictorial evidence may offer ; some of the woodcuts are obviously badly drawn, ill-proportioned and inaccurate, and inferior artists have made grievous blunders when depicting instruments which they did not understand ; better artists have sometimes succeeded in making the wind instruments in their pictures look more convincing, and if the detail may not always satisfy the musician, it must be remembered that the instrument is there for the sake of the picture and not for the purpose of providing future musical historians with reliable evidence.   Good photographs of existing specimens, such as are found in some of the more recent catalogues, supply useful and dependable evidence ; much may be lost, however, if an instrument is inexpertly posed.

17th-century music written for wind instruments demonstrates the limitations of musical art at that period quite as much as it does the limitations of contemporary instruments, but an abundance of 18th-century wind parts show not only what was expected of the executants and instruments at that time but also what could evidently be done on instruments equipped with only very few mechanical facilities. With the 19th century the amount of evidence obtainable from such sources as have already been reviewed becomes almost embarrassingly abundant, and to these are added such as Patent Records with diagrams, catalogues of exhibitions, trade advertisements, a quantity of the more precise records of more recent happenings, and memories stored with knowledge of events which even now are not too remote for human recollection. Much has been written about wind instruments during the last century of which accumulation the greater part is only to be found scattered about in scores of books, catalogues, pamphlets, periodicals and so forth. Too much of it consists of the mere repetition of statements which have been handed on from one book to another, through edition after edition of musical dictionaries, by authors who were not in touch with original sources and have been content to accept the printed words of other writers without verifying or investigating the truth of such statements afresh ; in this way, as the result of constant repetition and amplification, many statements which originated as mere suggestions or surmises have gained currency and are now accepted as historical facts.

In view of the vast accumulation of evidence from all sources it might be supposed that there is little of the history of wind instruments that is not known. This is far from being the case ; there are still many gaps in the historical sequence of events which cannot be filled up ; many significant names and important dates are missing ; not even all the wind instruments named in 18th-century scores can be identified with certainty. The answers to some awkward questions will not be found in these or in any other pages ; sources of information hitherto unknown may yet be discovered and some of the blanks may be filled up, but, probably because it was nobody's business to record such things or because their importance was not realised at the time, it is to be feared that many pertinent questions which still confront the enquirer into the history of wind instruments will remain for ever unanswered.

For their readiness to impart information, and for kind assistance which has considerably lightened the labour of research, the author is much indebted to the following : W. H. F. Blandford, Esq., R. B. Chatwin, Esq., A. Falkner, Esq., Canon Galpin, L. G. Langwill, Esq., Professor Dayton C. Miller (Cleveland, U.S.A.) and F. G. Rendall, Esq., and for preparing eleven line-drawings and diagrams he wishes to acknowledge the kind help of his brother, A. D. Carse, Esq.

ADAM CARSE

GT. MISSENDEN, 1938

CONTENTS

xi

PLATES

FINGERING CHARTS

ABBREVIATIONS, DEFINITIONS, ETC.

THE notes of the musical staff are normally given in Roman capitals, but when it is necessary to indicate the notes in any particular octave the following plan is adopted :

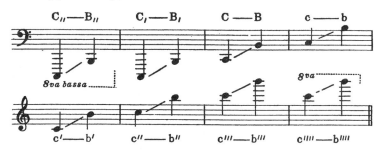

R. = Right or right hand.   L. = Left or left hand.

(E.) = English.   (G.) = German.   (F.) = French.   (I.) = Italian.

The *head* or *upper end* of an instrument = the end at which it is blown.

The *foot, lower end* or *bell* of an instrument = the opposite end, even though it may be uppermost when the instrument is being played.

The *right* or *right-hand side* ⎫ of an instrument = these sides from the
The *left* or *left-hand side* ⎭ standpoint of the player.

The *top, upper side* or *front* of an instrument = that which faces upwards or forwards when the instrument is being played.

The *bottom, under side* or *back* of an instrument = that which faces downwards or towards the player when the instrument is being played.

Fingers are named thus : thumb, first, second, third and little finger, and not as in " continental " piano-fingering.

In the Bibliography will be found the titles of books, etc., which are referred to in the text by the authors' names.

Public collections of instruments are named according to the town where they are situated.

CLASSIFICATION OF WIND INSTRUMENTS

WIND instruments are popularly divided into two large classes, namely, " wood-wind " and " brass " ; this classification is serviceable because it is concise and it is generally understood ; thus, for ordinary purposes it is convenient to regard all of the flute, oboe, clarinet, saxophone and bassoon families under the general heading of wood-wind instruments, and those of the trumpet, cornet, horn, trombone, tuba or bugle types as belonging to the family of brass instruments. Any classification of wind instruments which is based on the material from which they are made is, however, both inaccurate and unscientific ; the so-called " wood-wind " may be made of metal, ivory, glass, or of artificial compounds such as ebonite, and the " brass " may be made of silver, copper, ivory, horn or even of wood.

A two-group classification of wind instruments might be attempted according to whether the sounding-length of the tube is *shortened* by the use of finger- or key-holes in the side of the tube, or *lengthened* by the use of valves or slides which normally add tubing when they are operated. The prospect seems inviting at first sight, yet when put to the test this method of classification soon breaks down ; in the first place, it does not accommodate a large class of obsolete instruments which were musically of the " brass " type yet which employed the shortening-hole system, namely, the old cornetts, the serpents, bass-horns, keyed bugles and ophicleides ; it allows no place for " natural " brass instruments which are not mechanically either shortened or lengthened, such as bugles, fanfare trumpets, hunting horns, etc., and the ascending or shortening valve also steps in to upset any two-group classification which is based on shortening or lengthening devices. A two-group division based on the proportions of the tube, that is, whether conical or cylindrical, or both, offers no hope of a classification which corresponds to the popular conception of " wood-wind " and " brass ", for both varieties of tube occur inextricably mixed up in a way which would bring widely different instruments into the same class.

It would be almost feasible to embrace in a wood-wind class all instruments of which the bore is wide in proportion to its length and which therefore make use of the fundamental and only a few of the lower sounds of the natural harmonic series, and in a brass class all those of which the tube, being narrower in proportion to its length, will produce more freely the higher harmonics up to the eighth or even the sixteenth open notes while at the same time losing facility in sounding the fundamental and the lower harmonics. Such a classification, however, would prove to be not quite watertight owing to the fact that certain wide-bored brass instruments do make some use of the fundamental while at the same time they may easily reach the eighth sound of the harmonic series. Certain brass signalling instruments of a rather primitive type which are so wide-bored that they can sound little more than the fundamental would also find out a weak place in a classification which is based on the proportions of the tube.

There remains only one other system of classification which will correspond to the popular wood-wind and brass groups ; that is to divide the instruments into classes according to the method of sound-generation which is employed in playing them. This offers the best hope of a satisfying theory, and provides two classes which may be distinguished as follows :

CLASS A. (Brass).—All instruments on which the sound is generated by *lip-reeds* in conjunction with a cupped or conical mouthpiece. [Trumpets, horns, trombones, cornets, tubas, bugles, etc.]

CLASS B. (Wood-wind).—All wind instruments which employ other means of sound-generation, i.e. *air-reeds* or *cane-reeds*. [Flutes, oboes, clarinets, saxophones, bassoons, etc.]

The latter class, however, includes two such widely differing methods of sound-generation that a further subdivision is imperative ; hence, instead of only two classes which are covered by the common expressions brass and wood-wind, a division of wind instruments into *three* classes, one of which is brass and the other two wood-wind, seems to offer the only quite satisfying theory, and is moreover quite free from the weaknesses inherent in any other system of classification :

CLASS A. *Brass or lip-reed*. [Trumpets, horns, trombones, cornets, saxhorns, tubas, bugles, serpents, keyed bugles, ophicleides, etc.]

CLASS B. *Wood-wind with air-reed*. [Transverse flutes, fifes, recorders, flageolets, etc.]

CLASS C. *Wood-wind with cane-reed*. [Oboes, clarinets, bassoons, saxophones, sarrusophones, etc.]

The above classification is accurate and scientifically sound, although it may not altogether satisfy the musician, who will always be inclined to group the two classes B and C in one large wood-wind class. A further subclassification of the above three classes according to their methods of sound-generation cannot be made in the case of class A, but classes B and C both demand further subdivision, thus :

CLASS B.
(1) *The free air-reed*. [Transverse flutes, piccolos, fifes, etc.]
(2) *The confined air-reed*. [All whistle-flutes, i.e. recorders, flageolets, etc.]

CLASS C.
(1) *The single cane-reed*. [All clarinets including basset-horns, saxophones, octavins, etc.]
(2) *The double cane-reed*. [Oboes, cor anglais, etc., bassoons, sarrusophones, Heckelphones, etc.]

No further grouping can be made without falling back on methods which have already been rejected in forming the three main groups of wind instruments ; but, as it is necessary to differentiate between instruments which in their methods of sound-generation are alike, yet which differ in other respects, some smaller subclasses must be formed by taking into consideration essential features which have considerable effect on the characteristic tone-quality and the technique of the various types.

In class A (lip-reed or brass) three important methods of subclassification are necessary ; these are made by grouping the instruments according to : (a) the proportions of the tube ; (b) the mechanical means of either shortening or lengthening the tube, or the absence of any such device ; (c) the shape of the hollow or " cup " of the mouthpiece. According to (a) the lip-reed instruments may be classified as follows :

(1) *Instruments with mainly cylindrical bore.* [Trumpets, trombones.]

(2) *Instruments with mainly conical bore.* [Cornets, valved French horns, saxhorns or valved bugle-horns of all sizes, tubas, etc.]

(3) *Instruments with almost entirely conical bore.* [Bugles, hunting horns, coach horns, posthorns, and all " brass " instruments with keys or finger-holes, such as cornetts, serpents, keyed bugles, ophicleides, etc.]

A regrouping of the same instruments can be made according to the comparative width of the bore ; this, however, cannot be carried out with any great precision owing to many variations which are in some cases too small for exact classification :

(1) *Narrow bore.* [Trumpets, cornets, French horns, trombones.]

(2) *Wider bore.* [Bugles, flügelhorns and keyed bugles ; alto, tenor and baritone saxhorns or bugle-horns ; (still wider) euphoniums, tubas and bombardons ; (very wide) serpents, ophicleides.]

According to (b) the brass instruments are grouped as follows:

(1) *Tube shortened by finger- or key-holes.* (All obsolete.) [Cornetts ; serpents and bass-horns ; keyed bugles and keyed trumpets ; ophicleides, etc.]

(2) *Tube lengthened (normally) by valve-systems.* [Trumpets and cornets ; all sizes of valved bugle-horns, saxhorns, tubas, etc. ; French horns ; valved trombones.]

(3) *Tube lengthened by slide-systems.* [Slide trumpets and trombones.]

(4) *Tube of fixed length* (or only alterable by crooks or shanks). [Natural, cavalry and fanfare trumpets ; hand and French hunting horns ; bugles ; posthorns and coach horns ; stop-trumpets.]

Finally, according to (c), the brass or lip-reed instruments can be only approximately grouped as follows :

(1) *Shallow, cupped mouthpiece.* [Old trumpets, medieval cornetts.]

(2) *Deep, conical mouthpiece* (funnel-shaped). [French horns.]

(3) *Mouthpieces in varying degree between* (1) *and* (2). [All other instruments in class A.]

The so-called wood-wind classes (B and C) require further subdivision according to the nature of the bore ; this may be almost entirely cylindrical, partially cylindrical, or almost entirely conical, and in the latter case the wide end may be either at the head (mouthpiece end) or at the foot or bell end :

(1) *Cylindrical or largely cylindrical bore :*

Class B. (a) *Free air-reed.* [Boehm flutes, fifes.]

Class C. (b) *Single cane-reed.* [Clarinets of all sizes including basset-horns.]

(2) *Conical bore, widest at the head :*

Class B. { (a) *Free air-reed.* [Non-Boehm flutes, piccolos.]
{ (b) *Confined air-reed.* [Recorders, flageolets, etc.]

(3) *Conical bore, widest at the bell :*

Class B. (None).

Class C. { (a) *Single cane-reed.* [Saxophones, octavins.]
{ (b) *Double cane-reed.* [Oboes, etc., bassoons, sarrusophones, Heckelphones.]

The wood-wind classes B and C do not admit of classification according to the method of shortening or lengthening the tube, for all the instruments in both of these classes employ only the system by which the sounding-length of the tube is reduced by opening finger- or key-holes ; they can, however, be roughly divided into groups of which the bores are comparatively wide or narrower in proportion to the lengths of the tubes, thus :

(1) *Cylindrical bore :*

    (a) *Wider.* [Cylindrical or Boehm flutes.]

    (b) *Narrower.* [Clarinets.]

(3) *Conical bore :*

    (a) *Wider.* [Saxophones, sarrusophones, Heckelphones.]

    (b) *Narrower.* [Oboes, etc., bassoons.]

Another feature of classes B and C which can be taken into account is the size of the finger- or key-holes (note-holes) in proportion to the length of the tube. A precise classification under this heading is hardly feasible owing to the fact that the size of a note-hole generally varies according to its situation in the tube, those nearer the mouthpiece end being rather smaller than those situated near the bell or foot. The size of a note-hole also varies more or less according to the period of the instrument, and may depend on whether it is closed by a finger or by a key. Nevertheless, a rough classification under this heading would be as follows :

(a) *Large note-holes.* [Modern flutes, saxophones, sarrusophones, Heckelphones.]

(b) *Medium note-holes.* [Clarinets, old transverse flutes, whistle-flutes.]

(c) *Small note-holes.* [Oboes, etc., bassoons.]

On the same basis, the instruments of class A which are shortened by opening note-holes in the side of the tube fall into two sections according to whether the holes are closed by the fingers or by keys, thus :

(a) *Small finger-holes.* [Cornetts, serpents, bass-horns, etc.]

(b) *Larger key-holes.* [Keyed bugles, ophicleides, etc.]

The foregoing methods of classification still leave in the same class some instruments which, however closely allied they may be in principle, still demand separation when regarded from a musical standpoint ; for example, oboes and bassoons have gone hand in hand through all the subclasses in a way which may satisfy the scientist but will not convince the musician who (quite rightly) cannot regard a bassoon as being merely a large-sized oboe. Individual features which make one instrument different from another, although they may seem more or less insignificant, are nevertheless often vital, and if every peculiarity were to be taken into account, the classification of wind instruments might be carried on to such lengths that in the end almost every instrument would be found to stand in a class by itself.

Indeed, it seems as if it were impossible to make a classification which would be both scientifically and musically quite convincing. A difference of pitch (register) alone is enough to make a musical classification opposed to one which is purely scientific ; the musical function of a soprano instrument differs so much from that of a bass instrument that their kinship, although scientifically of the closest, may be musically quite remote.

It would serve no useful purpose to carry the classification to such extremes that every slight variation in tone-quality, proportions, mechanism, material, shape or register would be recognised. The following is an attempt to summarise the foregoing classification by methods which are rational even though not always artistically true :

Class A. Lip-reed (Brass)

Mechanism	Bore		Instruments	Mouthpiece
None	Mainly cylindrical. Narrow		Old trumpets Cavalry and fanfare trumpets	Cup Deeper cup
	Conical	Wide Narrow Narrow	Bugles Coach and posthorns Hand horns French hunting horns	Various Cornet or bugle Cone or funnel
Finger- or Key-holes (Shortening)	Conical	Wide Very wide Wide Wide Wide	Cornetts (Zinken) Serpents Bass-horns Keyed bugles Ophicleides	Cup Cup Intermediate Intermediate Intermediate
Valves (Lengthening)	Mainly cylindrical. Narrow		Valve trumpets Valve trombones	Cup to intermediate Intermediate
	Conical and cylindrical. Narrow.		Modern cornets Old cornets	Intermediate Conical (Lily-shaped)
	Mainly conical	Narrow Wider Wide	Valved French horns Flügelhorns, alto, tenor and baritone saxhorns and bugle-horns Euphoniums, tubas or bombardons	Cone or funnel Intermediate Intermediate
Slides (Lengthening)	Mainly cylindrical. Narrow		Slide trumpets Slide trombones	Cup Intermediate

CLASSES B AND C (WOOD-WIND)

CLASS	SOUND-GENERATOR	SUBDIVISION	BORE	INSTRUMENTS
B	Air-reed	Confined air-reed (whistle)	Conical, blown at wide end	Flûtes-à-bec, plockflöten, recorders, flageolets, etc.
		Free air-reed (mouth-hole)	Conical, blown at wide end	Flutes, piccolos, late 17th century to 19th century
			Cylindrical	Early transverse flutes, fifes, modern flutes
C	Double cane-reed	Reed in air-chamber or pirouette	Conical or cylindrical	Shawms, pommers, krumhorns, etc.
		Reed directly controlled by the lips	Conical, blown at narrow end	Dulcians (early bassoons)
				Oboes with expanding bell
				Oboes with bulb-bell (cor anglais, etc.)
				Bassoons
				Sarrusophones (metal)
				Heckelphones
	Single cane-reed		Conical	Saxophones (metal) Octavins (wood)
			Cylindrical	Clarinets, basset-horns, etc.

SOUND GENERATORS AND RESONATORS

A WIND instrument is made to sound by causing air to vibrate inside a hollow container. The most serviceable form of container is a tube enclosing a column of air which is thus separated from the surrounding air by the walls of the tube. The column of air, however, must not be completely isolated ; it must be in touch with the surrounding air, therefore some part of the tube, usually one end of it, must be open.

The bore or inside of the tube may be of the same width throughout (cylindrical) or it may expand or contract (conical), or it may be partially cylindrical and partially conical, and the whole may be straight or curved. To be of any practical use the tube must be made of some sufficiently hard and rigid material, and the inside must be smooth ; therefore, wind instruments are commonly made of either hard close-grained woods, of metal, or of hard composite substances such as ebonite ; they have also been made of ivory or horn. The choice of material is governed largely by its suitability to stand the process of manufacture, by its weight and ability to wear well when in use, and sometimes by its capacity for being bent or coiled into shapes convenient to handle and play.

In addition to a tube or *resonator*, all wind instruments except those of a very primitive type are provided with some means of assisting the player to make the column of air vibrate inside the tube. Musical sound will not be created by merely pushing a quantity of air *through* a tube ; actually, very little air passes through a wind instrument when it is being played. The air-stream or wind from the player's mouth must be compressed or intensified as it is injected into the instrument, otherwise it will fail to set up the vibration which is communicated to the column

of air in the tube, and which creates musical sound. This state
of vibration may be initiated at any part of the tube, but it is
most conveniently done at or near one end, and, in the case of
a conical tube, it is usually, but not necessarily, generated at the
narrow end.

The quality of the sound (*timbre*) of a wind instrument is
governed mainly by the nature of the means employed to generate vibration. Other conditions which influence the tone-quality
are the proportions of the tube, whether wide or narrow for its
length, and whether expanding (conical) or cylindrical ; the
material of which the tube is made, provided it is sufficiently
dense and rigid, has either little or no effect on tone-quality.

To the two foregoing essentials, namely, a *generator* of vibration and a *resonator*, must be added (on all but the simplest
form of wind instrument) some means of instantaneously either
decreasing or increasing its sounding-length ; this may conveniently be called its *mechanism*. The shortening mechanism
(finger- or key-holes) is applied to wood-wind instruments, and
the lengthening mechanism (valves or slides) to brass instruments.

The various means of generating vibration have been classified in the previous section, and will now be described.

The free air-reed (or non-reed) is a compressed and flattened
stream of air proceeding from a suitable formation of the player's
lips and directed against the edge of a mouth-hole (*embouchure*)
bored in the upper side of the tube ; there it is, so to speak, split
against the edge of the hole, and sets up the state of vibration
which is communicated to the column of air in the tube. This
form of vibration-generator is employed to sound all the various
sizes of transverse flutes, piccolos and fifes. The mouth-hole
is placed for convenience near the closed end of the tube, but it
can be situated actually at the end of the tube, or the open end
of a tube may serve the purpose of a mouth-hole as it does on
the primitive pan-pipes. Another form of air-reed, the confined
air-reed, is that which is formed by the use of a whistle-mouthpiece ; this was used to generate vibration on the obsolete *flûtes-
à-bec*, recorders, etc., and is now found only on instruments of

minor musical status such as flageolets and " tin-whistles ". The air-stream, instead of coming direct from the player's lips, passes through a flat channel cut in the mouthpiece which directs it automatically to the sharp edge of a sound-hole, just as it does on an ordinary whistle or an organ flue-pipe. The resulting tone-quality of both types of air-reed is distinguishable from that of all other wind instruments by a certain " windy " or whistling quality, but the tone created by means of the free air-reed is fuller, more resonant, more expressive and capable of more undulation between loud and soft than is the even and rather expressionless tone produced by the whistle-mouthpiece.

The two sorts of actual or cane-reeds, the single and the double, are associated with the tone-quality, respectively, of the clarinet and the oboe or bassoon.

The single reed is a flat piece of cane shaved down to almost paper-thinness and flexibility at the end which is placed in the player's mouth ; it is fixed over an oblong aperture in the top of a beak-like mouthpiece by a screw-device (ligature) which clamps the thick end of the reed firmly over a flat " table ", leaving the thin flexible end poised just above the end of the mouthpiece, where it vibrates when a stream of air is forced between it and the end of the mouthpiece. The latter is cut away slightly towards its end so that the thin end of the reed is free to vibrate ; this is called the " lay " of the mouthpiece, the exact slope of which is the most vital and sensitive part of this particular form of sound-apparatus.

The double reed consists of two pieces of cane, both shaved down like the single reed to a flexible thinness at the ends which are placed between the player's lips. The thicker ends are bound firmly round a small metal tube (staple), and the thin ends spread out slightly fan-wise so that their sides meet, and the whole becomes gradually flatter till the two reeds almost meet, leaving, however, a small opening at the extreme end. In the case of the bassoon the end of the metal crook takes the place of the staple. In playing, some pressure is applied by the lips of the player to both single and double reeds as the stream of air is forced into the small opening where it sets up a state of vibration which sympathetically communicates itself to the column of air in the tube of the instrument.

The tone-qualities produced by both types of cane-reed have a certain reediness in common which is absent from the whistle-quality of the air-reed, yet the two are clearly distinguishable ; the single-reed produces a rounder and richer tone than the double reed ; the latter is thinner, incisive and penetrating, slightly nasal, and without the fullness and body of the single reed. All single-reed instruments have a certain kinship of tone-

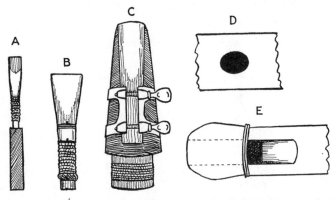

FIG. I.—A. Oboe reed (double). B. Bassoon reed (double). C. Clarinet reed (single) and mouthpiece. D. Mouth-hole of transverse flute. E. Whistle-mouthpiece.

quality ; thus, clarinet-tone, which is the result of a single reed associated with a cylindrical tube, has something in common with saxophone-tone in which it is associated with a conical tube. Oboe and bassoon-tone, again, are allied because of their double reeds which differ mainly in size, yet each has an individuality which is due to the different proportions of their respective tubes and note-holes. The several obliquely-bored note-holes, and the thickness of the walls they penetrate, give a rather veiled or choked quality to many sounds of the bassoon which distinguishes them from the open and more direct quality of oboe-sounds. Both, however, are united by a family tie closer than that which relates them to the single reed family.

The mouthpiece of a brass or lip-reed instrument is a cup or cone-shaped hollow with an outlet at the bottom which then expands slightly and leads into the narrow end of the instrument. The wide end of the cup or cone is placed against the almost closed lips of the player, and a stream of air forced between them causes the lips to vibrate as reeds ; this vibration is communicated to the air-column in the main tube through the neck or " throat " of the mouthpiece. The shape of the hollow of the cup of a mouthpiece varies infinitely between that of a hemispherical cup and a conical (or funnel-shaped) opening, the two extremes being the true cup of the old trumpet mouthpiece and the gently contracting cone of the French horn. The shallower cup, which makes almost a right angle with its lower outlet, tends to produce a tone-quality which is bright and assertive, and extremely forcible when loud ; the deep cone, which merges gradually into the neck of the mouthpiece without making any appreciable angle, favours the production of a more mellow and veiled tone-quality. The following are the characteristics of the various lip-reed mouthpieces which, however, are liable to vary considerably according to the taste or habit of individual players and also according to period, or to local or national custom :

Trumpet (old).—A more or less shallow cup making a clearly defined angle with the opening at the bottom ; the rim or lip is broad and more or less flat.

Trumpet (modern).—Slightly deeper and more conical at the bottom of the cup without making a clearly defined angle at the throat, the lip is slightly rounded.

Bugle.—The cup is deeper than the old trumpet and slopes more gradually at the throat.

Cornet.—Rather deeper and more conical than the modern trumpet, merging more gradually into the neck of the mouthpiece.

Horn.—A long cone or funnel, merging imperceptibly into the neck ; sometimes slightly cupped ; narrow rounded lip.

Trombone.—Varying from a deep cup to almost a cone.

Saxhorn, Tuba, etc.—All more or less conical but cupped to some extent.

Flügelhorn.—Almost a cone, but not so deep as the French horn.

Serpent, bass-horn.—A deep cup.

Cornett.—A more or less shallow cup.

Ophicleide and keyed bugle.—Similar to trombone or tuba, but varying considerably.

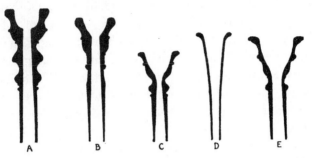

Fig. 2.—A. Old trumpet.   B. Modern trumpet.   C. Cornet.   D. French horn.   E. Trombone.

The smaller the diameter of the mouthpiece the more easily are the high sounds produced, and the larger the circumference the more readily do the lower notes sound ; similarly, a small opening at the bottom of the cup facilitates sounding the notes of the higher register, while a larger opening eases the production of the sounds in the lower register of the instrument. Lip-reed mouthpieces are usually detachable from the body of the instrument, and are now turned from castings in brass, silver or white composite metals ; formerly some mouthpieces were wrought from sheet metal hammered to shape and joined down the side. Ivory, horn or even hard woods were formerly often used to make mouthpieces.

Each type of lip-reed mouthpiece will influence the tone-quality of an instrument to some extent, the more so when they are united to tubes of different proportions ; thus, each type of brass instrument has some individual tone-character apart from its pitch or register, but all of them have a family resemblance and a weight of tone which is quite different from the tone-quality of any wood-wind instrument.

The main tubes of all wood-wind instruments are now either entirely conical or partially cylindrical, and, except in the case of flutes and fifes, the tube expands more or less at the lower end. Some varieties of the oboe family have bells which after expanding contract again, forming a sort of bulb or internal swelling near the lower end of the instrument ; the Heckelphone, a sort of bass oboe, is provided with a globular bell with an outlet in the side of the globe. The bulb-bell affects the tone-quality more particularly in the lowest register of the instrument, but its influence wanes as the sounds get higher. Except in the case of non-cylindrical flutes and piccolos, all conical wood-wind now in general use are blown at the narrow end.

Brass instruments are now all either entirely conical, conical-cylindrical-conical, or cylindrical-conical, and all are blown at the narrow end. The greatest expansion of the bore is in the lower fourth of the tube, and with few exceptions all are provided with a more or less pronounced bell. While the presence of a final sudden expansion or " flare " may not vitally affect the tone-quality of a brass instrument, the expansion of the bore *towards* the bell is essential, for without it the tone sounds stifled and lacks resonance.

PRACTICAL ACOUSTICS

THE pitch of a musical sound produced on a wind instrument depends on the rate or frequency of the vibrations which cause the sound. In obedience to Nature's law, the column of air in a tube can be made to vibrate only at certain rates, therefore, a tube of any particular length can be made to produce only certain sounds and no others as long as the length of the tube is unaltered. Whatever the length of the tube, these various sounds always bear the same relationship one to the other, but the actual pitch of the series will depend on the length of the tube.

The player on a wind instrument, by varying the intensity of the air-stream which he injects into the mouthpiece, can produce at will all or some of the various sounds which that particular length of tube is capable of sounding ; thus, by compressing the air-stream with his lips he increases the rate of vibration and produces higher sounds, and by decompressing or slackening the intensity of the air-stream he lowers the rate of vibration and produces lower-pitched sounds. In this way the fundamental, or lowest note which a tube is capable of sounding, can be raised an octave, a twelfth, a double-octave, and so on, the sounds becoming higher and higher by intervals which become smaller and smaller as they ascend. These sounds are usually called harmonics or upper partials, and it is convenient to refer to them by number, counting the fundamental as No. 1, the octave harmonic as No. 2, and so on. The series of sounds available on a tube approximately 8 feet in length is as follows :

FIG. 3.

A longer tube would produce a corresponding series of sounds proportionately lower in pitch according to its length, and on a shorter tube the same series would be proportionately higher. The entire series available on any tube is an octave lower than that of a tube half its length, or an octave higher than that of a tube double its length ; thus, the approximate lengths of tube required to sound the various notes C are as follows :

Fundamental	Length of tube
C,	16 feet
C	8 ,,
c	4 ,,
c′	2 ,,
c″	1 foot
c‴	$\frac{1}{2}$,,

The addition of about 6 inches to a 4-foot tube, of a foot to an 8-foot tube, or of 2 feet to a 16-foot tube, will give the series (Fig. 3) a tone lower (in B flat), and a proportionate shortening of the C tubes will raise the series a tone (D) ; on the same basis, tubes which give any F as the fundamental of a series must be about midway in length between those which give the C above and the C below as fundamental. Examples :

Trumpet (modern) in C—length about		4 feet
,, in F	,, ,,	6 ,,
,, (old) in C	,, ,,	8 ,,
Horn in F	,, ,,	12 ,,
,, ,, C	,, ,,	16 ,,

It will be noticed that the two lower octaves of the harmonic series (Fig. 3) are very sparsely provided with sounds ; the third octave has little more than an arpeggio, and only in the fourth octave do the sounds run consecutively or scale-wise, while semitones only appear at the upper end of the fourth octave. The series, however, does not end there, and is continued in the fifth octave in semitone and smaller intervals, but however favourably proportioned a tube may be, the production of sounds above the 16th note becomes more and more difficult and uncertain, therefore it is only rarely that any wind instrument is required to produce these extremely high harmonics. The sounds of Nature's harmonic series do not all coincide exactly with the notes of the musical or tempered scale ; Nos. 7, 11 and 13, for example, are noticeably out of tune, but the remainder are either perfectly true or near enough in tune for practical purposes.

For the present purpose it is not necessary to enquire into the number of vibrations per second which are required to sound any fundamental or its harmonics, nor need the exact lengths of tubes be taken into consideration. The player on a wind instrument does not count his vibrations nor does he measure his tube-lengths, but in order to understand wind instruments at all, to know their capabilities, their limitations, and why they are fingered and manipulated as they are, it is necessary to be familiar with the harmonic series (Fig. 3) and to be able to transpose it to suit any fundamental sound.

Although the entire series of harmonics is nominally available on any tube, in actual practice the human lip can hardly vary the pressure to such an extent that all of them can be sounded on the same tube with the same mouthpiece. How many of them can be produced on one instrument depends mainly on the width of the tube in proportion to its length. A tube can be so wide or so narrow that no musical sound can be extracted from it ; there must be some sort of reasonable proportion between width and length, and a tube which is not considerably longer than it is wide would be of no practical use as a musical instrument. A wide-bored tube will yield its fundamental more easily than a narrow one, and if not too wide can be made to sound its fundamental and a few of the lower harmonics, whereas a narrower tube can be made to sound up to the 16th note of the series but will then probably fail to sound the first two. For example, a primitive instrument made from an ox-horn or an elephant's tusk may be so short and so wide in proportion that it will only give one note (the fundamental), whereas an orchestral horn is long and proportionately so narrow that it will sound from the second note of the series up to even the 16th note.

Herein lies the main essential difference between wood-wind and brass instruments ; the wood-wind are comparatively wide for their length, and therefore play freely at the lower end of the harmonic series ; indeed, most of their notes are fundamentals and octave-harmonics ; the brass instruments, on the other hand, are narrow for their length and play freely in the middle or upper part of the harmonic series.

The above are Nature's laws, and, in obedience to them, all wind instruments with a conical or partially conical bore can sound the series of harmonics, or part of it, shown in Fig. 3, the actual pitch of which will vary according to the length of the tube. Cylindrical instruments with an opening at both ends, such as a Boehm flute or a fife, also obey the same laws, but when one end of a cylindrical tube is virtually closed, as in the clarinet type (or a " stopped " organ pipe) another law of Nature steps in and modifies the relations between length of tube and pitch, also the sequence of available harmonics. Where another instrument requires a certain length of tube to sound a particular note, instruments of the clarinet family require only half the length of tube to sound the same note. (A stopped organ pipe is half as long as an open pipe sounding the same note.) It is as if the sound coming up against the closed end had to find its way back again to the open end, so covering double the distance : an unscientific explanation, no doubt, but a convenient illustrative fiction. This explains why a clarinet, say in C, although shorter than an ordinary flute, can sound a sixth lower. Another peculiar property of the stopped cylindrical tube is that the alternate harmonics, Nos. 2, 4, etc., are not available ; therefore, when a fundamental on a clarinet is overblown, the note a twelfth higher will sound instead of the octave. All lip-reed instruments sound all the harmonics, and of the wood-wind only the clarinets sound alternate harmonics.

If the foregoing principles are appreciated, the limitations of any wind instrument which cannot be instantaneously either lengthened or shortened will be easily understood. Instruments used for signalling, such as bugles, cavalry trumpets, hunting

and coach horns, are plain tubes without any apparatus for altering the pitch of the fundamental, therefore the notes they can
sound are confined to those of Nature's harmonic series (Fig. 3),
or of some part of it. An ordinary British bugle, for example,
consists of about 4½ feet of conical tubing with a bore rather
wide for its length ; the fundamental for that particular length
of tube is B flat, and the wide bore permits free use of the
harmonics up to No. 6 of the series ; thus, a bugle-call consists
only of various arrangements of the sounds *b* flat, *f'*, *b'* flat,
d'' and *f''*. With considerable pressure two more harmonics
(*a''* flat and *b''* flat) can be sounded, and if the lips are loosened
enough the fundamental (B flat) can be produced ; but loosely
produced sounds on brass instruments are inferior in quality,
and sounds requiring great lip-pressure are difficult and uncertain, so the effective compass of a bugle is limited to the five
notes given above.

The following will help to illustrate the relation between the
width of a tube and the number of harmonics it will sound. An
ordinary English hunting horn is a very short tube about 9 inches
in length with an expanding bore of rather over half an inch at
the midway point ; this short but proportionately wide tube will
sound only its fundamental (*e''* flat) ; if the tube were gradually
lengthened while retaining the same average bore, the fundamental would gradually get lower and lower in pitch, and the
numbers of harmonics obtainable would gradually increase, till,
at a length of about 8 feet, the fundamental would be C, and
almost the entire series of harmonics up to about No. 16 would
be playable, while at the same time it would become less easy to
produce the fundamental, or that note might even refuse to
sound at all.

It should not be supposed that the production of harmonics
on any given tube-length and width is rigidly prescribed. An
instrument which gives freely up to its 8th harmonic is not incapable of sounding a few notes higher provided sufficient pressure is exerted, and many instruments on which the fundamental
is never used on account of its rough quality can be made to

sound that note if the *embouchure* is sufficiently relaxed. Some players will exceed the ordinary upward compass of an instrument with greater ease than others ; with a narrow mouthpiece the normal compass of any brass instrument may be extended a little upwards, but only at the cost of ease in producing the lower sounds. Each instrument has a normal register where the tone is at its best, and that is where neither extreme pressure nor excessive looseness of *embouchure* is required.

Just as the capacity of the human ear for receiving vibrations is limited, so there are limits to the capacity of the human lips for making vibrations. A narrow tube of about 8 feet can be made to sound its 16th harmonic (*c'''*), but a 2-foot tube, however narrow or wide, could not be persuaded to yield its corresponding note (*c'''''*).

Whatever its length, a column of air set into vibration by the lips requires a certain amount of width if it is to produce musical sounds. The bore of shorter instruments is not decreased proportionately to that of a longer instrument of the same type. The bore of a trumpet in 4-foot C is *not* half as narrow as that of a trumpet in 8-foot C, nor is the bore of a clarinet about 19 inches long (high E flat) half as narrow as that of a clarinet which is twice as long (alto in E flat).

Nature allows very little tampering with the pitch of the sounds available on any given tube ; she allows a little latitude as to the length of the tube, and still more as to its width, yet the general principle holds good that the wide tube yields more readily the lower sounds of Nature's series, and the narrow tube gives forth more freely from its higher sounds.

THE SHORTENING-HOLE SYSTEM OF THE WOOD-WIND INSTRUMENTS

IF a brass instrument without lengthening apparatus has certain limitations, a wood-wind instrument which was without means of shortening its tube-length would be still more severely handicapped, for its resources would then be confined to playing one fundamental sound and a few of the lower and more widely separated harmonics. Even in a comparatively primitive state, however, instruments of the wood-wind class have been provided with a simple means of shortening the sounding-length of the tube in a moment, and of thus creating several additional fundamentals at the will of the player. The system, which may be called the shortening-hole system, is indeed so much part of the instrument itself that it is almost impossible to regard as musical instruments any of the wood-wind class which are without this equipment.

When a lateral hole is opened in the side of a tube the sounding-length is reduced to that portion of the tube which is above the hole, or, in other words, it is as if the tube were cut off at the point where the open hole is situated. The opening of a hole, therefore, in effect shortens the tube and a new and higher fundamental is created. By cutting a series of holes in the upper side of a tube at such intervals as will shorten its sounding-length by diatonic degrees, and by then covering the holes with the finger tips, a means of instantaneously creating a number of new fundamentals is obtained, for a finger need only be raised practically to cut off the end of the tube from the open hole downwards.

A tube pierced by six holes, and held so that the first, second and third fingers of one hand can cover the three lower holes and the same three fingers of the other hand can cover the three upper holes, is thus capable of being shortened by successive degrees so that it will sound a rising diatonic scale when the fingers are raised one by one, beginning at the lowest hole. Although it is immaterial which hand is used to control the lower three or the upper three holes on such a simple instrument as has been imagined, it is more convenient to associate the R. hand with the lower and the L. hand with the upper part of the instrument, for all wood-wind instruments are now held and played in that manner. The following figure will help to demon-

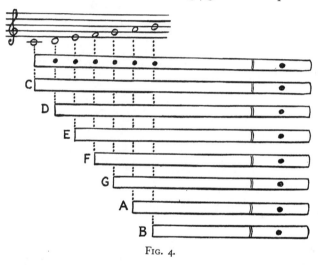

Fig. 4.

strate the fact that a tube with six finger-holes provides the equivalent of seven tubes of different lengths, each sounding a different fundamental but with the advantage that the pierced tube can be instantaneously shortened without interrupting the playing.

An instrument being thus provided with a scale of fundamentals, any of which can be sounded at will, all that is necessary to continue the scale upwards is to compress the wind-stream (overblow) and sound the octave-harmonics of each fundamental with the same fingering. The scale can then be extended into the third octave by a further compression of the wind-stream so as to sound the third and fourth notes of the harmonic series which raise the fundamentals, respectively, a twelfth and a double-octave. (See Fig. 3.)

It has been pointed out in Section III that instruments of the clarinet family do not sound the octave harmonics (No. 2) when overblown, but leap at once to the twelfths (No. 3) above the fundamental. This would leave a gap in the scale were it not filled up by means which will be explained later. Instruments with the clarinet mouthpiece (single reed), but with a conical bore, however, act in the way that has been described, and produce their second octave with the same fingering as for the primary scale ; thus, saxophone fingering is similar to that of the flute and oboe.

The above, in its simplest form, is the shortening-hole system of all wood-wind instruments, from the " tin whistle " with its six finger-holes to the modern orchestral instrument covered with an elaborate filigree of key-work. On the instruments of today the same six fingers still control the holes (even though covered by keys) which provide a diatonic succession of fundamentals and their harmonics just as they did on the simple instruments of the Middle Ages. It is helpful to the understanding of wood-wind instruments if the primary or six-finger-hole scale of each instrument is known ; Fig. 5 shows the notes (fundamentals) which are sounded on the ordinary flute, oboe, clarinet and bassoon by successively raising the fingers from the six holes (or keys) which they cover.

In order completely to blot out the effect of that part of a tube which remains below an open hole, the latter should be as wide as the inside diameter of the tube. There are several reasons, however, why finger- and key-holes have always been made smaller than the bore of the instrument. Originally the holes were all closed by the finger-tips, and, as a finger could barely cover one which was more than half an inch wide, it was obviously impracticable to make the finger-holes as wide as the bore on any but the very smallest of instruments, for the covering must be air-tight. Again, unless the instrument was very small, holes placed in acoustically correct positions would lie too far apart for

the lateral stretch of the fingers. By placing them further up the
tube and at the same time reducing the diameter of the holes, a
sort of compromise was arrived at which served well enough to
preserve something approximating to true intonation, although
on certain instruments which require large note-holes in order to
give their full tone-power there was necessarily some sacrifice
of tone, both in quality and quantity. Another reason for making

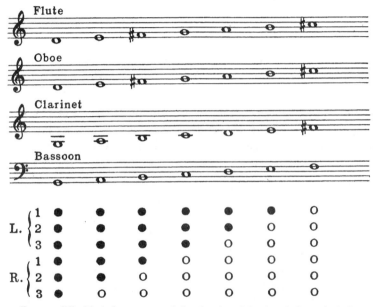

FIG. 5.—[The black dots represent holes closed, and the rings indicate the holes
which are uncovered by the fingers.]

them smaller than the bore of the tube is that small note-holes
undoubtedly contribute something to the particular tone-character of certain instruments ; oboes and bassoons, for example,
would not be the instruments they are if the note-holes were
much larger. With the aid of modern key-work it is possible
to control note-holes which are situated well out of the reach of
the fingers and which may be of almost any reasonable width ;
thus, it would not be mechanically impossible to make and control note-holes which were as wide as the bore of the tube, or to
place them in acoustically correct positions. All the note-holes

on modern instruments, however, even though controlled by
key-work, are smaller than the bore of the tube ; partly for
the reason already given—that is, the preservation of a certain
tone-character—but sometimes also because the holes have to
serve not only as note-holes for fundamentals but also as vent-
holes for the surer production of harmonics. Holes used in this
way (vent-holes) assist the formation of nodes in the segmental
vibration of the air-column, and are in some cases indispensable
for the certain production of octave, twelfth and double-octave
harmonics. The resources of pierced wood-wind instruments
do not end with the production of a diatonic series of fundamentals and the extension of the scale upwards by means of
harmonics. An extension downwards, below the first note of
the primary (six-finger-hole) scale, is available on all instruments
of the wood-wind class by adding to the length of the tube at its
lower end, and by piercing this extension with note-holes which
have to be controlled by keys worked by either the R. little
finger, or in some cases also by the L. little finger, or even by
one of or both the thumbs. The following are the downward
extensions now found on the four typical instruments :

Instrument	Extension downwards	Lowest Note	Fingers
Flute	2 semitones	c'	R. little finger
Oboe	4 semitones	b flat	R. and L. little fingers
Clarinet	3 semitones	e	R. and L. little fingers
Bassoon	9 semitones	B͵ flat	R. little finger and both thumbs.[1]

The semitones between the notes of the diatonic scale were
formerly produced on wood-wind instruments by means of the
device known as *forkfingering*,[2] which, although still a useful
asset, has been to some extent superseded by the addition at a
later period of appropriately placed note-holes covered by keys.
Forkfingering may be explained as follows : when a finger is
raised from a hole (all the holes above it being closed) the sound
will issue clearly and in tune only when the holes immediately

---

[1] Also L. little finger on German bassoons.
[2] (G.) *Gabelgriffe.* (F.) *Doigté fourchu.*

below it are uncovered ; but, when the hole immediately below the one which is sounding is closed by a finger, the pitch of the sounding hole is lowered approximately a semitone. Sounds produced in this way are not generally so resonant,[1] nor is the intonation so true as when the lower holes are all open, but, until chromatic note-holes and keys were introduced, these " forked " sounds were the players' only means of producing sounds which were not in the primary scale of the instrument. A simple six-holed instrument without any keys can be forked so as to sound all the chromatic notes in the octave *except that one which lies between the first and the second notes of the primary scale*; obviously, this note cannot be forked because there is no lower hole to close. The following diagram shows the fingering for a chromatic

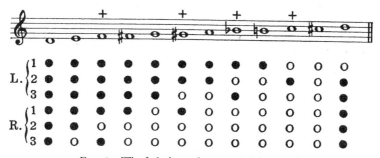

Fig. 6.—[The forked sounds are marked thus : +.]

scale on an instrument without either keys or downward extension of which the primary scale begins on *d'*.

When all but the uppermost hole are closed, the octave above the lowest note of the primary scale sounds more easily than when all the holes are closed. The opening of that hole (or partial opening) assists the formation of a node in the segmental vibration of the air-column. This way of fingering the octave is used on all wood-wind instruments except the clarinets, on which a thumbhole is provided to sound the octave above the first note of the six-finger-hole scale.

When two or more holes below the sounding hole are closed, the pitch will be further lowered and the intonation may be

---

[1] They are called " veiled notes " by flute-players.

improved, but the quality of the sound will be still more veiled.

It was the lack of the first chromatic semitone in the primary scale which led to the introduction of the first chromatic key on wood-wind instruments during the course of the 17th century, and it was the imperfect intonation and poorer quality of the forked sounds which subsequently brought about the addition of the remaining chromatic keys at the end of the 18th and early in the 19th century. These chromatic keys cover holes which are bored in between the diatonic note-holes. The primary scale, therefore, requires five keys in addition to six finger-holes in order to make it fully chromatic without having recourse to forkfingering. Unfortunately there are not enough fingers on the human hand to allow one finger to each hole or key required by the completely chromatic wood-wind instrument. While the two little fingers lie conveniently over two of the chromatic keys, the remaining three can only be manipulated by making use of the L. thumb and two other fingers, which for the time being have to be moved away from their usual positions over their respective note-holes. Except in the case of the bassoon, the R. thumb is fully occupied in supporting the instrument and can hardly be spared to work a key. Modern key-mechanism has to some extent remedied Nature's mistake of not allowing the wood-wind player at least eleven digits, yet one or more fingers even on the most up-to-date instrument has the duty of controlling more than one note-hole or key. The gap between the end of the primary scale (g to f' sharp) and the beginning of the overblown scale (sounding a twelfth higher) on the clarinet is filled up as follows : the primary scale is carried upwards another degree by a note-hole bored in the underside of the tube and covered by the L. thumb ; this hole, when opened, sounds g'. The scale is also carried downwards to e by an extension of the bell-joint, which is provided with note-holes and keys which are controlled by the two little fingers. With these additions a scale of fundamentals from e to g' is provided for. On being overblown, this scale begins again at b' (a twelfth higher than e), still leaving a gap between g' and b'. This gap is filled by keys covering holes near the upper end of the instrument, and controlled by the L. first finger and thumb. Of these keys, the one which is worked by the L. thumb serves not only as a note-hole for b' flat, but also as the vent-hole or " speaker " which is indispensable for the production of harmonics on this type of instrument. Thus, the speaker-key must be opened when the scale ascends above b' flat. From b' natural upwards the scale ascends for just over an octave by using the same fingering as was employed for the scale of fundamentals a twelfth lower, the speaker-key being kept open by the L. thumb. Above c''' sharp several higher notes are obtained by various fingerings involving the use of the next available harmonic (No. 5), and the opening of note-holes as vent-holes.

Amongst other keys used on wood-wind instruments generally, there are some which control small vent-holes which are not note-holes, but which assist the sounding of harmonic octaves or twelfths. Some duplicate keys or levers, and some special shake-keys are usually added to the varied assortment of mechanical helps with which most modern instruments are loaded. These will be noticed under the sections devoted to the history of keys and the historical development of the various instruments.

THE LENGTHENING SLIDE AND VALVE SYSTEMS OF THE BRASS INSTRUMENTS

THE tone of instruments in which vibration is generated by lip-reeds in conjunction with a cupped or conical mouthpiece suffers to some extent when the sounding-length of the tube is shortened by means of lateral holes. All instruments which embody a combination of the lip-reed and the shortening-hole system are now obsolete ; they form a hybrid species which includes medieval cornetts, serpents, keyed bugles and ophicleides. If the tone is to be clear, even and resonant, a lip-reed instrument must employ the full sounding-length of the tube for every note of its scale.

Any brass instrument can be lengthened by inserting an extra piece of detachable tubing at some convenient point ; such pieces are called crooks or shanks, and have been in use for over three centuries for the purpose of altering the pitch of brass instruments. This method of lengthening necessarily interrupts the playing ; therefore, until the valve was invented, or unless a slide was employed, it did not serve as a means of supplying the adjacent sounds which are missing in all but the highest part of the harmonic series (Fig. 3). Both the slide and the valve also lengthen the tube, and thus provide additional fundamentals just as do the crooks or shanks, but they accomplish the lengthening process so quickly that the player can pass from one series to another without interruption. Of the two systems the slide system is the older.

The slide system, commonly associated with the trombone family, requires that the cylindrical part of the tube be cut in two and the two pieces be placed parallel to one another, in which position they are held by a stay or cross-piece which is not part of the sounding tube; the actual slide is another tube with a slightly wider bore bent in the shape of a U with long parallel arms which are also steadied by a stay; these two arms are telescoped over the two ends of the other tube so that they can slide freely to and fro; thus, when the slide is pushed outwards the whole tube is lengthened and the entire harmonic series is lowered in pitch. The two arms of the inner tube and those of the slide or outer tube are made so long that the pitch of the instrument can be lowered to the extent of a diminished fifth, that is, by six semitones; therefore the player can command the harmonic series of seven different fundamentals. An instrument, for example, sounding the harmonic series of B flat can be lengthened by means of the slide to sound the fundamental and harmonics of A, A flat, G, G flat, F and E, in addition to the B flat series; thus, all semitones from a diminished fifth below the second or octave harmonic, and upwards, are available without leaving any gap in the chromatic succession of sounds. Each semitone-stage at which the slide may be stopped is called a *position*, and there are seven positions of the slide:

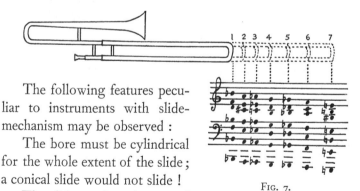

The following features peculiar to instruments with slide-mechanism may be observed:

The bore must be cylindrical for the whole extent of the slide; a conical slide would not slide!

The slide need not be moved

FIG. 7.

in fixed stages; it can be moved to any position within its radius of action; therefore, intonation can be adjusted to a nicety.

A movement of the slide can hardly be accomplished in an instant; a slight break between successive sounds is almost inevitable unless the movement is very short.

The amount by which the slide lengthens the tube must become progressively greater as the position becomes lower ; it should be remembered, however, that the slide has two arms, therefore the alteration of the total length of the tube by a certain amount is accomplished by moving the slide only half that distance. As applied to the trumpet the slide-system is similar in principle but more limited in scope ; this will be noticed in the Section devoted to the history of the trumpet.

It has been seen that the slide system provides six additional harmonic series, but that it is left to the player to find the exact position of the slide which will add the necessary amount of tube-length. The valve system also provides the same six additional harmonic series, but with the difference that it automatically

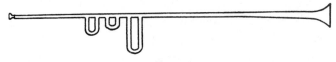

Fig. 8.

adds tubes of fixed lengths when the pistons or keys are operated by the player. For this purpose a mechanical door or tap (the valve) is connected with a loop-way of tubing (the valve-tube) which enables the air-passage through the instrument to be diverted through the loop-way or valve-tube. Three such valves, each with a valve-tube, are provided which, when opened, increase the sounding-length of the instrument by, respectively, a semitone, a tone and a tone and a half. The length of each valve-tube or loop-way must, of course, be proportionate to the original length of the instrument. The above (Fig. 8) shows approximately the amount of tubing required to make the three loop-ways, but does not show the mechanism by means of which the air-passage may be diverted through the loop-ways.

The valves are placed so that the first or tone-valve is nearest the player, and is operated by the first finger ; the second or semitone-valve is in the middle, and is operated by the second finger ; the third or tone-and-a-half valve is furthest away from the player, and is operated by the third finger. Each valve can

be used separately or they can be used together in any combination of two or three ; thus, the player is able to lower the harmonic series of the instrument by any interval from a semitone
to a diminished fifth :

No valves	= original harmonic series.	
2nd valve	= a semitone lower	
1st valve	= a tone lower	
1st and 2nd valves	= a minor third lower	than any sound
2nd and 3rd valves	= a major third lower	in the original
1st and 3rd valves	= a perfect fourth lower	harmonic series.
1st, 2nd and 3rd valves	= a diminished fifth lower	

This provides a complete chromatic scale from a diminished
fifth below the octave harmonic (or second open note) and
upwards as far as it is possible to play. The valves fulfil the
same purpose as the slide on a trombone, but the valve acts
immediately ; it leaps into position, so to speak, at once, whereas
the slide has to be moved progressively into its position. The
valve-tube may be too long or too short ; or, in other words, it
may be in tune or out of tune, flat or sharp ; in either case, it
cannot be readjusted without interrupting the playing to alter
the length of the valve-tube ; the slide can be adjusted at the
moment of playing. In this respect the two systems may be
likened to a piano and a violin ; the intonation on a piano is fixed
(by the tuner), on the violin it is entirely controlled by the player ;
the intonation of the one is ready-made, on the other it is depend-
ent on the player. When an instrument is lengthened by means
of a crook the valve-tubes must be proportionately lengthened ;
each is therefore provided with an adjustable tuning-slide.

The particular form of mechanism employed to open or close
the passage through a valve-tube varies more or less according
to national custom. Of the two devices now in general use, the
piston-valve is popular in France and England, whereas the
rotary-valve is generally favoured in Germany, Austria and
Italy. These two devices, and some others which are no longer
in use, will be explained in the appropriate historical section
(Section VIII).

Fig. 9 shows the use of the valves for a chromatic scale on a four-foot instrument with the usual three valves. The numerals indicate the valves and the ciphers the open notes or harmonics of the natural series.

The valve system has one imperfection which was very pronounced in the earlier types and which has since been mitigated to some extent by means of extra valves or compensating devices. The fault lies in the fact that, although a valve-tube may be exactly long enough to lower the pitch of the open notes of the original tube by the amount required, it cannot at the same time be long enough to lower the pitch by the right amount when the original tube is already lengthened by the use of one or other of the valves. If we suppose that the semitone valve-tube on a 4-foot

Fig. 9.—[The hollow notes are the open notes, namely, Nos. 2, 3, 4, 5, 6 and 8 of the harmonic series. No. 7 is not used because it is out of tune with the tempered scale.]

instrument is exactly 3 inches long, and that the tone valve-tube is 6 inches long, when the tone-valve is used the tube of the instrument measures 4 feet 6 inches, it is in fact in B flat ; but an instrument of that length would require rather more than 3 inches to lower it a semitone, therefore the valve-tube of exactly 3 inches is not long enough when both valves are used together, and the intonation is a little sharp in consequence. The discrepancy is very slight in the case of the first and second valves, but it becomes more pronounced when the third valve comes into use in combination with the others. On the shorter instruments, such as trumpets and cornets, the difficulty is met by making the third valve-tube rather longer than is necessary for a minor third, so that the extra tube-length compensates more or less for the shortage when the valves are used together ; for that reason players generally use the first and second valves combined rather than the third valve alone for sounds that are a minor third below any open note (see Fig. 9). On the large brass instruments the faulty intonation due to insufficient tube-length becomes very pronounced when the valves are used together, and some sort of compensation is almost imperative. This is usually supplied by one or other of the various compensating systems which automatically add extra tube-length when the valves are combined, or by the addition of a fourth, a fifth or even a sixth valve which serve not only to compensate for lack of tube-length, but are also used to carry the chromatic compass right down to the fundamental. Trumpets, cornets and horns are usually provided with three valves, but wide-bored instruments which make use of the fundamental are commonly given a fourth valve equivalent to a perfect fourth ; these are the euphonium, tubas or bombardons.

Valves have been used more recently for the purpose for which formerly only crooks and shanks were used. In this case a valve-tube takes the place of a crook or shank, and the change is accomplished more quickly than by the process of removing the mouthpiece and inserting a new crook.

Shortening or ascending valves are those which, instead of adding length to the tube, cut off a loop-way of tubing and so raise the pitch of the open sounds.

SUMMARY

CLASS B

Transverse Flute (Free Air-reed)

Cylinder or Boehm Flute.—Straight tube of wood or metal 26½ inches long. Sounding-length (from foot to stopper) is about 2 feet. Cylindrical bore about ¾ inch (19 millimetre) from foot to lower end of the head joint, then contracting very slightly in a parabolic curve till cut short by the stopper. Shortening-hole system with large note-holes. Primary scale d' to c'' sharp. Sounds fundamental and a few harmonics. Downward extension (usually) to c'. Key system is usually Boehm or modifications of that system.

Conical Flute.—The same but with cylindrical head, then tapering gradually to the foot. Key systems are based on the old eight-key system.

Larger Flutes.—Alto and Bass, usually a fourth and an octave below the normal flute. Otherwise the same, but the tube is sometimes bent for convenience in holding the instrument.

Smaller Flutes.—Usually a semitone or a minor third above the ordinary flute, but otherwise the same.

Piccolo.—Same as the flute but half the length and usually conical bore. Sounds an octave higher. Generally made without the downward extension of the flute. Also made a semitone and minor third higher.

Fife.—A small cylindrical flute with six finger-holes and sometimes with one or more keys. Usually a tone below the piccolo. For military " drum and fife " bands conical flutes of a simple type are now used.

Whistle Flute (Confined Air-reed)

Recorders, Flûtes-à-bec, Flageolets, etc.—Various lengths of tube with conical bore tapering towards the lower end. Shortening-hole system with or without a thumb-hole, sounding fundamentals and only a few harmonics. Extension, a tone downwards by little-finger hole or key. Modern flageolets are sometimes fitted with modern key-mechanism.

Fig. 10.—A. Cylinder flute.   B. Conical flute.   C. Recorder or whistle-flute.

CLASS C

Oboe (Double Reed)

Oboe.—Straight conical tube of wood expanding at the lower end to a small bell. Length 23 inches, but the sounding-length is increased to about $25\frac{1}{2}$ inches by the reed and staple. Bore is from $\frac{3}{16}$ inch at the upper end to $\frac{5}{8}$ inch at the top of the bell-joint. The bell expands to about $1\frac{1}{2}$ inches. Shortening-hole system with small note-holes. Primary scale d' to c'' sharp, sounding fundamentals and a few harmonics. Extension down to b flat. Key systems are developments of the original simple system.

Larger Oboes.—*Cor Anglais* and *Oboe d'amore*, respectively, a fifth and a minor third below the normal oboe. The same as the oboe, but proportionately larger and usually with bulb-bells. The staple or " crook " of metal is slightly curved for convenience in holding. Downward extension may be a semitone less than the oboe.

Heckelphone.—An octave below the oboe ; wide conical bore. Straight tube with bent metal crook. Globular bell with outlet(s) at the side. Downward extension a semitone more than the oboe. Key-system similar to the oboe.

Sarrusophones.—All-metal, wide-bored conical tubes in a variety of sizes from high soprano to contrabass. Shortening-hole system, sounding fundamentals and a few harmonics. Primary scale (written) *d'* to *c''* sharp. Downward extension

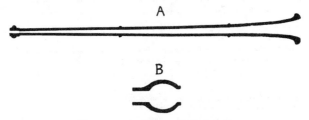

A

B

FIG. 11.—A. Oboe.   B. Bulb-bell.

to (written) *b* flat. The smaller sizes are straight tubes with the reed on a staple, but from the alto downwards the tube is doubled or redoubled, and the reed fits on to a crook.

BASSOON (DOUBLE REED)

Bassoon.—Wooden or (rarely) metal conical tube about 8 feet long with metal crook at the narrow end, all being sound-ing-length. The tube makes a U-bend about the middle of its length. The bassoon is jointed in a manner peculiar to the type (see Fig. 12.) The butt [1] is an oval piece of wood about 17 inches long in which are bored two parallel passages which meet at the bottom to form the U-bend ; from the narrower end of the passage through the butt the tube is continued in the wing or tenor-joint,[2] and in the narrower end of that joint is inserted the curved metal crook [3] which continues to taper till the bore

[1] (G.) *Stiefelstück, Doppelloch.*   (F.) *Culasse.*
[2] (G.) *Flügel.*   (F.) *Petit corps, Petite branche.*
[3] (G.) *S-rohr, Mundrohr.*   (F.) *Bocal.*

is reduced to about $\frac{1}{8}$ inch at the tip where the reed is fixed ; from the wider end of the passage through the butt the tube is continued through an expanding bass or long-joint,[1] and further through a final bell-joint [2] which may expand slightly or remain cylindrical. The measurement at the end of the bell is about $1\frac{1}{2}$ inches. The note-holes are small, and those of the primary

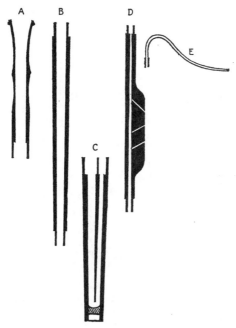

FIG. 12.—A. Bell-joint.   B. Long-joint.   C. Butt.   D. Wing-joint with note-holes.   E. Crook.

scale pierce the tube diagonally. The note-holes of the primary scale G to f are situated three in the narrower passage through the butt (R. hand), and three in the wing-joint (L. hand). The wing is a projection from the joint, and contains the three note-holes. The downward extension is to B, flat, the note-holes for which are all on the widening passage through the butt, the bass-joint, and the bell-joint. The shortening-hole system sounds

[1] (G.) *Bass-röhre, Mittelstück.*   (F.) *Grands corps, grande branche.*
[2] (G.) *Kopfstück, Stürze, Schallstück.*   (F.) *Pavillon, Bonnet.*

fundamentals in the primary scale, octaves and a few more harmonics. Two key-systems, respectively, the French and the German, are now in use.

Smaller Bassoons.—The same, but proportionately smaller ; usually a fifth or an octave above the normal instrument.

Larger Bassoons.—The same, but proportionately larger ; the double-bassoon is usually an octave below the ordinary instrument, but the downward extension may be only to C. The tube may be metal-jointed and may make one or more additional U-bends.

CLARINET (SINGLE REED)

Clarinet.—Straight tubes of wood or metal varying in length according to pitch. The B-flat clarinet is about 26 inches long, all of which is sounding-length. The bore is mainly cylindrical, about $\frac{9}{16}$ inch, but contracting in the mouthpiece, and expanding at the lower end towards the bell. The shortening-hole system is employed with medium-sized note-holes. The primary (six-finger-hole) scale is from (written) *g* to *f''* sharp, sounding fundamentals and harmonics Nos. 3 and 5. Extension downwards to (written) *e*, and the necessary upward extension to meet the lower end of the overblown (12th) scale. Key-systems are either based on the simple (13 keyed) or on the so-called Boehm system.

Smaller Clarinets.—The same, but proportionately smaller. The commonest, in high E flat, is about 19 inches long.

Larger Clarinets.—Alto or tenor are usually a fifth or a major sixth below the C clarinet. Bass clarinet is usually an octave below the ordinary B-flat instrument ; otherwise the same, but proportionately larger. *Basset-horns* (a fifth down) have an additional downward extension to (written) *c*. Contrabass clarinets are an octave below the bass clarinet. All larger clarinets are bent either at the mouthpiece end or at both ends (upturned bell) for convenience in holding, and the bends and bell are generally of metal.

Saxophone (Single Reed)

Saxophone.—All-metal, wide-bored conical tubes in a variety of sizes from high soprano to contrabass. Shortening-hole system with large note-holes, sounding fundamentals and all the lower harmonics. Primary scale (written) *d″* to *c″* sharp, with downward extension to *b* or *b* flat. The smallest are usually (but not invariably) straight, but from the alto downwards they are

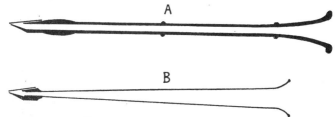

Fig. 13.—A. Clarinet. B. Saxophone.

bent at both ends (upturned bell), and on the largest the tube makes two U-bends near the narrow end. Key-system is somewhat similar to those of the oboe and sarrusophone.

CLASS A

Trumpet (Lip-reed)

Old Trumpet.—Metal tube from 6 to 9 feet long with a cylindrical bore about $\frac{7}{16}$ of an inch wide, expanding in the last quarter to a bell 4 or 5 inches across the mouth. Sounds from No. 2 to No. 16 (or higher) of the harmonic series. Valve, slide or no mechanism. Usually made with two or four U-bends.[1]

Modern Trumpet.—Tube from 4 feet (or less) to about 4 feet 10 inches long ; cylindrical bore the same as old trumpet but tapering slightly towards the mouthpiece. Sounds from No. 2 to No. 8 (or higher) of the harmonic series. Piston or rotary valve mechanism. Usually made with two U-bends, or quite straight.

[1] For mouthpieces, see Section II.

CORNET (LIP-REED)

Cornet (*à-pistons*).—Tube about 4 feet 7 inches (when in B flat), or longer according to shank. Bore at the narrow end starts at about $\frac{5}{16}$ of an inch, and expands slightly to a little over $\frac{7}{16}$ inch at the valves and tuning-slide where it is more or less cylindrical ; then expands again towards the bell. Sounds harmonics from No. 2 to No. 8 (or higher) of the harmonic series. Valve mechanism, piston or rotary. Usually made with four U-bends.

HORN (LIP-REED)

French Horn (*valved*).—Circular-coiled metal tube about 12 feet long when in F ; at the narrow end the bore is about $\frac{1}{4}$ inch, increasing through the crook to about $\frac{7}{16}$ of an inch at the valves and tuning-slide where it is more or less cylindrical ; expanding again towards the bell, which finally opens out to about 11 inches. Sounds harmonics up to about No. 16. Piston or rotary valve mechanism.

Hand Horn.—Circular-coiled metal tube from about 9 to 18 feet long according to the crook employed. The bore is about $\frac{1}{4}$ inch at the narrow end, increasing very gradually to about $\frac{7}{16}$ inch at the tuning-slide, which is cylindrical ; expanding again towards the bell as on the valved horn. Harmonics are the same as the valved horn, but there is no mechanism. French hunting-horns are similar, but without crooks or tuning-slide.

Tenor Cor.—Circular-coiled metal tube from about 6 feet to 6 feet 9 inches (F or E flat). Bore at narrow end is about $\frac{3}{8}$ of an inch increasing to $\frac{7}{16}$ inch at the valves, where it is cylindrical ; expanding again (but cylindrical at tuning-slide) to the bell which opens out to about 8 inches and points *downwards*. Sounds harmonics No. 2 to No. 8. Valve mechanism.

TROMBONE (LIP-REED)

Tenor Trombone.—Straight metal tube with two U-bends, about 9 feet long (B flat) when the slide is drawn up ; cylindrical bore of about $\frac{7}{16}$ of an inch for two-thirds of its length, then expanding to 6 inches across the mouth of the bell. Sounds harmonics No. 2 to No. 8 (or higher) but can sound the fundamental. Slide mechanism, but also made with valves.

Alto Trombone.—The same, but smaller. Length about 6 feet 9 inches (E flat) ; bore about $\frac{7}{16}$ inch, bell $4\frac{1}{2}$ inches.

Bass Trombone.—The same, but proportionately larger. Length about 11 feet when in G. Bore just over $\frac{1}{2}$ inch, bell 8 inches.

SAXHORNS, BUGLE HORNS, TUBA, ETC. (LIP-REED)

Flügelhorn.—Metal tube about 4 feet 6 inches long (B flat) ; bore about $\frac{3}{8}$ inch expanding slightly to the valves where it is cylindrical ; then expanding again like a bugle to about $5\frac{1}{2}$ inches across the mouth of the bell. Can sound fundamental and up to harmonic No. 6 or higher. Valve mechanism, piston or rotary. Usually in bugle form.

Tenor Horn.—Metal tube about 6 feet 9 inches long (E flat) ; bore rather over $\frac{3}{8}$ of an inch at narrow end expanding slightly to the valves ; cylindrical through valves, then expanding again to a bell about 6 inches across the mouth. Sounds harmonics No. 2 to No. 8. Valve mechanism. Now usually made in tuba-form with the bell pointing upwards.

Baritone.—The bore increases very slightly from rather under $\frac{1}{2}$ inch at the narrow end to $\frac{1}{2}$ inch in the middle of the valve-system ; after leaving the valves the tube expands to about 9 inches across the bell-mouth. Sounds from the second to the eighth open note, or higher.

Euphonium.—The bore starts at about $\frac{1}{2}$ inch, increasing to nearly $\frac{10}{16}$ inch in the valve-system, after which a considerable expansion leads to a wide bell of about 10 inches across the mouth. Fundamental is used and a fourth valve is generally supplied.

Tuba.—When in F the bore is just over $\frac{1}{2}$ inch at the narrow end, expanding slightly to about $\frac{11}{16}$ inch in the middle of the valve-system where it is more or less cylindrical ; leaving the valves the tube expands generously to about 13 or 14 inches across the bell-mouth. Tuba or helicon-form. Dimensions and pattern vary considerably according to make and nationality. Fundamental is available.

CORNETT, SERPENT, OPHICLEIDE (LIP-REED)

Cornett.—Short, wide-bored, conical tubes of various lengths made of wood or ivory ; straight or curved. Shortening-hole system sounding fundamental and one or two harmonics.

Serpent.—Conical wide-bored tube in zigzag curves, about 8 feet long when in C. Bore at the narrow end is about $\frac{1}{2}$ inch expanding steadily to about 4 inches at the wide end. Shortening-hole system with small finger-holes, sounding fundamentals and five or six harmonics. Usually of wood, but sometimes of copper.

Bass Horn.—Similar to serpent but generally made in two straight pieces joined by a butt or U-bend at the bottom, and with a long metal crook at the narrow end. Made of wood or metal.

Ophicleide.—Metal (rarely wood) wide-bored conical tube 8 or 9 feet long (C or B flat). Two straight tubes with U-bend about halfway ; coiled or folded crook at narrow end. Bore from about $\frac{1}{2}$ an inch at the narrow end, expanding to 8 or 9 inches at the bell mouth. Shortening-hole system with large key-holes. Sounds fundamentals and from six to eight harmonics.

BUGLES AND VARIOUS (LIP-REED)

Bugle.—Conical wide-bored metal tube usually from 4 feet to 4 feet 6 inches in length, expanding from about $\frac{7}{16}$ inch to 3, 4 or 5 inches across the mouth of the bell. Some are almost funnel-shaped at the wide end, and in any case the greatest expan-

sion is in the last quarter of the length. Sounds harmonics No. 2
to No. 6 freely. Made with two, four or six bends. A valved
bugle is practically a flügelhorn.

Keyed Bugle.—Bugle tube with shortening-hole system ;
fairly large key-holes.

Post Horn.—Conical metal tube from about 28 to 32 inches
long, expanding from about $\frac{5}{16}$ inch to 3 or 4 inches across the
bell. Sounds harmonics from No. 2 to No. 6. The tube is either
straight, bugle-shaped, or circular-coiled. No mechanism, but
may have tuning-slide or bits.

Coach Horn.—Much the same as a straight post horn but
from 3 to 4 feet long ; the bell is often funnel-shaped. Sounds
harmonics No. 2 to No. 6. No mechanism.

English Hunting Horn.—Conical metal tube about 9 inches
long, expanding from about $\frac{3}{8}$ inch to 2 inches. Sounds fundamental. No mechanism.

THE MECHANICS OF WOOD-WIND INSTRUMENTS

HAD Nature supplied us with only a few more and some rather longer and larger fingers it is improbable that there would have been any necessity for keys on wood-wind instruments. Keys are used to remedy the shortcomings of the human hand, for the fingers are too few, and they are neither long enough nor broad enough to serve all the purposes for which they are required ; therefore, keys are used to close note-holes where fingers are not available, to control holes which lie out of the reach of the fingers, or to close holes which are too large for the fingers to cover.

The two ends of a key may be distinguished as the key-cover or flap which actually closes the note-hole, and the fingerplate or touchpiece on which the finger presses ; the two ends are connected by a stem or shank, and the whole acts as a lever rocking on a fulcrum or axle. Keys are of two sorts, namely, the *open* and the *closed* key. The open key is one which stands open when it is not touched, leaving the hole uncovered ; the closed key seals up the hole when the lever is not touched, and only uncovers it when the fingerplate is pressed down. The open key acts in exactly the same way as a finger over a hole, for when a finger *falls* on a hole, that hole is closed ; similarly, when a finger *falls* on the fingerplate of an open key it causes the hole to be closed. The closed key acts in the opposite way and opens the hole when the finger falls on the fingerplate.

It has always been customary to identify keys according to the note which sounds when the fingerplate is pressed down ; thus, open keys are named, not by the note which sounds from the hole they cover, but by the note sounded from the next open hole further down the tube when the key is closed. The " C key " of a flute (an open key) is that one which actually covers

46

the c' sharp hole, but which, when closed, will cause the instrument to sound c' natural through the open end of the tube. Similarly, the " F key " on a bassoon is the open key which covers the G hole, and which, when closed, will cause the sound to come from the next lowest hole, namely, the F hole. Closed keys, on the other hand, are named by the note which sounds from the hole they open when the fingerplate is pressed down ; thus, the " D-sharp key " of a flute is that one which actually opens and closes the d' sharp note-hole.

The first open keys were used on the larger wood-wind instruments in the 16th century for the purpose of controlling note-holes which were situated out of reach of the little finger,

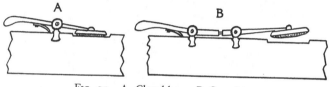

FIG. 14.—A. Closed key.   B. Open key.

and were required to carry the compass of the instrument downwards below the primary or six-finger-hole scale. These keys acted as elongated fingers, closing the holes by a downward pressure of the finger.

An open key requires two levers, each pivoting on its own axle, and placed end to end so that one acts on the end of the other ; thus, when the fingerplate is up the key-cover is also up, and the hole is open ; conversely, when the fingerplate is pressed down the key-cover descends on the hole and closes it.

A closed key is a single lever rocking see-saw-wise on an axle ; when the fingerplate is up the key-cover is down and the hole is closed, but when the fingerplate is pressed down the key-cover rises and opens the hole. Both open and closed keys are kept in their normal positions by springs pressing upwards which keep the fingerplate up till it is depressed by a finger.

The earliest open keys which appear on 16th-century instruments were commonly made of brass and at that time were provided with a fingerplate which branched out in two directions, swallow-tail fashion ; the two branches were designed to suit both the players who preferred to use the R. hand for the lower part of the instrument and also those who were in the habit of playing with the L. hand below and the R. hand above. This swallow-tail (or fish-tail) key was consistently made till towards the end of the 17th century, and even after that time it survived for certain keys of oboes and bassoons throughout the 18th century.

Sixteenth- and 17th-century keys were generally covered by a perforated protecting box[1] of either wood or metal ; this was usually in the form of a barrel or cylinder without ends which

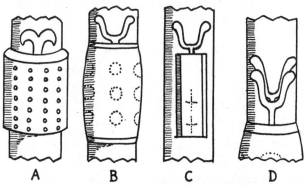

FIG. 15.—Protecting boxes and swallow-tail fingerplates.

was slipped over the whole tube and key-mechanism, leaving only the fingerplate exposed (Fig. 15, A and B). Another form of key-protection is also found on the early bassoons, cornetts and krumhorns, and on some of the very long shawms and *flûtes-à-bec* ; this is a metal oblong box covering the key-work but not encircling the whole tube (Fig. 15, C). The perforated wooden boxes were often barrel-shaped and were sometimes bound with brass bands at both ends.

Exceptionally, the compass of some of the very longest bass instruments was carried downwards below the primary scale to the extent of four additional note-holes, each of which required a key in order to control it. Two of these were operated by the

[1] (G.) *Schutzkapsel.* (F.) *Poche* or *Fontanelle.*

little finger, and were so placed that the higher of the two keys was kept closed whenever the lower one was depressed. This was accomplished by placing the fingerplate of the higher key just underneath that of the lower one, but allowing it to project a little so that it could be depressed independently of the lower key (Fig. 15, D). The other two of the four were on the underside of the instrument and were worked by the thumb. Mersenne (1636) shows the last two keys each in a separate protecting box and so situated that they could be worked by the player's feet.[1]

The characteristic protecting box survived till towards the end of the 17th century; it was then generally discarded, but was revived in modified form near the end of the 18th century in order to guard certain keys[2] which were liable to come in contact with the player's body when the instrument was being played; it still exists in the skeleton protection now placed over the large lower keys on saxophones, large clarinets and other instruments.

Although there is evidence that the closed key was known early in the 17th century,[3] it did not come into general use till after the middle of that century, when it was applied to the early jointed flutes and oboes in order to control an additional notehole for d' sharp, the only chromatic note in the primary scale of these instruments which could not be produced by fork-fingering.

The history of keys from the end of the 17th century is most conveniently traced along three independent lines: (a) the actual lever or key, (b) the key-mount or supports for the axle, (c) the means of transmitting the movement from fingerplate to key-cover.

---

[1] Illustrations showing the working of the early open keys may be seen in Mersenne; also reproduced in Hawkins, *History*, vol. iv, pp. 132 and 136; in Welch, *Six Lectures*, pp. 25 and 46, and in Sachs, *Berlin Cat.*, p. 251.

[2] Notably the low D key on bassoons.

[3] Closed keys are shown in the illustration of an instrument named the *Sourdeline*, by Mersenne, Book V, Prop. XXXIII, p. 305; reproduced in Welch, *History*, p. 220.

Eighteenth-century closed keys were cut from one piece of metal, commonly brass, occasionally silver, and more rarely from wood or ivory. The key-cover was either square, round, octagonal or oval in shape, and to the undersurface of the flap was fixed a piece of leather in order to make the hole air-tight when it was closed. Open keys were necessarily made of separate pieces so that the end of the first lever could work freely in a hole or recess bored in the end of the second lever. The rounded surface of the instrument at the top of the note-hole was generally flattened and slightly recessed to fit the shape of the key-

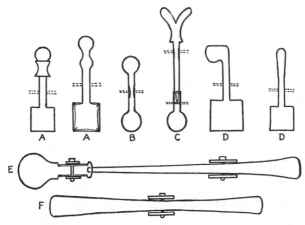

Fig. 16.—A selection of 18th-century keys. A. Flute. B. Oboe, round closed key. C. Oboe, open key. D. Short clarinet keys. E. Bassoon, open key. F. Bassoon, closed key.

cover. Owing to their length, bassoon keys were of a pattern rather different from those of the other wood-wind instruments, as is shown in Fig. 16.

Although many modifications and improvements to keys were introduced during the first half of the 19th century, the old flat key-cover was still used on many instruments made up till the middle of that century ; the square flap, however, gradually gave way to the round key-cover after having survived longest at the lower end of flutes and clarinets. Early in the 19th century the flat key-covers were often either soldered, riveted or screwed on to a shank made from a thicker piece of metal. Near the end of the 18th century a soft grey metal (pewter ?) was sometimes used for key-making instead of brass or silver.

A key provided with a conical plug of soft metal instead of the usual flap enjoyed some popularity from near the end of the 18th century till after the middle of the 19th century. In this case a corresponding recess, countersunk at the top of the note-hole, and sometimes lined with metal, received the conical plug and closed the hole more securely than the flat key. The idea is said to have been due to a German maker named Boie of Göttingen, but it appears to have been adopted (or re-invented) by the London maker Richard Potter who included the plug amongst his flute-patents of 1785. While it was very commonly

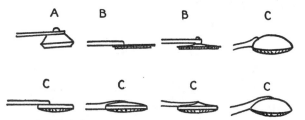

Fig. 17.—A. Metal plug.   B. Flat keys, soldered and riveted.   C. Cupped keys with stuffed pads.

used for flutes, especially for the foot-keys, by English makers for a considerable period, the plug does not appear to have been in favour for other wood-wind instruments.

An important improvement in key-making was the saucer-shaped or cupped key-cover which began to be used in the first or second decade of the 19th century ; a softer, thicker or stuffed pad fixed in the hollow of the cup or plate closed the hole much more securely than the flat leather, and with slight modifications this is the form of key which is now almost universally used. The exact shape of the cup has varied considerably, the general tendency being to flatten the base of the cup till it assumes the form of an inverted flat-bottomed plate with a low rim.   In its earlier stages the cupped key-cover was sometimes screwed or riveted on to the shank, but in its later form the cup and the shank are firmly soldered together.

What might be termed the " hinged key " is another form of open key which made its appearance about the middle of the 18th century and was used sporadically till after the middle of last century. This consists of a single lever attached at one end to the instrument by some sort of hinge, with a key-cover either in the middle of the shank and the fingerplate at the other end, or else with a fingerplate in the middle and the key-cover at the end.

Rudimentary open-centred or ring-keys appeared in connection with improvements to the flute mechanism as early as 1808 [1] and after some tentative experiments [2] were adopted by Boehm for the mechanism of his 1832 conical flute in association with horizontal rod-axles. Round about 1840 the ring-keys found a

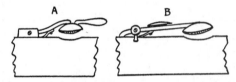

FIG. 18.—Hinged keys.   A. Fingerplate at the end.   B. Fingerplate in the middle.

place on clarinets and oboes, and since that time have become an essential part of the key-mechanism of many wood-wind instruments, especially of oboes and clarinets.

Almost all the important improvements in key-making were initiated during the period 1810–1850 ; some of these were designed only to aid the manipulation of particular keys on certain instruments. Amongst the devices which date from that period and are still in use, there is the perforated key-cover (now used on the oboe) which has the effect of half-closing a hole when the finger is drawn slightly to one side, thus uncovering the perforation without allowing the key-cover to rise. Rollers on the fingerplates of keys, designed to reduce friction when one finger has to pass from one key to an adjacent key, began to be applied to the L. little-finger-keys of the clarinet in 1823,[3] and

[1] Nolan's patent.
[2] Pottgiesser (1824), Gordon (1831), Boehm (1831).
[3] Said to have been invented by a Paris maker named Janssen.

soon after the same device appeared on the little-finger-keys of flutes and bassoons. It was also early in the second quarter of the 19th century that a white composite metal, sometimes called German silver,[1] first began to replace brass as the common material for the key-mechanism, and generally, for all the metal work of wood-wind instruments. Although brass was still largely used after the mid-century, for the last sixty or seventy years little else but German silver (or real silver) has been used for that purpose.

The history of the key-mount begins with the primitive contrivances which form the axle and supports for the open keys found on 16th- and early 17th-century instruments. These were contrived by running a wire axle through the holes bored in two wings of the key-cover bent over at right angles.[2] This somewhat rickety arrangement was followed by the late 17th-century device by which the keys lie in a channel cut in a raised ring or ridge of wood which runs right round the instrument. This ring forms, as it were, a sort of swelling [3] on the outer surface of the tube which was left standing when the instrument was turned on the lathe. A small metal pin (the axle on which the key pivots) runs across the channel and through a hole in the middle of the key-lever, the two ends being firmly embedded in the wood of the ring. This form of key-mount served almost throughout the 18th century for the keys of flutes, oboes and clarinets ; it continued to be used in the early 19th century for the keys at the lower and upper ends of these instruments. When, near the close of the 18th century, additional chromatic keys began to be added to wood-wind instruments, a reduced form of the wooden ring was adopted, no doubt owing to the inconvenience of having a number of thick wooden rings running round the middle of the tube ; instead of a ring encircling the whole tube only two *blocks* [4] of wood were left standing, one on either side of the

---

[1] An alloy, mainly composed of copper, zinc and nickel, first used commercially in 1823. (G.) *Neusilber.*

[2] The detail can be seen in Welch, *Six Lectures*, p. 25.

[3] (G.) *Wulst.*   [4] (G.) *Bock.*

channel in which the key lay ; these blocks received the two
ends of the pin or key-axle. Rings and blocks together remained
in use till about the middle of the 19th century in spite of the
growing use, in the meantime, of metal supports. The two
sides of the channel between the wooden blocks were subject to
considerable wear, and keys mounted in this way were very

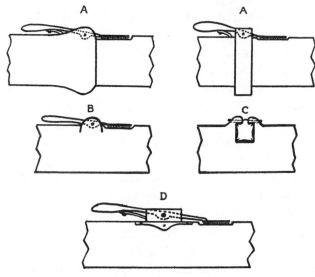

Fig. 19.—A A. Keys mounted in wooden rings. B. Key in blocks. C. Cross-
key in blocks. D. Key in brass saddle.

liable to develop side-play as the wear increased ; to obviate
this defect, some makers lined the inside of the blocks with small
metal plates.

Metal supports for the key-axle began in a primitive way with
the rather clumsy device used for the 16th- and 17th-century
open keys, but in a more serviceable form were adopted for
mounting bassoon keys from fairly early in the 18th century.
The use of metal supports was probably due to the awkwardness
of having (or of making) wooden rings or projections in the
form of blocks round the thick bassoon tube. This form of
key-mount, sometimes termed a *saddle*,[1] consists of a brass base

---

[1] (G.) *Kapsel.*

or floor and two upstanding walls between which the key-lever lies and pivots on an axle supported by the upright walls of the saddle. Although blocks are found in company with brass saddles on some of the earlier 18th-century bassoons, before the end of that century bassoon keys were commonly mounted in saddles with round-ended sides, and the axles were screwed in ; the base of the saddle was likewise fixed to the wood of the instrument by two screws. The same form of saddle rather lighter and more neatly finished made its appearance on clarinets and oboes in the second quarter of the 19th century, and is often found on these instruments in that period in company with blocks and rings. In the meantime, the sides of the saddle were made square-ended instead of round. Metal saddles of this sort are very rarely found on flutes.

A much more uncommon way of mounting keys, which occurs towards the end of the 18th century, was to carve out a channel in the wood of the instrument and to sink the middle of the key-lever in the depression thus formed, with a pin running across it as the key-axle. This was only possible when the wood of the instrument was fairly thick, as it is in certain parts of the bassoon tube.

All the foregoing key-mounts were destined to be superseded by the metal pillars [1] which are now in general use on all wood-wind instruments. It seems as if pillars were first made by the Paris maker Laurent to mount the keys on his glass flutes as early as 1806 (Pl. I, E) ; they were adopted by a few French makers during the first quarter of the century, but it was not until after Boehm's 1832 flute had become fairly well known that the pillars began to be used for other wood-wind instruments.[2] The old devices, rings, blocks and saddles, however, lingered during the third quarter of the century, but eventually gave way to the now almost universal pillar-mounts. These supports are small uprights provided with round heads into which the axle

[1] (G.) *Kugeln.*
[2] Boehm had already used pillars in 1828, four years before he completed the key-system with which his name is associated.

is firmly screwed [1] after passing through a small tube or " sleeve " which is fixed across the key-lever. Some of the earlier pillars stood in pairs on a metal footplate which was screwed down on to the instrument, yet it has generally been found more satisfactory to screw the pillars into the wood. On all-metal instruments, however, the pillars are fixed in a footplate or strap of metal which is soldered to the surface of the instrument.

The two levers which constitute an open key lie longways or parallel to the axis of the tube, while the lever of a closed key

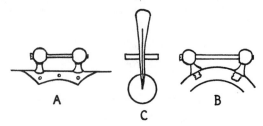

Fig. 20—A. Pillars on footplate. B. Pillars without footplate. C. Key with " sleeve ".

may lie either longways or across the instrument ; in either case, the axle, on which the key pivots, lies at right angles to the key-lever, and the movement is communicated from one side of the axle to the other. The *horizontal rod-axle* is one which lies parallel to the axis of the tube, while the fingerplates and key-covers project at right angles from it. This important form of key-movement was first made practicable on the Boehm flute of 1832, and by the mid-century was being applied wherever it was of service to the mechanism of other wood-wind instruments. Both ways of transmitting key-movement, the older rocking lever and the rod-axle, have remained in use ever since that time.

The first rod-axles were solid metal rods pivoted at both ends on the points of small screws which were driven through the round heads of the supporting pillars, and could convey only one sort of movement from finger to key-cover ; thus, any keys, rings or fingerplates attached to the same rod-axle were either

[1] Some German makers have used plain pins without screw-ends.

all raised together or all depressed together, although a note-hole
fitted with a ring-key could be opened by raising a finger without
letting the ring rise, provided another ring or fingerplate attached
to the same axle was pressed down. A later type of rod-axle
was that which appears to have been first introduced by the
Paris maker Buffet, jun., about 1838, and which enabled two sorts
of movement to take place on the same axle. This was accomplished by making the axle hollow (tubular) and by passing a
second solid rod through the tubular rod. By this means, the

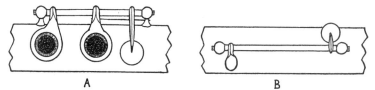

A   B

FIG. 21.—A. Rod-axle with open and ring-keys. Pillars and needle-spring.
B. Rod-axle with fingerplate and closed key.

outer or tubular rod might be made to move independently of
the inner rod, or the two might be coupled together by means
of a connecting pin or a " clutch ".

The rod-axle can be made to operate both open and closed
keys ; in the former case, the fingerplate and key-cover project
on the same side of the rod, but, for closed keys, they project on
opposite sides. The rod-axle can communicate movement over
any distance within reason, and several keys with independent
movements may be attached to the same axle when regulated by
stops, clutches or interlocking devices controlled by separate
springs. There is a saving of weight in the rod-axle mechanism,
and side-play is practically eliminated.

The early 16th and 17th century open keys were provided
with springs of which one end was fixed to the instrument while
the free end pressed downwards on the further end of the first
lever, keeping that end down and the fingerplate up. From near
the end of the 17th century, when keys were mounted in wooden
rings, and later in blocks, a flat brass spring was riveted to the
underside of the key-lever, pressing upwards, thus keeping that

end up when the key was not touched. Steel springs began to
be used before the middle of the 19th century and eventually
superseded the brass springs. Keys mounted on rod-axles and
pillars were at first regulated by flat springs, but in 1837, or soon
after,[1] Buffet of Paris introduced the steel needle-springs which
are now always associated with rod-axles.

Wood-wind instruments in the 16th and during part of the
17th century were made as far as possible from one piece of wood,
that is, without detachable joints. Although the first signs of
jointed instruments occur early in the 17th century, it was not
till towards the close of that century that it became customary to
make instruments in several detachable pieces. Those pieces
(joints) were united by joints of the tenon-and-socket type. To
make the tenon, the end of one piece was thinned to about half

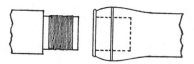

Fig. 22.—Tenon-and-socket joint with ferrule and thread-lapping.

its normal thickness, and a corresponding amount was taken
away from the inside of the piece which received the tenon, thus
forming a socket. In order to give it greater strength, the wood
round the socket was turned rather thicker than the rest of the
tube, and the end was generally protected against strain and
consequent splitting by a ring or ferrule of ivory, bone or metal.
This extra thickness round the socket also served as the ring or
swelling which was made use of to mount the key or keys at the
lower end of the instrument. The tenon was wrapped round
with waxed thread (lapping) in order to make the joint air-tight.

No serious effort seems to have been made during the 18th
century to improve on the thread-wrapped tenon and wooden
socket ; in fact, joints of that sort were still made after the middle
of the 19th century, although by that time the ivory ferrule was
beginning to be replaced by a narrow band of metal which served

[1] First used in England by Ward, the London flute-maker, in 1842.

the same purpose, and it was no longer considered necessary to thicken the joint round the socket. Soon after 1800, improved joints began to appear, more particularly on the more expensive flutes. The inside of the socket was sometimes lined with metal, and the tip of the tenon was strengthened and protected by a ring of metal. A cork-covered tenon made its appearance early in the same century, also a metal inner tube in place of the wooden tenon. Since that time the joints have varied considerably according to the type and class of instrument. The wooden tenon with thread-lapping is not by any means obsolete at the present time, although good-class instruments are usually provided with metal-lined sockets and either cork-covered or thread-wrapped tenons and a protective ring of metal on the tip.

Devices for tuning or slightly modifying the pitch of wood-wind instruments have been known from soon after the middle of the 17th century, if not earlier. They were very necessary adjuncts to the instruments before pitch began to be stabilised during the course of last century. These devices took the form of either alternative middle-pieces of varying lengths or of sliding tenon-and-socket joints. The first of these methods can never have been quite satisfactory, because with the lengthening of any one part of the instrument there should be a corresponding increase in the distances between the note-holes. Nevertheless, many flutes, oboes and clarinets may be found, dating from early in the 18th century till towards the middle of the 19th century, for which two or more alternative middle-pieces were provided. The pieces were generally numbered or marked with a sharp, natural or flat sign in order to distinguish them one from the other. For the same purpose alternative head-joints were sometimes provided for flutes, and short detachable pieces at the upper end of oboes occur on instruments made in the first half of last century. An alternative wing-joint or crook, or a movable upper part of the wing are amongst the devices which occur for tuning bassoons. In the second half of the 18th century, a short extra piece, inserted between the mouthpiece and the upper middle-piece, made its appearance on clarinets ; on account of its shape this was called the "barrel",[1] and by using barrels of varying lengths slightly varying pitches could be accommodated.[2]

The telescopic tuning-slide first makes a tentative appearance on flutes about the middle of the 18th century, but was evidently not found to be a very efficient tuning device as long as the joint was entirely of wood. The thickness of the wooden tenon left a cavity in the inside of the tube when the slide was drawn out ; this was sometimes filled up with little rings of wood specially made for the purpose, even as late as the time of Boehm. The tuning-slide became more common and more efficient rather late in the 18th century, when a thinner metal tube sliding in a metal-lined socket began to replace the thick wooden slide. Tuning-slides of this nature also occur on clarinets, rather less commonly on oboes, and still more rarely on bassoons made during the first half of the 19th century. These sliding joints were sometimes graduated and numbered.

The increased number of keys and the mechanical devices connected with them which appeared on the various wood-wind instruments in such large numbers during the first half of last century demanded increasingly accurate workmanship in the making of them, for, unless they had proved their reliability and efficiency, they would have been condemned by players on the instruments as encumbrances and dangers rather than as aids to playing. As it was, there was considerable opposition on the part of many players to the various devices as they were introduced, partly on the ground that the more mechanical appliances there were on an instrument the more liable it was to get out of order, and partly from a not unnatural disinclination to accustom themselves to new movements of the fingers, or even to entirely new systems of fingering. The tests of reliability and efficiency, when applied to the key-work of that period, would

---

[1] (G.) *Birne*. (F.) *Baril*.

[2] In the price lists issued by makers, both before and during the first half of last century, the extra cost of alternative joints is almost invariably quoted.

easily find out weaknesses which were due to mechanical short-comings, and it is quite certain that without improved methods of manufacture and an ever-increasing precision on the part of the makers, key-work such as we now know would never have become a permanent part of the instruments' outfit.

THE MECHANICS OF BRASS INSTRUMENTS

Two varieties of valve-mechanism are now in use to divert the air-passage of a brass instrument through the extra loops of tubing (valve-tubes) which, when they are added to the original sounding-length, serve to lower the pitch of the instrument ; these are the *piston* and the *rotary* valve. Both are mechanical contrivances which achieve the same end by different means.

The piston valve consists of a cylindrical piston which can move freely up and down in a close-fitting tubular case ; a spiral spring keeps the movable piston up when the button or finger-plate at the top of the piston is not pressed down. There are three channels running transversely through the piston, one of which connects the main inlet tube (coming from the mouth-piece) with the main outlet tube (going towards the bell), and when in a position of rest the air-passage through the instrument merely passes through (across) the piston and does not enter the valve-tube. When the piston is pressed down a second channel connects the main inlet tube with one end of the valve-tube, and the other end of the valve-tube is at the same time connected by a third channel in the piston with the main outlet tube, which then leads either to the next valve or towards the bell of the instrument.

The rotary valve consists of a cylinder revolving in a horizontal plane and enclosed in a case ; it is put into motion by means of cranks or a cord connected with a key or fingerplate, and is regulated by a spring. There are two channels running transversely and parallel to one another through the cylinder, one on either side of the axis on which it rotates. When the key is untouched one of these channels connects the main inlet tube with the main outlet tube, and the air-passage passes through the cylinder without entering the valve-tube. When the key is depressed the cylinder rotates a quarter of a circle and one of the two channels connects the main inlet tube with one end of the valve-tube, while the other channel at the same time connects the other end of the valve-tube with the main outlet tube.

In both types of mechanism the two ends of the valve-tube are soldered to the outer piston or cylinder case, and pressure on the button or fingerplate causes the valve-tube to be added to the original sounding-length of the instrument. All valve-tubes are provided with tuning-slides which can be drawn out, thus lengthening the valve-tube, when necessary ; when a longer crook or shank is put on an instrument all the valve-tubes must be lengthened proportionately, otherwise the valve-produced sounds would be too sharp.

Although the valve-system, consisting of a tubular loopway and a controlling mechanism, dates only from the second decade of the 19th century, the idea of instantaneously lengthening the tube of a brass instrument by diverting the air-passage through additional tubing seems to have had its birth already before the end of the previous century ; it then took the rather clumsy form of joining together two complete instruments of different sounding-lengths so that either one or the other could be sounded without interrupting the playing. Gerber (1792) tells us of one Maräsch [1] who combined two horns, sounding a minor third apart, in some such way. In 1788 Charles Clagget of London patented his idea of uniting a D and an E flat horn or trumpet to a common mouthpiece ; the following is from the patent specification dated August 15, 1788 : " My Sixth New Improvement on Musical Instruments relates to the French horns or trumpets, and consists in uniting together two French horns or trumpets in such a manner that the same mouthpiece may be applied to either of them instantaneously during the time of performance, as the music may require ". Clagget then explains that the narrow ends of the two instruments are brought together

---

[1] Johann Anton Maresch, 1719–1794. See Theo. Rode, " Die russische Jagdmusik ", *Zeitschrift für Musik*, May 27, 1859.

in a box, and that " In the cover of this box, what is commonly called the mouthpiece is fixed by means of a joint, by means of a piece of elastic, gum, or leather, or otherwise, so that the point of the mouthpiece may be directed to the opening of either of the horns or trumpets at pleasure, at the same time that another piece of elastic, gum, or leather, or other proper material, stops the aperture of the horn or trumpet which is not in use ". This rather suggests a movable mouthpiece which could be switched from one instrument to the other, but the nature of the mechanism inside the box is not revealed, nor did Clagget explain how " an entire chromatic scale " could be produced, for the open notes of a D and an E flat instrument combined do not provide all the notes of a chromatic scale until the fourth octave of the harmonic series is reached. There is nothing to show that Clagget's device was anything more than an unsuccessful experiment ; no instruments made according to his plan are available for examination, and there is not the slightest sign that either players or composers took advantage of an invention which, if it had been of any practical use, would surely have been further exploited. It is probable that the writer in Busby's *Concert Room and Orchestra Anecdotes* was not far wrong when he described Clagget as one " the misfortune of whose life it was, to have ideas theoretically sublime, but deficient in practical utility."

Unless fresh evidence comes to light, it will never be known who was actually the originator of the valve-system and the piston mechanism, but it is certain that it was either Heinrich Stölzel or Friedrich Blühmel, and that it was in Berlin that the new device was first exploited during the second decade of last century. The birth of this most important and far-reaching invention cannot be placed much before or after the year 1815.

The earliest evidence of the existence of the valve occurs in a short article written by G. B. Bierey of Breslau which appeared in the *Allgemeine Musikalische Zeitung* (Leipzig) of May 1815, headed " New Discovery " ; the statement therein is to the effect that the *Kammermusikus* Heinrich Stölzel of Ples had invented a simple contrivance by means of which all the sounds of the chromatic scale, over a compass of nearly three octaves, could be played with good effect on a horn without hand-stopping. Again, in an issue of the same paper dated November 1817, under the heading "Wichtige Verbesserung des Waldhorns", an article written by Friedrich Schneider names Stölzel as the inventor of a valve (*ventil*), and rather vaguely hints that the device was a form of air-tight piston which was depressed by the player's finger and which, when released, was restored to its original position by the action of a spring. Yet another short article appeared in the same paper of July 1818, and announced that "Kammermusikus Stölzel und der Berghoboist[1] Blühmel, in Berlin" had invented devices by means of which all the chromatic notes of the scale could be played on the horn, trumpet and trombone without the use of crooks or hand-stopping, and that a patent had been granted protecting the invention in Prussia for a period of ten years. According to Mahillon, who stated that he had procured a copy of the document from Berlin, the patent stands jointly in the names of Blühmel and Stölzel; Mahillon added that the diagrams accompanying the specification were unfortunately lost.

Wilhelm Wieprecht (1802–1872), who settled in Berlin in 1824 and was eventually charged with the reorganisation of the bands of the Prussian Cavalry Guards, wrote some letters which appeared in the *Berliner Musikalische Zeitung* in 1845; in one of these[2] he gave an account of the invention of the valve. According to Wieprecht it was in 1816 or 1817 that Stölzel appeared in Berlin with a three-valved chromatic horn which he claimed to have invented, and for which he was granted a patent in Prussia for a period of ten years. In order to exploit his invention, Stölzel associated himself with the Berlin instrument-makers Griessling und Schlott, who then proceeded to make all manner

---

[1] At that time the word *hoboist* in German was applied to any player in a wind-band, or as one might say, a bandsman; it did not necessarily indicate an oboe-player.

[2] Quoted by Kalkbrenner, p. 88.

of valved brass instruments which, however, proved to be defective and failed to find acceptance. Stölzel then tried to improve on his first design and devised some "push-box-valves" (*Schiebekastenventile*) which were found to be impracticable ; he therefore fell back on " tubular push-valves " (*Röhrenschiebeventile*). From this, it would appear that Stölzel's first valves were tubular piston-valves, and that the rectangular box-valve was an unsuccessful attempt to improve on the cylindrical pistons. Wieprecht stated, incidentally, that musicians in Berlin strenuously opposed the introduction of valved instruments, but that they were more readily welcomed in Russia, France and Austria. Wieprecht continues the story as follows : In 1828, when the patent expired, Blühmel appeared on the scene with his " conical turn-case-valves " (*konischen Drehbüchsenventile*), and on asking for patent rights, was refused on the ground that Stölzel had already been granted a patent for chromatic brass instruments. Blühmel then produced documents purporting to show that he had sold his first invention to Stölzel ten years previously ; he was nevertheless refused a patent, and Stölzel continued to pass as the inventor of the valve. Blühmel's new valve was said to differ from Stölzel's piston-valve only in outward appearance, but the inner construction was the same, and both formed the fundamental basis of the invention. Wieprecht went on to say that Blühmel's valves gave a more even tone than did Stölzel's, because on the former the valve-tubes took a circular course, while on the latter the air-passage encountered a sharp right-angled bend in the tube, but that on the other hand the Stölzel valves were more handy to manipulate. In order to combine the advantages of both types, Wieprecht, later on, himself devised what he called *Stecherbüchsenventile* (pricker-case-valves), and these, being found practicable and satisfactory, were quickly adopted by military bands, and especially by Cavalry bands.

The foregoing account, while it is certainly more specific than the articles of 1815, 1817 and 1818 in the *Allgemeine Musikalische Zeitung*, is nevertheless not quite conclusive because of some uncertainty as to the exact meaning of Wieprecht's expressions *Röhrenschiebeventile, Schiebekastenventile, konischen Dreh-büchsenventile* and *Stecherbüchsenventile.* The first two and the last of these strongly suggest piston-valves, and the third seems to indicate that Blühmel was the originator of the rotary valve. Wieprecht added that, although he knew both Blühmel and Stölzel personally, he never succeeded in finding out which of the two was actually the inventor of the first device for instantaneously lengthening or shortening the tubes of brass instruments. Both claimed the idea as their own and a quarrel ensued which was carried on for many years, not only during the period of the patent, but also after its expiry in 1828. If Wieprecht— who was on the spot, who championed the valve-system in its early stages against considerable opposition, and who was instrumental in introducing valved instruments into Prussian cavalry bands — could not disentangle the problem, it would be unwise now to pronounce in favour of either claimant for the distinction of having initiated the most far-reaching reform in the history of brass instrument making and playing.

The uncertainty which surrounds the invention of the valve was not cleared up by a lengthy footnote which appeared in Kastner's *Manuel général de Musique Militaire* (p. 190), published in Paris in 1848. Therein it is stated that according to a letter written by Spontini (who was conductor at the Royal Opera in Berlin) Blühmel sold his invention at first to Stölzel and later on to Wieprecht. This statement is followed by an abbreviated version of Wieprecht's letter which had appeared in the *Berliner Musikalische Zeitung* in 1845.

Whatever the nature of the earliest valve-mechanism devised by Blühmel or Stölzel, or by both, it is tolerably certain that it embodied a piston movement of some sort, and that the rotary valve was a later invention. Mahillon,[1] whose conclusion was based on the specification of the 1818 patent and on a solitary valve-trumpet in the Brussels collection, supposed that the original mechanism took the form of a rectangular box piston-valve, whereas Wieprecht's letter of 1845 distinctly points to a

---

[1] Cat. Brussels Coll., vol. i, p. 282.

tubular piston-valve. In support of the latter view, it may be remarked that nearly all the earliest valve instruments now surviving are provided with tubular piston-valves, whereas only two specimens with box-valves are known to exist.[1]

The two box-valves [2] with which the trumpet in the Brussels collection is provided are connected with valve-tubes which when in operation lower the pitch of the open sounds by, respectively, a tone and a semitone, the tone-valve being that which is situated nearest the mouthpiece. The piston is a solid rectangular block of brass which moves up and down in a brass case of a similar shape ; it is regulated by a spring and is worked by a thin

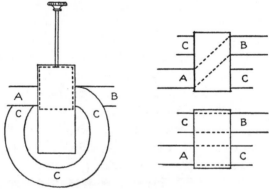

FIG. 23.—A. Main inlet tube. B. Main outlet tube. C-C. Valve-tube.

shank with a button or fingerplate on the upper end. When the button is untouched, a channel, bored diagonally through the brass block, connects the main inlet and outlet tubes, and when depressed two parallel channels in the block connect the inlet and outlet tubes with the two ends of the valve-tube so that the air-passage goes through the valve-tube. On this particular instrument one of the valve-tubes curls round below the box and the other makes a circuit above the box.

The valve which became known in Germany as the *schub-ventil* (push-valve), and for some time was, rightly or wrongly,

[1] Brussels Cat. vol. ii, p. 482 and R.M.E. Cat. Plate x; Berlin Cat. p. 212, No. 3104.
[2] (G.) *Büchsenventil.* (F.) *Piston à boîte carrée.*

associated with the name of Stölzel, was a slender cylindrical piston-valve very similar in appearance to the present-day pistons. Large numbers of trumpets, cornets, horns and other instruments made from about 1830 to 1850 were provided with at first two, and later on with three valves of this type.

Referring to Fig. 24 (a), it will be seen that the air-passage (A) enters the valve at the side and turns sharply downwards through the hollow piston, finding its outlet through the bottom of the

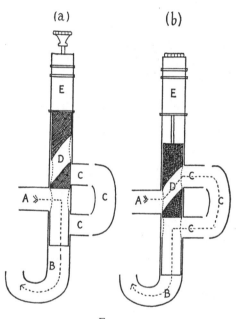

Fig. 24.

piston-case (B) when the button is untouched, and that when the piston is pressed down (Fig. 24 (b)) the air-passage is diverted through the channel (D) into the valve-tube (C), and returning to the piston, finds its outlet through the bottom of the valve (B) after making a sharp turn downwards. A spiral spring in the cylinder at (E) keeps the piston up when the button is untouched. For an adjacent valve the direction of the air-passage was reversed, and the inlet was then through the bottom of the valve (B) while the outlet was at the side (A).

There is plenty of evidence that by about 1830 the piston-valve was becoming known in France, Belgium, Russia, Austria and England. The composer Spontini claimed that he sent from Berlin to Paris a number of instruments with two and three valves (the first known in Paris) between 1823 and 1831 ; [1] there they were speedily copied by French makers, who then began to add improvements of their own and to re-invent valves which undoubtedly owed their existence to the German piston or *schub-ventil*. It seems that the valve reached England via Russia ; [2] valve-trumpets, in fact, were first known in this country as " Russian valve or stop trumpets ".[3] Soon after 1830 valved instruments were being freely made in France, Belgium, Holland, Italy and England, as well as in Germany and Austria.

It has frequently been stated that the third valve was first added by C. A. Müller of Mayence in 1830 ; the specification of the patent granted to Labbaye (Paris) in 1827, however, shows a drawing of a trumpet with three valves, and the Spontini document, already referred to, specifically mentions instruments " à deux ou trois pistons ou ventiles ".

A number of improvements or modifications of the first piston-valves, also some new mechanical contrivances designed for the same purpose, were introduced by various makers between about 1830 and 1850. Some of these held their own until well after the mid-century, notably the *Berliner-pumpen* [4] devised by Wieprecht and Moritz of Berlin in 1835, the Vienna-valve (*Wiener-ventil*) probably due to Uhlmann of Vienna shortly before 1830, and the improved piston-valve known by the name of its designer, the Périnet-valve (Paris, 1839). The first of these was a short wide-bored cylindrical piston-valve in which the two ends of the valve-tube were placed opposite each other in the same horizontal plane as the main inlet and outlet tubes. The Vienna-valve may have been based on a somewhat similar device invented

1 Kastner, *Manuel,* p. 192.
2 Farmer, *Rise and Development of Military Music,* p. 103.
3 Harper, *Instructions for the Trumpet* (1835–1837).
4 Probably the *Stecherbüchsenventile* mentioned by Wieprecht.

by John Shaw of Glossop and patented as early as 1824 under the name Transverse Spring Slides.[1] As made by Uhlmann,[2] this type was in the form of a U-shaped tube, placed at right-angles to the main tube, in which a double piston moved up and down by the action of a lever or key not unlike that which actuates the rotary-valve of the present day. These valves are still in use in Vienna at the present time, although their popularity generally declined soon after the middle of last century. On Périnet's valves, the two ends of the valve-tube were placed one above and the other below the plane of the main inlet and outlet tubes. On

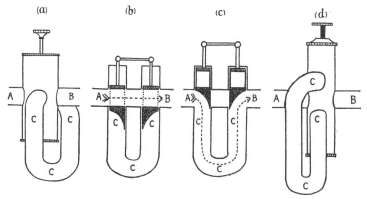

Fig. 25.—(a) Berliner-pumpen. (b) Section of Vienna-valve, closed. (c) The same, open. (d) Périnet-valve.

all the above types, the inlet and outlet tubes were at the side of the piston-case ; the use of the bottom of the piston case as an inlet or outlet passage was discontinued in all the newer and improved types of piston-valves.

After 1850 there was not much scope left for inventors of piston-valves, and the efforts of makers were then devoted rather to improving the design and mechanical details of the device which was first exploited in Berlin by Stölzel and Blühmel. These improvements were largely concerned with preserving a uniform bore throughout the valve-channels, with avoiding sharp turns

[1] Patent No. 5013 (1824).

[2] Joh. Tob. Uhlmann made trombones with Vienna-valves in 1830. (Nemetz, *Posaun-Schule.*)

in the passages, and with many small improvements in connection with the springs, the slots which keep the piston from rotating in its case, the washers which prevent a noisy action, and other mechanical details. Prominent amongst those who contributed towards perfecting the piston-valve before and round about the middle of last century were the Paris makers Halary, Labbaye, Besson and Courtois, the Belgian Adolphe Sax (then settled in Paris), Wieprecht and Moritz of Berlin, Embach of Amsterdam, Riedl and Uhlmann of Vienna, Dr. Oates, an English doctor of medicine, and the London maker Henry Distin, whose " light-valve " was patented in 1864.

In the meantime another mechanism for diverting the air-passage through the valve-tubes had made its appearance, one which in the end proved itself the only serious rival of the piston-valve ; this was the rotary valve.[1] Grove and Day (R.M.E. Cat.) place its appearance as early as *c.* 1820, but there seems to be no evidence to support this early estimate. If Wieprecht's expression *Drehbüchsenventil* can be identified as a rotary valve, the credit for inventing the latter is certainly due to Blühmel in 1827, but Wieprecht's account of how he improved that valve and as the result produced his *Stecherbüchsenventil*, which was almost certainly a piston-valve, creates some doubt as to whether Blühmel's valve of 1827 was really of the rotary type. Failing Blühmel, credit for inventing this valve-mechanism must go to Jos. Riedl of Vienna, whose *Rad-maschine*[2] of 1832 was undoubtedly a rotary valve. However it may be, there are surviving instruments enough to prove that this sort of valve-mechanism was being made in the 'thirties, and that German and Austrian makers eventually adopted it as their standard valve after the *schubventil* and the *Berliner-pumpen* had become merged in the piston-valve common to French, Belgian and English makers. Fig. 26 shows the working of the cylinder which is turned or pulled round by means of cranks or cords connected with a key or fingerplate.

---

[1] (G.) *Drehventil, Zylinderventil.* (F.) *Cylindre à rotation.*
[2] Th. Rode, *Neue Berliner Musikzeitung*, 1860.

Although the patent records of the period 1850–1870 reveal the fact that some English makers and inventors were then occupied in designing and making rotary valves, those valves have never been generally adopted in this country ; some surviving instruments supply evidence that they were being made in Paris about that time both by Ad. Sax and Antoine Courtois.[1]

The foregoing is an outline of the history of the valve-system controlled by either pistons or rotary action. Both of these devices are in use today ; they are the fittest survivors of several attempts made during last century to provide an apparatus by

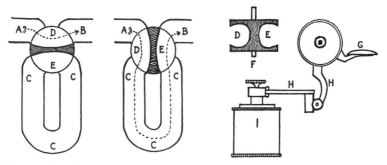

Fig. 26.—A. Inlet tube. B. Outlet tube. C-C. Valve-tube. D E. Passages through rotating cylinder. F. Section of rotating cylinder. H H. Cranks. I. Cylinder case.

means of which the air-passage through the valve-tubes or loopways on a brass instrument could be instantaneously opened or closed.

A number of less successful valve mechanisms are on record, including amongst English devices the " disc-valve " and the " finger-slide ". The former seems to have been first attempted by Halary of Paris in 1835 [2] under the name *plaques tournantes* ; the same principle underlies a similar device introduced and patented by John Shaw in 1838.[3] These valves, first known as " patent levers ", were used for some time on cornets and

[1] French instruments with rotary valves were sold in London by Henry Distin and Arthur Chappell soon after 1850.

[2] Pierre, *Les Facteurs*, p. 335.

[3] Patent No. 7892 (1838), Wind Musical Instruments.

trumpets made by Köhler of London, and, after having been given a fair trial, were eventually rejected on account of mechanical shortcomings. The arrangement as shown in the diagrams of the patent specification differs slightly from that of the actual instruments made by Köhler ; on the latter there are two circular plates or discs placed face to face, and one of these, rotated by a lever and finger-button, is provided with two short loopways of tubing one of which connects the main inlet and outlet tubes ; when the button and lever are pressed down, the movable disc revolves a quarter of a circle and the same loopway then connects the inlet tube with one end of the valve-tube, while the other loopway connects the other end of the valve-tube with the outlet tube. A specimen of one of these disc-valve cornets is often to be found in collections of old wind instruments. (Pl. XXII, c.)

The finger-slide, invented by Samson in 1862 and improved later on by C. A. Goodison, is rarely seen. It was made by Rudall, Rose, Carte and Co., London. On these the piston-case contained only a lever, which, through an opening in the side of the case, communicated an up and down movement to the actual valve, which was situated inside a part of the valve-tube lying parallel to the piston-case.[1]

The middle of last century marks the beginning of a long series of attempts made by many makers and players to remedy the inherent weakness of all three-valve systems. (See Section V.) The various compensating valves or systems, as they are called, sought to correct the shortage of valve-tube length by contriving that some extra tubing was automatically added whenever two or three valves were used simultaneously. As well as by compensating valves, efforts were made to ensure better intonation, that is, sufficient tube-length, for every valve-produced sound by providing separate valves and valve-tubes for every semitone stage below the open notes of the harmonic series. Thus, a number of schemes were devised which involved

[1] Specimens in Brussels Coll., No. 1272, and in the author's Coll., No. 102.

the addition of two or three extra valves. Some of these systems were carried out by means of *shortening* or *ascending* valves, which, contrary to the principle of the lengthening-valve, cut off so much tubing when they were operated, thus raising the pitch instead of lowering it by means of added tubing. Some of the most important of these schemes are the following :

1852. *Adolphe Sax.* A six-piston system with shortening-valves.

1853. *Gustav Besson (Paris).* Each valve was provided with an extra piece of tubing which could be added to the ordinary valve-tube ; the control of the extra tubing was by means of a rotary cylinder-valve and a key placed alongside the piston.

1856–1857. *Gustav Besson. Registre.* A horizontal lengthening-valve (in addition to the usual three) which when used substituted another set of longer valve-tubes.

1858–1859. *Besson-Giradin. Transpositeur.* A similar, but improved *Registre.*

1856. *de Rette and Courtois (Paris).* Two extra piston-valves providing additional tube-length.

1873. *Léon Cousin (Paris).* A five-valve system in which the fourth and fifth valves lowered the pitch, respectively, a perfect fourth and a major third.

1874. *Thibouville-Lamy.* Two keys were used to adjust the length of the air-passage when valves were used in combination.

1874. *D. J. Blaikley (London).* Boosey's compensating valves. A device by means of which extra tubing was automatically brought into use when the valves were combined ; this was done without the use of any additional pistons or keys.

1881. *Sudre (Paris).* Another device for automatically lengthening the valve-tubes.

1883. *Arban (Paris).* A compensating scheme involving the use of the L. middle finger to work a fourth valve, and a lever for the L. index finger which transformed the third valve into a major third instead of a minor third.

1884. *Daniel and Sudre* (*Paris*). Automatic addition of tube-
length when the valves were combined.

1885–1888. *Arban-Bouvet* (*Paris*). A series of modifications of
the Arban (1883) and Daniel (1884) devices which ended
in a compensating system without any extra valves.

1886. *Mahillon* (*Brussels*). Compensating devices, the first
requiring a fourth valve ; later improved, and by inter-
connection of valves and the addition of two extra loopways
on the first valve, becoming automatic, thus dispensing
with the fourth valve.

Most of the above devices were applied to tubas, bombardons,
saxhorns and cornets. The list is not complete, but it will suffice
to show how much concern has been shown for the imperfections of the three-valve system. In the end, however, it may be
said that compensating devices have never come into general use
for the smaller and higher-pitched brass instruments, while for
the wide-bored bass instruments on which the useful range lies
so low in the harmonic series that valve-combinations are necessarily more often used, it is almost imperative to seek the aid of
either compensating devices or extra valves.

Mention of many details and side-lines in the history of the
valve must necessarily be omitted here, for they are too many
and have often been too transient to figure in a general survey of
the subject. Makers have experimented from time to time, for
example, with shortening-valves, with conical valves, with combined valve and slide systems, and many of their efforts may
now be seen reposing in the glass cases of the principal European
collections of musical instruments, there giving silent testimony
to much ingenuity and fertility of invention.

Valved brass instruments were adopted first by military and
brass bands, and then only rather slowly and grudgingly were
they admitted into orchestras.[1] That it took nearly half a century

---

[1] Wieprecht reorganised a Prussian cavalry band, and included some
valve instruments, about, or soon after, 1825. About the same time Gott.
Rode began to make use of valves in the band of a *jäger* regiment at
Potsdam.

for the valve to become firmly established as an essential part of the mechanism of brass instruments was probably due to the mechanical inefficiency of the early valves. The makers of brass instruments, accustomed, as they were, to fashioning only the plain brass tube without any mechanism, had to learn a new craft when they embarked on the construction of valves. New processes, new tools and new machinery had to be devised in order to make a mechanism which required not only careful and accurate workmanship, but also involved problems in the cutting, bending and joining of metals such as did not arise in the pre-valve period. The making of air-channels running diagonally in curves through the piston was not a matter which could be accomplished by casual or improvised methods; it is even now intricate, specialised and highly skilled work which requires special tools and machinery. Small wonder, then, that the early makers of valves failed to produce mechanism that was dependable in its action, free from leakage, and based on principles that were both acoustically and mechanically sound; a valve must not only work well, but it must wear well; not until all these requirements were fulfilled did players finally abandon the " natural " instruments, of which they knew the shortcomings and pitfalls only too well, in favour of new instruments which, unless they lived up to the claims made on their behalf, opened up possibilities of mechanical failure such as could not have befallen the plain unmechanised tube.

The tuning-slide[1] on a brass instrument now usually consists of a detachable U-shaped tube of cylindrical bore, the two arms of which must be strictly parallel, although the shape of the bend at the bottom of the U may vary infinitely. The two parallel arms of the slide fit closely either inside or outside of two parallel ends of the main tube of the instrument, which must be broken or interrupted at the point where the tuning-slide is fitted. When the slide is drawn out the sounding-length of the instrument is increased, and the pitch is lowered accordingly. The tuning-slide now usually fits inside the ends of the main tube, but on the

---

[1] (G.) *Stimmzug*. (F.) *Coulisse d'accord*.

earlier 19th-century instruments and up to about fifty or sixty years ago, the slide was sometimes on the outside, or one arm might be inside and the other outside. These slides are used for making small adjustments of pitch and should not be confused with crooks or shanks the purpose of which is to alter the harmonic series, or in other words, to put the instrument into another key.

The tuning-slide first appears late in the 18th century and is said to have been invented by a German maker named Haltenhof

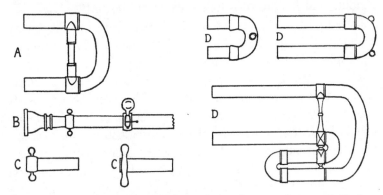

Fig. 27.—A. Tuning-slide.   B. Tuning-slide (single) at mouthpiece.   C. Tuning "bits".   D. Slides for tuning valve-tubes.

in 1781.[1] Similar slides began to be fitted to valve-tubes soon after the valve-system came into use ; these serve to tune each valve individually, and may vary in shape from the short U such as is used for the middle valve of trumpets and cornets, to a long-armed U, or the many bent and curled shapes found on the third valve of the longer instruments. Tuning-slides are often strengthened by a cross-stay, and are sometimes provided with a ring or a knob or two knobs at the end of the bend so as to give a better grip when the slide is to be drawn out.

Another form of tuning-slide is that which is sometimes found on the earlier saxhorns, on flügelhorns, posthorns, etc., also on some of the later keyed bugles. This is a single slide inserted at the narrow end of the instrument so that the mouth-

[1] *Sachs, Real-Lexikon.*

piece fits into one end of it. The extreme end of the main tube is generally split and a ligature screw serves to keep the slide in position when it has been readjusted. A screw and ratchet wheel was sometimes provided to regulate and fix the slide.

An older method of tuning brass instruments is to provide them with a selection of short pieces of tubing of slightly varying lengths. One or more of these are inserted between the narrow end of the instrument and the mouthpiece. One end of the tuning " bit " is slightly tapered so that it just fits inside the tube, and the end which receives the mouthpiece is strengthened by an encircling band with two projecting lugs for the more convenient handling of the bit. Tuning bits were much used on 18th-century trumpets, and have been largely employed to tune 19th-century valve and slide-trumpets, also keyed-bugles, ophicleides, saxhorns, etc.

A crook [1] is a bent or coiled detachable tube, and a shank a straight tube, by means of which a brass instrument can be temporarily lengthened, and thereby lowered in pitch. The earliest evidence of the use of crooks seems to be that given by Praetorius (1619), who shows illustrations of oblong tone-crooks for trumpet and trombone, a circular crook on a *Jägertrommet*, also a straight shank evidently belonging to a trombone.[2] In the text Praetorius states that *Krummbügel* were of recent origin.

The early crooks were usually fitted at the mouthpiece end of the instrument, but after about 1750–1760 they were also made in the form of sliding crooks with parallel ends fitting into the middle of the tube of horns, as on the *inventions-hörner* of Hampel. Straight shanks have latterly been used only for trumpets and cornets to lower the pitch a semitone, but tone-shanks were evidently used late in the 18th century on trumpets.[3] The usual tone-crook, however, was coiled in a small circle, or, when it was required to lower the pitch more than a tone, was

---

[1] (G.) *Stimmbogen, Krummbügel, Aufsatzbogen, Aufsteckbogen, Einsatzbogen.* (F.) *Corps de rechange.*

[2] *Theatrum Instrumentorum*, pl. viii.

[3] Altenburg, 1795.

bent in an oblong with rounded corners. Horn crooks have
generally been coiled in from one to three complete hoops.

The term " crook " is also used to denote the narrow metal
end of the bassoon tube, and the bent or coiled metal tube which
forms the narrow end of serpents, bass-horns and ophicleides.

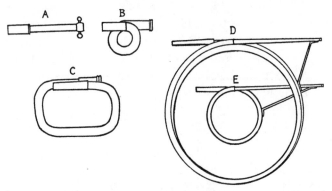

FIG. 28.—A. Cornet shank.   B. Trumpet E-crook.   C. Trumpet D-crook.
D. Horn F-crook.   E. Horn high B-flat-crook.

When keys were used on brass instruments they were mounted
on brass saddles (see Section VII), but in the final stage of their
existence the keys were sometimes supported in pillars standing
in footplates.

The bells [1] of brass instruments from the 16th century till
about the middle of last century were always finished off with a
broad band of metal fixed outside the bell and overlapping its
extreme edge. After that time the rim of the bell has been turned
over backwards so as to make a rounded edge, and latterly a wire
has been enclosed in the turn at the rim.

[1] (G.) *Schallstück, Stürze.* (F.) *Pavillon.*

THE TRANSVERSE FLUTE

(E.) German flute (18th century). Cross flute. Flute.
(G.) Querflöte. Flöte.
(F.) Flûte d'Allemagne. Flûte traversière. Traversière. Flûte.
(I.) Flauto traverso. Flauto.

THE origin of the flute which is sounded by means of an air-stream directed against the edge of a hole in the side of the tube is hidden away in some period which is far too remote for musical-historical research. The quite recognisable representations of this type of instrument which occur in the carvings, manuscripts and pictures of the Middle Ages suggest that it was then a cylindrical tube with six finger-holes and a stopper or plug at the head, and that it was held, according to taste or custom, either to the right or to the left of the player's face. Actual instruments of the Middle Ages are not available, and even the 16th and 17th centuries have left remarkably few specimens of an instrument which is too often mentioned and depicted to have been at all an uncommon type. Early in the 13th century the association between the flute or cylindrical fife and the small side-drum as the characteristic musical accompaniment for the infantryman on the march seems to have been already established; such terms as *Schweitzerpfeiff* (Swiss-pipe), or *zwerchpfeiff*, occurring in the 14th, 15th and 16th centuries, place the instrument in the hands of the Swiss soldier.

THE KEYLESS, CYLINDRICAL FLUTE

The very few 16th- or early 17th-century flutes which survive in some of the continental collections [1] are made from one piece

[1] Vienna, Brussels, Verona.

of wood, without any joints ; they are cylindrical, and are provided with a mouth-hole and six finger-holes. The specimens
are too few to form the basis of any satisfying conclusion as to
a standard length and pitch, yet from early in the 17th century
there are signs that the instrument of just under 2 feet in length,
sounding the primary scale of D major, was to become the
standard flute of the future.

A few particulars about these one-piece cylindrical and keyless flutes, dating from about 1500 to 1650, may be gleaned from
the pages of the earliest books devoted to musical instruments,
namely, those by Virdung (1511), Agricola (1528 and 1545),
Praetorius (1619–1620) and Mersenne (1636).

Virdung shows a crude woodcut of a (too) narrow flute
with six finger-holes placed unusually close together ; this he
names a *zwerchpfeiff*, and associates it with a small drum as the
instrument of the soldier (*kriegsknecht*). Agricola shows rather
better proportioned representations of four flutes of different
sizes, named *schweitzerpfeiffen* ; the two middle members of the
group, the *tenor* and *altus*, hardly differ in length and share the
same table of fingering. From the latter it would appear that
there were only three sizes, and that these were pitched a perfect
fifth apart. The three tables of fingering show that each flute
had a compass of a little over two octaves, and that forkfingering
was already practised. Praetorius is more specific ; he makes a
distinction between the flute proper (*Querflötten*, *Querpfeiffen*,
(Ital.) *Traversa*) and the small military fife (*Schweitzerpfeiffen*,
Feldpfeiffen). His family of flutes are in three sizes, the largest
of which appears to be jointed between the mouth-hole and the
finger-holes. According to Praetorius, each of these flutes had a
" natural " compass of two octaves, and in addition, four more
" *falset* " notes which only unusually skilled players could produce. The following shows the pitch, compass and approximate
lengths of the three flutes which constitute the complete group
(*ganz stimmwerck*) :

	Natural Compass	Falset	Mouth-hole to Foot
Discant . .	$a' — a'''$	$b''' — e''''$	14 inches
Alto or tenor .	$d' — d'''$	$e''' — a'''$	22 ,,
Bass . .	$g — g''$	$a'' — d'''$	32 ,,

It was the middle member of this family of three, the tenor or alto in D, which was destined to become the standard flute of the 18th century.

Mersenne cites two transverse flutes which he names *Flûtes d'Allemands*, respectively in d' and g. The shorter of the two measures nearly 23½ inches from the end of the stopper just above the mouth-hole to the end of the foot. A curiously warped specimen is depicted, and a table of fingering gives the diatonic scale of D over two octaves (fundamentals and octave-harmonics) extended to a''' by using the twelfth and double-octave harmonics.

After Mersenne's contribution, our knowledge of the history of the keyless cylindrical flute comes to a sudden end, and, after a period regarding which the historian must either remain silent or fall back on his imagination, the instrument emerges near the end of the 17th century in a practically standardised form which was to hold good for about a hundred years.

It is worthy of note that the division of Praetorius' bass flute into two joints foreshadows what was going to happen to all flutes except the small military fife. A 17th-century keyless flute in the Vienna Collection [1] is divided into three parts ; the head-joint contains the mouth-hole, a middle-piece has no holes, and a lower piece has the six finger-holes. This, however, appears to be a solitary specimen and may not represent a common type. Moreover, the divisions of the tube are not made in the same places as on the late 17th-century one-keyed and jointed flute.

THE ONE-KEYED CONICAL FLUTE

The new type appeared during the second half of the 17th

[1] No. 187.

century. It is not known by whom or where it was first made ; dates which are sometimes advanced may be taken as guesses which are probably not far wrong, yet which cannot be supported by incontrovertible evidence. All that can be stated with certainty is that the conical one-keyed flute was unknown early in the 17th century, and that by the end of that century it was known and used. There is no definite proof that the one-keyed flute originated in France, yet it is highly probable that, in common with the jointed oboe, it owes its origin to that country, and it seems that the first well-known performers on the instrument were Frenchmen.[1]

Johann Joachim Quantz, a famous German player and teacher of Frederick the Great, writing in 1752, stated that the D sharp key was first added to the flute in France, and that it was then (1752) not yet a hundred years old ; Quantz also remarked that this key was adopted in Germany about " fifty or sixty years ago ". From this it would appear that the advent of the key occurred after the middle of the 17th century, and that it found its way to Germany just before the beginning of the 18th century. The first tutor for the instrument was that by Louis Hotteterre (*Le Romain*), published in Paris in 1707. As the author in his preface states that this was one of the most agreeable and fashionable of instruments, there seems to be no doubt that the one-keyed conical flute, for which these instructions were written, was by that time well established in France.

The principal features of the new instrument were :

(a) The *conical bore*, widest at the head and tapering towards the foot, thus adopting the bore of the *Flûtes-à-bec* or recorders.

(b) The *closed D sharp key*, covering a hole bored below the E hole and controlled by the R. little finger, thus providing the only chromatic note in the primary scale of D which could not be produced by forkfingering.

(c) The *division of the flute* into at first three, and later on,

---

[1] Philibert, La Barre, Louis Hotteterre, Buffardin.

four pieces, fitted together by means of tenon-and-socket joints.

(d) The *tonality of D major*.

The bore of the 18th-century flute was not entirely conical ; the head was cylindrical, with an inside diameter of just under ¾ inch (18 to 19 mm.), a measurement which shows very little variation at any period. The taper begins at the top of the upper-middle joint and continues to the beginning of the foot, where it is approximately just under ½ inch in diameter ; thence to the end of the foot the bore varies considerably, being sometimes cylindrical and sometimes expanding.

The earlier instruments were made in three pieces with the six finger-holes on the middle-piece. Later on, the middle-piece

FIG. 29.—Early 18th-century flute with convex foot.

was divided into two joints between the third and the fourth finger-hole, probably so that different lengths of middle-pieces might be used alternatively in order to suit the variable pitches of the period. The very earliest of these flutes can be distinguished by the convex exterior of the foot [1] ; the later and more common model has a straight or slightly tapering foot. The usual material for making flutes during the 18th and early 19th century was boxwood ; ebony and other hard woods or ivory were also used. The keys were of brass or silver, and the ferrules, likewise the cap over the end of the head, were generally of ivory, bone or silver. The mouth-hole was at first round and small, later, sometimes oval and tending to increase in size, but always varying according to the taste or habit of the player.

The finger-holes were small and variable in size, those for both third fingers being smaller than those for the two second fingers, and placed so far up the tube that they could be covered

[1] See the illustrations in Hotteterre (1707) ; *The Modern Musick Master* (1731) ; Eisel (1738) ; Cat. Berlin Coll. Nos. 2667, 2670 ; Galpin, plate xxxi, No. 2 ; Welch, *History*, pp. 225 and 226.

without much discomfort rather than with a view to good intonation and an even tone. The stopper was an ordinary cork ;
although even as early as Quantz's time some sort of screw device
for regulating the position of the cork was known, this convenience is not commonly found on flutes till near the end of the
18th century.

Following that of Hotteterre (1707), quite a number of instruction books for the one-keyed transverse flute (German flute)
were published ; several of these appeared in England, where the
instrument had become a great favourite with amateurs. The
following are the authors or titles of some of these tutors, not
all of which were devoted entirely to the flute : Hotteterre
(1707). Corrette (*c.* 1730). Schickhard (1730). *The Modern
Musick Master* (1731). Eisel (1738). Majer (1741). *Compleat
Tutor* (several, from *c.* 1750 to 1800). Quantz (1752). *The
Muses' Delight* (1754). Mahaut (1759). Granom (1766). Heron
(1771). *New Instructions* (several, *c.* 1780–1802). Gunn (1793).
Devienne (1795).

The fingering charts given in these 18th-century tutors show
that the compass expected of the flute was from d' to a''', completely chromatic for the first two octaves, but lacking the high F
in the earliest charts.[1] A slight extension of the upward compass
is shown in the charts towards the end of the century, and by
that time the F in the third octave was also included.

Such was the simple one-keyed flute of the 18th century, the
instrument for which Bach, Handel, Mozart and Haydn wrote.
Numbers of these instruments can be seen in nearly all collections of wind instruments, from the cheapest boxwood instrument with brass keys to the expensive and elaborate ebony or
ivory flutes of the wealthy amateur. To the collector they have
an indefinable charm ; to the modern player they are useless old
things which, if they arouse any interest at all, awaken only
feelings of sympathy for the old players who had to manage
with such inferior instruments. With all their imperfections,
however, they evidently served their purpose quite well, for till

[1] See Fingering Chart No. 1 (Hotteterre).

the last quarter of the century very little effort was made really to improve on the instrument which had made its appearance about a hundred years earlier. Provided they were not called upon to play in keys very remote from the foundation key of D, they evidently satisfied the players and composers of several generations.[1] (Pl. I, A, B and C.)

That some of the forked sounds were dull and out of tune seems to have been philosophically accepted as a natural weakness of the instrument which it was the player's duty to conceal by skilful manipulation; the wind-players of that period accepted their instruments as they accepted (we hope) their wives — for better or for worse. The doubtful intonation did not escape the notice of musicians; the English historian Hawkins, writing in 1776, remarked scathingly of the German flute that it " still retains some degree of estimation among gentlemen whose ears are not nice enough to inform them that it is never in tune ", and Burney (1772) knew that it was " natural to those instruments to be out of tune ".

An enormous quantity of music, original and " adapted ", for one or two flutes, was issued during the 18th century; much of it may now be found lying undisturbed in musical libraries all over Europe. These publications, together with numbers of old instruments and an abundance of contemporary instruction books, testify to the great popularity of the transverse flute during the 18th century.

In spite of the chromatic keys which began to be added to the flute in the last quarter of the 18th century, the one-keyed instrument held its own well into the early part of the 19th century; contemporary instruction books and numerous surviving instruments demonstrate that the one-keyed flute was by no means obsolete when Beethoven was writing his symphonies. The early 19th-century makers were prepared to supply flutes with almost anything from one to eight keys; the more keys there were, the higher the price of the instrument. Several tutors

---

[1] Tromlitz, writing near the end of the 18th century, stated that keys with more than three sharps or flats were *difficult and unsuitable* for the flute.

after 1800 continued to treat the one-keyed flute as the standard instrument, and added supplementary information for the use of players whose up-to-date instruments included the new " additional " keys.

Attempts to improve the flute between 1700 and 1775 appear to have been both few and transient. Quantz, it is true, added an E flat key alongside the D sharp key in 1726, but even on German instruments this extra key is rarely found.[1] There was some sort of an attempt to prolong the downward compass of the flute in the first half of the 18th century,[2] and Majer's fingering chart (1741) demands a low C. The foot-keys were not approved by Quantz, and are not to be found on flutes till the last quarter of the century.

The following are some of the makers of transverse flutes in the 18th century, roughly divided into an earlier and a later group :

Early Group	*Later Group*
Denner (Nürnberg)	Lot (Paris)
Hotteterre (Paris)	Scherer ——
Bressan (London)	Rottenburgh (Brussels)
Stanesby, T. (London)	Willems (Brussels)
Stanesby, jun. (London)	Cahusac (London)
Boie (Göttingen)	Eisenbrant (Göttingen)
Bizey (Paris)	Grenser A. (Dresden)
Anciuti (Milan)	Schlegel (Basle)
	Potter (London)

Four to Eight-keyed Flutes

In the last quarter of the 18th century a consciousness seems to have arisen that the flute *was* capable of being improved. The veiled, forked chromatic notes were poor in quality and intonation, and would be improved if each could sound from a note-hole of its own. The L. little finger was unemployed, and lay conveniently handy to work a key between the G and the A holes ;

---

[1] Tromlitz was one of the few who retained Quantz's E flat key.

[2] About 1722 (Quantz).

so a hole for G sharp was bored below the A hole on the far side at the lower end of the upper middle-piece, and was provided with a closed key for the L. little finger lying longways down the flute. The L. thumb was also handy to control a B flat hole bored on the near side of the tube below the B natural ; this was covered by a closed key lying longways. For an F natural there was no finger to spare, but, of the forked sounds, this was the worst and its improvement was urgent ; so a hole was bored between the E and the F sharp holes, and it was covered by a closed cross-key which had to be worked by the R. third finger in addition to controlling the E hole. The only remaining chromatic note in the scale of D was the C natural, played with all holes open except one ; this was not such a bad note, so for the time being it was left alone. Makers did not want to encumber the instrument with any more rings or swellings on its surface, so they mounted the new keys in small wooden blocks. (See Section VII.)

So the four-keyed flute came into being, a pioneer amongst wood-wind instruments in adopting additional chromatic keys in its primary scale. A number of flutes, most of them made between 1785 and 1820, survive to tell of the popularity of the four-keyed instrument during the period which covered most of the working-life of Beethoven. To the instruction books current at the time, supplementary scales, instructions and shake-fingerings involving use of the new keys were added. The new keys were not accepted without opposition by players who knew from experience that one key could fail to function, and who were rather reluctant to multiply that danger by four. There is some evidence that the new keys were known as early as 1774,[1] but surviving instruments and contemporary instruction books suggest that they did not begin to be generally adopted till about ten or fifteen years later. Even then players were reluctant to change their accustomed fingering, and used the new keys for shakes rather than for improving the quality of the forked sounds. (Pl. I, D and E.)

[1] See Rockstro, p. 244 ; Welch, *Six Lectures*, p. 96.

Despite some opposition and distrust of these new-fangled inventions, some flutes made during the last quarter of the 18th century are provided with not only the four chromatic keys, but also with two additional foot-keys which carry the compass of the instrument down to C. There cannot have been any great urgency for increasing the downward range of the flute ; it had been attempted before, but apparently without any great success. Yet the oboe had its low C, and the starting-point of the whole musical system seemed to be C, so the flute was lengthened by about two inches and the added portion was pierced by two note-holes which were necessarily covered by open keys. The R. little finger was put in charge of them, and was now responsible for working three keys. In order to sound the low C, the C sharp key had to be closed, and for that reason the fingerplate of the latter key was placed underneath that of the former so that the two went down together when the C key was depressed, but the fingerplate of the C sharp key was allowed to project a little in front of the other so that it could be pressed down without moving the C key. The oldest known flutes with foot-keys appear to be those by the London maker Richard Potter.[1] Except that they work on rod-axles, the three keys at the lower extremity of the flute remain just as they were at the end of the 18th century. The up-to-date flute at the close of the century, therefore, was a six-keyed instrument with two open foot-keys and four closed chromatic keys. Numbers of these six-keyed flutes were made round about 1800, and instruction books began to provide for the " newly-invented " keys. (Pl. I, F and G.)

Yet another key remained to be added in order to make the key-system of the flute fully chromatic ; this was the closed key for c'' natural. It had been advocated by Ribock in 1782, and after some uncertainty as to its position, the hole was bored on

---

[1] Historical Soc. Coll. (Chicago), with only one foot-key, dated 1776 ; Carse Coll. (London), dated 1777 ; Dayton C. Miller Coll. (Cleveland), dated 1778. The last two have both foot-keys, and on the one dated 1777 the two fingerplates are independent, thus, to sound low C, both fingerplates would have to be depressed at the same time.

the near-side of the flute, between the B and C sharp holes, and a long shank brought the fingerplate so far down the instrument that it could be operated by the R. first finger. (Pl. I, H.)

The eight-keyed flute, the up-to-date instrument of the early 19th century, was completed by the addition of a duplicate F natural key. The difficulty which is always experienced when one finger is required to move sideways from a key to an adjacent hole (or *vice versa*), arose in connection with the R. third finger, which had to control the E hole and the F natural cross-key. It was almost impossible to slur from F to D or D sharp (or *vice versa*) without sounding an involuntary grace note (E) in between. In order to overcome this difficulty another F natural hole was bored on the far side of the flute, and this was covered by a long closed key worked by the L. little finger.[1] (Pl. I, I.)

Claims for the credit of having " invented " the additional keys of the flute have been made on behalf of many players and makers, rather many, in fact, for the number of added keys.[2] Now, after the passage of about 150 years, any attempt to disentangle these claims would be both tedious and inconclusive, and any attempt to pin down to any particular year the advent of the various keys, would be equally futile.

The flutes made and played on during the period of Beethoven, Weber and Schubert were provided with either one, four, six or eight keys [3] ; they also occur with seven keys, for some players would not have the long duplicate F natural. The instruments were generally made of boxwood, ebony, cocuswood or ivory, with keys of brass, silver or pewter. The ferrules were usually of ivory or silver, and many flutes were fitted with graduated screw-stoppers, metal tuning-slides, metal-lined heads, and more rarely with a graduated and movable slide at the

[1] On some German flutes only an extra lever was provided ; this lever acted on the cross F natural key and saved boring another hole.

[2] Kusder, Tacet, Florio, Petersen and Wolf, Richard Potter, Tromlitz, Ribock. (See Rockstro, Welch, Fitzgibbon.)

[3] Three- and five-keyed flutes occur more rarely.

extreme end of the foot.[1]   They are in four or five pieces, the fifth being a short extra piece containing the tuning-slide inserted between the head and the upper middle-piece.   Some English flutes of the period combine in one piece the lower middle-piece and the foot.

The first half of the 19th century was very fertile in flute improvers and inventors, and many makers and players, both professional and amateur, were busy tinkering with the instrument.   Some keys other than the usual eight occur, the most common being an extra lever to work the B flat key, operated by the R. first finger.   (Pl. I, J.)

A small hole with a key for making the C sharp — D shake (hitherto an awkward affair) also occurs, and is said to have been invented by Capeller of Munich, Boehm's teacher ; this eventually became an indispensable adjunct.   Efforts were persistently made to carry the compass of the flute down to B or even lower ; the keys for the extra holes in the lengthened foot were given either to the R. or to the L. little finger.   This extension was most favoured in Germany, Austria and Italy.   (Pl. II, E and F.)

The 19th-century eight-keyed flutes vary slightly in width of bore, and more so in the size of the finger-holes.   Each type had its adherents ; large-holed instruments were used by the famous English player Charles Nicholson, but such as Drouet, a well-known French player, preferred to play on a flute with small note-holes.

The eight-keyed instrument is still the basis of nearly all non-Boehm flutes.   While taking every advantage of the facilities afforded by improved key-mechanism, the designers of these have preserved the conical bore and as much as possible of the old system of fingering, and in so doing they have not neglected to adopt features of the Boehm *mechanism* when it served their purpose, even if they rejected his *system* of fingering and the cylindrical bore.   Many systems based on the eight-keyed finger-

[1] The " register " ; this was amongst the features of Richard Potter's patents of 1785.

ing have been and are still made and used, particularly in Germany, where the Boehm flute has never been accepted so readily as it was in France and England.

The following are some of the names which occur most frequently on one to eight-keyed flutes made in London from the end of the 18th century till about 1830 :

Astor	Metzler
Clementi	Milhouse
Drouet	Monzani
Gerock and Wolf	Prowse
Goulding	Potter (Willm. Henry)
D'Almaine	Wood (James)

The number of tutors which were issued for flutes with from four to eight keys during the first half of the 19th century is considerable, and an amazing quantity of music for the popular instrument was published in France, Germany and England.

In the first quarter of last century the flute went from strength to strength in England. Thousands of flutes were made and sold in London by an increasing number of makers ; every music-shop sold flutes, often marked with the shopkeeper's name, but not necessarily made by him, and unscrupulous makers endeavoured to imitate as nearly as possible the names of well-known makers. The instrument was greatly favoured by amateurs, and London became the happy-hunting-ground for distinguished " professors " of the flute, each of which was in possession of the one and only true method, while the others (they did not hesitate to suggest) were ignorant impostors. Distinguished players from abroad made a point of visiting London, and the instrument was constantly discussed, written and argued about, sometimes with quite unnecessary ill-feeling. It was into this hive of flute-blowing busybodies that Theobald Boehm came when he visited London in 1831.

THE BOEHM FLUTE

Theobald Boehm (1794–1881) was not disposed to regard the flute as a finished product, a perfect instrument which it would be presumptuous to try to improve. If it was out-of-tune, if the tone was uneven, and if its range of tonality was limited, he regarded these as faults of the instrument, but not of the player. Trained to his father's trade, a jeweller, he was skilled in handling metal, and for many years before visiting London had turned that skill to good account in making flutes. He was an accomplished flute-player of professional standing, and had occupied the position of first flute in a Munich theatre. Boehm was also a thinker with a scientific bent, in fact, he was the ideal man to reform the flute.

Hearing Nicholson play in London, Boehm made up his mind that a flute must have large note-holes more or less uniform in size, well placed for intonation, and capable of serving the instrument well in all three octaves, rather than of varying sizes and placed mainly for the convenience of the fingers.

A flute made to his specification in 1831 by the London makers Gerock and Wolf paved the way for the first real Boehm flute which he made in his workshop at Munich early in 1832. This was a conical flute with note-holes the size and situations of which were determined by experiments conducted with the object of securing evenness and sufficiency of tone, good intonation, and general utility over the whole compass of the instrument. Whether the holes lay so that they were convenient for the fingers to cover was not taken into consideration. Having made a tube pierced with holes which satisfied these demands, Boehm then turned his attention to devising a mechanism with which to control the holes. He decided on an open-keyed system in order to avoid the veiling of many notes, which he considered was one of the integral faults of the old system. Except one hole which was required for a shake-key, his tube had thirteen note-holes, one for every semitone from c' sharp to c'' sharp, and he had only nine fingers to cover them. Boehm decided that the two little fingers should continue to occupy the same positions as they did on the old flute, so the R. little finger remained in charge of the three lowest keys, while the L. little finger continued to work the G sharp key as heretofore. That fixed the positions of the two hands and left him four note-holes (E, F, F sharp and G) to be controlled by the three remaining fingers of the R. hand, and five note-holes (A, B flat, B, C and C sharp) for which the three fingers and the thumb of the L. hand were available. A finger was not to be allowed to move away from its appointed place over one note-hole or key, so there was a shortage of one finger on each half of the key-system. The Boehm *mechanism* is that of key-covers and ring-keys mounted on

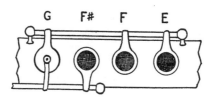

Fig. 30.—Boehm flute of 1832, R.-hand mechanism (omitting the little finger keys).

horizontal rod-axles, and the Boehm *system* is the arrangement of the fingers in relation to the keys.

With the R. little finger situated as it was, the third, second and first fingers of that hand lay comfortably over the E, F and F sharp holes, but there was no finger to cover the G hole. A key-cover placed over the G hole was attached to a horizontal rod-axle from which projected two ring-keys over the E and F holes. In that way the G hole could be kept closed by the action of either the second or the third finger or by both. A ring-key placed over the F sharp hole was attached to the end of another rod-axle which was carried up as far as the B hole, and from that rod-axle an arm projected over the G key-cover so that the G hole would be kept closed when the F sharp ring-key was pressed down. Thus, three fingers controlled four holes without moving away from their places. It was the third finger of the R. hand which performed a double duty, for it opened the E hole by simply uncovering, and it opened the G hole by releasing the ring over the E hole.

On the upper half of the flute, the L. little finger lay over the G sharp key, and the third finger over the A hole. A ring-key over the B flat hole and a key-cover over the B natural hole were attached to a common rod-axle, and an arm over the B natural key-cover projected from the rod-axle which ran down the flute to the F sharp ring-key, so that the B hole could be kept closed by pressure of the R. first finger. The L. second finger lay over the B flat hole and ring. The C hole was bored on the near side of the flute and was controlled by an open key worked by the L. thumb. The C sharp hole was rather too

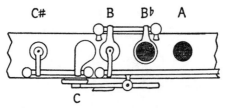

FIG. 31.—Boehm flute of 1832, L.-hand mechanism (omitting the little-finger key and the shake-key.)

high up the flute to be comfortably covered by the first finger, so a key-cover was placed over the hole, while a fingerplate for the first finger was placed a little lower down, and the two were attached to a short rod-axle. Thus, five holes were controlled by bringing into action the R. first finger, and by the three fingers and the thumb of the L. hand.

The G sharp key was an open hinged-key, and the D sharp was, as before, a closed key. The outfit was completed by a shake-key (C sharp — D) for which a small *d″* hole was necessary, and a long rod-axle communicated with a fingerplate situated so that it could be operated by the R. second finger. Another rod-axle with a fingerplate for the R. third finger was connected to the C natural key for shakes which could not be managed very well by the L. thumb. All the keys and rings stood up and open by the pressure of springs when they were untouched, excepting, of course, the closed D sharp key and the shake-key.

The joint between the two middle-pieces of the flute was abolished on account of the rod-axles which connected the lower and the upper keys, so the flute was again made in only three pieces. (Pl. I, κ.)

For some years after completing his flute in 1832, Boehm played and exhibited his new instrument, visiting both London and Paris. Shortly after that he turned his attention to other matters, so for some years little progress was made. By about 1840, however, there were signs that the merits of the Boehm flute were beginning to be appreciated ; several players of good standing in both Paris and London had adopted it. In 1843 Boehm made arrangements to have his flute made in London by Rudall and Rose, and in Paris by Clair Godfroy. These instruments were very similar to those made by Boehm in Munich, except that they included a *d″* sharp shake-key, and because the French players did not take kindly to an open G sharp key, a closed key was substituted. The veiling of the A caused by a closed G sharp hole was then improved by the introduction of the Dorus key,[1] a device employing a weaker and a stronger spring, which kept the G sharp hole open when the A hole was opened ; this remained for a long time a popular key with those players who would not accustom themselves to an open G sharp key.

In the meantime flutes modelled on that of Boehm were made in Paris by Buffet in 1838 and in London by Ward in 1839, with some mechanical modifications, the most important of which were those devised by Buffet, who was associated with the player Coche. They included the hollow sleeve or tubular rod-axle and its auxiliary the clutch, also the needle-springs and the *d″* sharp shake-key ; all these have become part of the regular mechanism of Boehm flutes.

The success and diffusion of the Boehm flute were not achieved without some unseemly disputes which appear to have

---

[1] Invented by Dorus, a French flautist, in 1838.

been rooted in either jealousy or a desire for self-advertisement. The French player Coche asserted that the credit for the new flute was due to an amateur named Capt. Gordon, who had been trying to reform the mechanism of the flute at the time when Boehm was busy devising his new system. Coche's statement, that Gordon *invented* the new flute, that Boehm *improved* it, and that he himself *perfected* it, seems to have been widely accepted in France. Then, and later at intermittent periods, the " Boehm-Gordon controversy " was carried on with considerable ill-feeling and some display of rather childish vituperation through the medium of the press, by letters, articles and even in books. The pro-Gordon cause was espoused by Rockstro in his com-prehensive treatise *The Flute* (1890) in which he displayed a violent prejudice against Boehm. This attack was effectively countered by Welch in his *History of the Boehm Flute* (1896).

Just when the 1832 conical flute of Boehm was becoming widely known and appreciated, and when many other improvers and inventors were busy with it, altering, adding or substituting pet devices of their own, Boehm again turned his attention to the instrument which he did not yet regard as incapable of further improvement. According to his own words : " As regards the sounding and the quality of the lower and the higher tones, there was yet much to be desired, but further improve-ment could only be secured by a complete change in the bore of the flute ".[1] With the help of a German scientist, Dr. Carl von Schafhäutl, he devoted some time (1846–1847) to probing deeper into the acoustical properties of tubes, supplementing theory by a long series of practical experiments carried out with metal tubes. The result of these investigations satisfied him that a cylindrical bore with a slight contraction at the upper end would serve the instrument better than the conical tube which had been accepted without question as the correct bore for flutes for over 150 years. After continued experiments Boehm decided on a tube with a diameter one-thirtieth of its sounding-length,

---

[1] From *Die Flöte und das Flötenspiel*, translated by Dayton C. Miller, D.Sc.

viz. 19 millimetres, contracting with a slight outward curve [1] in the upper quarter of the tube (the head) to 17 millimetres at the stopper. With these dimensions he made flutes of metal, silver or German silver, and launched the Boehm cylindrical flute on its career in 1847. From that time the conical flute with the Boehm system of fingering gradually retired into obscurity. In fitting out his cylindrical flute with the necessary key-work, Boehm took advantage of the mechanical improvements which had in the meantine developed (between 1832 and 1847), but retained his system of fingering. The use of tubular axles (sleeves) hinging on rod-axles which, with the stops or clutches and connecting pins had made an independent movement of the keys possible, did away with the necessity for ring-keys, for a key could now be coupled with another when pressed down, yet could rise independently when untouched. Large open-standing key-covers, therefore, replaced the ring-keys and the two projecting arms of the 1832 flute. (Pl. I, L.)

Boehm assigned the right to make his cylindrical flute in England to Rudall and Rose, and in France to Godfroy and Lot (Paris); these instruments were made either of metal or of wood. The first to use the cylindrical flute in England was Richard Carte, who in 1850 joined the firm of Rudall and Rose.

Boehm's reform of the flute was practically completed by the middle of last century. An accumulation of experience has brought about certain modifications of the original 1847 model, but no vital changes. The rod-axles have been moved from the far side to the near side of the flute, and needle-springs have been universally adopted. The question of an open versus a closed G sharp key has remained unsettled; for those who prefer a closed key the disadvantage of a veiled A has been overcome by making a duplicate G Sharp hole and key-cover which opens automatically when the A hole is uncovered. The Briccialdi B flat lever,[2] a lever for the L. thumb which duplicates the action of the R. first finger on the B natural key, has become

---

[1] This is usually described as a parabolic curve.
[2] Invented in 1849 by Briccialdi, an Italian flautist.

a very general addition to the outfit of the modern Boehm flute, and the customary shake-keys are now likewise regarded as indispensable mechanical helps.

Soon after the appearance of the cylindrical flute in 1847 a number of improvers, all apparently eager to have a finger in the pie, set to work making additions and alterations of their own ; some of these have been used by players who have accustomed themselves to certain fingering devices.[1] The only important and lasting modification of the Boehm flute is that devised by Richard Carte in 1867. On this instrument the interlocking of the F, F sharp and B flat keys was rearranged, giving some fingering facilities which include an F sharp with the first finger as on the old flute, as well as the usual Boehm-fingering for that note ; a closed F natural key was also re-introduced on this model.

With the mid-century the period of boxwood and ebony flutes was well over. Just at that time ebonite made its appearance, but on the whole cocuswood (*grenadilla*), silver or German silver, has been the favourite material for flutes of the modern type. Ivory heads were at one time in favour, but these, like the all-ivory flute, are now things of the past. The metal-work on flutes is now of either real or German silver.

Some of the most important makers who were active during the period when the flute was undergoing transformation (from about 1830 to 1860) were the following :

Boehm (Munich)	Maino (Milan)
Buffet (Paris)	Rudall and Rose (London)
Collinet (Paris)	Uhlmann (Vienna)
Godfroy (Paris)	Ward (London)
Greve (Munich)	Ziegler (Vienna)
Lot (Paris)	Sax (Paris)

A short-lived success in England was achieved by the

[1] Pratten, Clinton, Rockstro, Radcliff, Barrett, Collard (London), Lot, Colonieu (Paris).

Diatonic flute of Siccama (1847). This was an eleven-keyed flute on which the E and A holes were placed lower down the tube, and were covered by hinged keys with the fingerplate in the middle of the lever, thus keeping the two third fingers in their accustomed places. (Pl. II, G.)

Amongst the curiosities of the 19th-century flutes perhaps the most peculiar were those devised by an Italian named Giorgi, in 1888. Made of ebonite,[1] with the mouth-hole on the *end* of the tube, there were eleven finger-holes, one for each semitone in the octave *d'* to *d''*; with no keys or mechanism of any sort, each finger and thumb was responsible for covering a hole, and the L. first finger enjoyed the privilege of stopping one hole with the tip and another with the upper joint of the finger. These flutes were also made with open keys over every note-hole. (Pl. II, H.)

The foregoing history of the transverse flute from near the end of the 17th century for about two hundred years, shows how for the first hundred years little or no progress was made, while during the next hundred years the instrument was the subject of unceasing attention by numbers of well-meaning improvers who, if they frequently strayed up blind alleys, have among them transformed the instrument from a very simple affair to an elaborately built-up piece of mechanism. Probably no one instrument has ever attracted the attention of so many "inventors" as did the flute during the period from 1775 to 1875; of no other wind instrument are there so many surviving specimens in our collections, nor of any other has so much been written. The cult of flute-playing by amateurs in England probably accounts for the fact that so much of the important flute-literature is in English.

A summary of the history of the flute shows the following main periods:

(a) *Prehistoric*. The plain tube or reed blown across one end.

---

[1] Made by Wallis and Son; demonstrated by the inventor in London in November 1896. (*Musical Opinion*, Dec. 1896.)

(b) *Middle Ages.* The cylindrical tube closed at one end, blown across a side mouth-hole and provided with six finger-holes.

(c) *c.* 1675–1775. The conical tube with six finger-holes and one key.

(d) *c.* 1775–1850. The conical four- to eight-keyed flutes.

(e) *From* 1832. The Boehm-flute, at first conical, and from 1847, cylindrical.

Smaller and Larger Flutes

Transverse flutes both shorter and longer than the normal instrument have been made and used almost at all periods in the history of this species ; mechanically and acoustically they share the history and development of the ordinary (so-called) concert flute.

While it is impossible to say exactly at what length and pitch the instrument ceases to be a flute and becomes a piccolo,[1] in the sense of that word as it is generally understood, a piccolo or octave-flute is one which is half the size and consequently sounds an octave higher than the normal instrument.

The short military fife of the later Middle Ages may be counted the progenitor of the piccolo, yet the former survived till fairly recent times more or less in its original form with a cylindrical bore, six finger-holes and possibly one or more keys, quite independently of the miniature flute which we now call a piccolo. The 19th-century military fife was pitched in B flat (a tone below the octave-flute) and was sometimes given a D sharp key ; the two ends of the tube were protected by brass bands.[2] (Pl. II, Q.) Soon after the middle of last century fifes were replaced in the British Army by small conical flutes or piccolos. These are now made with one or five keys and are pitched a tone below, also a semitone and a minor third above, the octave flute.

As distinguished from the true fife, the piccolo, with its

[1] (G.) *Kleine Flöte.* (F.) *Petite Flûte.* (I.) *Flauto piccolo, Ottavina.*

[2] All-metal fifes were also made. (Patent, 1810, George Miller.)

conical bore and a primary scale from *d″* to *d‴*, cannot be traced so far back as the cylindrical instrument, in fact, it came into prominence as an orchestral instrument only in the 19th century.[1] Its history is the same as that of the flute from about the end of the 18th century, except that the piccolo did not gain the two additional foot-keys, nor has the cylindrical bore of the Boehm flute been generally adopted. Piccolos with foot-keys and a cylindrical bore, however, do occur, and are therefore in every respect miniature flutes. Piccolos (without foot-keys) with one, four or six keys correspond to the one-, four-or eight-keyed flutes of the early 19th century, but the smaller instrument was not usually made in more than two pieces. The Boehm system has been applied to the piccolo just as to the flute. (Pl. II, L to P.)

When the organisation of military bands developed towards the end of the 18th and in the early part of the 19th century, flutes were made to sound a semitone and a minor third[2] higher than the ordinary orchestral flute. Just as the ordinary flute was formerly said to be in D because its primary scale was D major, so the higher flutes were said to be, respectively, in E flat and F. Being treated as a non-transposing instrument, the flute is now said to be in C, and the two higher flutes are therefore more correctly described as being, respectively, in D flat and E flat instead of in E flat and F. (Pl. II. B, C and D.) The old misleading nomenclature was used in this country till quite recently and may not yet be quite extinct. Piccolos have also been made for use in military bands a semitone and a minor third above the ordinary octave instrument, and were similarly called E flat and F piccolos, whereas from the point of view of transposition they are really in D flat and E flat. Both the E flat (formerly F) flute and piccolo are now more or less obsolete, but the D flat (formerly E flat) instruments are still used in some military bands.

---

[1] The parts for *flauto-piccolo* which occur in 18th-century scores were written for small flageolets, i.e. whistle-flutes.

[2] (G.) *Terzflöte.* (F.) *Flûte tierce.*

A small flute pitched a minor sixth above the ordinary flute is frequently found amongst the boxwood instruments of the late 18th and early 19th centuries. They were called small B flat flutes, but would now be described as flutes in high A flat. These little flutes (or large piccolos) were no doubt used in military bands. (Pl. II, I, J, K.)

A flute sounding a minor third below the ordinary flute was known as the *Flûte d'amour* in France and the *Liebesflöte* in Germany ; it occurs from about the middle of the 18th century till early in the 19th century.

A flute pitched a tone lower than normal (in B flat) occurs sporadically at various periods ; it is now sometimes made with modern mechanism for the purpose of playing the lowest part in drum and flute bands. The head is generally bent back.

A flute pitched a fourth lower than normal has been variously called Alto flute, Bass flute or Bass flute in G. This instrument can trace its descent back to the 16th or 17th century ; it enjoyed only a rather precarious existence during the 18th and early 19th centuries. (Pl. II, A.) The distances between the finger-holes on these large flutes made it almost necessary to employ some sort of key in order to enable the fingers to control the note-holes. For this purpose open or hinged keys were often placed over one or more of the six holes of the primary scale, and a " D sharp " key was provided for the same purpose as it was on the ordinary 18th-century flutes. Similar flutes occur in the first half of the nineteenth century without foot-keys ; these instruments would at that time be called flutes in A, the low A corresponding to the lowest D of the ordinary flute, but according to the modern nomenclature they would now be described as alto flutes in G.[1]

When the modern mechanism with rod-axles came into use, the difficulty of placing the holes correctly and of controlling them on these long flutes was easily overcome, so the alto or

---

[1] These alto flutes should not be confused with ordinary flutes provided with extra length and extra foot-keys which take the compass down to B, B flat, A or G.

bass flute in G seemed as if it were assured of enjoying an independent and useful existence ; yet it is still only rarely demanded in orchestral scores, and has hardly reached in the orchestral family the status that seemed open to it. Alto flutes in G are now usually made of metal, either quite straight or with the head bent back ; they can be made with any modern key-mechanism that is desired.

A few old flutes below the alto in G have occurred, and a real bass flute in D, an octave below the ordinary flute, has turned up like a rare sea monster at intervals during the last two centuries. On these long instruments the head is generally bent back and of the six finger-holes two at least are covered by open keys. An English effort of this sort was the bass flute of MacGregor (London), patented in 1810. Modern mechanism has banished the difficulty of controlling note-holes placed so far apart as they must be on these very long flutes, and several such instruments with foot-keys have been constructed during the last fifty years.[1] On one by Bartoli of Milan the head is doubled back ; another designed by Albisi in 1910 and named *Albisiphone*, is bent so that the mouth-hole lies transversely, but by means of two bends near the head, the body of the flute points downwards in front of the player. The fingering is on the Boehm system and includes a low B. The latest bass flute is that introduced in 1932 by Rudall Carte, Ltd., of London. In this case the head lies transversely, and by means of some bends in the tube the straight body of the instrument is held diagonally downwards and a projecting crutch, which fits over the player's thigh, takes the weight of the instrument off the player's arms.

The foregoing does not exhaust the list of different sized flutes which have been made from time to time. They occur in a bewildering variety of lengths, and are difficult to classify owing to the variable and unstable pitches which have been in use at various times and places. A price-list issued by a Belgian

---

[1] Four bass flutes going down to low C were exhibited at the Paris Exhibition of 1900.

maker [1] about 1830 shows that he was prepared to supply flutes in no less than twenty different sizes. Yet, from the early 17th century, the flute which sounds the scale d' to c'' sharp when the six fingers are successively raised to uncover the note-holes, has remained the dominating member of the family ; the instrument pitched an octave higher has an equally secure position in the orchestra and military band, and the flute sounding a fourth below normal barely manages to exist on the fringe of the orchestra.

[1] Tuerlinckx of Malines.

WHISTLE-FLUTES

The Recorder

(E.) Recorder. Common flute (18th century). English flute.
(G.) Blockflöte. Plockflöte. Plockpfeife. Schnabelflöte.
(F.) Flûte douce. Flûte-à-bec. Flûte d'Angleterre.
(I.) Flauto dolce.

As more thought and skill must have gone to fashioning the whistle-mouthpiece than to making the simple mouth-hole of the transverse flute, it may be presumed that of the two flute types the whistle-flute had its birth at a later period. It has been found pictorially represented as early as the 11th century; actual specimens made in the 16th century survive in several collections, and mention of the instrument occurs frequently in the literature and records of the intervening centuries.

The main branch of the family lost its musical status and became obsolete during the 18th century, but a side branch, under the name of flageolet, survived during the 19th century, and still exists.

The recorders, *Plockflöten* or *Flûtes-à-bec* which flourished during the 16th and 17th centuries occur in a variety of sizes, from a few inches to over 4 feet in length; their principal characteristics are : (a) a conical bore tapering towards the lower end ; (b) six finger-holes on the upper side of the tube for sounding the primary scale ; (c) a thumb-hole on the underside near the upper end used to complete the primary octave and also to act as a " speaker " or vent-hole for the second octave ; (d) an extra note-hole near the lower end which extended the downward compass of the instrument one tone lower when it was closed by the little finger or by a key. These instruments could sound some or all of the octave-harmonics all the more freely when the thumb-hole was opened or partially opened,[1] and all the usual forkfingerings were available.[2]

On the smaller and earlier recorders the little-finger-hole was bored in duplicate, one slightly to the right and the other slightly to the left side of the tube, in order to accommodate both those players who were in the habit of using the R. hand for the lower part of the instrument and those who preferred to play with the L. hand below the R. hand ; the hole which was not required was filled up with wax. When, at a later period, the recorders were made with detachable joints, the duplicate holes became unnecessary, for the lower piece could be twisted

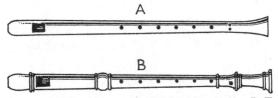

Fig. 32.—A. Treble recorder, 16th and early 17th centuries. B. Treble recorder, late 17th and early 18th centuries.

round so as to bring the hole within reach of either the R. or the L. little finger. On the larger sizes this extra hole lay out of reach of either little finger, therefore an open key with a swallow-tail fingerplate was provided in order to control it either with the R. or the L. little finger.

The earlier instruments made in the 16th and early 17th centuries can be recognised by the plain unornamented exterior, and by the twin little-finger-holes, or the protecting box which covered the key on the larger sizes ; these were made from one piece of wood ; they were unjointed. The later recorders, which belong to the late 17th and early 18th centuries, are jointed, and the exterior of the tube is ornamented by turned rings ; the key was then mounted in a wooden ring in the same way as the D sharp key of the contemporary transverse flute.

The protecting box is not found on the later pattern, and

---

[1] " Pinched ", as the old players called it.
[2] " Govern these ventages with your fingers and thumb " (*Hamlet*).

on these the lower end takes the shape of a more pronounced bell which, however, is a bell only in appearance, and is not accompanied by any expansion of the inside of the tube. Owing to their length the larger recorders were blown through a metal tube or crook which curved downwards and made it possible to hold the instrument so that the finger-holes could be conveniently reached.[1] The distance between the holes on the larger instruments was reduced to some extent by boring the holes diagonally, much as they are on a bassoon, so that the holes on the outside surface were rather closer together than they were in the inside of the tube. Some of the later specimens of the bass recorders were closed up at the lower end, and the instrument rested on the floor while being played ; in that case an outlet was provided at the side of the bell. Others, which although long and somewhat heavy did not quite reach the floor, were provided with a detachable solid rod of wood made to fit into the lower end of the tube so that it might rest on the floor, and a side-outlet provided that the air-passage through the instrument was not blocked up.

Recorders were often made of boxwood, also of walnut, maple, oak or ebony, and the smaller instruments were frequently made entirely of ivory. Rings or ferrules of ivory became common on the later wooden recorders. The mouthpiece is generally of wood, but sometimes of ivory or bone, and the keys are of brass or silver. A few very long bass recorders survive on which the downward compass is extended by means of four open keys, two for the little finger and two for the thumb ; the keys are arranged as described in Section VII. Mersenne depicts one with the two lowest keys worked by the player's feet. Specimens of these long four-keyed instruments are preserved at Munich and at Antwerp.[2]

Recorders occur in sets of from three to eight instruments,[3]

[1] See Frontispiece.

[2] Munich, National Museum ; Antwerp, Musée de Steen. Facsimile copies of both in the Brussels Coll.

[3] Chester, Grosvenor Museum (four) ; Nürnberg, Germanisches Museum (eight in five different sizes).

designed to form little harmonically self-contained wind-bands.

The earliest particulars available are those given by Virdung (1511), who shows rough woodcuts of four instruments, of which the alto and tenor are apparently the same size. Only the bass has a key and protecting box. The three sizes are pitched a fifth apart, and their compass is from a tone below the lower end of the primary or six-finger-hole scale, up to the sixth note of the second (harmonic) octave for the discant and tenor, but only up to the fifth note for the bass :

	Primary Scale	Downward Extension	Highest Note
Discant .	a' — g'' sharp	g' natural	f'''
Tenor . .	d' — c'' sharp	c' natural	b''
Bass . .	g — f' sharp	f natural	d''

Fingering Chart No. 2 shows the complete scale for the discant instrument transcribed into the form which is now customary. It will be seen that the scale produced by opening the six finger-holes in succession is that of A major, and that all the other notes are forked ; the thumb-hole was partially opened for that part of the second octave which was playable, and the little-finger-hole gave an additional note at the bottom of the scale.

Agricola depicts the same three instruments as Virdung, and provides similar fingering-charts in the editions of 1528 and 1545.

Praetorius (1619) specifies no less than eight sizes of *Plockpfeiffen*, of which numbers 4, 5 and 6 correspond to the three shown by Virdung about a hundred years earlier :

1. *Exilent, klein flöttlein*   Lowest note g''
2. *Discantflöt*   ,,   ,, d''
3. *Discantflöt*   ,,   ,, c''
4. *Altflöt*   ,,   ,, g'
5. *Tenorflöt*   ,,   ,, c'
6. *Basset*   ,,   ,, f
7. *Bassflöt*   ,,   ,, B flat
8. *Grossbassflöt*   ,,   ,, F

The lower instruments, according to Praetorius, could ascend four notes above the primary scale, and the smaller ones reached the fifth note above, making a compass of, respectively, 13 and 14 diatonic degrees.

Mersenne (1636) describes two sets of these instruments, a *petit jeu* and a *grand jeu*; the smaller set corresponds to the three described by Virdung and Agricola, and to Praetorius' numbers 4, 5 and 6.

Later in the 17th century it seems that the common group was a set of three, the lowest notes (when all holes were closed) of which were, respectively, f' c' and f; thus, the soprano instrument was pitched a tone lower than previously. According to Mattheson (1713) the set of three was as follows:

> Discant; compass f' to f'''
> Alto; „ c' to c'''
> Bass; „ f to f''.

It was the discant or soprano of this group that was much favoured by amateurs in the late 17th and early 18th centuries, and for which several instruction books with fingering charts were issued. The term "recorder" had gone out of use in England by the 18th century, and the instrument was then known as the "flute" or "common flute", while the transverse instrument was distinguished by the prefix "German". (P. III, A and B.)

The following are some particulars of the scale of the soprano instrument gleaned from the charts given by their respective authors:

1683. *Salter, "The Genteel Companion" (Recorder).* Compass f' to g'''; a diatonic scale of C major with a forked f'' natural; thumb-hole "pinched", i.e. half-closed, for the second octave.

1697. *Speer (Quart Flöte).* Compass f' to f'''; transposed notation written a fourth below the real sounds. All fork-fingerings for the chromatic notes and thumb-hole half-opened for the second octave. (This identical chart was given by Schneider in 1834 for the *Flauto douce* or *Stille flöte*.)

1707. *Hotteterre* (*Flûte-à-bec*). Compass f' to g''', fully chromatic except f''' sharp. The lowest f' sharp is made by
half-closing the little-finger-hole, and g' sharp by half-closing
the A hole ; other chromatic notes are forked. The thumb-
hole is half-opened from a'' sharp and upwards.

1731. "*The Modern Musick Master*" (*The Flute*). Compass
f' to f''', chromatic except f' sharp and g' sharp. Thumb-
hole half-opened from a'' and upwards.

1738. *Eisel* (*Fleute douce*). Compass f' to g''', chromatic except
f' sharp and f''' sharp. Forkfingering for chromatic notes.
Thumb-hole half-opened from g'' sharp and upwards.

1754. "*The Muses' Delight*" (*Common flute*). Compass f' to
g''', chromatic except f' sharp and f''' sharp. Chromatic
notes forked. Thumb-hole half-opened from a'' and
upwards.

Other English instruction books are the following :

1679. *Lessons for the Rechorder* (Hudgebut).

1681. *The Most Pleasant Companion*, by John Banister (Hudgebut).

1684. *The Delightful Companion*. Recorder or flute (Playford).

1690 ? *The Compleat Flute-Master*. Rechorder (Hare and
Walsh).

1750 ? *The Complete Flute Master* (Tyther).

1779-1798. *Compleat Instructions for the Common Flute* (Longman
and Broderip).

The fingerings of these books frequently differ in detail ;
this would probably be accounted for by slight differences in
the bore, the size and the situation of the note-holes on different
instruments.

The following are amongst the makers of recorders or
common flutes in the late 17th and 18th centuries whose instruments are preserved in the principal European collections ; [1]

---

[1] Makers' names do not usually appear on the earlier wood-wind instruments. No instrument by Pepys' pipe-maker " Drumbleby " is known.

Rafi ——	Rykel (Amsterdam)
Haka (Amsterdam)	Bressan (London)
Hotteterre (Paris)	Stanesby (London)
Denner (Nürnberg)	Anciuti (Milan)
Steenbergen (Belgium)	Schlegel (Bale)
Heitz (Berlin)	Walch (Berchtesgaden)
Oberlender (Germany)	Rottenburgh (Brussels)
Kenigsperger ——	

When the orchestra was developing in the 17th century, both whistle-flutes and transverse flutes were in use ; parts for either one or the other of them occur in some of the later 17th century scores, the former being designated simply " flutes ", the latter always distinguished by some such term as " transverse " or " German ". Lully wrote for both types, also Scarlatti, Purcell, and in the first half of the 18th century Bach, Handel and many of their contemporaries. Though not invariably, it seems to have been the treble instrument in f' which was most commonly employed. Its quiet and expressionless tone, however, was not fit for the growing sonority of the 18th-century orchestra ; the recorder, of which Shakespeare and Milton wrote, the sound of which was " sweet ", " solemn " and " pleasing ", was doomed ; so it gradually faded out of existence, leaving the transverse flute in full possession of the orchestral field. The recorders or common flutes then retired into the quiet seclusion of museums and private collections, there to await the interested attentions of historians, and to serve as models for the revival of their type in our own time. The instrument will probably never again figure in the orchestra, but for music of its own period, as an amateur's and a children's instrument it is now being made in England and in Germany, and the old tutors and music books are being searched in order to provide it with suitable music to play.

The Flageolet

Small high-pitched whistle-flutes have been, and still are frequently called flageolets ; the name properly belongs to one

particular type, the French flageolet, which is a whistle-flute
with about 6 to 7 inches of sounding length, four finger-holes
on the top of the tube and two thumb-holes on the underside.
It is said to have been "invented" by one Juvigny in Paris
about 1581. Small whistle-flutes, however, were known before
that time, for Virdung (1511) shows a small pipe with four holes
called the *russpfeif*; Agricola depicts a similar *rüspeyfe* (which
he also calls *klein flötlein*); it has three finger-holes on top and
a thumb-hole underneath, and he states that the end of the tube
may also be half-stopped in order to act as a note-hole. Very
similar is the tiny *gar-klein plockflötlein*, about 4 inches long
with three finger- and one thumb-hole, shown by Praetorius.

Mersenne shows the French flageolet made in a form very
like the early recorders, but with six note-holes arranged so that
the L. thumb controls the 6th or highest hole, the L. first and
second fingers the 5th and 4th holes, the R. first finger the
3rd hole, the R. thumb the 2nd hole, and the R. second finger
the 1st or lowest hole. The R. little finger supports the instrument and is placed underneath the lower end, while the R. third
finger helps to steady it on top. A fingering chart is supplied
by Mersenne, also by Speer (1697), and by 1661 the instrument
must have been used in England, for in that year was published
" *The Pleasant Companion, or New Lessons and Instructions for
the Flagelet*, by Thomas Greeting, Gent ".[1] Greeting's flageolet
is similar to Mersenne's and is held in the same way with the R.
little finger underneath the lower end.

Some late 17th-century and a number of 18th-century French
flageolets are preserved in various collections ; they vary from
about 4½ inches to a foot or more in length, and are made, usually
in one piece, of boxwood or ebony with ivory ferrules, or entirely of ivory. About the middle of the 18th century they
began to be divided into two joints, and the upper piece, above
the whistle, was lengthened and widened so as to form a chamber
intended to contain a sponge which was to absorb condensed

---

[1] Pepys bought a copy on April 16, 1668, and arranged that his wife
should be taught by Mr. Greeting to play the flageolet.

moisture from the player's breath. At the same time a separate
mouthpiece of ivory, bone or mother-of-pearl was added, so
that the instrument grew to be nearly twice as long as its
sounding-length. In this form the French flageolet was made
throughout the 19th century. Following the transverse flute,
it gained closed chromatic keys and even shake-keys. Modern
French flageolets are made to sound the primary scale a'' to
g''' sharp, and have a compass of just over two octaves ; they
may be fitted with a complete key-system mounted in pillars,
with ring-keys, rod-axles, Boehm mechanism, and two foot-
keys like the flute. (Pl. III, G.)

This little instrument seems to have led an independent
existence of its own quite apart from the recorders, keeping
rather to the lighter side of musical art during the 17th, 18th and
19th centuries. It was in the hands of amateur musicians and
in dancing circles in France, Belgium and in England, where it
found most of its admirers. Possibly its high-pitched sounds
were too frivolous for German taste, for it does not seem to
have gained any foothold in that country. In the first half of
the 18th century, before the transverse piccolo had begun to
assume the position of highest amongst the wood-wind instruments, composers sometimes wrote for the French flageolet
under the name of *Flauto piccolo* or *Flautino*, generally for the
purpose of underlining the meaning of the words when the
subject was birds.[1]

The English Flageolet

A somewhat similar whistle-flute is the so-called English
flute or flageolet which appeared late in the 18th century as a
high-pitched and somewhat belated successor to the recorder.
The upper part, which has a separate ivory mouthpiece and
sponge-chamber, is very similar to the French flageolet, but the
six finger-holes all lie along the top of the slightly tapering
tube. The sounding-length is usually about 11 inches, giving

[1] " Hush, ye pretty warbling quire " (Handel, *Acis and Galatea*).

a primary scale of *d″* to *c‴* sharp, but the total length of the instrument is about 18 inches. Some of these flutes have a thumb-hole at the back and may, therefore, be classed as recorders. A feature of these flutes, which must have been popular in England during the early part of last century, is a set of ivory studs placed between the finger-holes and evidently intended as guides to keep the fingers from losing their places over the small holes. These instruments gained chromatic keys, corresponding to those of the transverse flutes of the same period, but are without foot-keys. A patent "New C key" (1819) is often found situated just below the sound-hole of the whistle. (Pl. III, E and F.) Modern versions of the flageolet made of cocuswood with German silver keys are still sold, and in company with the "tin whistles" are classed as toys rather than as musical instruments.

THE TABOR-PIPE

A one-handed whistle-flute, known in England as the Tabor-pipe [1] on account of its association with a small drum or tabor, dates from the Middle Ages, and was used for several centuries in France and England as the musical accompaniment of the Folk dance. It appears in Virdung (1511) as the *Schwegel*, in Praetorius as the *Stamentienpfeiff* (in three sizes), and is named *La flûte à trois trous* by Mersenne. The instrument is fingered by the L. hand of the player while the R. hand taps a small drum which is suspended from the L. arm, thus providing a sort of one-man drum and fife band. The three note-holes are bored near the lower end of a narrow-bored cylindrical tube, the two lowest being covered by the first and second fingers and the third (on the underside) by the thumb. The narrow bore of the tube, which is only about one-fortieth of its length, favours the production of harmonics at the expense of the fundamentals ; the scale therefore really begins with the four octave-harmonics produced by over-blowing the four fundamentals ; it is con-

[1] (G.) *Schwegel.* (F.) *Galoubet.*

tinued without a break by the four twelfth-harmonics, and the double-octave harmonics provide a further continuation of the diatonic scale to the extent of an octave and a half ; this can be exceeded by employing still higher harmonics and may comprise two octaves or even more. By employing forkfingerings, half-closing holes, and even by using the end of the tube as a note-hole, several chromatic notes can be produced. The length and pitch of the tabor-pipe has varied ; [1] even in the 18th century, however, the larger instruments seem to have been already abandoned in favour of those round about a foot in length. The tabor-pipe and its companion drum have never died out altogether in France ; although they languished and became more or less extinct in this country during the last century, both are now being successfully revived by folk-dancing enthusiasts.

THE DOUBLE FLAGEOLET

The idea of one person playing on two pipes is a very old one. From time to time double whistle-flutes have been made, either in the form of two tubes fastened together or else by cutting two passages through the same block of wood, in either case with the upper ends meeting in one common mouthpiece ; the idea seems to have been to enable one person to play a tune in thirds, or a tune with a drone, or possibly to echo the sound of one pipe on the other. None of these double pipes have at any time been taken very seriously, but as an amateur's instrument the double flageolet, as it is commonly called, must have enjoyed a considerable vogue in England during the first half of last century. Isolated specimens of double pipes dating from before 1800 occur in some collections, but no collection of wind instruments seems to be complete without a specimen of the English 19th-century double flageolet. This was devised by the London flute-maker Bainbridge early in the century, and

---

[1] A solitary specimen of the bass *Stamentienpfeiff* is preserved in the Brussels Coll., it has a sounding-length of over 2 feet, and is blown through a long bent metal crook.

served as a model for many of the same sort made by his pupil
or apprentice Simpson, and by his successor Hastrick ; they
also occur bearing the names Metzler and Clementi. Bainbridge
issued a " Preceptor " (1820) for the double flageolet in which
he calls it " that fashionable and sweet-toned instrument ".
(Pl. III, c and d.)

These instruments are made on the same pattern as the
boxwood English single flageolets of the same period, but there
are *two* air-channels leading from the wind-chamber through
which a current of air is directed to two separate sound-holes.
The two flute-tubes, normally of the same length and detachable
from the whistle-apparatus, fit into two sockets below the two
sound-holes, and a pair of " wind-cutters ", controlled by the
thumbs, provide that either tube can be shut off so that the
other may serve as a single flageolet. The conical bore and
ivory studs are characteristics of the double as well as the single
flageolet. The pitch is usually round about the one-foot octave ;
those with the primary scales of either *d''* to *c'''* or *b'* flat to *a''*
are perhaps the most common, but both larger and smaller
sizes were also made. While they differ slightly in detail, the
English double-flageolet is generally planned as follows :

The L.-hand tube is pierced with six finger-holes in line,
which provide for the primary scale as on a single flageolet.[1]
When both tubes are being played together the four fingers of
the L. hand cover only the upper four of the six holes, the
others being left uncovered. The tube for the R. hand has
four finger-holes, these being the lower four of the primary scale.
By this arrangement the two hands are situated, so to speak,
a third apart ; therefore, when both tubes are fingered in the
same way the sounds produced will always be in thirds. In
addition to the finger-holes one or both tubes are generally
provided with closed keys which correspond to the D sharp
and F natural keys of the contemporary transverse flute. The

---

[1] The uppermost hole is nearly blocked up by an ebony pin ; this
causes the seventh note of the primary scale to sound the minor seventh
above the key-note instead of the leading-note of the scale.

L.-hand tube is also given a closed key at the top to complete the octave, and the R.-hand tube has two closed keys which can be used to carry the scale upwards. It will be understood that some of the keys and holes can only be used when one of the tubes is in action, the other being shut off by the wind-cutter. Sundry improvements appear on the later instruments ; the " New C key " (1819) often occurs on the L.-tube, and on some instruments the R.-hand tube is made longer than its fellow, and the compass is carried down two semitones lower by means of open foot-keys.

Triple flageolets [1] of similar pattern contrive to give a some-what limited control over the sounds of three tubes by the combined efforts of the fingers and thumbs of both hands. Bainbridge also made a double flageolet blown through a mouth-piece projecting from the side of the wind-chamber ; these instruments are held in the manner of the transverse flute, but are, nevertheless, whistle-flutes.

Probably the smallest of all whistle-flutes is the Picco pipe, a tiny shrill whistle about $3\frac{1}{2}$ inches long with two finger-holes on the upper side and a thumb-hole underneath. It was played by a blind Sardinian named Picco in London about the middle of last century, and is said to have had a compass of about three octaves.

[1] Called " trio flageolet " by Bainbridge.

THE OBOE

(E.) Oboe.   (G.) Oboe.   (F.) Hautbois.   (I.) Oboe.

THE history of the oboe divides itself into two main periods ; the 17th century marks the end of the first and the beginning of the second period.   During the course of that century the instrument was transformed from the earlier into the later type from which the modern oboe has developed.   The varied nomenclature of the two types may be summarised as follows :

Earlier Type (Shawm)	Later Type (Oboe)
England. Shawm, Shalm, Schalm, Chalme, Bumbarde, Howboye, Hoyeboye, Howeboie, Hautboit, Hoeboy, Hoboy, Hautboy	Oboe, Hautboy
Germany. Schalmei, Schalmey, Schalemie, Schalemeye, Pommer, Bomhard, Bombart, Bomhardt, Bombardt, Pumhart	Oboe, Hoboe
France. Hautbois, Haulxbois, Bombarde, Chalamie, Chalumeau, Calemelle, Chalemel, Chalemie	Hautbois
Italy. Piffero, Bombardo, Bombardone, Bombardino	Oboe

It will be seen from the above that the use of some form of the French word *Hautbois* does not necessarily distinguish between the earlier and the later type.   In these pages, however, for the sake of clearness, the older type will always be referred to as shawms, and the newer type as oboes.

The origin of instruments sounded by means of a double reed reaches far back into the remote past ; they appear to have come from the East and to have reached Europe in the later Middle Ages, where they took root and flourished especially during the 15th and 16th centuries.   During the 17th century the shawms were refined and improved ; the oboe emerged in a form which remained practically unaltered till the end of the 18th century. The first half of the 19th century saw the oboe developing its key-system which was completed soon after the mid-century.

The Shawms

Although not so many as the contemporary recorders, a number of the 16th- and 17th-century shawms are preserved in several European collections of musical instruments.[1] An examination of these relics, together with the written descriptions and the illustrations which occur in Virdung, Agricola, Praetorius and Mersenne, will give some idea of the form and the capabilities of a class of instrument which belongs to a pre-orchestral era, to the small open-air wind bands and Church bands which pre-dated both the orchestra and the military band of the last two or three centuries.

Shawms occur in sizes varying from a little over 1 foot to about 9 or 10 feet in length. They are made from sundry hard woods, usually in one piece. The bore is conical, narrowest at the upper end and expanding to a trumpet-like bell at the lower extremity.

Owing to the fact that it was detachable, the reed or sounding apparatus of these old instruments is generally lost, but contemporary illustrations suggest that they were not played with the reed actually held between the player's lips as is done on the oboe and bassoon of the present day. The most common arrangement seems to be that which required the use of a *pirouette*. This was a small detachable wooden lily-shaped contrivance (like

---

[1] Disregarding a number of small pastoral instruments of the shawm type, there are probably not a hundred of these instruments now in existence. They occur singly or in groups scattered about the various museums on the Continent. Specimens may be found in Berlin, Vienna, Munich, Salzburg, Hamburg, Breslau, Basel, Innsbruck, Paris, Middelbourg, Stockholm, Leipzig, Frankfurt, Darmstadt, Brussels, Nürnberg, Copenhagen and Prague. Several collections also exhibit facsimile copies of the old instruments.

an upturned bell) which was inserted in the narrow end of the instrument ; the reed was fixed in the centre of the *pirouette* and projected above the rim of the bell. When being played the reed was, therefore, inside the cavity of the player's mouth, and his lips were pressed against the rim of the *pirouette* so as to form an air-tight wind-chamber. Sound generated in this way is rough and bagpipe-like [1] because the player cannot com-

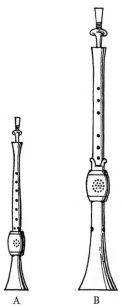

press the reed, and therefore cannot pro-perly control the vibration nor make any undulation between a loud and a soft tone. The *pirouette* and reed are shown in the illustrations of Virdung, Agricola, Prae-torius and Mersenne. Another arrange-ment which occurs on some of the shawms is a blowing apparatus similar to that of the contemporary krumhorns. This is a wooden or ivory case, perforated at one end, which completely encloses the reed and forms a wind-chamber into which the player blows. It acts very similarly to the *pirouette*, but that it provides an artificial wind-chamber instead of using the cavity of the mouth as such.

A   B

FIG. 33.—Shawms with *pirouettes*.

The shawms were pierced with the usual six finger-holes, which gave a primary scale of one octave. The holes are fairly evenly spaced on the smaller instruments, but on the larger sizes they are arranged in two groups of three each, and they pierce the tube diagonally in the same way as the holes of the bass recorders and bassoons. In addition to the six finger-holes there is sometimes a thumb-hole on the underside, and very generally a seventh or little-finger-hole situated lower down the

[1] Mersenne remarked of the tone, " ils ont le son le plus fort et le plus violent de tous les instruments, si l'on excepte la trompette ". The experi-ment may be tried of placing an oboe or bassoon reed right inside the mouth and blowing with the lips closed.

upper side of the tube, and pierced in duplicate on the smaller instruments so as to accommodate either the R. or the L. little finger. This hole, when closed, carries the scale a tone downwards. On the larger shawms the seventh hole is controlled by an open swallow-tail key covered by the usual protecting box. A few tenor, bass and double-bass shawms are provided with four open keys, two for the little finger and two for the thumb, arranged under perforated protections as they were on the very largest of the older bass recorders. These four-keyed instruments could sound four notes below the lowest note of the primary scale.

A peculiarity of all the shawm family, and one which was handed on to the 18th-century oboe, is that below the lowest of the note-holes the tube is pierced with from two to six " tuning-holes " ; these are situated down towards the bell, well out of reach of the fingers and have no keys to control them. These holes could only serve the purpose of adjusting the pitch and tuning of the instrument. They could not (as has been suggested) be closed by the player's knees.

The larger shawms were blown through a metal crook similar to that used for the bass recorders ; the instrument was then held, as is shown in contemporary pictures, diagonally, like a bassoon.

The existing shawms vary considerably in length and pitch. They fall roughly into six groups of which the soprano or treble (*discant pommer*), the alto, the tenor and bass, pitched a perfect fifth apart, are the most common. A group smaller than the soprano includes many instruments of a purely rustic or pastoral type, and a double-bass monster shawm is represented by only two complete specimens [1] and the remains of another.[2]

Virdung in 1511 apparently knew only two shawms, a treble, (*schalmey*) and a tenor or alto (*bombardt*) pitched a fifth lower. The treble has the duplicate little finger-holes, and the tenor a swallow-tail key and protecting box ; both are blown with a *pirouette*. Agricola in 1528 and 1545 shows the same two

[1] Berlin, No. 289. Salzburg, No. 187.   [2] Breslau, No. 91.

instruments, and allows them each a limited compass which ends at the top of the primary scale. It will be understood that when the reed could not be compressed by the lips the octave harmonics would be difficult or impossible to produce. Early in the 17th century the shawm family seems to have reached its apogee, for Praetorius (1619) mentions seven sizes which were, moreover, capable of reaching upwards to the fourth note of the second octave, and downwards by means of four keys. Only the lower three instruments are provided with four keys; the others have either one key or duplicate little-finger-holes, while the highest member of the group appears to have only six note-holes.

The following is Praetorius' group, named collectively *Bombyces*, *Pommern*,[1] *Piffari* and *Schallmeyen* :

Instrument	Extension downwards by Key or Keys or by Little-finger-hole	Primary or Six-finger-hole Scale	Extension upwards by Octave Harmonics
Gar klein discant Schalmey	..	$b'-b''$	to b''' (?)
Discant Schalmey (little-finger-hole)	to d'	$e'-e''$	to b''
Klein Alt Pommer (one key)	to g	$a-a'$	to d''
Tenor Pommer Nicolo (one key)	to c	$d-d'$	to g'
Tenor Pommer Basset (four keys)	to G	$d-d'$	to g'
Bass Pommer (four keys)	to C	$G-g$	to c'
Gross bass Pommer (four keys)	to $F_{,}$	$C-c$	to f

Of these the alto and discant are also available, pitched a

[1] Praetorius gives *Houtbois* as French, *Hoboyen* as English (!) and *Bombardo* as Italian for the German word *Pommern*.

tone lower. From the tenor downwards the instruments are depicted with crooks, and all are sounded with a *pirouette*.

Mersenne describes two sorts of shawms ; the group named *Hautbois de Poitou* corresponds to the true shawm type and is shown in three sizes, a treble, a tenor with one key, and a bass with four keys. A treble " *haut-bois* " depicted by Mersenne, however, appears to be a more advanced instrument which foreshadows the coming change, and lends colour to the generally accepted theory that the modern oboe originated in France. This instrument has no *pirouette* ; the reed was presumably held between the lips. Eight finger-holes are shown in addition to what appear to be two pairs of tuning-holes. It is by no means clear how the eight note-holes were controlled by the fingers, unless both little fingers were used. This instrument is outwardly rather like the later oboe type, and may mark the beginning of the transformation from shawm to oboe.

It is unfortunate that the second half of the 17th century produced no Praetorius or Mersenne to tell us of the progress of events at this important period in the history of wood-wind instruments. The old cylindrical flute was transformed into the 18th century jointed, one-keyed, conical flute not very long after Mersenne wrote in 1636 ; similarly, it may be in the same place, at the same time, and possibly by the same hands that the true oboe emerged, jointed, keyed and ready to take its place and to form the nucleus of a wood-wind section in the orchestra during the second half of the 17th century.

When Lulli and other composers of French opera and ballet were writing for a pair of oboes, and when Purcell and Scarlatti began to admit the double reeds into their orchestral group, the coarser shawms receded into the background.[1] They had not long to wait before the recorders joined the family of discarded instruments ; practical musicians were finished with them ; worthless and out of date, many of the old shawms must have perished before interested historians and collectors in the 19th

---

[1] " Nothing need be said about the German shawms, because they are amongst the obsolete instruments " (Eisel, 1738).

century began to rescue the few which had survived the 18th century. The *pirouettes*, the wind-caps and the barrel-shaped protecting boxes all died with the 17th century, but the swallow-tail key lived on and survived the 18th century, even though one branch of the tail had for some time been quite useless.

Krumhorns, Rauschpfeifen, Bassanelli and Schreierpfeifen

Amongst some other instruments which were closely akin to the shawms, and like them did not outlive the 17th century, probably the most widely used were the krumhorns.[1] These were straight cylindrical wooden tubes bent round at the lower end like the letter J and generally pierced with the usual six finger-holes and a duplicated little-finger-hole on the upper side, also a thumb-hole on the underside. The sound was generated by means of a double reed encased in a detachable wind-chamber, and the instrument was blown through an opening in the end, or in the case of some of the larger krumhorns, through an opening in the side of the wind-chamber. Because the reed could not be compressed by the player's lips it was hardly possible to sound any harmonics,[2] so the scale of the krumhorns was limited to fundamentals, of which a diatonic succession of nine sounds was available. No doubt a few intermediate semi-tones would be produced by means of forkfingering or by half-opening note-holes.

Except for a very slight expansion at the lower end, the tube being cylindrical and virtually closed at the upper end, the krum-horns acted in accordance with the principles of a stopped pipe and produced their sounds an octave lower than those of conical tubes of the same sounding-length.

Like all the wood-wind instruments of their period, the krum-

---

[1] (E.) Krumhorn, Cromorne. (G.) *Krummhorn, Krumphorn.* (F.) *Cromorne, Tournebout.* (I.) *Cromorne.*

[2]   " Die Kromhörner aber nicht höher gan
        Denn die acht löcher werden auffgethan " (Agricola, 1528).

horns were made in different sizes; Virdung and Agricola show a group of four, and Praetorius gives the compass of six sizes as follows :

	Primary Octave	Downward Extension to
Klein Cant. .	d' to d''	c'
Cant. . .	a to a'	g
Alt. Ten. .	d to d'	c
Bass Chorist .	G to g	F
Grossbass .	$\lbrace$ D to d	C
	C to c	B flat

In order to control the lowest note-hole the larger krumhorns were provided with a swallow-tail key under a protecting box, and from one to three tuning-holes pierced the lower and curved part of the tube.

Not very many krumhorns have survived to the present day. Some genuine old specimens are shown in the Berlin, Vienna, Brussels, Leipzig (Heyer), Paris, Munich and Copenhagen collections, and several museums display replicas copied from original instruments or made according to Praetorius' descriptions and woodcuts. One or two of the bass krumhorns occur with two little-finger-keys, and one unique specimen in the Brussels collection (No. 615) has, in addition to these two keys, yet another pair of holes still lower down the tube covered by sliding shutters like those shown in Praetorius' woodcut of the *Bass Krummhorn*. The second little-finger-key added another note to the downward compass of the instrument, and no doubt still lower sounds could be obtained when the shutters over the lowest holes were closed, although it is evident that these shutters could not be moved by the player whilst the instrument was being played.

Krumhorns are depicted in many 16th- and 17th-century paintings and engravings, and are rarely missing in the groups of instruments which so frequently adorn the title-pages of printed musical works of that period. They are shown associated with other reed instruments, and even with trombones, and were evidently much used in the small wind bands of the later Middle Ages. By the end of the 17th century the day of the Krumhorns was over, and in the 18th century they figured in musical and other dictionaries merely as antiquities.

Two instruments of the shawm type figure in one of Burgkmair's famous series of woodcuts "Kayser Maximilians I Triumph" (c. 1516) and are there named *rauschpfeiffen*.[1] In his *Real-lexikon* (1913) Sachs refers to this as the only occasion on which the word *rauschpfeife* occurs, and in the catalogue of the Berlin collection (1922) he gives that name to a set of six instruments exhibited there. (Pl. 28.) These are a set of shawms in three sizes, with a slightly conical bore, the usual finger-holes, and sounded by means of a double reed encased in a windchamber. It may be that the Berlin instruments can be identified with those shown in the woodcut ; in that case they are the only known specimens, although, it is true, very similar instruments occur in other collections under different names.

A group of reed instruments, said to have been invented by the Venetian composer Giovanni Bassano, and named *bassanelli*, are depicted and described by Praetorius. They are rather elaborately turned cylindrical tubes with six finger-holes and an open little-finger-key, but no thumb-hole, and were sounded by means of a double reed on the end of a bassoon-like crook which was inserted in the upper end of the instrument. The reed was apparently held between the player's lips, and three octave-harmonics are included in the compass of eleven diatonic degrees which Praetorius allows these instruments. The lowest sounds of the three *bassanelli* were, respectively, *d* (*diskant*), G (*alt-tenor*) and C (*bass*), and the tone was said to be quieter than that of the contemporary bassoons and shawms. It is claimed in the catalogue of the Vienna collection that an instrument shown there (No. 218, Pl. 39) is a *bassanello*. The Vienna instrument, however, has no key, and the crook is missing. Apart from this rather doubtful specimen, no others are known.

---

[1] See *A History of Music in Pictures*, p. 76, No. 4, where the instruments are named *Windkapselschalmeien*.

Still more shadowy are the *schryari* or *schreierpfeifen* of which Praetorius gave a brief description, illustrations of three sizes, and the compass for four instruments. Not a single specimen is known, but Praetorius' woodcuts show that the exterior of the tube was widest at the upper end, and that in addition to the usual six finger-holes, a little-finger-hole or key and a thumb-hole at the back, another key was situated on the front of the instrument near the upper end ; the latter key, however, is not shown on the discant instrument for which Praetorius gave no upward compass. The lowest notes of the three instruments were, respectively, F, *c* and *g* ; judging by the low pitch and short tube-length—the bass appears to have been just a little over 3 feet long—one may conclude that the bore of the *schreierpfeifen* was cylindrical if it did follow the shape of the exterior of the tube. The discant instrument, curiously enough, was closed at the lower end. Praetorius' woodcuts show no sounding apparatus, but as he makes it clear that no harmonics were available, it may be supposed that the *schreierpfeifen* were sounded with a double reed in a wind-chamber.

The 18th-century Oboe

" Das gleichsam redende Hautbois, Ital. oboe, ist bey den Frantzosen / und nunmehro auch bey uns / das / was vor diesem in Teutschland die Schalmeyen (von den alten Musicis Piffari genandt) gewesen sind / ob sie gleich etwas anders eingerichtet." So wrote the North German composer Mattheson in 1713. The first instructions for playing the oboe are in French,[1] and the word *Hautbois* is French. No doubt this improved and refined shawm came from France, but it had found its way to Germany, the Netherlands and England before the beginning of the 18th century. Very few 17th-century oboes survive,[2] but the first half of the 18th century provides a fair number of examples, while those made towards the end of that century are available

---

[1] Freillon-Poncein (1700) ; Hotteterre, in the flute tutor (1707).

[2] No. 2933 in the Berlin Coll. is possibly the oldest extant.

in abundance. The instrument underwent no important change during the whole of the 18th century.

The oboe known to Bach and Handel, to Haydn and Mozart, even to the young man Beethoven, was made in three pieces, of boxwood, ebony or ivory, with keys of brass or silver.[1] Ivory ferrules usually go with the boxwood instruments, but the more costly instruments of ebony or ivory are often provided with silver keys and ferrules. The key-covers are usually round, more rarely square, and octagonal only on the later oboes. They are mounted in two wooden rings turned on the lower end of the middle-piece.

Six finger-holes provide the primary scale of D major as on the contemporary flute, and a closed key sounds d' sharp when the hole it covers is opened by the R. (or L.) little finger. Below that key there is another note-hole covered by a swallow-tail open key (also worked by the R. or L. little finger) which gives c' natural when it is closed. On the earlier 18th-century oboes the D sharp key is provided in duplicate, one on each side, so that either the R. or the L. hand might be used for the lower half of the instrument. Although these duplicate keys are still to be found on some oboes made late in the century, the key on the L. side is usually absent on those made in the second half of the 18th century, indicating that most players were then in the habit of playing with the L. hand on the upper part of the instrument. The swallow-tail C key, however, persisted long after the duplicate D sharp was abandoned.

The upper piece contains the three upper note-holes, the lower of which (A hole) consists of two very small holes bored so close together that either both or only one of them might be covered by the L. third finger. When only one is covered the instrument gives a g' sharp or a' flat. The middle-piece contains the three lower finger-holes and the two keys. On many of the earlier oboes, and occasionally on those of a later date, the g' hole is also doubled, no doubt for the purpose of sharpening the f' sharp which is generally rather flat, or of lowering the

---

[1] Ivory keys occur rarely. Pewter keys appear at the end of the century.

g' which is sometimes sharp. On the bell-joint there are one or two tuning-holes situated about $3\frac{1}{2}$ to 4 inches from the end of the bell. It is from these holes that the low c' sounds, but they cannot be closed, so that note is the lowest the instrument can sound.[1] Interchangeable upper-pieces were provided, as on other instruments of the period, to suit the varying pitches then in use.

A characteristic of the early oboes is a funnel-shaped profile at the top end, no doubt a relic of the old *pirouette* ; this feature disappears fairly early in the 18th century, and the extreme end eventually becomes cylindrical. Another mark of the earlier 18th-century oboes is a pair of turned rings on the bell-joint, one above and the other below the tuning-holes. (Pl. IV, A, B and C.) The later instruments have only one of these rings placed above the tuning-holes. A swelling on the exterior of the tube about one inch from the top end is a mark of the 18th-century oboe which is very slight on the earlier instruments, but which becomes very pronounced and onion-like towards the end of the century (Pl. IV, D and E) ; that feature, and a slight incurve of the interior of the bell at its lower extremity, are characteristics which were not abandoned till towards the middle of last century. The usual ornamental rings and swellings of the profile are typical external features of the 18th-century instrument which contrast strangely with the plain profile of some oboes made by English makers at the end of the century. (Pl. IV, F.)

The three finger-holes on the middle-piece are rather larger than those on the upper-piece, and the two uppermost holes are sometimes bored in a slightly upward direction, while the pair for the L. hand third finger incline to turn downwards. The very small holes on the upper piece give a distinctly flat c'' sharp, but this note was generally played with only the top hole open and the low C key closed,[2] in fact, as a lowered d''.

---

[1] An experiment will show that if both tuning-holes are closed, the instrument will sound b natural through the bell.

[2] Eisel (1738) shows c'' sharp played with all finger-holes open ; this is unusual.

By compressing the reed with the lips the octave-harmonics of the primary scale are available, but not without some modifications of the fingering at the upper end of the second octave. The *f'* natural, *b'* flat and *c''* natural and their octaves were forked much in the same way as on the contemporary one-keyed flute, thus, the scale was completely chromatic except that the low *c'* sharp was missing ; that note was unplayable unless attempted by half-closing the C key.[1]

Of the reeds used on these early oboes very little can be stated with confidence. Detachable from the instrument, very easily lost or destroyed, such frail things as oboe reeds do not usually survive for such long periods as 150 or 200 years. The little evidence there is suggests that the reeds used in the 18th century were broader than those now in use.

Fingering charts for the two-keyed oboe are given in the following instruction books :

1707. Hotteterre (*c'—d'''*)
1731. *The Modern Musick Master* (*c'—c'''*)
1738. *Eisel* (*c—c'''* sharp)
c. 1750. *The Compleat Tutor*
        (*c'—c'''*)   These appear to be taken from *The*
1754. *The Muses' Delight*   *Modern Musick Master.*
        (*c'—c'''*)
1754. *Minguet* (Spanish) (*c'—d'''*)
c. 1800. *New and Complete Instructions* (*c'—d'''*)
c. 1808. *The Compleat Tutor* (*c'—d'''*)

Fingering Chart No. 3 is taken from the *New and Complete Instructions* (c. 1800) ; it is for a two-keyed oboe.

Played with a broader reed, the tone of the 18th-century oboe was probably heavier than that of a modern instrument, but there is no reason to suppose that it was coarse or strident as is often suggested. In his *Musikalischer Almanach* of 1782, C. L. Junker described the oboe as being suitable for the expression of " soft, tender and mildly sad feelings ".

[1] *Freillon-Poncein, Méthode* (1700).

The following are only some amongst a number of makers' names which appear on 18th-century oboes :

Early Group (with duplicate D sharp keys)	*Later Group* (with only one D sharp key)
Hotteterre (Paris)	Rottenburgh (Brussels)
Denner (Nürnberg)	Willems (Brussels)
Stanesby (London)	Schlegel (Bale)
Anciuti (Milan)	Cahusac (London)
Richters ——	Lot T. (Paris)
Lehner ——	Delusse (Paris)
Bizey (Paris)	Goulding (London)
	Milhouse (Newark)
	Grenser (Dresden)
	Grundmann (Dresden)

Two-keyed oboes were still made and used early in the 19th century. There are no signs that the 18th-century composers regarded the instrument as being at all imperfect ; the players accepted the instrument with all its limitations and imperfections just as the flautists accepted the one-keyed flute. Their life's work was to play on it, and their duty was to cover up its faults with all the skill at their command. No effort was made to improve the oboe mechanically till after the flute had gained its additional keys, so the instrument of Bach and Handel in the early 18th century remained practically the same when the famous player Fischer [1] delighted his audiences at Vauxhall Gardens with his " celebrated Rondo " at the end of the same century.

In almost every book that touches on the history of the oboe, and in nearly all Dictionaries of Music,[2] the statement appears that one Gerhard Hoffmann added a G sharp and an A sharp (or B flat) key to the oboe in 1727. No trace of these keys can be found on any oboes made till near the end of the

---

[1] " The tone of Fischer was soft and sweet, his style was expressive, and his execution was at once neat and brilliant " (Parke's *Musical Memoirs*, 1830).

[2] Grove (1927), Riemann, Koch (1802), Gassner, Terry (1932), Galpin (1937).

18th century, nor do the fingering charts give any hint that such keys were in use till the 19th century. The statement appears to be based on a misunderstanding and persistent mis-quotation or mistranslation of a notice regarding Hoffmann which first appeared in print in Gerber's *Lexikon* of 1792 ; it seems that the latter derived his information from some MS. addenda made by Walther, who evidently intended them to be included in a later edition of his *Lexikon* of 1732. Gerber's statement is to the effect that Hoffmann improved the intonation of the notes G sharp and A flat (enharmonics) by means of a valve (*ventil*) ; the German for key is, and has always been, *klappe* ; and the note *as* in German means A flat, not A sharp. So Hoffmann's improvement was not a key or keys, nor did it affect the notes A sharp or B flat. Whatever the *Bürgermeister* Hoff-mann did to improve the oboe, it is certain that he did not anticipate the advent of the chromatic keys on the oboe by sixty or seventy years. The twin-holes for the third finger of the L. hand (which certainly did improve the intonation of G sharp or A flat) seem to have been known before 1727, so it is improbable that Hoff-mann can be given credit for having initiated that useful device.

The 19th-century Oboe

With the flute as pioneer amongst the wood-wind instru-ments, the addition of chromatic keys to the oboe followed in due course, but rather irregularly, during the first quarter of the 19th century. Two prominent German makers, Grundmann and Grenser, both of Dresden, began to make these additions in the last few years of the 18th century, yet on the whole the oboe started the new century with its mechanical equipment very much in the state that it had been throughout the previous century.

Amongst the earliest additions were the octave-key,[1] a closed G sharp key for the L. little finger, a closed F sharp key for

---

[1] (G.) *Schleifklappe*, i.e. slurring-key. Usually worked by the L. thumb, exceptionally by the L. first finger.

the R. little finger which improved the intonation (flat) of that note, and a closed key for the missing low C sharp. The old swallow-tail key disappeared with the advent of this last key. Subsequent additions were the closed cross-key for F natural (as on the flute), a closed B flat key sometimes worked by the L. thumb, but eventually allotted to the R. first finger, and a closed key for the upper C natural, also worked by the R. first finger.[1] Thus, an oboe made in the first twenty years of the 19th century might be provided with any number from two to nine keys. (Pl. IV, G and I. Pl. V, J.) The tuning was adjusted either by using alternative joints or by means of a longer or shorter staple.

Yet another important addition was made in the first quarter of the 19th century; this was a long-shanked open key covering a hole in the bell-joint situated just where one of the tuning-holes had hitherto been bored. When this hole was closed the instrument sounded B natural through the bell, and an extra semitone was added to the downward compass of the oboe. With the advent of this key tuning-holes disappeared from all but German oboes; on these one may still be found. The low B key was at first worked by the L. thumb, as on the first Sellner-Koch oboes; this arrangement was no doubt found to be inconvenient, and the control of the key was eventually transferred to the L. little finger. (Pl. V, L.) The twin-hole for the L. third finger survived long after the G sharp key was added, and may be found on oboes made late in the 19th century.

When provided with all the above keys, the oboe had fifteen note-holes, of which nine were controlled by keys and six were finger-holes. The octave-key made a total of sixteen holes. Of the keys only the lower two stood open. The new keys were mounted at first in wooden blocks, but later on in metal saddles. Old 18th-century oboes are sometimes found with added 19th-century keys; this was usually done by mounting the new keys in saddles or even on pillars, but instances do occur of neatly added blocks fitted on to the surface of the old wooden tube.

[1] On some old instruments by the L. third finger.

By about 1825 the most advanced and fully-equipped oboes were possibly those devised by the well-known player Joseph Sellner, and made by the Viennese maker Koch. In addition to the nine keys and the *schleifklappe*, Sellner added extra levers to work the B flat key (L. thumb), the F natural (L. little finger) and the D sharp keys (also L. little finger). This was the instrument for which he wrote his tutor, first published in 1825, and afterwards translated into French and Italian. A tuning-slide at the top of the instrument was also included in the Sellner-Koch oboe. (Pl. V, K.) Some German makers made oboes on the lines of Sellner's instrument, and for a while it seemed as if they were going to take the lead in providing the oboe with mechanical facilities. Some prominent French players apparently distrusted these many keys, and were content for a while to play on two- or four-keyed oboes.[1] However, the time was near when Paris makers and players were to begin reshaping and refitting the instrument, and it is to them, and in particular to Triébert, Barret and Lorée, that the modern French oboe owes most of its well-deserved high reputation. In the meantime, from about 1800 to 1835, although the bore was being slightly narrowed at the upper end of the tube, the instrument retained many of its 18th-century characteristics. Oboes were at that time still being made of boxwood with ivory ferrules and flat brass keys, and the old outward profile as well as the incurve of the interior at the bell-end was retained. The very earliest Triébert oboes have many of the old features, but the white metal keys are slenderer, working in neat saddles, and are slightly cupped in order to accommodate small stuffed pads. (Pl. V, M.)

Cupped keys with stuffed pads, pillar-mounts and the ring-keys and rod-axles of Boehm's 1832 flute began to spread to other wood-wind instruments about 1840, and the newer oboes were destined to benefit by these mechanical conveniences, also to acquire some key-devices which since that time have become recognised adjuncts to the mechanism of all the oboe family.

[1] Sallantin and Vogt. Tuerlinckx, a maker of Malines, in 1830 offered oboes with only 2, 4 or 5 keys.

Prominent amongst the latter is the perforated key-cover over the c'' sharp hole ; this device seems to have been due to the Paris player Brod (1799–1839), who found that his pupils experienced great difficulty in half-closing the very small finger-hole with the L. first finger. Both forms of the older F sharp key (cross and longitudinal) were abolished when two ring-keys over the E and F sharp holes and a small F sharp key (the " spectacle ") were attached to the same rod-axle ; this useful device simplified the fingering for the second and third fingers of the R. hand, and retained the old forkfingering for F natural. Both of these improvements were embodied on new oboes made before the middle of the 19th century, and were sometimes added to box-wood instruments of the old school. Cocuswood, with German silver keys and ferrules, began to take the place of the old yellow boxwood, brass and ivory, as materials for making oboes.[1] As well as cocuswood, pearwood and ebony were beginning to be used about that time, and some all-metal oboes made their appearance, but apparently without any great success.[2] The following are makers of oboes (1800–1850) whose instruments cover the period during which the number of keys grew from two to thirteen or more :

D'Almaine (London)	Tuerlinckx (Malines)
Goodlad (London)	Brod (Paris)
Grenser H. (Dresden)	Buffet (Paris)
Golde (Dresden)	Triébert (Paris)
Koch (Vienna)	Maino (Milan)
Ziegler (Vienna)	Piana (Milan)

Beethoven, Schubert, Weber and their contemporaries cover the period when the oboe was gaining its keys ; they would know the instrument in its 18th-century form, with but two keys ; they would also see it with a complete set of chromatic

---

[1] The Triébert Oboe (Pl. V, N) is of painted boxwood, and still has the incurve in the interior of the bell-end.

[2] Von Gontershausen (1855) remarks that the tone of the brass oboe is hard and pointed (*hart und spitz*) ; it loses the " heartgripping " tenderness of the wooden instrument.

keys, a low B natural and an octave key. To the next generation, to Schumann, Mendelssohn and Berlioz, the two-keyed oboe would seem old-fashioned and inefficient ; they would see the instrument with its new key-system, increasing its compass and beginning to look something like the oboe of today. Berlioz would know well the difference between a German and a French oboe, and would no doubt follow the progress of the latter in the hands of Frédéric Triébert with keen interest.

It may be that it is possible to trace back to the 18th century the tendency of the oboe to develop along national lines, namely, a French and a German type. A close comparison of instruments by Th. Lot or Ch. Delusse of Paris with those of Jacob Grundmann or Carl Grenser of Dresden, might reveal subtle differences which would show how French taste was then already seeking to cultivate a thin, refined and sensitive tone-quality, while German taste leaned towards a heavier and more robust tone. However that may be, there can be no question that when F. Triébert took under his special care the welfare of the French instrument, the difference between the two schools was clearly established, and that their respective tendencies were not only mechanically, but also aesthetically governed. The nerve-centre of the oboe lies in its reed, and in the bore is its soul. A narrower and finer reed favoured the French ideal ; meticulous care in adjusting the diameter and expansion of the bore, together with minute measurements in determining the situation and size of the note-holes, gave the French oboe its character rather than the growth of mechanical devices on the exterior of the tube. These measurements are only to be expressed in millimetres and fractions of millimetres, and will reveal their secrets only under micrometrical treatment.

Mechanically the French instrument progressed step by step ; one key-device followed another till, when the process culminated in the *Conservatoire Model*, the exterior of the oboe was covered with mechanism just about to the extent of its capacity. Only the most important and permanent of these improvements will be noticed here.

An early Triébert oboe of about 1840 still retains the incurved interior at the extreme end of the bell, but the bulges and undulations on the outside of the tube have been smoothed away. The keys are all mounted on pillars, and needle-springs regulate those which are attached to rod-axles. The R. little-finger-keys work each on a separate lever. The finger-holes for the R. second and third fingers are provided with ring-keys attached to the same rod-axle as the small F sharp key. The cross F natural key and the note-hole for the R. first finger remain unaltered. The L. little-finger-keys for low B and D sharp (duplicate) work on separate levers. The fingerplate of the upper C key overlaps the lever of the B flat key so that both holes are open when the C is played. A perforated key for the L. first finger, a shake-key and the octave-key complete the outfit. (Pl. V, N.)

With the above simple system as a basis, a further series of improvements follows ; the period is roughly from 1840 to 1880.

The incurve at the end of the bell disappears.

(a) The R. little-finger-keys are made to work on rod-axles, and are grouped as is now customary, with the round fingerplate of the C sharp key in the middle.

(b) A shake key for d'' (and later for d'' sharp) works on a rod axle.

(c) The L. little-finger-keys are made to work on one rod-axle.

(d) A second octave-key (used from a'') is added. (Pl. V. o.)

(e) The upper B flat and C natural holes are placed in line with the other note-holes along the top of the tube, and both keys work on a common rod-axle controlled by a single fingerplate for the R. first finger. (The Barret-action.) [1]

(f) A thumb-plate for the L. thumb is added ; this plate duplicates the action of the R. first finger but in the reverse direction, that is, it opens the upper B flat and C keys when the thumb-plate is released.

[1] Devised by Apollon Barret (Barrē) of Paris and London.

   (g) The instrument is lengthened and an additional note-hole
        is added lower down on the bell-joint ; this hole is con-
        trolled by an open key worked by the L. little finger and
        sounds low B flat when it is closed. Thus, another semi-
        tone is added to the downward compass of the oboe.[1]
        (Pl. V, P.)

   (h) *The Conservatoire Model*, known as No. 6. By means of
        a connecting rod-axle, the first, second and third fingers
        of the R. hand control the upper B flat and C keys. The
        action of the F natural and G sharp keys are duplicated,
        respectively, by the L. little finger and the R. first finger.
        The second octave-key works automatically. (Pl. V, R.)

To the above catalogue might be added a few extra keys
or levers which facilitate the performance of certain shakes
which were formerly very awkward to negotiate or even quite
impossible.

When the *Conservatoire Model* was complete (*c.* 1880) the
last word in French oboes had been spoken. Triébert's successor Lorée, and the player Gillet, had taken some part in the
final stages of the development of the instrument, and a few
other players and makers have since had a finger in the pie,
adding facilities, altering here and there, and endeavouring to
remove every possible awkwardness which might hamper the
player. Oboes are now made and used in all stages from the
simplest system with thirteen keys to the elaborate *Conservatoire
Model* ; the French type is favoured in England, Belgium and
Italy, and each player has just as many or as few of the various
key-facilities on his instrument as he wishes. His choice may be
governed by habit, by conviction, by experience, perhaps by
fancy, or even by the length of his purse, for the modern oboe is
an expensive instrument. The full *Conservatoire Model* is by
no means universally used, and not every device invented for it
will be found on the same instrument, even if room could be

----

[1] The low B flat key occurs exceptionally at a much earlier date. An
oboe by Power (Pl. IV, H), with a bulb-bell, is an unusually early example.

found for them all. Players recognise that it is better to have good control over a limited number of devices than to have imperfect control over too many facilities.

In the meantime the German-Austrian oboe developed along its own lines. Makers of the mid-19th century took advantage of the ring-keys, the rod-axles and all the new mechanism which was then finding its way on to all wood-wind instruments, and made use of them on the cruder and more robust tube of the German oboe. Combined with modern mechanism, some quite old-fashioned features are found on German oboes made towards the end of last century. The incurve at the bottom of the bell, and a tuning-hole in the bell, were not extinct when the French oboe was already well advanced and approaching its culminating stage. (Pl. V, Q.) In his amplification of Berlioz's *Instrumentation* (1904), Richard Strauss compared the French and the German oboe, also their respective tone-qualities and the style of playing on them in a way which was distinctly unfavourable to the latter. He described the German tone as " thick and trumpet-like," unaccommodating in the matter of blend, and often unpleasantly prominent. Coming from such a weighty source, German makers have taken this reproof to heart, and now offer to supply French oboes made in Germany.

Oboes are now usually made of blackwood, rosewood, or more rarely of ebonite or metal.

The ordinary instrument in C is universally employed in both orchestras and military bands, but smaller oboes pitched a semitone and a minor third higher than normal, also a larger variety pitched a tone down, have been used in continental military bands at various times. The higher oboes are said to be, respectively, in D flat and E flat, and the lower one on B flat.

The Oboe d'amore

(G.) Liebesoboe. (F.) Hautbois d'amour. (I.) Oboe d'amore.

THE *oboe d'amore* is pitched a minor third below the ordinary oboe and is provided with a bulb-bell. According to Walther's

Lexikon (1732), this instrument first appeared about 1720, and is described as being in every way similar to the oboe except that the bell was contracted at the lower end, leaving an opening just wide enough to admit a man's finger. The compass given by Walther, namely, from *a* to *b″*, corresponds to the range of the oboe of that period.[1] Specimens made up till near the end of the 18th century are fairly common in large collections ; after that time there are only a few scattered traces of the instrument till the last quarter of the 19th century, when it was revived for the purpose of playing the parts that Bach wrote for it. Koch (1802), who calls it also *Oboe luongo*, states that it was then seldom used. A specimen by Winnen, made about 1830, figures in the Paris collection (No. 326). In the Koch-Dommer *Lexikon* (1865), it is said that the difficulty of playing in tune on the *oboe d'amore* was probably the reason why it was allowed to fall into disuse. The 18th-century instruments have the same two (or three) keys, also the usual tuning-holes of the contemporary oboe. Bach wrote freely for the *oboe d'amore*, especially in his Church works, and occasionally exceeded the compass given by Walther.

Mahillon in 1878, and Lorée in 1889, revived the *oboe d'amore*, and it is now made complete with modern oboe-mechanism, but is not usually supplied with the low B flat key.

The Cor Anglais

(G.) Englisches Horn.   (F.) Cor Anglais.   (I.) Corno Inglese.

Tenor or alto oboes in general are larger oboes which sound a fourth or a fifth lower than the ordinary treble instrument. They can all trace their descent from the alto shawm (*pommer* or *bombard*), and even if the transformation did not take place at the same time and in the same place as the transformation from treble shawm to oboe, it must have been accomplished

---

[1] Mattheson (1713) does not mention the *oboe d'amore* ; both Majer (1741) and Eisel (1738) merely repeat Walther's statement.

before the end of the 17th century, for in his music to " Dio-clesian " (1691), Purcell asks for a " tenner Hautboy." It was the instrument sounding a fifth below the oboe which, after having figured as the *oboe da caccia, Taille* or *Hautecontre de Hautbois*, became the *cor anglais* some time after the middle of the 18th century.

Neither Speer (1697), Mattheson (1713), Walther (1732), Eisel (1738) nor Majer (1741) seem to have known the tenor oboe, although Walther knew the *oboe d'amore* ; yet such instruments, apparently made in the first half of the 18th century, survive in several collections,[1] and Bach wrote parts for *oboe da caccia* and *taille*.[2] The existing specimens are straight or curved tubes slightly prolonged by metal crooks at the narrow end. They occur both with and without the bulb-bell, and are provided with the same keys as the contemporary oboe, namely, the open C and the closed D sharp keys, sounding, of course, a fifth lower. As on the oboe, the D sharp key is duplicated on the earlier examples.

It was no doubt the awkwardness of holding such a long straight tube that caused makers to bend the tube of the tenor oboe, and it was when the instrument was made in a curved form with a bulb-bell that it began to acquire the name *cor anglais*. Why a continental tenor oboe should have been named an " English horn " has never been quite satisfactorily explained. That it was curved does explain why the instrument was called a horn, for horns were usually curved or coiled, but no con-vincing reason has yet been offered why it should have been associated with the name of this country. It has been suggested that *anglais* is a corruption of *anglé* (angular, or bent at an angle) ; if that were so one would certainly expect to find the term *cor anglé* at an earlier period than *cor anglais* ; as a matter of fact, *anglé* does not occur at all till it was offered as a possible origin of *anglais* in the 19th century. In any case it is as the

---

[1] Berlin, Vienna, Salzburg, Leipzig (Heyer), Basel, Breslau, Brussels ; specimens by Denner at are Berlin and Leipzig.

[2] From 1723 (Terry, *Bach's Orchestra*).

Corno Inglese that the instrument first appears in a few scores just before, and after the middle of the 18th century.[1] The two names *cor anglais* and *oboe da caccia* (hunting oboe) remain unexplained ; there seems to be no reason for supposing that the former originated in England, nor that the latter was associated with the sport of hunting.

The curve of the tube, which varies from a gentle bend to almost a semicircle, brought the lower hand of the player nearer to his body, but the necessity for placing the finger-holes within reach of the fingers (i.e. too close together) remained an acoustical weakness of the *cor anglais* till modern mechanism came to the rescue and enabled the note-holes to be properly spaced while keeping the finger-plates comfortably under the fingers. The curved tube could only be made (as were the medieval cornet, the serpent and the curved basset horn) by hollowing out two transverse halves of the wooden material, and then glueing them together again ; the whole was strengthened by a leather binding, and the bulb-bell was turned on a lathe in the usual way and was attached to the curved tube by means of an ordinary tenon-and-socket joint. The instrument was also jointed in the middle of the curve, and the two usual oboe-keys were provided. (Pl. VI, B.) At a later period the upper and the lower of each group of finger-holes were bored diagonally outwards, as on a bassoon, in order to mitigate to some extent the disadvantage which ensues when the note-holes are situated too close together for the length of the tube. In spite of the difficulty of making this hollowed-out tube, the curved *cor anglais* persisted till about the middle of last century ; curved specimens occur, with quite advanced key-mechanism mounted on pillars, which cannot have been made much before 1850. (Pl. VI, C.) The curved tube was avoided on some 19th-century instruments by using straight tubes united in the middle by a small knee-joint. (Pl. VI, D.)

The key-work of the *cor anglais* has always gone hand in hand with that of the oboe, except that the low B flat key of

[1] Jomelli (1741), Haydn (1764), Gluck (1767).

the oboe is not always provided. From about the middle of last century the *cor anglais* has become straight again, and a small bend in the metal crook is sufficient to keep the instrument near enough to the player. (Pl. VI, E.) Although the bulb-bell (G. *Liebesfuss*) has for long been considered an essential feature of the larger oboes, the tenor instrument with an expanding bell never completely died out. Straight tenor oboes with ordinary bells occur as the work of some English makers during the 18th century,[1] and quite recent instruments with modern mechanism and expanding bells have been made. The bulb-bell also occurs on 18th- and 19th-century oboes (Pl. IV, H), yet *Liebesoboe* or *oboe d'amore* is understood to denote only the oboe which sounds a third lower than normal.

Bass or Baritone Oboes

Bass or baritone oboes are those which are twice the size of the ordinary oboe, and sound an octave lower. One by Denner (*c.* 1700) is preserved at Nürnberg[2] and, according to Mahillon, sounds the primary scale *d* to *c'* sharp. It has the usual six finger-holes and two keys of the 18th-century oboe, and a crook with a right-angled bend. Sachs mentions an 18th-century English bass oboe, now in a New York collection, and the Paris collection displays a two-keyed specimen bearing the name Bizey (No. 334).

Little more is heard of bass oboes till about 1775 when a basset oboe[3] made a brief appearance. The maker and presumably the designer of this instrument appears to have been J. J. Riedlocker of Paris. Made with a very wide conical bore, the narrow end of the tube is continued in a circular-coiled brass crook. All the note-holes excepting those for the two middle fingers are covered by open keys, and a seventh and lower hole is controlled by a swallow-tail open key worked by the little

---

[1] Stanesby, jun., Cahusac, Milhouse, Longman and Broderip.
[2] A facsimile is shown at Brussels, No. 985.
[3] (G.) *Musettenbass.* (F.) *Basse de Musette.*

finger. (Pl. VI, A.) If it ever had any active life, which is very doubtful, this instrument soon settled down to an uneventful career as a curiosity in a few museums.[1]

After another interval the baritone oboe again crops up in Paris about 1825, when the elder and the younger Triébert made some attempts to give life to an instrument which seemed determined to languish and die. An eight-keyed specimen, made by the elder Triébert for the oboist Vogt, now reposes in the Paris Collection (No. 335), and some further efforts by the younger Triébert met with no better fate. This type was apparently made with an upturned bell which emerged from an abbreviated bassoon-like butt. In 1889 Lorée again revived the instrument, this time with a bulb-bell, a curved crook and modern mechanism.[2]

Early in the present century the intermittent and precarious existence of the baritone oboe was seriously threatened by the appearance of a robust German rival, which itself has found the struggle for existence none too easy. This was the *Heckelphon*, a product of the well-known firm of bassoon-makers, Wilhelm Heckel of Biebrich-am-Rhein. The *Heckelphon* was introduced in 1904 and has found a place in the scores of a few works by modern German composers. The instrument has a wide conical bore and is pitched an octave below the ordinary oboe, but with yet another semitone added to its downward compass. The lowest note is A below the four-foot C, and the compass extends upwards to g'', or even a little higher. Made of maplewood, the wide tube ends in a globular bell closed at the lower end by a perforated stopper ; in the side of the bell, at first one hole, but later three holes, were bored. A bent metal crook carries a reed almost as large as a bassoon reed. The large note-holes are all covered by keys, the fingerplates of which are brought

[1] Leipzig (Heyer), No. 1352; Basel, No. 77 (dated 1777); Munich, No. 66; Paris, No. 468; London (Donaldson); London (Carse Coll.), No. 214. Facsimile copy at Brussels, No. 979.

[2] Pierre (1893) cites a contrabass oboe (1781) by Delusse in the Paris Coll., and states that Lorée contemplated making some such monster, but had not yet carried out the project.

up to the upper half of the instrument, and are so disposed that the fingering is that of the ordinary German oboe.

A *piccolo-Heckelphon* in high F followed soon after the bass instrument, and is similarly constructed. The written compass is from *b* to *e'''*, sounding a fourth higher. Any system of fingering can be adapted to this instrument, or to the *Terz-Heckelphon* in E flat, the latest of the family, which is pitched a tone lower.

THE CLARINET

(G.) Klarinette.   (F.) Clarinette.   (I.) Clarinetto

Clarinetto is a diminutive of *clarino*, the Italian for trumpet ; this word was associated more particularly with the upper register of the trumpet in the 17th and 18th centuries ; Walther (1732), and many who repeated his statement almost in the same words, remarked that the clarinet sounded from afar like a trumpet ; hence the name " small trumpet " or *clarinetto*.

In its rudimentary form the single reed was merely a flexible tongue cut from the side of a hollow reed-pipe, leaving one end attached while the other end was free to vibrate. As a means of generating sound it is said to have originated in the East, from whence it came by various routes to Europe at periods which cannot be even vaguely indicated. It is found on a variety of rude instruments both Eastern and European, also in some forms of bagpipes, and when united to a cylindrical tube or pipe it is commonly said to have been in use in Europe during the 17th century under the name *chalumeau*. That word is a French form of shawm or *Schalmey*, and has been loosely applied to a number of pipes or reed instruments, both single and double, and generally of a rustic or primitive character, also to some of the bagpipes family. It is, therefore, unsafe to assume that *chalumeau* implies only an instrument sounded by means of a single reed.

In 1732 Walther defined *chalumeau* as (a) a shawm (*schallmey*), shepherd's pipe (*Schäfer-pfeiffe*) ; (b) the pipe of a bagpipes ; (c) a small wind instrument with seven holes ; (d) a small box-wood wind instrument with seven holes on top, one underneath, and two brass keys. Although the last three of these *may* have been single-reed instruments, there is no evidence which proves beyond doubt that a *chalumeau* previous to the 18th century was necessarily an instrument with a cylindrical bore and a single reed. Only in the 18th century, after the invention of the clarinet, can such an instrument be definitely associated with the word *chalumeau*; as far as it goes, Walther's definition (c) corresponds to the 18th-century *chalumeau*, but there is no mention or hint of a single reed. In the Diderot and Alembert *Encyclopédie*, published in 1767, a *chalumeau* with cylindrical bore and single reed is described and depicted.[1] A similar instrument, but now with one key on the upper side, is described as the *chalumeau* in Reynvaan's *Musijkaal Konst-Woordenboek* published at Amsterdam in 1795,[2] and a chart is supplied which shows the instrument and the fingering of its scale. (See Fig. 34). Reynvaan's *chalumeau* is a cylindrical reed-pipe about a foot long, with six finger-holes on the upper side and a thumb-hole underneath; the upper end is stopped with a cork, and a flexible tongue has been split down the top of the pipe with the free end towards the player. The seven note-holes give a diatonic series of fundamentals from f' to f'', to which a g'' may be added when an additional note-hole, covered by a closed key, is opened. The key is situated on the top of the tube and is worked by the L. first finger. (See Fingering Chart No. 4.) Thus, the evidence of Diderot and Reynvaan definitely pins down the 18th-century *chalumeau* with a cylindrical bore and a single reed, but does not justify the assumption that this instrument was in use in the 17th century. Even in its 18th-century form this elusive instrument has left all too few traces of its existence. Some parts for *chalumeau* occur in a few earlier 18th-century scores, but in view of Walther's definition (d), it seems highly probable that these were written for the clarinet in its earliest form. The curators of museums are unable to produce a single specimen

---

[1] *Lutherie*, Figs. 20, 21, 22. Laborde's description of the *chalumeau* or *Zampogne* (1780) is too obviously taken from Diderot and Alembert to be of any value as additional evidence.

[2] An earlier edition, dated 1789, is extant.

of this will-o'-the-wisp amongst wind instruments. The tantalis-
ing uncertainty as to what was meant when the earlier writers
used the word *chamuleau*, has led to many speculative suggestions and unauthenticated statements, which, by constant repetition, have gradually become crystalised, and are now often
accepted as historical facts.

In the year 1730 Doppelmayr's *Historische Nachricht von den
Nürnbergischen Mathematicis und Künstlern* was published at
Nürnberg ; this book contains an account of Johann Christoph
Denner,[1] a flute-maker, and includes the statement that Denner
invented the " so-called " clarinet at the beginning of the 18th
century ; later on it is also stated that he eventually improved
the *chalumeau* and other instruments. This reads as if Denner
accomplished two things ; he invented one instrument, and
improved another. Doppelmayr's account of Denner was
repeated word for word by Walther in his Lexikon, who also
added some information about the clarinet and, incidentally,
managed to contradict himself when giving the compass of the
new instrument. Walther's description was repeated in almost
the same words by Eisel in 1738 and by Majer in 1741.[2] Since
then, the statement that Denner invented the clarinet, has been
handed on from book to book, and from one musical dictionary
to another, till in the course of time there was added to it the
gratuitous information that Denner's clarinet has been based on
the *chalumeau*. Doppelmayr's statements that Denner invented
the clarinet, and that he also improved the *chalumeau*, provide no
evidence for supposing that the clarinet was an improved *chalumeau*, or even for assuming that the latter was an instrument of
the single reed family. There is no reason to doubt the correctness of the information supplied by Doppelmayr ; his book,
which must have taken a long time to compile, was published
at Nürnberg only twenty-three years after Denner's death ; in
it he states that two sons of Denner, whom he does not name,

---

[1] Born 1655 at Leipzig, died 1707 at Nürnberg.

[2] 1741 is the date of the second edition ; the original book, which
appears to have been published in 1732, is unknown.

successfully carried on their father's craft in the same town after his death. But for Doppelmayr, the name of the originator of the clarinet would never have been known, for there is no independent evidence to support his statement. All the later writers took their information from Walther, who in turn had it from Doppelmayr.

In spite of the fact that Praetorius, Mersenne and other 17th-century writers appear to have known nothing of the instrument on which Denner is alleged to have based his clarinet, it is not unreasonable to suppose that some such instrument with a cylindrical tube and a single reed was used in Europe before the 18th century, and that Denner did not create a new type. The logical course of events would be that the primitive type existed before the more advanced type, but the hard fact must be faced, that no trace of the *chalumeau* as it was described in the 18th century by Diderot and Reynvaan can be found before Denner's time.

That Denner began to improve the *chalumeau* in 1690, or that the clarinet dates from that or any other specific year, are amongst several estimates made by 19th-century writers which have eventually been cited as facts, and have been repeated over and over again, but in support of which no historical evidence can be produced; Doppelmayr's words are : " zu Anfang dieses lauffenden Seculi ".

If Denner based his clarinet on some single-reed instrument of a more primitive type, his vital discovery was, that by opening a vent-hole near the upper end of the tube, the scale of fundamentals might be made to sound a twelfth higher.

In the following history of the clarinet the note-holes and keys are identified by the notes they sound as fundamentals. It is convenient to regard the instrument as being always in C, and to take for granted that the L. hand is placed above the R. hand.

The earliest clarinet was evidently a two-keyed instrument. A few specimens bearing the name of Denner [1] (father or sons),[2]

---

[1] The names I. C. Denner and I. Denner are found on a number of old wood-wind instruments. It is generally *presumed* that I. Denner was a son of I. C. Denner.   [2] Munich, Berlin, Brussels, Nürnberg.

and some by other makers who were probably working in the first half and round about the middle of the 18th century,[1] survive in some continental collections ; these, together with the fingering charts provided by Eisel and Majer, give a fairly adequate idea of the instrument in its earliest stage.

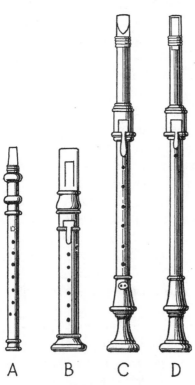

The tube was pierced with eight finger-holes ; six of these lay in line on the top, and a hole for the L. thumb was bored in the underside. These seven holes provided the primary scale *g* to *g'*. A twin-hole for the R. little finger, bored in a thickening of the wood near the lower end, carried the scale downwards to *f* when it was closed. No doubt an *f* sharp would be forthcoming when only one of the twin-holes was closed. A ninth hole, covered by a closed key for the L. first finger, carried the scale of fundamentals up to *a'* when the key was raised. Yet another hole on the underside, placed directly under the *a'* hole, was covered by a closed key for the L.

A   B   C   D

Fig. 34.—A. Diderot's Chalumeau.
          B. Reynvaan's Chalumeau.
          C. Two-keyed Clarinet (front).
          D. Two-keyed Clarinet (back).

thumb ; when this was opened the scale was carried up to *b'* ; the same hole was also the speaker or vent-hole for the twelfth harmonics ; thus, the whole series of fundamentals was from *f* to *b'*. The scale was continued upwards to *c'''* by opening the

[1] Oberlender, Rottenburgh, Willems, Boekhout, Kelmer, Klenig, Liebhav.

speaker and compressing the wind-stream, while repeating the same fingering as from f to f'.

A change in the situation and size of the speaker-hole must have been made at a later stage, for on the later instruments, and according to Eisel (1738), the speaker then gave b' flat instead of b' natural. (See Fingering Chart, No. 5.) That the a' and b' flat should be fingered alike seems incorrect, yet in his text Eisel distinctly says that it is so ; [1] Eisel also adds that some " *virtuosen* " could play a fifth or a sixth higher than the given compass. The speaker-hole on the improved instruments was moved nearer to the mouthpiece ; it was reduced in size and was lined with a small brass tube which projected up into the bore with the object of preventing moisture from coming through the hole. That this improvement and the addition of a third key were due to one of Denner's sons in 1720, are statements which seem to have gained credence only fairly recently ; they are probably based on some suggestions made by Mahillon towards the end of last century, and on his guess that a likely date was round about 1720. [2]

An advance in the development of the clarinet was made when the bell was lengthened and another and lower hole was added ; this hole was controlled by an open key which gave the low e through the bell when all holes were closed, and b' natural (the 12th), when the speaker was opened ; the long stem of the key was carried up within reach of the L. little finger. While it is quite likely that this key made its appearance in the first half of the 18th century, there is no evidence to support the suggestion that this innovation dates from as early as 1720, or that it was initiated by one of Denner's sons. As neither Eisel (1738) nor Majer (1741) described any but the two-keyed clarinet, and Diderot and Alembert illustrate only a two-keyed

---

[1] Neither Walther, Eisel nor Majer appears to be quite sure of his ground when describing the clarinet ; their statements cannot always be implicitly trusted.

[2] Altenburg (*Die Klarinette*, 1904) seems to have relied largely on Mahillon's surmises.

instrument in the *Encyclopédie* published in 1767, it seems unlikely that the addition of the third key could have been made
as early as 1720. Some three-keyed clarinets by Kelmer, Lindner,
Scherer, Walch, I. S. W., Triften and Kenigsperger, are preserved
in the collections at Berlin, Brussels, Salzburg, Munich and Nürnberg, but no fingering chart for the three-keyed clarinet is known.

Some four-keyed clarinets made in the second half of the
18th century by German, Belgian, Dutch and French makers
show the advent of the short closed key for the R. little finger
which gave *g* sharp when opened. It is improbable that this
key dates from much before the mid-century, although there was
ample precedent for it in the corresponding D sharp key of the
oboe and flute. (Pl. VII, A.) Towards the end of the third
quarter of the 18th century the up-to-date clarinet would be
provided with four keys. In the supplement to Diderot's
Encyclopédie (1776) a four-keyed clarinet is depicted and a fingering chart is supplied.

The instrument had made little progress artistically, and was
still far from being the important member of the orchestra which
it was destined to become by the end of the century. It had
found its way to the Netherlands at quite an early stage in its
career,[1] but it appears to have been unknown in England and
France much before the mid-century. Laborde, writing in 1780,
states that the clarinet had become known in France during the
" last thirty years ". Curiously enough, the new instrument had
been heard in Dublin as early as 1742 ; in May of that year the
" Hungarian, Mr. Charles " (!) played a concerto on the clarinet
at a Grand Concert of Music at which Handel may have been
present.[2]

An *f* sharp key had appeared by about 1780 ; this was a
closed key placed on the left side, and worked by the L. little

---

[1] The earliest known clarinet part is in a Mass by Faber which was
preserved at Antwerp ; this is said to have been composed in 1720.

[2] Announced in the *Dublin Mercury*, April 1742. An overture for two
clarinets and horn in Handel's handwriting is preserved in the Fitzwilliam
Museum at Cambridge.

finger. Credit for " inventing " these last two keys in or about 1750 is often given to an organ-builder named Barthold Fritz of Brunswick,[1] but many clarinets made after that year were still without these new keys. The five-keyed clarinet, the instrument which, towards the end of the 18th century, was the standard type, and which just then was establishing itself as a permanent member of the orchestra, was made in large numbers by continental makers, and was now also being made in England. It was then made in high F, E (rarely), E flat and D ; the normal sizes were in C, B flat and A, more rarely in B and low G. Tutors were provided for the five-keyed clarinet, and Mozart gave it higher musical status by composing a concerto for it. Military bands absorbed large numbers of these instruments ; this no doubt accounts for the many surviving specimens. (Pl. VII, B.) The five-keyed clarinet was commonly made in six pieces, namely :

(a) The ebony *mouthpiece* ; rather narrow, with a " table " for a short reed which was tied on, and might be placed either against the upper or the lower lip.

(b) The *barrel* ; varying slightly in length, for tuning purposes.

(c) The *upper middle-piece* ; with three finger-holes and two keys mounted in wooden rings or blocks.

(d) The *lower middle-piece* ; with the three R.-hand finger-holes.

(e) The *lower piece* ; with the R. little-finger-hole and the three keys mounted in a wooden bulge which went right round the tube.[2]

(f) The expanding *bell*.

The usual material was boxwood, and ivory or bone ferrules were generally provided to strengthen the joints and protect the end of the bell. The square keys were of brass, flat, and furnished with a piece of leather as a pad. Handsome instru-

---

[1] Schneider, 1834. Fritz died in 1766.
[2] (d) and (e) were sometimes made in one piece.

ments of ebony or ivory also occur, suitably fitted with silver keys and ferrules. The cylindrical bore (when in B flat) was about 13 millimetres, expanding in the lower piece to 18 millimetres or more at the top of the bell-joint.

The compass was creeping upwards at the end of the 18th century ; d''', e''' and f''' are shown in the early 19th-century tutors, and soon after, a''' and c'''' appear in the fingering charts. Koch (1802) mentions clarinets with a downward compass to C (by Stadler of Vienna), but no such instrument has ever been found.

The five-keyed clarinet remained for some time the standard type ; [1] it was for this simple instrument that the following tutors were written : [2]

> c. 1780–82. Vanderhagen (Paris).
> c. 1800. *Compleat Instructions* (London).
> 1803. Backofen (Leipzig).
> 1811. Fröhlich (Bonn).
> 1813. Antolini (Milan).
> c. 1820. *Clarinet Preceptor* (London).

The list of makers would be a long one if every name which is found on a five-keyed clarinet were included. The following is a selection from many names which occur on instruments made between 1775 and 1825 :

Astor (London)	Baumann (Paris)
Goulding (London)	Winnen (Paris)
Cramer (London)	Amlingue (Paris)
Metzler (London)	Rottenburgh (Brussels)
Grenser (Dresden)	Willems (Brussels)
Embach (Adorf)	Raingo (Mons)
Eisenbrant (Göttingen)	Tuerlinckx (Malines)
Martin (Paris)	

[1] *Ziegler* of Vienna advertised five-keyed clarinets as late as 1855.
[2] Fingering charts for five-keyed clarinets are given by Gehot (*c.* 1784–1786) and Reynvaan (1795).

Despite its five keys, the clarinet was no better off than the one-keyed flute or the two-keyed oboe, which could produce only the chromatic notes in their primary scales by forkfingering, for the clarinet could do no better in its primary scale. These sounds suffered in the same way from the veiling effect of a closed hole immediately below the sounding-hole. Like the f' sharp of the oboe, and for the same reason, the b natural of the clarinet was woefully flat.

The classical composers, whose parts are now played well in tune with an even tone on the modern Boehm clarinet, knew nothing better than these old boxwood relics with yellowed ivory ferrules and tarnished brass keys, which may still be found amongst the unwanted lumber of today. No doubt in their day these old instruments sometimes missed fire and squealed unpleasantly. An anonymous author (said to have been C. L. Junker) in his *Musikalischer Almanach* of 1783 wrote of a clarinet player named Wagner and his instrument as follows :

" Playing this instrument, which can sound so softly and sweetly, is beset with difficulties which if not overcome can result in the most indescribable coos and squeaks ! Run away, then — whoever can run ! ! But Wagner is master of his instrument and produces a pure tone. His notes are languishing, his perform- ance soft and tender." There can be little doubt that to our ears the old clarinets would have sounded dreadfully out of tune ; but according to Burney (1772) pure intonation was not to be expected from the wind instruments of the 18th century : " I know it is natural to those instruments to be out of tune."

THE 19TH-CENTURY CLARINET

Before the end of the 18th century a few odd keys, additional to the usual five, had begun to appear on clarinets ; but the greatest growth of the key-system took place in the first quarter of the 19th century. Round about 1800 six-keyed clarinets became fairly common ; the extra key on English instruments was invariably the long shake-key for the R. first finger

(Pl. VII, c and e); on continental clarinets it was usually a cross-key for c' sharp worked by the L. little finger.[1]   (Pl. VII, d.) During the next twenty years all the semitones in the fundamental scale, which could only be forked on the old instruments, were provided with note-holes and closed keys, so that by about 1825 the up-to-date clarinet had an outfit of from eleven to thirteen keys.   An intermediate stage, however, is marked by a large number of English clarinets with eight keys.   These were the usual six, and in addition a closed cross-key for the R. hand second finger covering a small hole designed to improve the intonation of the faulty b natural.   The other was a closed cross-key for the L. third finger which gave a better e' flat than the forked note.   (Pl. VII, f and h.)   A ninth key, sometimes found on English clarinets, was the c' sharp, which was already fairly common on the continental instruments.   The remaining forked notes, namely, the fundamentals b flat, f' natural and g' sharp, then came in for attention, and were provided with closed keys, respectively, for the R. third finger (cross-key), R. first finger [2] (lying longways) and the L. first or second finger.   On English clarinets of about 1825 (and later) a thirteenth is an additional b natural key for the R. third finger (lying longways) similar to the corresponding key on the oboes of the same period. The two b natural keys offered certain facilities in fingering, but the difficulties of slurring in that part of the instrument were never quite overcome till about the mid-century, when the rod-axle and ring-keys came into general use.   The R. little finger was still without an f key, and the hole retained its old irrational position above the g sharp hole.   (Pl. VII, g, i, j.)

The twelve- or thirteen-keyed clarinets of about 1825–1835 retained many of the old characteristics, and were still made of boxwood with ivory ferrules and brass keys. A few improvements, however, began to appear on the newer instruments: the joint

---

[1] The Paris player Lefèvre is generally given credit for "inventing" this key about 1790; it was quite common (g sharp) on the flute at that time. (See Lefèvre's *Méthode*, 1802.)

[2] Also found on German clarinets for the L. third finger.

between the lower middle-piece and the lower piece was abolished, so the two pieces became one ; the new keys were mounted in blocks till, when they grew too many, brass saddles were employed ; the square key-cover gave way to a round cover, and the key-holes were sometimes metal-lined ; the long L. little-finger-keys were often improved by devices designed to make the passage of the finger from one fingerplate to the other smoother and easier, included amongst these were the rollers; the mouthpiece tended to increase slightly in breadth at the tip, and metal ligatures [1] began to take the place of the thread which formerly held the reed in position ; there was, perhaps, a very slight increase in the width of the cylindrical part of the bore and at the top of the bell-joint.

A typical advanced German clarinet (*Inventions-Clarinette*) of about 1825–1830 is that shown by Backofen in the second edition of his tutor (1824). The instrument has twelve keys and two extra levers, but the R. little-finger-hole still remains uncovered by a key. The reed is tied on with thread [2] and is placed on the upper side of the mouthpiece. A wooden projection for the R. thumb is provided to help to support the instrument. Although Backofen knew the thirteen-keyed clarinets of Ivan Müller, he considered those by Bischoff of Darmstadt greatly superior. Contemporary English instruments are the thirteen-keyed boxwood clarinets made by D'Almaine, Key, Bilton and other London makers. (Pl. VIII, L.) These were also without the R. little-finger-key, but they had the short *b* natural key which was missing on the German instruments.

French efforts to provide the clarinet with an adequate key-system in the first quarter of the 19th century are represented mainly by the work of the maker J. F. Simiot of Lyons, and of the player Ivan Müller of Paris. Already in 1808 Simiot had provided several additional keys ; [3] he is credited with having

[1] (G.) *Blattschraube.* (F.) *Ligature.*

[2] The metal ligature was known, but Backofen disapproved of it. Many German players of the present day still bind their reeds on with cord.

[3] " Tableau explicatif des innovations et changements faits à la clari-nette " par Simiot, facteur à Lyon (1808).

been the first to move the hole of the speaker to the upper side of the instrument. A clarinet with nineteen keys was exhibited in 1828 by this enterprising maker.

More influential in the end was the thirteen-keyed system of Ivan Müller (1786–1854), launched in 1812. When he devoted himself to improving the old five- or six-keyed clarinet which was used in France at the beginning of the 19th century, Müller was concerned not only with giving it an adequate key-system, but also with the acoustical betterment of the instrument.[1] The hole for the R. little finger had always been bored obliquely in a bulge of the tube with the base of the hole inclined slightly towards the bell. The hole was small because it had to be closed by the tip of the little finger ; it was the hole from which *g* sounded, yet in order to bring it within reach of the little finger it was situated higher up the tube than the *g* sharp hole. Müller remedied this acoustical fault by enlarging the hole and by placing it lower down the tube, where it was controlled by means of an open-hinged key. The situation and size of each of the six finger-holes were also reconsidered, and some modifications were made. The rest of Müller's key-work was much the same as on other twelve- or thirteen-keyed clarinets ; it included the key which improved the intonation of the *b* natural, all the chromatic keys, the usual shake-key and some duplicating levers. Stuffed pads replaced the flat pieces of leather which were still generally used at the time. Although its advent is dated as early as 1812, there is no evidence to show that Müller's thirteen-keyed clarinet was generally adopted, even in France, till towards the middle of the 19th century. The official Commission appointed in Paris to examine the new instrument (1812) reported none too favourably, and Müller's claim that his B flat instrument was *omnitonique*, and therefore competent to replace the C and A clarinets, was not allowed. The first makers of the thirteen-keyed clarinets on the Müller-system seem to have been Gentellet of Paris and Wünnenberg of Cologne.

---

[1] " Herr Müller has remedied all the faults and may be regarded as a second inventor of the clarinet " (Fröhlich, *Allg. Mus. Zeitung*, Leipzig, 1817).

It was from about 1840, and round about the middle of the century, that the brass key-work of the old clarinets gave place to German silver keys mounted on pillars. Cupped keys had already been gradually superseding the old flat keys, and had become very general by that time. The reed was no longer tied on to the mouthpiece, but was held in position by metal ligatures. (Pl. VII, K; Pl. VIII, M, N.) Rod-axles and ring-keys then became more and more part of the essential mechanism of the clarinet, and instruments began to be equipped with the two rings (the "*brille*" or "spectacle") which have since become indispensable adjuncts of the key-work of the simple system or thirteen-keyed clarinet. (Pl. VIII, O to R.) Although it lingered for some time after the mid-century, boxwood was eventually discarded in favour of dark and harder woods such as cocuswood; so the clarinet lost its old-world look and became more like the familiar instrument of to-day. (Pl. VIII, S.)

The simple thirteen-keyed clarinet remains today much as it was in the third quarter of last century. A few modifications have now become standardised: both keys for the R. little finger now work on rod-axles, and the hinged key is a thing of the past; the small hole of the speaker is now on top of the tube, and is prolonged outwards instead of projecting into the bore of the tube by means of the small lining-tube which is found on the old boxwood clarinets. An addition to the thirteen-keyed system which is now universal is the extra *f* sharp key ("patent C sharp key"); this opens when the R. little finger is raised, but the note-hole immediately above it can be kept closed by pressing down the low E key with the L. little finger. (Pl. VIII, T.)

All-metal clarinets of brass are recorded as early as 1818; soon after the middle of last century these were made of sheet metal, with inner and outer tubes corresponding to the bore and the exterior surface of a wooden tube. (Pl. VIII, P and R.) Another form of metal clarinet is that which is built with a single tube (representing the bore) but with note-holes raised above the outside surface so as to give the necessary depth to the holes. Such instruments were made by Ad. Sax soon after

1850 (Pl. VIII, Q) ; clarinets are now again being made of metal, both with a single and with double tubes.

The foregoing by no means includes every effort which was made to improve the clarinet mechanism in the first half of last century. Many makers and players have taken a share in developing the instrument from the five-keyed to the thirteen-keyed stage, and in the course of experimenting with and designing further improvements, have, from time to time, evolved a number of different clarinets. In the end, these have been either rejected or have lost their identity through becoming merged in one or other of the standard types which were to become the eventual outcome of all these efforts. Amongst others, Ad. Sax was busy planning clarinet-mechanism from about 1838, and his patents of 1840 and 1842 are for instruments elaborately fitted with key-devices ; these include ring-keys and rod-axles, and seem to have been inspired by those which not long before that time had made their début on the 1832 Boehm flute. It is quite likely that more would have been heard of these Sax clarinets had not the Klosé-Boehm instrument appeared on the scene just about the same time.

The following are some of many makers who worked during the period in which the clarinet progressed from the five- or six-keyed type to the fully-equipped instrument with thirteen or more keys :

Bilton (London)	C. Sax (Brussels)
Clementi (London)	Ad. Sax (Brussels, Paris)
D'Almaine (London)	Simiot (Lyons)
Key (London)	Lefèvre (Paris)
Metzler (London)	Gentellet (Paris)
Wünnenberg (Cologne)	Aug. Buffet (Paris)
Griessling and Schlott (Berlin)	Uhlmann (Vienna)
Euler (Frankfurt)	Ziegler (Vienna)
Stengel (Bayreuth)	Piana (Milan)
Bachmann (Brussels)	Miano (Milan)

To these may be added a later generation who made and

developed the thirteen-keyed system of Müller after the mid-century :

Rudall, Rose & Carte (London)	Buffet-Crampon (Paris)
Meyer (Hanover)	Mahillon (Brussels)
Mollenhauer (Fulda)	Albert (Brussels)

Taking the thirteen-keyed clarinet as a basis, many makers and players in the second half of last century produced systems which ranged from slight modifications involving only the addition of a few key-facilities, to more or less radical and elaborate rearrangements of the key-work of the instrument. The Barret-action, borrowed from the oboe, has been freely used on the clarinet, and several arrangements embodying certain features of the Boehm system have been combined with those of the simpler system. The work of Albert of Brussels has been successful and influential since about 1860 ; the systems devised by Richard Carte, Spencer and Clinton in England, by Romero, Rampone and Pupeschi in Italy, as well as a number of schemes by German and French makers, would make altogether a lengthy list of clarinet-systems, some of which have enjoyed a limited or local measure of success, while others have proved to be quite uninfluential and transient. The main line in the history of the clarinet, however, does not lose itself in the endless ramifications of varied key-work which belongs to the second half of last century. Before then the story of the clarinet had already taken two distinct courses ; one of these is that which has just been outlined, namely, the simple system or thirteen-fourteen-keyed instrument, and the other is that of the instrument now commonly known as the Boehm clarinet.

The so-called Boehm clarinet was devised by the player Hyacinthe Klosé in association with the Paris maker Auguste Buffet soon after the former had been appointed Professor at the *Conservatoire* in 1839. The date of the completed instrument is generally said to be 1843, and the patent was granted in 1844.

The new instrument was not a wholesale adaptation of the Boehm flute system to the clarinet ; only certain features were borrowed from that system, but free use was made of the Boehm mechanism in order to control the twenty-four holes which Klosé considered it was necessary to bore in his newly-planned clarinet.

Just as Boehm had left the two little fingers in their former positions when he planned his flute-mechanism, so Klosé did not interfere with the customary duties of the two little fingers on the clarinet. Both control the same keys as they do on the thirteen-keyed instrument, but duplicating levers are provided so that the little finger of one hand may, when desirable, take over the duties of the other. Thus, on the Boehm clarinet the three lowest note-holes can be controlled by either little finger. It was in order to control the four holes which lie between the two little fingers that Klosé took over the system of fingering from the Boehm flute of 1832. A somewhat similar mechanism is used, namely, three ring-keys and a key-cover projecting from a solid rod-axle, and the same flute-fingering produces the four successive semitones on the clarinet. As an extra facility Klosé provided a closed *b* key for third finger covering a separate note-hole. On the upper half of the instrument, the third finger and the little finger of the L. hand act as on the thirteen-keyed clarinet. The next four holes of the ascending chromatic scale are controlled by rings and key-covers on rod-axles (with some alternatives) arranged in a manner peculiar to the Boehm clarinet, and when the thumb-hole (*g*) is reached, the fingering again reverts to that of the ordinary clarinet. The speaker is in its old position on the underside of the tube, and two shake-keys complete the outfit.

The elaborate key-system of the Boehm clarinet gave control over note-holes which were more evenly spaced, and therefore acoustically better situated than they were on the simpler instrument, and the gains were a more even quality and better intonation. The generous array of keys gave facilities for almost every shake, and every convenience for slurring from note to note ; on it much could be accomplished which could only be negotiated with great difficulty, or not at all, on the older instrument.

Klosé's problems were much the same as those which faced

Boehm when he planned his flute in 1832, but Klosé had before him the example of Boehm ; Buffet also had knowledge and experience derived from Boehm's flute, and had himself contributed to the advancement of the rod-axle mechanism. No doubt Klosé owed much to Buffet for carrying out his ideas and providing a key-mechanism which was thoroughly workable, and for its period, quite remarkable ; both owed much to Boehm for providing both the acoustical and the mechanical principles which made the reorganisation of the clarinet a practical possibility. (Pl. VIII, U and V.)

As the new key-system required changes of the established fingering, it is not surprising that the Boehm clarinet was not at once accepted with open arms by all and sundry players. In Paris, however, where it originated, the new instrument soon began to be adopted by prominent players, a tutor by Klosé was published, and with official recognition by the *Conservatoire* the Boehm clarinet established itself in France during the third quarter of the 19th century. An English translation of the Klosé tutor was published in 1873, and slowly but surely, about the end of last century, most of the foremost orchestral players in this country discarded their old instruments and adopted the Boehm clarinet. German players, on the whole, have remained true to the clarinet based on Müller's thirteen-keyed system, but supplied with additional key-facilities which are mostly designed to aid the rendering of awkward shakes and to ease the passage, in *legato* playing, from note to note.

In spite of the Boehm clarinet, the ordinary thirteen-fourteen-keyed instrument still carries on an independent existence. It is much used in military bands, by beginners, and in industrial and boys' bands, and will probably always be used on account of two virtues which it possesses, namely, simplicity and comparative cheapness.

The 19th century produced clarinets in a great variety of different sizes ; including the alto and bass instruments, about twenty different sizes can be counted. An instrument in high A flat has been used in German, Austrian and Spanish military bands, but on the whole the miniature clarinets pitched above high E flat have never enjoyed much favour, and are now practically obsolete. The high E flat clarinet still thrives in military bands and is occasionally required in the orchestra. The C clarinet retired into obscurity towards the end of last century, but has recently emerged again as an associate of saxophones in dance-band circles. Whatever the future of the C clarinet may be, those in A, B flat and high E flat seem assured of eternal life. Several attempts have been made to combine the C and the B flat, or the B flat and the A clarinet in one instrument, but so far makers have not succeeded in persuading players that it is wise to carry economy to such lengths.

In spite of intermittent efforts to extend the downward compass, the lowest note of the clarinet remains what it was when the long little-finger-key was first added to the two-keyed instrument about two hundred years ago.

Clarinets are now made of either African blackwood, cocuswood, ebonite or metal. The mouthpiece was formerly of ebony, or more rarely of ivory or glass, but is now usually of ebonite, a material which is not so sensitive to warmth and moisture as the more porous wood.[1] Since about the middle of last century the tip of the mouthpiece has been made broader and the aperture wider. The reed is now about $\frac{3}{4}$ of an inch longer than those used in the early 19th century, and is commonly placed on the lower lip of the player. Not until the clarinet had reached the four- or five-keyed stage was any attempt made to construct larger instruments in the alto-tenor or bass registers. The former have been made in A flat, G, F and E flat, and amongst them two distinctive types have appeared, namely, the *clarinette d'amour* and the basset-horn. Of the bass group, there have been instruments pitched an octave below the soprano clarinets, the Batyphone in low C, a contrabass in E flat an octave below the alto in E flat, and yet a lower contrabass in B flat sounding an octave below the ordinary bass clarinet.

---

[1] Metal mouthpieces have also been used. Klosé recommended a glass mouthpiece. Berlioz mentions one of " gilt metal " introduced by Sax.

The Alto or Tenor Clarinet

The *clarinette d'amour* (G. *Liebesklarinette*) was an alto clarinet with a bulb-bell, in either A flat, G or F. It belongs to the latter end of the 18th century, and must have gone out of use early in the following century. The upper end is slightly curved towards the player ; surviving specimens suggest that it rarely got beyond the five- or six-keyed stage. Laborde in 1780, Francœur in 1772, and Backofen in 1803 each mention an alto clarinet in G, and may possibly have been referring to the *clarinette d'amour*, which was known just at that time and was often made in G. The alto instruments in F begin to appear in the first quarter of the 19th century.[1] The earliest are of boxwood, and have the usual five keys of the contemporary clarinet. In order to bring the rather long instrument closer to the player a slight bend was made at the upper end of the wooden barrel, or by means of a curved brass neck.

Towards the middle of the century the alto clarinets acquired all the usual twelve or thirteen keys of the period and were also made in E flat, in which key they were introduced into English military bands as tenor clarinets. They remained in use in England till fairly recently, but have now been more or less driven out of the military band by the alto saxophone.

In its early career, the alto clarinet seems to have been rather overshadowed by the basset-horn. After the middle of the century it was made in F or in E flat, with a metal bell either straight or upturned, and a bent metal neck at the upper end. (Pl. IX, B.) The thirteen-keyed system and the Boehm system have both been applied to it, and instruments of cocuswood, ebony or ebonite, with modern key-work, still figure in the catalogues of instrument-makers. As on the bass clarinet, two speakers are now provided on the alto instrument. (Pl. IX, C.)

[1] Ivan Müller designed an alto clarinet in F embodying his thirteen-keyed system about the same time as he introduced his newly-planned clarinet. These were made by Gentellet of Paris.

The Basset-horn

(G.) Bassethorn.[1]   (F.) Cor de Bassette.   (I.) Corno Bassetto.

According to Gerber (1792) the basset-horn was invented in 1770 at Passau in Bavaria. It has been repeatedly stated that the name of the inventor was Horn;[2] there is no authority for this, and no such name is found either on instruments of the period nor in contemporary musical literature. There is every reason, however, for supposing that the originator of the basset-horn was, not the mythical Horn, but an instrument-maker (or makers) named Mayrhofer who worked in Passau at the time. Two early specimens[3] bearing that name survive, and on the one which is preserved at Hamburg the following inscription will be found : " Ant, et Mich : Mayrhofer Inven. & Elabor. Passavii ".

The basset-horn is an alto clarinet, usually in F (a fifth lower than the C clarinet) but provided with an extension of the lower part of the tube which carries the compass two notes (or four semitones) below the (written) *e* of the clarinet family ; the actual sound of the lowest note is therefore F.

Up till about 1800 the basset-horn was made in the same curved shape as the early *cor anglais*, and it was no doubt owing to the curve of the tube that it was given the name " horn ", while " basset " indicates the register (small or high bass) of the instrument. The tube was constructed in the same way as the curved tube of the early *cor anglais* by hollowing out two transverse halves and then glueing them together.

A characteristic of the basset-horn, from the time when it was first known till even after the middle of last century, is the peculiar way in which sufficient tube-length was provided without making the instrument inconveniently long and awkward to hold. At the lower end of the curved tube the air-passage entered a sort

---

[1] Sometimes called " *Bassklarinette* " in Germany during the early 19th century.   [2] Lavoix ; R.M.E. Cat. ; Forsyth.
[3] At Nürnberg and Hamburg (No. 159).

of wooden box,[1] wherein it zigzagged up and down before making its exit through the bell, which was attached to the bottom of the box. There were three parallel passages in the box, connected by U-bends similar to that in the butt of a bassoon; thus, the air-passage went first *down*, then *up*, and then *down* again before reaching its outlet in the bell. This box, which sometimes had the appearance of a closed book, contained the note-holes for the extra " basset notes ".

The earliest basset-horns were provided with seven keys, of which only four corresponded to the four keys of the contemporary clarinet; these were the "speaker" and the *a'* key at the upper end, and the closed *g* sharp and open *e* key at the lower end; the fifth key was an open *f* key covering the hole which on the clarinet was then closed by the tip of the R. little finger. This hole was out of reach of the little finger on the basset-horn, hence an open key was a necessity. The levers of the two " basset-keys " (*d* and *c*) were brought up underneath the instrument to the thumb of the R. hand. An eighth key soon made its appearance; this was the closed *f* sharp key of the five-keyed clarinet. The eight-keyed basset-horns of about 1800 had therefore the five usual clarinet keys, an open *f* key, and two thumb-keys for the extra low notes *d* and *c*. The bell was either of brass or of boxwood like the rest of the instrument, and it might be quite round or oval; it seems that the bell was sometimes held between the player's knees, and that an oval or slightly flattened shape was easier to grip than the round one. Otherwise the instrument was held with the bell resting on the R. thigh, or, like a bassoon, to the right-hand side of the player. A cord attached to a ring on the instrument was passed round a button on the player's clothing and helped to support the instrument. Conventional Dictionary statements (all derived from Gerber) are that the basset-horn was improved by Theo. Lotz of Pressburg in 1782, and again by the brothers Stadler of Vienna.[2] These may refer to the addition of keys.

---

[1] Backofen (1803) calls it " *Kästchen* ".
[2] Backofen states that Lotz was the inventor of the basset-horn.

Shortly before 1800 the upper part of the basset-horn was made in an angular form, instead of curved. The two middle-pieces were then straight *bored* tubes joined together by a knee-joint at an angle which varied on different instruments from a slight inclination to a right angle. Numerous specimens of these angular basset-horns survive. (Pl. IX, A.)

During the course of the first half of the 19th century all the keys of the clarinet were gradually added to the upper part, and two additional keys on the " box " provided for the two missing semitones in the extension. Any number of keys from eight to seventeen occur on basset-horns made between 1800 and 1850 ; the seventeen-keyed instrument had all the usual keys of the thirteen-keyed clarinet, and in addition, the four low " basset-keys ".

While most of the instruments of that period still retained the characteristic box which gave the early basset-horn its peculiar appearance, some, however, were made on which the tube was bent at an angle in the middle (as before) but also again just above the bell ; the old box-arrangement was then discarded. Others, again, were made quite straight except for a gentle bend just below the mouthpiece and a right-angled bend just above the bell. Several of the latter were given the globular or bulb-bell of the *clarinette d'amour* ; others had an upturned expanding bell emerging from a small bassoon-like butt. There is probably no instrument, unless it be the bass-clarinet, which has been made in so many peculiar shapes as the basset-horn, and all with the object of bringing the finger-holes and keys within reach of the player's arms without undue discomfort.

Although commonly made in F from its earliest days up to the present time, basset-horns in other keys also occur during the first half of last century. A few are in G, and others in E, E flat and D are mentioned.[1]

The basset-horn is perhaps best known because of the parts

[1] Von Gontershausen (1855), G, F, E, E flat, D ; Antolini (1813), G, F, E flat.

which Mozart wrote for it. Up to the time of Mendelssohn it made occasional appearances, and then, except for the purpose of playing the Mozart parts, the instrument was rather neglected and forgotten till R. Strauss included it in the score of *Electra* (1909).

From the time of its invention in 1770, however, the basset-horn has never quite vanished. It is still made in the usual form of all the larger clarinets, with a straight wooden tube, a slightly curved metal neck which receives the mouthpiece, and in France and England with an upturned metal bell. In Germany, except for the slight curve of the metal neck at the upper end, the basset-horn is sometimes made quite straight, with a wooden or a metal bell. This instrument has been given all the usual key-facilities of the larger clarinets, and is made, or can be made, with any system of clarinet fingering that may be desired. The extra keys for the " basset-notes " are worked either by the R. thumb or by both little fingers.

THE BASS CLARINET

(G.) Bass Klarinette.   (F.) Clarinette Basse.   (I.) Clarinetto Basso, Clarone.

The earliest attempts to make clarinets sounding an octave lower than the ordinary instruments in C or B flat demonstrate the difficulty which was experienced in bringing the note-holes of a long tube close enough together to lie within reach of the fingers. The earlier attempts show that their makers generally sought to overcome the difficulty by doubling or bending the tube in some way or other. It was not until sufficiently advanced key-work came into use that the problem was satisfactorily solved ; the note-holes could then be bored wherever they were required, without regard to the limited stretch of the fingers, and the fingerplates could be brought together in two groups, one for each hand.

The earliest attempt to make a bass clarinet is said to be that made by Gilles Lot of Paris in 1772 ; little seems to be known about this instrument except that it was called *Basse-tube*.[1] The next is credited to Heinrich Grenser of Dresden in 1793. If an instrument bearing the name of Grenser exhibited at Darmstadt represents this effort, it would seem as if Grenser sought to bring the note-holes within reach of the fingers by doubling the tube in the manner of a bassoon. Two other early efforts date from shortly before or soon after 1800. On a strange-looking affair by the Italian Nicola Papalini, the tube makes a series of curved zigzag undulations in the manner of a serpent, and five keys are provided.[2] On another bass clarinet, which bears no name,[3] the finger-holes are diagonally bored through the breadth of a thick slab of wood, and reach the bore at considerably increased distances apart; the upper end is curved towards the player and an upturned bell is provided.

Several efforts to make bass clarinets are recorded in the first thirty or forty years of last century; some of these may be seen in various continental museums. They are either in the form of an angular basset-horn, or else contrived with a double tube meeting in a bassoon-like butt, and are generally curved towards the player at the upper end. According to Lavoix the bass clarinet part in Meyerbeer's *Les Huguenots* was played in Paris on an instrument made by Buffet in 1836. Just at that time Ad. Sax produced a bass clarinet which he took to Paris in 1839, where it at once outclassed the former instrument.[4] Compared with Sax's instrument, Habeneck declared that the old bass clarinet was a monstrosity. Sax's first effort appears to have had a straight bell pointing downwards, but later on he improved on that model and provided a large upturned bell.[5] This *Clarinette basse recourbée* in B flat was given on outfit of keys which covered all the note-holes, and was said by Kastner in 1848 to be perfectly in tune, even in tone-quality, and possessed of a *timbre magnifique*.[6]

[1] Pierre, *Les Facteurs d'Instruments de Musique* (1893), p. 103.
[2] Brussels, No. 940; Leipzig (Heyer), No. 1538; Grove, pl. lxxv, No. 1.
[3] Berlin, No. 2910; (facsimile) Brussels, No. 939.
[4] Kastner, *Manuel*, p. 232.
[5] "Concave metallic reflector" (Berlioz).   [6] *Manuel*, pl. xxvi, No. 5.

After the middle of last century, when the rod-axle mechanism was being applied to all wood-wind instruments, the bass clarinet with its large and widespread note-holes presented no more serious difficulties to makers, and from that time the model of today, the straight tube with metal bends at both ends and an upturned bell, became the standard type in France and England. The German model, like their basset-horn, was straight except for the bend at the upper end. Most instruments are now provided with an extra low semitone so that the lowest note written for a bass clarinet in A can be played on the B flat instrument ; this key is worked by the little finger or R. thumb. Bass clarinets are given two speaker keys, which are sometimes made to work automatically.

Bass clarinets have been made in C, B flat and A ; the first of these was more or less obsolete by the middle of last century, and although Wagner did write for the instrument in A, the bass clarinet in B flat is now very generally used, and seems to satisfy all requirements. The thirteen-keyed or the Boehm system are both available on modern instruments.

CONTRABASS OR PEDAL-CLARINETS

(G.) Kontrabassklarinette. (F.) Clarinette contrebasse. Clarinette-pédale.

Even before the bass register had been quite successfully conquered, efforts were made to construct clarinets still larger and lower than the bass instrument. The *Contrebasse guerrière* by Dumas (1808) is generally said to have been one of these monsters, although in Halary's patent of 1821 this instrument is described as being a sort of ophicleide.[1] Early in the field was Streitwolf of Göttingen with his *Kontrabassethorn*, about 1830 ; this sounded an octave below the ordinary basset-horn

---

[1] " Dans les instruments de M. Dumas, comme dans ceux de M. Halary, l'introduction de l'air s'opère de la même manière par une embouchure de métal " (French patent No. 1849, March 1821). See also *Le Moniteur Universel* (1811) and *Archives des Découvertes* (1810), where Dumas' instruments are described as bass and contrabass clarinets.

and included the extra " basset-keys ". Next on the scene was
the Bathyphon (1839) designed by Wieprecht, made by Skorra
of Berlin, and later on also by Kruspe of Erfurt. This wide
tube was doubled like a bassoon, and the eighteen note-holes were
all covered by keys working on rod-axles, and arranged in two
groups. The metal bell pointed upwards, and at the upper end the
bore was continued in a metal tube or crook bent over towards
the player. Made in C, two octaves below the ordinary clarinet
in C, the lowest sound was E.

A contrabass or *Clarinette-bourdon* by Ad. Sax dates from
about 1842-1846, and was pitched an octave below the alto
clarinet in E flat. This was an all-metal instrument of which
the tube was folded something like an ophicleide, but the bell
turned sideways. All the note-holes were covered by key-covers.

In 1890 a contrabass or pedal-clarinet in B flat by Besson
of Paris was launched hopefully on its career. One long and
two shorter wooden tubes were joined by metal U-bends ; the
upper end turned sideways towards the player, and like the
upturned bell, was made of plated metal. The fingering was
on the thirteen-keyed system with fingerplates arranged in two
groups, the movement being communicated by means of numerous long rod-axles. There is a separate note-hole for *b'* flat and
two speaker keys, all worked by the L. thumb. Every note-
hole is covered, but all except the usual closed keys of the
clarinet are open-standing keys. The lowest sound is D,[1] corresponding to the written *e* on the ordinary clarinet. (Pl. X, A.)
D'Indy wrote a part for this instrument in his opera " *Fervaal* "
(1897), and a few of these monsters found their way to England.

Other contrabass clarinets were those made by Albert of
Brussels, an instrument in F with fifteen keys ; the all-metal
contrabass by Evette and Schaeffer of Paris (1889), and the large
belled instrument by Heckel of Biebrich-am-Rhein, both in
B flat.[2]

[1] It was also designed to reach the A below by means of extra keys.
[2] A contrabass in B flat designed by R. Kohl of New York is mentioned
in *Musical Opinion* of September 1898.

Although they have been tried from time to time in military bands, these huge clarinets never seem to outlive their period of trial. They are necessarily very unwieldy, very heavy, and the key-work is easily damaged; moreover, very considerable effort is required to blow them. The enormous mouthpiece calls for the "capacious mouth" of a Polyphemus. It seems to be the destiny of contrabass clarinets to end their days as museum exhibits.

THE SAXOPHONE

DURING the years 1840–1841 Adolphe Sax, then working in Brussels with his father, produced his first saxophones. The early instruments were made only in the larger sizes ; the whole group was not completed till some time after Sax had established himself in Paris in 1842. The French patent is dated 1846.

The idea of the saxophone may have occurred to the originator as a metal clarinet with a conical bore, or possibly in the light of an ophicleide with a clarinet mouthpiece and reed, for the tube of the saxophone with its thin metal walls and wide conical bore has more in common with the bore of an ophicleide than with the narrower cylindrical bore and thick wooden walls of the clarinet tube. Two other possible sources of inspiration were, either the bass instrument with a wooden conical tube and a clarinet mouthpiece made in 1807 by one Desfontenelles of Lisieux,[1] or the Alto Fagotto [2] invented by William Meikle and made by George Wood of London in 1830, also a conical wooden tube shaped like a bassoon, but sounded by means of a single-reed attached to the end of a bassoon-like crook.[3]

The whole family of saxophones was completed about 1846 and was organised in two groups ; one, in which the instruments were alternately in F and C, was evidently intended for orchestral use, and the other, alternately in E flat and B flat, was designed for use in military bands. Each group was in seven sizes, as in the following table :

[1] Paris, No. 1136. Illus., Pierre, *La Facture*, p. 50.

[2] London (S. Kensington) ; Edinburgh (Glen Coll.) ; Brussels, No. 944. A tutor was published in London, *c.* 1830, by Geo. Wood.

[3] This instrument has been confused with the tenor bassoon and has been misnamed Tenoroon.

	MILITARY GROUP			ORCHESTRAL GROUP		
1. Sopranino	high E flat, sounding		a minor 3rd up	high F, sounding		a perfect 4th up
2. Soprano	B flat,	,,	a tone down	C,	,,	in unison
3. Alto	E flat,	,,	a major 6th down	F,	,,	a perfect 5th down
4. Tenor	B flat,	,,	a 9th down	C,	,,	an octave down
5. Baritone	E flat,	,,	a 13th down	F,	,,	a 12th down
6. Bass	B flat,	,,	a 16th down	C,	,,	2 octaves down
7. Contrabass	E flat,	,,	a 20th down	F,	,,	a 19th down

The orchestral group in F and C did not last very long, but the soprano and the tenor in C have both survived till the present time. The sizes most commonly used in military bands in England are the alto in E flat and the tenor in B flat.[1]

FIG. 35.—Alto, tenor and baritone saxophones from Kastner (1848).

The two smaller saxophones were made with a straight tube ;[2] from the alto downwards, the upturned bell and one or more bends at the narrow end served to reduce the length of the instruments to a manageable size.

[1] According to Kastner, the Alto in E flat and the Bass in B flat were adopted by French infantry bands in 1845.

[2] Curved sopranos have also been made.

Compared with a clarinet the difference in the bore is considerable. A soprano saxophone in B flat starts at the upper end with a bore about half as wide as the clarinet ; the conical tube, which is about three inches shorter than the B-flat clarinet tube, increases in width till it is nearly half as wide again as the cylindrical bore of a clarinet. The mouthpiece and reed are broader for the saxophone than for the clarinet, and the aperture is rounded at the tip ; the interior opening inside the mouthpiece is also wider on the saxophone, in spite of the narrow bore at the upper end of its conical tube. The note-holes are larger than those of the clarinet, and increase in diameter as the cone increases in width ; in this respect the saxophone tube much resembles the tube of an ophicleide.

Having no early history, the saxophone was at once provided with a covered-key system partly mounted on rod-axles. The primary scale (according to the notation in C) is the same as that of the flute or oboe, and when overblown the octave-harmonics sound as on both of these instruments. The key-system is much the same as that of the oboe except that the keys for the first, second and third fingers of the R. hand are arranged as on the Boehm flute. The two little fingers operate practically the same keys as they do on the oboe, and the R. first finger works the b'-flat key just as on the oboe. Two closed octave-keys are worked by the L. thumb, the first being used for the lower half, and the second for the upper half of the second octave. The original (written) compass was from b to f'''. (Pl. IX, D.)

Sax's original key-system has undergone some minor changes, but it remains the basis of several later systems devised by Paris makers, notably those of Goumas in 1879 and the more recent system of Evette and Schaeffer. The original downward compass was extended about 1887, when a low B-flat key was added.

The first saxophones were of brass, and without the plating and gilding which has recently become common. Since it became vulgarised by American dance bands the production of saxophones has increased by leaps and bounds, and silver-

plating, gilding, frosting and engraving have given the instruments a more showy if somewhat tawdry appearance. When
it became popular as a dance-band instrument the saxophone
lost status and dignity, and a style of playing developed which
was mercifully never known to the originator.

As early as 1844 a saxophone part was included in the score
of Kastner's opera *Le dernier Roi de Juda*, produced in that year
at Paris, and in 1845 the new instruments were introduced into
French Army bands. Several French composers, including
Thomas and Bizet, subsequently made use of the saxophone in
some of their operas, and since then it has figured frequently in
the works of French and Belgian composers, and only occasionally in German and English scores. The saxophone was first
introduced into England by Richard Carte of the firm Rudall,
Rose and Carte, about 1850. In Germany it was almost
ignored, and it is said that when Strauss' Domestic Symphony
was produced in Berlin the specified saxophone quartet could
not be recruited amongst local players. Till the end of last
century the instrument was really hardly known outside France,
but when the nature and organisation of dance bands underwent
radical change, and the saxophones were promoted to the position
of leading instruments, this one-time unknown and shy instrument rather suddenly found itself completely in the centre of
the stage, and it is now probably better known all the world
over than any other wind instrument.

The Octavin and kindred Instruments

Very similar to the saxophone is the wooden *octavin*, designed
by Jehring in 1894, and made by Adler of Markneukirchen.
(Pl. IX, E.) The instrument rather resembles the butt of a
bassoon ; two parallel passages are bored in an oval piece of
wood about 11 inches long, and are joined at the bottom by
a U-bend ; the bore is conical, but rather narrower than that
of a saxophone of the same pitch. The small end of the bore
is continued for a few inches above the " butt ", and ends with a
clarinet mouthpiece and reed ; at the wide end a small detachable

metal bell is inserted, facing sideways. The primary scale is d' to c'', and a key-system not unlike that of a simple-system oboe is provided. Keys for the two little fingers take the scale down to b natural, and three thumb-plates for the L. hand add three more semitones to the downward range. An octave-key is also worked by the L. thumb. The octavin has been made in C and B flat. According to a fingering chart published by Zimmerman (Leipzig), the full compass is from (written) g sharp to g'''. The tone is reedy, but not unlike that of a soprano saxophone. The octavin has also been made with a straight single tube, and a bass-octavin sounding down to G is mentioned by Altenburg. It is difficult to say exactly what was the purpose for which this quaint little instrument was intended ; there is nothing to show that it was anything but still-born in Europe, although it may have found some appreciation in America. Most musical dictionaries ignore the octavin, and very few musicians are aware that it ever existed.

Another instrument of the wooden saxophone type is the *Heckelphon-klarinette*, designed in 1907 by Heckel of Biebrich-am-Rhein. This is a very wide straight conical tube, continued at the narrow end by a slightly bent metal tube, into the end of which is inserted a single-reed mouthpiece ; the lower end is finished off with a slightly incurved bell of the *amore* type. This instrument is in unison with the alto saxophone and was intended to augment the lower clarinet-register in military bands.

Somewhat similar is the *Heckelklarina*,[1] another product of the same firm. Again, the tube is conical and very wide, and the bell expands slightly at the extreme end. It is in B flat, in unison with the soprano saxophone, and has also been made in high E flat under the name *Heckel-piccoloklarina*.

Yet another wide-bored conical wooden tube sounded by means of a single-reed is the Hungarian *Tárogató*. This was originally a primitive instrument with a double reed, but since the beginning of this century it has been modernised and given a complete key-outfit (Pl. IX, F.) by Schunda of Budapest.

---

[1] Misnamed *Heckelclarind* in some English books.

THE BASSOON

(G.) Fagott.   (F.) Basson.   (I.) Fagotto

THERE can be little doubt that the doubled tube of the bassoon was the outcome of efforts made to shorten an inconveniently long instrument, while still preserving the full sounding-length of the tube.   Straight tubes, when made long enough to cover the bass register, require a length of from 6 to 8 feet, and must necessarily be awkward to hold and play ; a long metal instrument could be shaped more compactly by folding or coiling the tube, but a wooden tube could not be either folded or coiled, so some other means of reducing the size of the instrument had to be found.

The idea of uniting two parallel passages bored through the same piece of wood, so that they make one continuous air-passage, cannot be traced further back than the 16th century. Instruments made in that way, and sounded by means of a double-reed fixed on the end of a metal crook which was inserted in the narrow end of the tube, made their appearance in the 16th century, and became known by names which were variants of either *kortholt*,[1] *dulzian* or *fagotto*.   The first of these (short wood) refers to the reduced size, *dulzian* to the tone, and *fagotto* to the supposed appearance of the instrument.   The French name *basson* refers to the register of the instrument, and as " bassoon " was adopted in this country during the course of the 18th century.

That the bassoon was invented early in the 16th century by Afranio, a Canon of Ferrara, was formerly accepted without question by musical historians ; the illustrations of Afranio's

---

[1] (F.) *Courtaud.*   (E.) *Curtal, Curtail*, etc.

Phagotum,[1] furnished by his nephew in 1539, are those of a strange contrivance which at first sight it is rather difficult to regard as representing the bassoon in its infancy. That the wind for the *Phagotum* was supplied by a bellows and air reservoir seems to place it in a class far removed from the bassoon type, and when we learn that its tubes were cylindrical, and that the sound was generated by a single-reed enclosed in an air chamber, the kinship between the two instruments seems more remote than ever. That the air-passage through the *Phagotum* took the form of tubes doubled up in parallel formation certainly brings it a little nearer to the bassoon, and is apparently the only ground on which the former may claim to be regarded as the progenitor of the latter. Even if the *Phagotum* had achieved any success, and had become so widely diffused that the internal arrangements of its tube would be well known and understood, it would still be difficult to recognise in this elaborate bagpipe the parent of the bassoon ; but Afranio's instrument was evidently an experiment which failed and left no successors. In any case it is extremely unlikely that it will ever be known whether the bassoon owes its origin to the doubled tube of the *Phagotum*, or whether the similarly doubled tubes of the trumpet or the trombone provided the idea, or whether the designer of the first bassoon just hit on a simple way of shortening his instrument quite independently of the suggestion supplied by the form of any pre-existing type.

The suggestion that the bassoon originated by doubling the tube of the long bass shawms, and that it was the successor of these long straight-tubed instruments, has been very generally accepted, and may be correct in the sense that the doubling of the bassoon tube very probably arose from a desire to shorten an inconveniently long and awkward instrument; but, as Sachs has pointed out,[2] there is no reason for believing that the long 6- or 8-feet shawms were made until after the bassoon had

[1] See Grove, pl. lviii ; Wasielewski, pl. v and vi ; Forsyth, pl. xii ; Galpin, *European Mus. Instruments*, p. 206.

[2] *Real-Lexikon*, Art. *Fagott*.

already appeared ; moreover, the bass shawms continued to develop and were improved for some considerable time after the advent of the bassoon type ; the two instruments, in fact, existed side by side and independently of each other for quite a hundred years ; it is therefore hardly possible to regard the bassoon type exactly as a continuation of the shawm type, though the former may well be regarded as the successful rival of the latter in the bass register.

Neither Virdung (1511) nor Agricola (1528–1545) gave any hint that they knew the bassoon ; Doppelmayr (1730) tells of one Sigmund Schnitzer of Nürnberg, who died in 1578, after having gained considerable repute in Germany, Italy and France as a bassoon maker. Not till 1596 is the instrument mentioned in any Italian book, and then by Zacconi.[1] It would seem that either Germany or Italy was the birthplace of the bassoon, and that the time of its appearance was either not very long before or soon after the middle of the 16th century.

Like the flute and oboe, the bassoon was originally made in one piece, without joints ; like the flute and oboe, it was transformed into a jointed instrument during the course of the 17th century.

Not very many of the early one-piece bassoons have survived the passage of some three hundred years or more ; from those that are still preserved in a few continental collections,[2] however, an idea can be formed of the instrument in its original state, when it was a contemporary of the shawms, krumhorns, *sourdines* and other instruments of the period, most of which have either completely disappeared or have lost their identity by becoming merged in a common type. The following describes the early bassoon with a conical bore :

The two passages, which together make one long conical tube, are bored side by side in a thick oval piece of wood, and are joined at the bottom ; the whole instrument is, as it were, an

---

[1] *Prattica di Musica*, Venice, 1596.
[2] Vienna, Berlin, Brussels, Leipzig (Heyer), Hamburg, Paris, Frankfurt, Nürnberg, Linz.

elongated butt. Ten note-holes, in addition to the full sounding-length of the tube, provide for a diatonic series of eleven fundamentals starting at C (8 ft.) and ending at *f*; of these the last seven (G to *f*) form the primary or six-finger-hole scale of the instrument, which is sounded on the narrower of the two tubes, while the four lower notes (extending the scale downwards) are sounded on the wider tube. The six finger-holes are placed in two groups of three each, and pierce the tube obliquely, so that

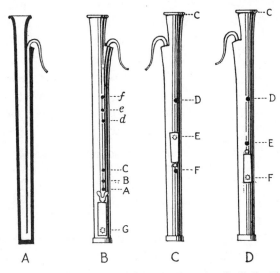

Fig. 36.—A. Section. B. Front. C. Back with " D-key ". D. Back with " E-key ".

they lie within reach of the fingers on the outside surface of the tube, but are more widely spaced where they meet the bore or inside of the tube. A seventh note-hole is situated at the lower end of the instrument near the U-bend, and is controlled by an open key for the R. little finger ; this is the note-hole which sounds G, but as the note F is sounded when it is closed, that key is usually called the " F-key ". The swallow-tail finger-plate of this key probably indicates that the instrument might also be held on the left-hand side of the player with the hands reversed. The three note-holes for F, E and D are on the back or near side of the bassoon, and are controlled by the two thumbs ;

for this purpose either the F or the E hole is covered by another open key worked by the R. thumb. Both keys are covered by protecting boxes.

In addition to the diatonic scale, most of the intermediate semitones were produced by forkfingering or by the less satisfactory device of half closing a note-hole. By compressing the reed, all or most of the octave-harmonics of the primary scale were available, and carried the compass up to f' or g', thus giving a total range from C to g', with all semitones except the low C sharp and possibly the low E flat.

The foregoing particulars refer to the bass or 8-foot instrument which was known in Germany as the *Chorist Fagott*, and is the predecessor of the ordinary bassoon of today. Both larger and smaller bassoons were made about the end of the 16th century; a double or contrabass instrument was pitched a fourth or a fifth lower, and a tenor or "basset" a fifth higher than the *Chorist Fagott*; the alto and soprano registers were also represented by still smaller bassoons. Praetorius (1619) gave the following list in the *Tabella universalis*:

FAGOTTEN.   DOLCIANEN

	Compass	Primary Scale
1. Doppel Fagott (Quint)	F, to g	C to B flat
2. Doppel Fagott (Quart)	G, to a	D to c
3. Fagott / Chorist Fagott / Corthol / Doppel Corthol	C to g'	G to f
4. Fagott Piccolo / Singel Corthol	G to g'	d to c'
5. ——	g to c''	——

In Plate X of the *Theatrum Instrumentorum* Praetorius shows woodcuts of a still larger bassoon family; in addition to those numbered 2, 3 and 4 in the above list, there is an alto pitched a fifth above the tenor, and a *discant* or *exilent* a fifth above the alto. The last two are without keys; the two little fingers could evidently reach the holes which on the larger instruments were covered by keys.

Amongst the surviving specimens are to be found both the open and the closed (*gedackt*) bassoons which Praetorius depicts; the latter was provided with a perforated cap which closed the outlet at the bell and served to mute or veil the tone. Unlike the contemporary shawm, it seems that the reeds of the early bassoons were not enclosed in wind-chambers, nor is there any sign of a *pirouette*; unless it was placed right inside the mouth, the reed must have been held between the lips as it is now.

The one-piece two-keyed bassoon was no doubt still used at the end of the 17th century, although by that time the jointed instrument with an extension to B, flat had appeared, and was causing the older type to fall into disuse. The fingering chart for the *Bass-fagott* given by Speer in 1697 is evidently for the two-keyed instrument of the original pattern. (See Fingering Chart No. 6.) Forty-one years later Eisel reproduced the same chart for what he called the *Teutschen Basson*, with the remark that the instrument was then (1738) no longer in use.

Although the one-piece bassoon remained on the whole a two-keyed instrument with C as its lowest note, a lengthened tube with an additional note-hole which carried the compass still lower seems to have been known in France fairly early in the 17th century, for Mersenne (1636) shows a bassoon of the old pattern with an additional note-hole sounding C which, when closed, caused the instrument to sound B, flat through the bell; for this note-hole another open key was provided.

The division of the bassoon into separate joints appears to date from after Mersenne's time. Neither the time nor the place of this innovation can be laid down, nor can the appearance of the overlapping " wing " projecting from the narrow tube with the three upper finger-holes bored obliquely through the thickness of the wood be fixed with any more accuracy than to conclude that it must have occurred after about 1640 and before about 1680, a period which corresponds with that in which the jointed flute and oboe first appeared. A single instrument in the Vienna Collection [1] shows a transition stage between the 16th- and the 18th-century types ; on this instrument there is a butt from which separate tenor and bass joints project, but there is no projecting " wing " on the tenor joint. A crude drawing of a " double curtal ", which is said to date from about 1688,[2] shows the complete jointed bassoon with a " wing " on the tenor joint, a butt and a long or bass joint, also three open keys for F, D and B, flat. Only a separate bell-joint was necessary to complete the subdivision of the bassoon tube into the five sections with which it started the 18th century.

The 18th-century Bassoon

The air-passage of the newer early 18th-century bassoons was carried through five detachable pieces, namely, the metal crook, the wing-joint, the butt, the long-joint and the bell-joint. Of the six finger-holes which provided the primary scale G to f, three were in the wing and three in the front of the butt ; the open F-key for the R. little finger, and the R. hand thumb-hole were also on the butt. On the long-joint there were two open keys, both for the L.-hand thumb, sounding respectively D and B, flat when closed, and in between the two fingerplates lay the L. thumb-hole from which D sounded when the D key was closed. The two long keys on the long-joint were mounted at first in wooden rings and later in blocks, while the axles for the levers of the F key were supported in blocks or in brass saddles. Eventually blocks were discarded, and all the keys were mounted in saddles.[3] The modern bassoon is based on the early 18th-century type ; it is an elaboration of the three-keyed bassoon which would be the up-to-date instrument during the childhood of Bach and Handel.

Mattheson in 1713 calls the instrument " the proud bassoon ", and gives it a compass from C to f' or g', but allows that some

---

[1] No. 201.   [2] Brit. Mus. Harl. M.S. 2034.
[3] Wooden keys occur on a few early 18th-century instruments.

bassoons could descend to B, flat, or even to A,. Not very many of these old three-keyed bassoons survive ; [1] at least two of them bear the name of J. C. Denner, and may have been made before the beginning of the 18th century.

Majer (1741) gives a fingering chart for the *Fagot-Bass* with three keys, and shows an absurdly bad sketch of a jointed three-keyed bassoon in which the L. hand keys and thumb-hole are placed on the wing instead of on the long-joint.

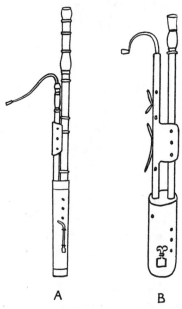

The next key to be added was the closed G sharp, worked by the R. little finger ; the hole was bored in the lower end of the butt, and the lever lay parallel with and to the right of the F key. This, the first chromatic key in the primary scale of the bassoon, was already well known on the contemporary flute and oboe ; both of these had their D-sharp key before the end of the 17th century, so there was ample precedent for the new bassoon key. It has often been stated that the G-sharp key was first added to the bassoon in 1751 ; it certainly made its appearance before that year,

A   B

Fig. 37.—A. Three-keyed bassoon, early
          18th century.
     B. Majer's deformed bassoon.

for not only is it prescribed in Eisel's fingering chart (1738), but it is found on at least two dated bassoons made before the mid-century.[2]

Fingering Chart No. 7 shows Eisel's fingering for a four-keyed bassoon. Another chart for a similar bassoon appears in

[1] Berlin, Brussels, Leipzig (Heyer), Breslau, Nürnberg.
[2] Brussels, No. 997 (1730) ; Galpin coll. (Stanesby, 1747). See also the Frontispiece.

The Muses' Delight (1754), where the four keys are described as follows : [1]

Great key on the Double piece, stopt with the little finger, R. hand (F key).

Little key on the Double piece, opened with the little finger, R. hand (G sharp key).

Lowermost key on the middle piece, stopt with the thumb, L. hand (D key).

Uppermost long key (Double B-mi key) stopt with the thumb, L. hand (low B-flat key).

Yet another chart for the four-keyed bassoon is that in Diderot's *Encyclopédie* (1767) ; this includes a low A, played with all holes closed as for the low B flat, but evidently by merely slackening the lip-pressure.

The best bassoon that Bach and Handel could know would be the four-keyed instruments ; the low B natural, C sharp and E flat were generally avoided in the parts of that period, although composers did not hesitate to write these notes when the bassoon was merely doubling the general bass part ; except in solo-work the higher register was ignored. (Pls. XI and XII, A and B.)

Two more keys make their appearance later in the 18th century. Five-keyed bassoons generally include a closed E flat key for the L. thumb placed alongside the long D key on French and English instruments, but on the front of the long-joint (little finger) on German bassoons.[2] A closed F-sharp key is situated below the R. thumb-hole at the back of the butt. These two notes, hitherto forked or played with half-closed holes, were no doubt much improved by sounding from separate note-holes. The wooden blocks which mounted the keys had gradually given way to improved brass saddles screwed down into the wood of the instrument, and by the beginning of the 19th century wooden key-mounts had almost disappeared. (Pls. XI and XII, C.)

A considerable number of six-keyed bassoons made during the last quarter of the 18th century are preserved, and show the

---

[1] Also in *The Compleat Tutor*. The matter in this and in *The Muses' Delight* appears to have been largely taken from *The Modern Musick Master* (1731).   [2] See Plate XI, E.

instrument as it would be known to Mozart and Haydn. The bassoon had then fourteen note-holes, of which six were finger-holes and two were thumb-holes ; three were controlled by open keys and three by closed keys. The compass was chromatic from B, flat to g', or even a' (Diderot), but there were no note-holes for B, natural or C sharp ; these notes could only be attempted by lip-pressure on the reed or by half closing note-holes.

The typical bassoon of the period is of maple,[1] with flat brass keys working in saddles.[2] A brass " shoe " covers the cork stopper at the lower end of the butt, and the end of each joint is protected by a brass ferrule. The uppermost finger-hole is sometimes lined with a small copper tube, the purpose of which is uncertain (see Pl. XI, A), and swallow-tail F keys still occur. The bore averages about 10 millimetres at the narrowest part and about 15 millimetres at the lower end of the wing-joint ; the long-joint increases from about 25 millimetres at the narrow end to about 30 millimetres at the bottom of the bell-joint. The following are only some of many makers' names which appear on bassoons with from three to six keys :

Denner (Nürnberg), late 17th and early 18th century.
Stanesby, jun. (London), first half 18th century.
Lott, D. (Paris), mid-18th century.
Bizey (Paris), mid-18th century.
Caleb Gedney (London)
Küsder (London)
Cahusac (London)   } second half 18th century.
Milhouse (Newark)
Grenser (Dresden)
Grundmann (Dresden)   } late 18th century.
Porthaux (Paris)
Astor (London)
Goulding (London)   } c. 1800.
Kirst (Potsdam)

---

[1] 18th-century bassoons (and serpents) are frequently worm-eaten ; it is unusual to find a flute, oboe or clarinet of the same period with worm-holes.   [2] Ivory, wooden or silver keys occur more rarely.

THE 19TH-CENTURY BASSOON

Just before the end of the 18th century the upward range of the bassoon was extended by opening two small holes near the upper end of the wing-joint ; these holes were covered by closed keys worked by the L. thumb. With the aid of these " octave " or " twelfth " keys, an upper register, which eventually reached e'' flat, was brought within the compass of the instrument, and the bassoon became a melodist in the higher register as well as a bass voice of the orchestra. Some of the instruments of round about 1800 have only one wing-key, but, on the whole, both the a' and c'' keys [1] are usually found on the eight-keyed bassoon which was the standard up-to-date instrument during the period in which most of Beethoven's symphonies were composed. (Pls. XI and XII, D to G.)

During the early part of the 19th century further chromatic keys appear ; these are commonly either the B flat or the C sharp keys, or both. (Pls. XIII and XIV, H and I.) Rather later the two missing notes in the lowest register (B, natural and C sharp) were given note-holes and closed keys. The story of the bassoon, however, from the end of the 18th century, can be more conveniently traced along national lines, for it was about that time when the French and the German types developed independently and drew apart, both as regards tone-quality and mechanism.

Even at its best the tone of the six- or eight-keyed bassoon was notoriously uneven and capricious; it varied in strength and quality from note to note and in its different registers, but was, nevertheless, strongly characteristic and peculiar to itself. The endeavour of those who took in hand the betterment of the bassoon in France was to preserve the individuality and inherent characteristics of the old instrument as far as possible, while giving greater executive facility and more certainty of control by means of improved mechanism ; the German aim was to

[1] On some of the earlier eight-keyed bassoons the wing-keys are lower down the tube (g sharp and b flat ?). A tuning-hole in the bell is found on some of the German bassoons of the period.

smooth away unevenness in the tone, to modify the strongly individual characteristics of the sounds, and to bring to them all a common roundness and mellowness which was designed to blend with the tone of other instruments rather than to emphasise the inherent peculiarities of the instrument.

Beginning soon after 1800, the French makers Simiot of Lyons and Porthaux of Paris were early in the field with new keys and other modifications ; Adler, Savary junior, and Triébert of Paris then took under their care the development of the instrument, and finally left it to the player Jancourt and the maker Buffet to consolidate the character and key-system of the French bassoon in the second half of last century. The work of Savary junior (*b.* 1786, *d. c.* 1850) covers roughly the second quarter of the century, and gained for his instruments a reputation which was destined to outlive his own period, and caused his bassoons to be prized and used for some time after they were mechanically out of date.[1]   (Pls. XIII and XIV, J.)

It is hardly possible to allot credit with any degree of certainty to particular individuals for the various improvements, mechanical and otherwise, which accrued to the French bassoon during the first half of the 19th century, nor can their contributions towards the betterment of the instrument be pinned down to particular dates, for the claims are many and often conflicting ; but the sum of their efforts can be stated and contrasted with the condition of the instrument as it was at the beginning of the century.

The bore is slightly reduced at its narrowest end, but increases in width at a rather greater rate throughout the rest of the tube ; the finger-holes show considerable variety of diameter, but little change of position and obliquity.

The key-additions on the long-joint are (*a*) an open key over the L. thumb-hole with a projecting lug which keeps the D key closed when the former is pressed down ; (*b*) a closed C sharp key for the L. thumb ; (*c*) the B, flat key overlaps the L. thumb-key and keeps it closed when the former is pressed

[1] Savary bassoons frequently show added key-work of a later period.

down ; (*d*) a closed key for B, natural is provided, covering a hole in the bell-joint, with a fingerplate covering the L. thumb-key ; (*e*) the E-flat key now lies to the right of the D key. The above arrangement forms the typical L. hand thumb key-mechanism which is a characteristic of the French bassoon, and requires fingering which differs from that of the German instru-ment. On the butt a closed B-flat key for the R. third finger is provided, and rollers make the passage of the R. little finger between the F and the G sharp keys easier. A closed C-sharp key for the L. little finger governs a hole bored at the lower end of the wing-joint, and later is moved up to the projecting wing itself.

The pin-hole in the crook makes its appearance about the period 1820–1840 and is at first uncontrolled by a key ; soon after, a key over the pin-hole was worked automatically by the two wing keys. Rather later additions are an *e*-flat key on the wing, two shake keys, and the L. little-finger key governing the crook key. (Pls. XIII and XIV, M.)

Other improvements which may be found prior to 1850 include a tuning-slide at the top of the wing-joint, also various and better arrangements at the lower end of the butt, such as a removable cork with a metal lining.

With the seventeen keys which have been described, the basis of the French key-system was established early in the second half of the 19th century. Cupped or saucer-shaped keys with stuffed pads had in the meantime replaced the old keys, and pillar-mounts were superseding the brass saddles of the older instruments. Rod-axles also began to be made use of to benefit the key-mechanism, and eventually German silver instead of brass was used for all the metal-work of the bassoon ; with that the instrument shed the last of its old-world appearance.

Some odd-shaped bells appeared on bassoons early in the 19th century. In military bands brass bells (see Pl. XI, G), sometimes expanding to 4 or 5 inches across the mouth, were fancied, and in France brass globular bells occur in military circles. Wooden bells expanding to about 6 inches occur more rarely.

The principal makers of French bassoons during the period 1800 to 1850, who saw the instrument through that stage of its history which has been outlined, were the following :

Simiot (Lyons)	Savary, jun. (Paris)
Porthaux (Paris)	Triébert (Paris)
Adler (Paris)	Ad. Sax (Paris)
Buffet et Crampon (Paris)	

English makers,[1] also Belgian and Italian makers, on the whole, adopted the French instrument as their model ; bassoons of the period 1800–1850 with from eight to seventeen keys occur bearing the following names :

Goulding and D'Almaine (London)	Tuerlinckx (Malines)
Milhouse (London)	Piana (Milan)
D'Almaine (London)	Maldura (Milan)
Key (London)	Maino (Milan)
Sax (Brussels)	

The French key-system was amplified during the third quarter of the 19th century by the addition of some duplicate keys and interlocking devices designed to facilitate the rendering of awkward shakes, or to ease the smooth passage from one note to another, without altering the general scheme of fingering ; important amongst these are the keys numbered 19, 20, 21 and 22 on the bassoons of the Jancourt-Buffet system. An acoustical flaw was rectified by lowering the position of the A hole (R. third finger), which then had to be controlled by an open key, and ring-keys for the second finger of each hand were added to improve the notes B and e. A U-shaped tube at the lower end of the butt, which preserves a more uniform interior at the point where the tube bends, the ebonite lining of the wing-joint and the R. hand thumbplate are features of the modern instrument which are common to both the French and the German bassoon.

[1] Instruments bearing English names were sometimes importations from France.

The fully equipped French bassoon has now twenty-two keys and possibly two rings ; instruments with less elaborate key-work are those with seventeen, eighteen or nineteen keys.

All-metal French bassoons have been made at various times during the 19th century [1] but have never successfully competed with the wooden instrument, which is now made of rosewood or maple.

Attempts, which were made about 1855 and renewed later, to adapt the Boehm system to the bassoon have not proved very successful. There would be no great difficulty now in making an instrument with large note-holes distributed rationally at proper intervals along the tube and controlled by key-work ; such an instrument, however, would hardly be a bassoon. The bassoon is more or less an acoustical freak, and if it were deprived of its irrational features it would lose its character and become something else ; it might be a wooden sarrusophone, but it would not be a bassoon.

In order to follow the history of the German bassoon it is necessary to go back to the end of the 18th century. The story is largely that of the instrument which developed according to the designs of the player Carl Almenräder (1786–1843), carried out at first by the makers B. Schott Söhne of Mayence and continued after 1831 by Johann Adam Heckel of Biebrich-am-Rhein, and subsequently adopted by other German bassoon-makers.

At the beginning of the 19th century the bassoons made by the Grensers of Dresden are said to have been known and preferred in Germany on account of their round and musical tone ; they still suffered, however, from the faults common to all bassoons of that period, namely, inequality of tone, faulty intonation, and some uncertainty of speech. The difficulty of fingering smoothly in all but a few favoured keys was also hampering the further development of the instrument at the time when Almenräder took it in hand, and amongst the wood-wind group the bassoon seemed likely to become the lame duck unless its key

[1] Halary (1818) ; Ad. Sax (1851) ; Lecomte (1889).

mechanism could be made to keep pace with that of the flute, oboe and clarinet. The Grenser bassoons had reached the eight-keyed stage, and were now also being provided with a closed C sharp key for the L. little finger.

The German theorist Gottfried Weber had made some investigations of problems connected with the acoustics of wind-instruments, and claimed that the theories as laid down in his *Akustik der Blasinstrumente* (1816) formed the basis of Almenräder's subsequent regeneration of the bassoon. The work of the latter begins in 1817, and by 1820 the bassoons made by Schott according to Almenräder's directions were provided with a mechanical outfit of fifteen keys ; the situations and size of some of the note-holes had been re-designed, and it was claimed for the new instrument that the intonation was much improved, and that the tone was now purer and more uniform in quality.

Almenräder's bassoon of that time, as described in his *Abhandlung über die Verbesserung des Fagotts*, was equipped as follows :

Long-joint and Bell.—An open B‚-flat key, covering a B‚-natural hole in the bell-joint, and worked by the L. thumb, was added ; this improved the tone of the low notes C to F.

The L. thumb-hole was covered by an open thumbplate (C key) and was therefore more easily and securely closed.

A long closed key for C sharp (turning on a central swivel) was provided, also a short closed key for E flat, both worked by the L. little finger.

Those keys, together with the old D key, established the fingering for the L. thumb and little finger, which became a characteristic feature of the future German bassoon.

The Butt.—On the back of the butt another closed key was placed just below the old F-sharp key ; this gave a good G sharp, and made slurring between F sharp and G sharp possible. On the front of the butt the most important innovation was the substitution of an open key (G key) for the old A-finger hole. The new key was provided with a double head covering two holes bored lower down the butt ; the fingerplate lay just under the R. third finger, where formerly the hole had been situated, and the upper end of the key-lever was sunk and hinged in the wood of the butt ; this key greatly improved the octave A to *a*, also the note *e*, and was of great service when playing in the keys of A, E and B major. The lever lay between those of the F- and G-sharp keys, and it was automatically depressed whenever the F key was closed by the R. little finger. A closed B-flat key for the R. third finger was now placed lower down the butt, and the hole was in a rational position above the A hole instead of, as formerly, below it.

The Wing.—A closed C-sharp key for the L. thumb was placed at the back of the wing-joint, covering a larger hole at the lower end of that joint ; in this situation the hole was less likely to become clogged with water. The wing-joint was lengthened and the butt shortened. The *a'* and *c''* keys remained as before.

Instead of flat leathers, stuffed pads were fixed under the key-covers, and the latter were slightly curved [1] so as to fit the rounded surface of the tube ; only the B,-flat, C and D keys remained quite straight and flat.

By 1828 Almenräder had further improved his bassoon by the addition of another F-sharp key for the R. little finger on the front of the butt, and had enlarged and moved the note-holes for D and E flat further towards the bell.

The L. thumbplate then became an open C key pivoting on two axles, and the E-flat key was turned into a short cross-key.

The bassoon was now provided with twenty-two note-holes, of which sixteen were controlled by keys, six being open and ten closed keys. (Pls. XIII and XIV, κ.)

The instrument shown in Plates XIII and XIV (*c.* 1825–1830) is made of ringed maple, with both flat and curved brass keys mounted in saddles. The total length is just over 51 inches, or about an inch longer than contemporary French bassoons. The bore increases from about 9 millimetres at the narrowest point of the wing to about 18 millimetres at the lower end of that joint ; the long-joint increases from about 25 millimetres to 34 millimetres at the bottom of the bell-joint. On the long-joint, the note-holes for C, D and E flat are situated further towards the bell, and the note-hole for E is further towards the butt when compared with contemporary French instruments. The three finger-holes

---

[1] These should not be confused with cupped keys.

on the wing are situated much as on the French bassoon, but the middle hole is distinctly larger, while the uppermost hole is smaller and less obliquely bored. The holes for the R. first and second fingers are rather smaller, and pierce the tube at an angle which is less acute. The crook increases in diameter from just over 3 millimetres to just under 9 millimetres, and is pierced by a pin-hole (since closed up), but there is no provision for a crook-key. The top of the opening of the wing-joint is lined with ivory to protect it against wear and consequent widening.

In 1831, Johann Adam Heckel, who had already worked on Almenräder's bassoons in the Schott workshop, established himself as a bassoon-maker at Biebrich, and in conjunction with Almenräder proceeded to further improve the instrument on the basis already established by the latter.[1] Before Almenräder died in 1843 the situation of the R. thumb-hole was readjusted, and a thumbplate was provided in order to give better control over it. The B-flat hole was then moved to the back of the butt and the key was worked by the R. thumb ; an additional lever running *through* the butt also enabled the R. third finger to work this key as before. Both of these devices were subject to several mechanical improvements later on, but both have remained essential parts of the key-system of the Heckel-Almenräder bassoon. Before the mid-century Heckel adopted the cupped keys and the pillar-mounts which were then replacing the old flat keys and saddles on all wood-wind instruments. Rod-axles were then used to improve the working of most of the keys on the butt, and of the C sharp and E flat keys on the long-joint. (Pls. XIII. and XIV, N.)

Heckel continued to improve the details of the key-work till his death in 1877. During that period another *c* sharp on the butt (first finger) and a crook-key added further facilities for managing the instrument. Heckel's son and successor, Wilhelm, was equally tireless in improving the bassoon both mechanically and acoustically. The bore of the most vital part

---

[1] The name of *B. Schott fils* still appeared on the bassoons made by Heckel till Almenräder's death in 1843.

of the instrument, namely, in the wing and in the narrower tube of the butt, was enlarged where necessary, and the conicity of the whole tube was more evenly adjusted ; the situations of the G and F holes were lowered, and certain disadvantages connected with the old double-headed G key were removed by remodelling the mechanism. The new shake-mechanism for F-sharp-G-sharp is said to date from about 1870, and that for C-sharp-D-sharp from about 1880. Wilhelm Heckel rejected the idea of covering all the note-holes of the bassoon with keys, and refused to alter the nature of the instrument by re-designing it on lines which might be acoustically sound, but would rob the bassoon of its individual character.

By about 1880 the Heckel-Almenräder or German bassoon was more or less a finished product. Its smooth and even tone, its mechanical facilities and fingering were peculiar to itself, and its reputation, already established in Germany, began to penetrate into some of the preserves which had hitherto been sacred to the French instrument. Many minor improvements and modifications have been made since then ; the ebonite lining of the wing, and the narrower tube of the butt dates from 1899, the crook-key for the R. thumb from 1905, and perforated keys for the R. second and L. third fingers are now generally adopted. A considerable variety of models are now available, differing in detail to suit the wishes of different players, but retaining the general key-system of which the foundation was laid about 1820–1830. A third generation of the Heckel succession now jealously guards the reputation of the instruments made in the workshop which had its small beginnings in Biebrich in 1831.[1]

Most of Almenräder's early improvements are found on the bassoons made by Wiesner of Dresden, Grenser's successor, in the first half of last century. Some instruments made about 1830–1840 according to the instructions of a player named Neukirchner by Schaufler of Stuttgart do not follow the Almenräder plan in every respect, notably in that the low B-natural

---

[1] See *Der Fagott*, by Wilhelm Heckel (1899), revised (1931) by W. Hermann Heckel (Leipzig).

hole is covered by a closed, instead of an open key (Pls. XIII and XIV, L), yet the design and mechanism of the Almenräder-Heckel bassoon has been very generally followed by German bassoon makers up to the present time.

Perhaps it need hardly be added that the German instrument is used in all orchestras in that country, and that French players are equally true to their national type. In this country at the present time both the French and the German types are in use, and both may sometimes be seen being played side by side in the same orchestra.

The Double Bassoon

(G.) Kontrafagott.   (F.) Contrebasson.   (I.) Contrafagotto

The first signs of bassoons made on a larger scale than the ordinary instrument are Praetorius' *Quart* and *Quint Doppel Fagott*, pitched, respectively, a fourth and a fifth lower. The same author also mentions a real double bassoon, sounding an octave below the *Chorist Fagott*, but does not appear to have had any practical knowledge of it. Two instruments in the Vienna collection dating from the 16th century, and one in the Heyer collection at Leipzig, lie between the bass and the contrabass register, and are of the early one-piece type with two keys.

Little more is heard of the larger bassoons till the 18th century, when it appears that a double bassoon made by Stanesby senior was used, apparently with no great success, at the coronation of George II in 1727. In 1739 it is recorded that a pair of these monsters were played at Marylebone Gardens. A four-keyed double bassoon by Stanesby junior, dated 1739, is now in the National Museum at Dublin ; it was evidently one of those instruments which was present at the Handel Commemoration in Westminster Abbey in 1784.[1]

---

[1] " No doubt, Ashley would do every justice to the powers of the instrument, if he could but once make it speak " (Busby, *Concert Room and Orchestra Anecdotes*, 1825). " This instrument, which rested on a stand, had a sort of flue affixed to the top of it, similar (with the exception

No doubt the difficulty of constructing such large instruments without adequate key-work accounts for the non-success of the double bassoon in the 18th century. In the first half of the 19th century determined efforts were made to overcome the difficulties which the double-sized bassoon presented, and quite a number of makers produced bassoons in the lower octave, also some *Quartfagotten* [1] pitched a fourth below the normal size. These are wooden instruments made in the same pattern as an ordinary bassoon, and corresponding to the six-keyed type which was the standard bassoon near the close of the 18th century, but without the low B flat. Most of these could therefore descend only to $C_{,}$, and some only reached $D_{,}$.

Some of these efforts by the following makers now repose in various museums :

H. Grenser (Dresden) (*Quart* in F)	Horák (Prague)
Schott (Mayence)	Doke (Linz)
Lempp (Vienna)	Stehle (Vienna)
Tuerlinckx (Malines)	Haseneier (Coblenz)
Koch (Vienna)	

By making additional bends in the tube, the great length and unwieldiness of the instrument was eventually reduced, and soon after the mid-century the use of keys working on rod-axles greatly eased the problem of how to bring the note-holes under the control of the fingers. It was not till then that the double bassoon made substantial progress, and in the last quarter of the century became a more reliable and tractable affair. French and German makers have produced a variety of models during the last sixty or seventy years, both of wood and entirely of metal.

of smoke) to that of a Richmond steam-boat. I am ignorant, however, whether it produced any tone, or whether it was placed in the orchestra to terminate the prospect. The name of this double *bass* and gigantic instrument, which was only fit to be grasped by the monster Polyphemus, did not transpire, and the double bassoon, which had never been *heard*, was never again seen after those performances were ended ! " (Parke, 1830).

[1] For military bands (Koch, 1802) ; rarely used (Gassner, 1838).

The founder of the firm of Heckel and his son began to remodel the shape and the mechanism of the instrument between 1870 and in 1880, and succeeded in evolving a compact model with a workable key-system and an extension of the former downward compass to B,, flat, or even to A,,. The Heckel double bassoon is now made of wooden tubes united by metal U-bends, and has a metal bell which usually points downwards and slightly outwards. French double bassoons have often been made entirely of metal, and retain the upturned bell, although the tube may make several turns before finally taking the upward turn. Amongst the French instruments those by Thibouville (1889) and Mahillon (Brussels) were of metal, and the model of 1889 by Evette and Schaeffer was mainly of wood. English efforts are represented by the double bassoon designed by Dr. Stone and made by Haseneier of Coblenz, and a similar instrument made rather later by Alfred Morton of London.[1] Only a few of those were made ; at least two are known, and are regarded as interesting curiosities.

SMALLER BASSOONS

(E.) Tenor bassoon, Tenoroon, Octave or Soprano bassoon.
(G.) Tenorfagott, Altfagott, Quintfagott, Discantfagott.
(F.) Bassoon-quinte, Basson-ottavino, Basson-soprano.
(I.) Fagottino, Fagotto piccolo.

The smaller bassoons fall into two groups, one of which is pitched either a fourth[2] or a fifth above the bass instrument, and may be considered the tenor of the family, the other sounds an octave above normal and can be regarded as the treble or soprano of the group.

Both sizes figure in Praetorius' list, and are represented in

[1] An earlier English effort is the "Bassoon in low G" by Samme of London, now in the Donaldson Coll.

[2] Almenräder (*Schule*, 1841) calls the smaller bassoon a *Quartfagott* ; others of the same period give that name to the instrument pitched a fourth *below* the ordinary bassoon.

their early one-piece form by a few specimens preserved in some continental collections. In the 18th-century form, jointed and keyed like the ordinary bassoon, the same two sizes are found, and the tenor inclines to settle down to a pitch which is a fourth above that of the bass instrument. In the first half of the 19th century the smaller bassoons were still made, and were provided with key-work similar to that of the larger instruments. In 1889 Evette and Schaeffer of Paris exhibited some small bassoons in high E flat, F and G, with modern key-work; but the smaller bassoons have practically died out, leaving the ordinary bass and the double-bassoon as the only survivors of a family which at one time was represented in all registers from soprano to double bass.

THE SARRUSOPHONES

Soon after the middle of last century a French bandmaster named Sarrus conceived the idea of creating a complete group of metal instruments sounded by means of double reeds; they were to be uniform in tone-colour, fingering and notation, and were intended to replace oboes and bassoons in military bands. In order to carry out his idea Sarrus enlisted the services of the Paris maker Gautrot, and between them they evolved the family of sarrusophones, patented in 1856.[1]

Made of brass, with a wide conical bore, the first group comprised a soprano in B flat (in unison with the B-flat clarinet), an alto in E flat, a tenor in B flat, a bass in B flat an octave lower, and a contrabass in E flat. The uniform (written) compass was from b to f''' for the three smaller, and from b to g''' for the two larger instruments, sounding, of course, in accordance with their respective pitches in B flat and E flat. The soprano was a straight tube like an oboe, while the others were doubled up like elongated tubas and were provided with crooks something like that of a bassoon. (Pl. XV, A and B.) Later on, the group was extended to nine different sizes, and a low B-flat key was added.

[1] A tutor was published by Gautrot in 1867.

The full compass for all sizes was then from (written) *b* flat to *g'''*. The complete family is as follows :

    Sopranino in high E flat } Straight tubes without a crook.
    Soprano in B flat

    Alto in E flat   } Two U-bends and a crook.
    Tenor in B flat

    Baritone in E flat.   Three U-bends and a crook.

    Bass in B flat
    Contrabass in E flat } Three or more U-bends and a crook.
    Contrabass in C
    Contrabass in BB flat

The bore of a soprano sarrusophone in B flat increases steadily from $\frac{3}{16}$ of an inch at the narrower end to nearly an inch at the wider end ; the bell then expands to rather over 2 inches across the mouth. On the larger sizes the rate of expansion is even greater ; a contrabass in E flat, for example, measures about $\frac{1}{2}$ an inch at the wide end of the crook and reaches a diameter of about 4 inches just before the final expansion which forms the bell. The note-holes are much larger than on the oboe and bassoon, and, like those of the saxophone, they increase in size as the tube expands ; on an E-flat contrabass the holes (disregarding the small holes of the octave-keys) range from 1 inch to $2\frac{1}{2}$ inches in width.[1]

Originally made with only seventeen holes, the subsequent addition of the low B flat and a pair of shake-keys increased the number of holes to twenty, including those of the octave-keys. The keys all work on rod-axles and, except in the case of the two smallest instruments, the fingerplates are brought together in two groups, one for each hand. The primary scale is the same as on the oboe and flute, namely, from (written) *d'* to *c''* sharp, and when the reed is compressed the octave-harmonics sound, aided by the two octave-keys which open small holes near the upper or narrower end of the tube.[2] The keys which provide

   [1] If the narrow crook is disregarded, the bore and note-holes of a contrabass sarrusophone correspond very closely to those of an ophicleide.
   [2] Three octave keys are provided on modern bass and contrabass sarrusophones.

the downward extension are controlled by both little fingers and one thumb. The fingering is very similar to that of the saxophones, or it might be described as being similar to the Boehm-flute for the R. hand, and to the oboe for the L. hand.

A rather broad and short reed, the wide bore and the large note-holes combine to give the sarrusophones a powerful if not very refined tone. When used in numbers they impart to the tone of a military band a strongly reedy character.

Sarrus' idea of a uniform group was possibly inspired by Sax's family of saxophones, and although they were introduced into French military bands, the oboes and bassoons managed to survive the attack on their status; it may be, owing to strenuous opposition on the part of Ad. Sax, who was powerful and influential in the military musical circles at Paris at the time when the claims of the sarrusophones were advanced. Nevertheless, sarrusophones have taken their places in French military bands, and the contrabass in C has been used in French orchestras instead of the double bassoon; but outside of France these instruments have never succeeded in gaining a foothold either in military bands or in orchestras. The non-success of the sarrusophone as an orchestral instrument has been accounted for thus: composers don't write for it because players don't use it, and players don't use it because composers don't write for it !

Sordune and kindred Instruments, Racket and Tartöld

A few instruments played with a double reed, which were contemporary with the shawms and pommers, and became obsolete before the end of the 17th century, may be counted as belonging to the bassoon family mainly because the tubes were doubled or coiled in some such way as to reduce the length of the instruments to a handy size. A group of four instruments in the Vienna collection (Nos. 226 to 229) are the only surviving specimens of a somewhat similar type which Praetorius called *sordini* or (G.) *sordunen*. On the Vienna instruments, two of which are basses and two contrabasses, the air-passage is narrow

and cylindrical ; it begins at a side-inlet near the upper end of
the instrument and proceeds downwards, making a U-bend at
the lower end and, turning upwards again, finds its outlet in
another side-opening near the upper end. The note-holes con-
sist of six finger-holes, a thumb-hole and six holes controlled
by keys, and near the lower end there is a water-outlet and plug.
According to Mahillon's reconstruction, the thirteen note-holes
gave a diatonic succession of fourteen sounds starting at B, on
the bass, and at E, on the contrabass. It is supposed that these
instruments were blown with a double reed on the end of a
metal crook inserted in the side-inlet near the upper end.

Praetorius' *sordunen* do not correspond in every respect to
the Vienna specimens ; the metal crook is shown to be inserted
in the upper end of the instrument, and the bass has only three
keys, while on the smaller instruments the corresponding note-
holes were evidently controlled by little fingers and thumbs.
Praetorius' group consists of five instruments, each with a
compass of thirteen diatonic sounds. Associated with the
sordunen is a somewhat similar instrument, but played with a
double reed in a wind-chamber, which Praetorius named *Kort
instrument*, *kortholt* or *kurʒpfeiff*, and a shadowy group of three
named *Doppioni*, concerning which he could give no first-hand
information and was obliged to depend on Zacconi (1596). That
these various instruments of short stature and cylindrical bore
should give forth such low-pitched sounds seems to have puzzled
the old German musician, for he admits that he could not as
yet offer any explanation of this phenomenon, nor had he been
able to find anyone who could enlighten him.

In the racket or sausage-bassoon[1] the air-passage is doubled
and redoubled to such an extent that the sounding-length of the
tube is quite nine times as long as the body of the instrument.
The use of a cylindrical bore. or nearly so, which causes the
tube to act as a stopped pipe, further emphasises the remarkable diversity between the low pitch of the instrument and its

---

[1] (G.) *Rackett, Ranket, Wurstfagott.*   (F.) *Cervelas, Cervelat.*   (I.)
Racketto.

short stature, and helps to account for the fact that an instrument about a foot long may be made to sound as low as 16 ft. C.[1]

The body of the racket was a short and thick cylindrical block of wood or ivory in which nine or ten cylindrical passages were bored, one in the centre and the others surrounding it ; each passage was connected to the adjacent passages by U-bends, alternately at the top and the bottom, so that they all formed one long continuous air-passage which zigzagged down and up several times, and finally found an outlet through the end of the block. A number of finger-holes, usually eleven,[2] were bored through the sides of the cylinder to the inner air-passage at suitable intervals apart, and the instrument was clutched with both hands so that these holes could be opened or closed by the fingers or thumbs, and even by other parts of the hand. Existing specimens are from a little under 5 to a little over 8 inches high, but Praetorius shows five different sizes ranging from about 5 to nearly 15 inches in height without the blowing apparatus ; to each of these he allows a scale of twelve sounds, of which the lowest notes are, respectively, G, C, F,, D, and C,. According to Mahillon, a reconstructed racket with a cylinder about $4\frac{3}{4}$ inches in height, copied from one of a pair in the Vienna collection (Nos. 224, 225), gave a scale from D to *a*.

There are probably not more than a dozen of these remarkable instruments now in existence.[3] On some of the old specimens the blowing apparatus is a double reed emerging from a sort of *pirouette*, and on others the reed is placed on the end of a rather long curved or coiled metal crook. It seems that no harmonics were available, and Praetorius describes the tone as very quiet (*gar stille*), and almost as if one was blowing on a comb (and paper ?).

The racket evidently interested some makers after its day

[1] Praetorius, *Tomi secundi*, first part, p. 40.

[2] A specimen in the Copenhagen collection has two keys.

[3] Berlin, Vienna (*Kunsthistorisches Museum* and *Gesellschaft der Musikfreunde*), Leipzig, Munich, Paris, Copenhagen. A few replicas are shown in some museums.

was over, for in the collection of the *Gesellschaft der Musikfreunde* at Vienna (No. 173) there is a specimen with a *conical bore*, dated 1709, said to have been made by one of the Denners of Nürnberg.[1] From Hawkins (vol. iv, p. 139) we learn that the London maker Stanesby (father or son ?), " who was a diligent peruser both of Mersennus and Kircher ", attempted to make some such instrument, but that " it did not answer expectation ; by reason of its closeness the interior parts imbibed and retained the moisture of the breath, the ducts dilated, and broke. In short the whole blew up ". Perhaps Stanesby neglected to provide the water-outlet which is found on the old specimens.

Somewhat similar to the racket, but more fancifully conceived, was the *tartöld* or *tartölt*, of which a set of five unique specimens is preserved in the Vienna collection (Nos. 219 to 223). Even Praetorius could tell us nothing about these instruments, and it may be that the Vienna specimens are just a solitary set constructed by some enterprising maker for some particular occasion. Instead of zigzagging up and down as in the racket, the cylindrical metal tube is wound round in a series of spiral coils, and the whole is enclosed in a metal case fashioned in the shape of a dragon, and painted red, green and gold. The conical tail of the dragon, twisted in a loose knot, forms a crook on the end of which, no doubt, a double reed was placed, and the animal's mouth, with bared teeth and protruding tongue, serves as a bell. Along the dragon's back there are seven finger-holes, and in its chest a thumb-hole, each of which communicates with one of the spiral coils in its interior. The set at Vienna comprises two discant, two alto-tenor and one bass instrument, and it may be surmised that the compass was limited, the pitch somewhat low, and that the tone matched the fearsome exterior. A few other bassoon or shawm-like instruments of the 16th and 17th centuries occur in various collections, labelled with names which are different forms of *short-wood*, such as *kortholt, courtaud, curtal*, etc. The use of such names, even by contemporary writers, is sometimes confusing, and it is obvious that they did not always

[1] Reconstruction at Brussels, No. 619..

indicate the same instrument. Mersenne's *courtaut*, for example, was a bassoon-like instrument with a doubled cylindrical bore, a double reed inserted in the end of the tube and, in addition to the usual finger- and thumb-holes, six hollow wooden projections which he named *tetines*; whereas to Praetorius the *corthol*, *korthol* or *kortholt* was a conical-tubed tenor bassoon on one page, and the *kortholt* or *kurzpfeiff* a cylindrical bassoon with the reed in a wind-chamber on another page. Similarly, Mersenne's *cornamusa* is a bagpipes, but Praetorius' instrument named *corna-muse* is a straight-tubed shawm something like his *bassanello*, but closed at the lower end. A distinction between *dolcian*, *dulcian* or *dulzian* and *fagott* or bassoon is made by some writers and in some modern catalogues, but to Praetorius they were all the same instrument.

THE HORN

(G.) Horn. Jagdhorn. Waldhorn. Ventilhorn.
(F.) Cor. Trompe de chasse. Cor de chasse. Cor à pistons.
(I.) Corno. Tromba da caccia. Corno da caccia. Corno a pistoni.

IN its broadest sense the word " horn " (*corno, cor*) covers a large variety of wind instruments, most of which belong to the lip-reed class, and are commonly metallic conical tubes fashioned in some curved, coiled or folded form. But neither the method of sound-generation, nor the bore or shape of the instrument, can be used as a means of confining or classifying such a diversity of musical instruments as come under this comprehensive heading. Primitive instruments made by boring through or opening a side-hole in the tusks or horns of animals have generally been called horns ; many simple, unmechanised instruments of bone, wood or metal are called horns ; straight tubes may be coach or post horns ; wooden alpine horns, bugles, sundry keyed or valved brass instruments, and even the originally curved *cor anglais* and basset-horn are not too diverse to be included under this convenient and all-embracing expression.

In its narrower sense the horn, that is, the orchestral or French horn, is the brass instrument with a long tube, a conical and proportionately narrow bore, a large bell and a funnel-shaped mouthpiece, which in its present state is a mechanised version of the 18th-century hunting-horn, the French *cor de chasse* or German *waldhorn*.

After having demonstrated its growing fitness for artistic use in the hunting field, and in a partially developed state, this instrument entered the sphere of cultured music at the beginning of the 18th century, and soon became an indispensable member of all orchestral and wind combinations.

The rudimentary horns of the later Middle Ages, short and wide for their length, and therefore capable of sounding only rhythmical signals on one note, were useless for artistic purposes ; the length had to increase till the fourth octave of the harmonic series could be approached, and as this required a tube-length which eventually reached as much as from 9 to 18 feet, the lengthening process was naturally slow ; moreover, it demanded a metal body, and skill in brazing and bending metal tubes, for increase in length had to be accompanied by some bending or coiling of the tube if the instrument was to be compact enough for use in the hunting-field. The circular form of the horn can be traced back as far as the 14th century, and by the 16th century a length was attained which was no doubt sufficient to sound a few of the lower harmonics. It is early in the 16th century that we find the first trace of the very compactly coiled horns which, towards the close of the 17th century, were superseded by the larger open-hooped model made in the style character-istic of the 18th-century *cor de chasse* or *waldhorn*.

Virdung's illustration of a snail-like *jegerhorn* does little more than prove that the closely-coiled horn existed early in the 16th century (1511), but conclusions based on his crude wood-cut cannot be other than speculative. Instruments of this type made in the 16th or 17th centuries are very rare, but the few which survive, and some pictorial representations, show the horn growing in sounding-length, increasing the taper of its bore towards the narrow end, and acquiring the characteristic conical mouthpiece. Two closely-coiled horns in the Historisches Museum at Dresden date from the first half of the 17th century or possibly earlier ; these instruments are four-times coiled, leaving only a small opening in the centre of the circle ; the bells are small (4 to 5 inches) and the bore decreases as it approaches the mouthpiece, although the taper is not quite so pronounced as on the fully developed 18th-century type ; the mouthpieces are distinctly of the characteristic horn pattern.[1] Pitched in high D and A flat, the sounding-length of these

---

[1] Particulars supplied by Mr Blandford.

instruments was still under 8 feet, and it is probable that the upward range would not reach much above the 8th note of the harmonic series. Horns of the same period and pattern are shown in some etchings by Wenzel Hollar (1607–1677) and in the picture " Hearing " (c. 1620) by Jan Brueghel in the Prado Gallery at Madrid. (See Fig 38, A.) The instruments depicted are three, four or five times coiled ; the bells are small and the mouthpieces distinctly conical ; their pitch may be estimated at round about the series based on 8 feet C. Praetorius (1619) shows only one close-coiled *jägertrommet* which, however, appears to be more trumpet than horn.[1] Mersenne (1636) gives a poor drawing of a many-coiled horn which is named *Le cor à plusiers tours*.

The foregoing supplies evidence enough on which to base the conclusion that the close-coiled horn, from which the larger open-hooped type eventually developed, was in use from about 1500 to 1650, and that it required a still greater tube-length, a wider bell, and a more pronounced taper of the bore before it became the instrument which began to be artistically employed in the orchestras of the early 18th century. The close-coiled horn has never completely disappeared ; it was still made for hunting in France during last century with eight coils arranged in two ranks (*trompe à huit tours*). (Pl. XVI, C.)

The second half of the 17th century marked the next stage in the development of the horn. The length of the tube was then increased, and reached as much as 12 feet (F), at which length the consecutive notes of the fourth octave of the harmonic series were available, and the instrument acquired melodic pos-sibilities which were denied to the short horns. The increase in tube-length was coincident with an increase in the diameter of the circular coils, and the number of coils was reduced to one, two or three, a number which varied according to the tube-length and the width of the coils. The diameter of the bell-

---

[1] A number of circular-coiled instruments, which cannot be strictly classified as either horns or trumpets, occur in several collections. (See Pl. XVI, A.)

mouth then also increased up to as much as 9 inches, and the taper of the bore towards the mouthpiece became still more pronounced. Thus, the larger open-hooped horns originated, probably in France, during a period which may be estimated as between 1650 and 1680.

From the following words in Ferdinand van der Roxas' *Life of Frantz Anton, Grafen von Sporck* (1662–1738), published in 1715, we learn that the *waldhorn* was first introduced into Bohemia by that nobleman about 1680–1682, on his return from Paris : " Es würden durch Se. Excellenz die jagd oder so genannten Wald-hörner in diesem Königreich das erstemal eingeführet und bekandt gemacht ". This probably marks the appearance of the open-hooped horn in Germany, for the close-coiled variety was already being made there long before that date. In Gerber's Lexikon (1792) it is stated that von Sporck sent two of his huntsmen to Paris to learn to play the instruments.

Mattheson wrote in 1713 that the *lieblich-pompeusen Wald-hörner* had lately come into vogue in Germany, that those in F were the most useful, and that the tone was better and " filled out " better than the " deafening and screaming trumpets ". A horn made by William Bull of London [1] in 1699 shows that the hooped horn was being made in this country before the end of the 17th century.

The earliest surviving dated horns of the open-hooped pattern belong to the last twenty years of the 17th century. The names inscribed on them show that these instruments were then being made in Germany, and by at least one maker in England. The table on the following page is a list of dated horns made between 1680 and 1725, with such measurements as are available ; they are all of the open-hooped pattern, and together they demonstrate the general tendency gradually to increase the length of the tube, the width of the hoop and the size of the bell :

[1] Galpin coll.

Date	Maker	Key	Width of Coils	Width of Bell	Coils
1682	J. W. Haas, Nürnberg	A	..	..	1
1689	..	B flat alto	..	..	..
1698	H. L. Ehe, Nürnberg	B flat alto	19¾ ins.	6½ ins.	1
1699	W. Bull, London	F	14¼ ,,	6¾ ,,	3
1710	..	F	17½ ,,	..	..
1713	M. Leichamschneider, Vienna	..	18½ ,,	9¼ ins.	2
1713	,, ,,	F	..	..	..
1713	J. C. Müller, Roda	D flat alto	9 ins.	6⅛ ins.	2
1718	M. Leichamschneider, Vienna	F	16½ ,,	..	3
1724	J. W. Haas, Nürnberg	F	16½ ,,	9 ins.	..
1725	J. Leichamschneider, Vienna	F (pair)	18 ,,	9½ ,,	2

To the above might be added a number of instruments which are of the same period but are not dated.[1]

Horn parts began to appear in orchestral scores soon after the beginning of the 18th century ; the earliest of these suggest that F was the standard key at first, but a number of actual instruments and some contemporary parts written for horns in G, F, E flat, D and C, show that further lengthening of the tube was in progress during the first half of the century. Eisel (1738) and Majer (1741) mention the F and C horns as the most common ; the English instruction books, *The Modern Musick Master* (1731), *The Muses' Delight* (1754) and *The Compleat Tutor* (c. 1754),[2] name horns in G, F, E (flat ?), D and C, and contemporary parts suggest that the favourite instruments for orchestral use were those in F and in D.

In the meantime the size of the bell was growing ; in his Musical Dictionary (1740) Grassineau describes the horn thus : " The French Horn, called in France the Corne de Chasse, is

[1] Specimens by Jacob Schmid and Michael Hainlein, both of Nürnberg, are in the Germanisches Museum in that city.

In Weigel's *Abbildungen derer gemeinnützigen Hauptstände* (Regensburg, 1698) a woodcut shows the interior of a trumpet-maker's workshop ; on the wall hangs a three-coiled open-hooped horn.

[2] The last two are practically reprints of the first.

bent in a circle, and goes two or three times round, growing gradually bigger and wider towards the end, which in some *Horns* is 9 or 10 inches over ".

Horns by members of the Ehe family of Nürnberg, and dated instruments by M. Schmied of Pfaffendorf (1726), M. Canepel of Brussels (1728), A. Buchschwinder of Ellwang (1738), J. H. Eichentopf of Leipzig (1738), J. Benith of London (1738), Joh. Werner of Dresden (1740), in addition to a number of contemporary but undated horns, may be seen in various continental collections. John Harris, Bull's successor, also made horns in London about the same time. The instruments of the

A   B

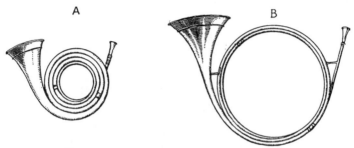

Fig. 38.—A. Early 17th century. B. 18th century.

period have the usual band [1] round the rim of the bell, and the coils are sometimes wrapped round with strips of cloth. The taper of the tube continues right up to the end which receives the mouthpiece, thus making no provision for the addition of crooks.

Crooks had been used for trumpets since early in the 17th century; their use on horns appears to date from soon after these instruments began to be used in orchestras. According to Fürstenau (1860–1861) and Rühlmann (1870), horns with six crooks were made in Vienna as early as 1718; these orchestral horns had a fixed tube-length of about 8 feet, twice coiled in a rather small hoop, and the addition of circular crooks, or combinations of two or even three crooks, inserted between the body of the horn and the mouthpiece, increased the sounding-length

[1] (F.) *Guirlande.* (G.) *Schallrand.*

so as to provide for almost all keys from C alto downwards. A pair of Viennese horns purchased by Sir Samuel Hellier in 1735 were exhibited at the Royal Military Exhibition in London in 1890, and are described in the catalogue [1]; on these instruments the six assorted crooks could be used singly, or assembled in various combinations, for practically all keys.[2] Horns with crooks made in the first half of the 18th century, however, are exceedingly rare, and there can be little doubt that the instruments commonly used in the orchestras of that period were the ordinary hunting-horns of fixed length.

The very large hooped hunting-horns or *Parforcehörner* appeared before the mid-century. These were coiled in a hoop large enough to be carried over one shoulder and under the other arm of the player when not in use. Such a horn in D has a tube-length of about 14 feet, wound in two coils in a hoop with a diameter of about 20 inches ; a horn of the same pitch closely wound in eight coils measures only about 8 inches across the outside of the coils. (Pl. XVI, B and C.)

In the hunting-field the horn was held resting on the up-raised arm of the player with the bell pointing over his shoulder, but in 18th-century engravings the bell is represented pointing upwards when the instrument was played in an orchestra.

Gerber (1792) states that horns with sets of crooks for B flat alto, A, G, F, E, E flat, D, C and B flat basso were made by Werner of Dresden in 1757. Just about that time (*c.* 1750–1760) Anton Joseph Hampel, a horn player in Hasse's famous orchestra at Dresden, is said to have initiated the practice of stopping the bell of the horn with the R. hand, by means of which device the notes in the middle register of the instrument could be lowered or raised a semitone. If the quality of the sounds so modified suffered to some extent, the resources of the instrument were thereby considerably increased, and a new technique, that of the hand-horn, developed, and was gradually diffused as the

[1] No. 308, p. 147.
[2] Majer (1741) mentions *Krum-bögen* and *setzstücke,* i.e. crooks and tuning bits, for horns.

practice of stopping the horn became more and more known. The instrument was then held, as it is now, with the R. hand inside the bell. The horn treated in this manner was heard in England soon after 1770, played by two of its most famous exponents, Punto and Spandau. In addition to the hand-stopping device, Hampel is sometimes credited with the idea of contriving that the crooks could be inserted in the middle of the hoop instead of at the narrow end of the tube. For this purpose the tube was carried across the inside of the hoop and back again, so that it made a large U-shaped bend ; this U was made as a slide, which could be removed and replaced by longer or shorter pieces of tubing ; the slide could also be used for adjusting the tuning. The new method of crooking the horn was sometimes adopted by both German and French makers towards the end of the century, and the new instruments were known in Germany as *Inventionshörner*. One of the Thürschmidt family is said to have improved the new arrangement by crossing the tube in the centre of the hoop, thereby avoiding some sharp turns.[1] The crooks inserted in the centre of the horn were generally limited to those for G, F, E, E flat and D, and it was by solo-players that these instruments were found most acceptable.

It was probably the introduction of sliding crooks that led to the addition of a U-shaped tuning-slide in the centre of the horn crooked by the more common method at the narrow end, and in order to accommodate these devices, the horns made towards the end of the 18th century were coiled in a rather larger circle measuring about 12 to 13 inches across. The bell had by then reached its full dimensions, namely, about eleven inches across the mouth.

Long before the end of the 18th century the orchestral horn had severed its connection with the hunting field ; the conicity of the slender tube, tapering from the wide bell to about $\frac{1}{4}$ of an inch at the mouthpiece end, was interrupted in the middle by a cylindrical portion at the point where the tuning-slide was inserted. The full set of crooks required to complete the outfit

[1] Theo. Rode, *Neue Berliner Musikzeitung*, 1860.

of the hand-horn were for B flat alto, A, G, F, E, E flat, D, C and B flat basso. (Pl. XVII.)

Early in the 19th century composers began to make more free use of the stopped sounds, and the technique of the hand-horn reached its full development in the first half of that century. It was towards the close of the 18th, and in the early 19th century, that the French-made horns reached their high-water-mark ; the instruments by Raoux, in particular, gained a reputation which still holds good.[1]

Beethoven, Schubert, Weber, Mendelssohn and their contemporaries all wrote for the hand-horn with crooks. Already in the time of Haydn and Mozart, the high-lying and rather florid parts written for the horn in the first half of the 18th century, had given place to a style which was more harmonic than melodic, and lay more in the middle and lower register of the instrument. The earlier 19th-century composers also wrote harmonically in the medium and lower registers, and, with the aid of stopped sounds, were able to give the horn some melodic passages.

Amongst the makers of hand-horns and *Inventionshörner*, from late in the 18th till about the middle of last century, the following names occur :

Haltenhof (Hanau)	Krause (Berlin)
Korn (Mayence)	Sattler (Leipzig)
Schmidt (Leipzig)	Roth (Adorf)
Gabler (Berlin)	Duirrschmidt (Markneukirchen)
Eschenbach (Markneukirchen)	Gambaro (Paris)
Riedl (Vienna)	Guichard (Paris)
Naumann (Vienna)	Kretschmann (Strasbourg)
Ripasoli (Pistoja)	Dubois and Couturier (Lyons)
Pelliti (Milan)	Bacher (Ghent)
Cormery (Paris)	Devaster (Brussels)
Dujarier (Paris)	Tuerlinckx (Malines)
Raoux (Paris)	van Engelen (Liége)
Labbaye (Paris)	

[1] Horns by Raoux, fitted with valves, are still in use.

An effort to fill up some of the gaps in the natural scale of the horn was made in 1760 by Kölbel of St. Petersburg ; his idea of reducing the sounding-length of the tube by opening side-holes controlled by keys was evidently found to be unsuitable to the long and narrow tube of the horn, but was more successful when applied later on to the wider bore of the bugle. Another attempt to achieve the same end was made by Dickhuth of Mannheim in 1812 ; in this case a lengthening-slide was employed, but no success attended this effort to graft the system of the trombone on to the slender and more tapering tube of the horn.

In the first half of the 19th century, some horns were constructed with all the crooks permanently fixed on to the instrument, and so contrived that any one of them could be embodied in the sounding-length of the tube without having to remove one crook and insert another. The idea is said to have been due to Dupont in 1818, and examples of these *cors omnitoniques* are extant made by Sax (father) of Brussels, Embach and Gautrot. The control of the additional tubes which represented the various crooks was managed by means of keys, or by a graduated valve or some other such mechanical contrivance. It may be that the added weight of so much extra tubing contributed to the non-success of the *cor omnitonique*, but in any case the scheme was pre-destined to failure, because the valve-system was already at that time being applied to the horn ; the valves accomplished the tube-lengthening process more rapidly and, in the end, more efficiently than the crook-changing apparatus, so the *cor omnitonique* was obliged to retire almost before it had any chance of proving its worth.

Like the trumpet, the horn had to wait for the valve-system before the intervals between the sounds of the harmonic series were successfully filled up. It was in the second decade of the 19th century that the valve-system was invented and applied to the horn, but it was not till towards the middle of the century that the valved instrument began seriously to undermine the position of the hand-horn in the orchestra. After a period, from about 1835 to 1865, during which both types were used concurrently, the hand-horn became obsolete during the third quarter of last century, leaving the valved horn in full possession of the field.

Very few valve horns made during the earlier and experimental stage are extant, in fact, it is tolerably certain that none of the existing specimens were made much before 1830. It is possible that not very many were made until after the expiry of the ten years' patent granted to Blühmel and Stölzel in 1818, and it is certain that all the early valve instruments were both mechanically and acoustically defective. Players, quite naturally, would not at once discard the instrument they knew for one which was unknown, and probably unreliable ; composers, too, almost ignored the new invention till about 1835, when the early parts written specifically for valve-horns began to appear in orchestral scores. On the other hand, the valved instruments found a much more ready welcome in military band circles, and the new horns were adopted by some Prussian military bands during the period 1825–1830.[1] By that time the valve was known in France, and Meifred, a prominent horn player in Paris, had already adopted a three-valved instrument made for him by Labbaye.[2] Viennese makers had also got hold of the idea, and were experimenting with more than one type of valve-mechanism. Between 1830 and 1850, a variety of valved instruments, including horns, trumpets, cornets and trombones, were being produced in most European countries where brass instruments were made. A number of valve-horns made during that period are preserved, and are presumably fair examples of the instruments which at that time were beginning to be used in orchestras and military bands.

In order that the R. hand should remain in the bell as hitherto,

[1] See Wieprecht's letters, and Th. Rode's articles in the *Neue Berliner Musikzeitung* and *Zeitschrift für Musik*, 1858, 1859, 1860.

[2] Catrufo (1832) names Meifred as the " artiste ", and Halary as the first maker of the valve-horn in France. Meifred's *Méthode pour le cor chromatique à pistons ou à cylindres* was published in 1840, and was recognised by the *Conservatoire*.

the valves of the horn were so situated that they could be operated by the L. hand. Both two- and three-valved horns occur amongst the instruments made round about the mid-century, and nearly all the current types of mechanism are to be found on them, namely, the early tubular piston or *schubventil* associated at that time with the name of Stölzel, an improved form of the same type as designed by Périnet, the double-tubed or Vienna-valve, the short stout *Berliner-pumpen* and the rotary valve or *drehventil*. Kastner [1] (1848) depicts the valve-horns known in France just before the middle of the century ; they include instruments with two or three valves of the slender *schubventil* type, some with rotary valves, and some with three short valves of the *Berliner-pumpen* type ; the latter were made by Ad. Sax, and the outfit included sets of seven or three (F, E and E flat) crooks. In 1855 von Gontershausen depicted a horn with Vienna-valves and sliding-crooks which, he stated, was the up-to-date instrument then being used in Germany [2] ; he added that the tone of the new valve-horns was hardly distinguishable from that of the wider-bored tenorhorns (saxhorns), and that the soft gentle tone of the old hand-horn was preferred by solo-players.

There are very few English-made horns of that period ; one instrument which bears the name Key, probably made about 1850–1860, is provided with two piston-valves of the early Stölzel type on which the inlet or outlet passage is through the bottom of the valve-case, and a set of crooks which, when used in various combinations, gave all keys from B flat alto to B flat basso. (Pl. XVIII, b.)

After the mid-century French and Belgian makers generally remained true to the piston-valve of a rather shortened Périnet type, and continued the practice of inserting the crooks at the narrow end of the instrument. The slender bore of the hand-horn was retained, but more cylindrical tubing necessarily occurred where the air-passage went through the valve-system and

---

[1] *Manuel*, plates xiv and xxiv.
[2] Ordinary pistons were abandoned in Germany from about 1840.

tuning-slide. (Pl. XVIII, c.) English makers modelled their horns on the French instrument. German and Austrian makers of the same period made either the Vienna-valve or the rotary valve ; although it is still used in Vienna, the former became less common in Germany towards the close of last century, and for the last fifty or sixty years the rotary valve has been the standard type for all horns of German make. Valve-horns made between c. 1830 and 1860 occur, bearing the names of the following :

Müller (Mayence)	Sax (Paris)
Kersten (Dresden)	Rivet (Lyons)
Moritz (Berlin)	Gautrot (Paris)
Schott (Mayence)	Labbaye (Paris)
Riedl (Vienna)	Delfas (Brussels)
Bauer (Prague)	Sax (Brussels)
Key (London)	

Berlioz (1848) and Gevaert (1863) both gave some attention to the valve-horn in their respective works on orchestration ; both treated the hand-horn as the standard instrument, and gave the impression that they regarded the valve-horn more as a useful addition to the orchestra rather than as a substitute for the older instrument. Both remarked on a difference between the tone-quality of the two types, especially with regard to the valve-produced sounds. Schumann, Berlioz and Wagner specified a pair of valve-horns in addition to a pair of hand-horns in their scores written round about the middle of last century ; the new instrument was evidently not yet regarded as fit to supersede entirely the hand-horn in the orchestra.

With the growing use of the valve-horn in the third quarter of last century, there began a corresponding decline in the usefulness of changeable crooks. The valve acted, in fact, as a quick way of changing the crook, and players began to realise the advantages of playing on an instrument of one particular tube-length, rather than on one which might vary in length between about 9 and 18 feet. The medium crooks were found to be the most satisfactory for all-round usefulness, and those of F, E and E flat were generally favoured, while the very long crooks were gradually discarded, and only some of the shorter crooks were used for special parts. Although horns were still provided with a whole battery of crooks, and composers continued to write for the instrument crooked in a variety of keys, orchestral players eventually settled the matter for themselves, and decided that the horn in F was the most useful and effective tube-length (12 feet) for the instrument. In military band scores, the parts were written for E flat horns, and that practice was continued long after the players were using only the F-horn. Only towards the end of last century did composers realise that their parts were always being played with one crook, and then began the custom of writing only for the horn in F. In the meantime a distinction between the French and the German type of horn had developed. The divergence probably began about the middle of last century, when the valve-horn was quickly super-seding the hand-horn in Germany, and the latter was as yet the standard instrument in France. The real difference lay in the width of the bore, and was quite independent of the fact that in France piston valves were favoured, while in Germany the rotary mechanism was preferred. For the French instrument the slender proportions of the old hand-horn were retained, but the tube of the German horn was made to expand more generously after leaving the valves, and in some cases was already widened by approximately 10 per cent at the passage through the valve system and tuning-slide. This national distinction still holds good. The German (and Italian) instrument is rather easier to control, and the rotary valve acts a little more promptly than the piston ; the typical French horn, though not so easily manageable, can rightly claim for itself a more refined and dis-tinctive tone-quality, and the piston mechanism has the advantage of being reliable and easy to keep in order.

In the last quarter of the 19th century the valve-horn entirely replaced the hand-horn in the orchestra ; the valve-system, if not perfect, was at any rate adequate, and gave a chromatic scale which was free from the inequalities caused by employing stopped sounds. Although the R. hand still takes some part in controlling the tone of the horn, the old technique of the hand-horn practically died out before the end of the century, except in France, where it still formed the basis of training for horn students at the Paris *Conservatoire* till about 1900.

Most modern horns are either of the French or the German type ; in this country the French type is still very generally used, but German horns are now finding their way into the hands of many English players. The French instrument is still played with a detachable crook at the narrow end ; [1] the German " double-horn " (*doppelhorn*) is now generally made so that it can be played in either F or B flat alto, and the change from one to the other is managed by means of a special valve which cuts off or adds the requisite amount of tubing which is necessary to turn the horn in F into one in B flat alto, or *vice versa*. The valve-tubes are simultaneously and automatically either lengthened or shortened to suit whichever tube-length is being used ; on some instruments a separate set of valve-tubes is brought into use when the horn is put into B flat alto, and on others the passages through the valve-tubes are automatically shortened when the change from F to B flat alto is made. Players on the *doppelhorn* generally switch over to the B flat alto for all notes above (written) *d″*, and most German 1st and 3rd horn players (*hoch-hornisten*) play entirely on the instrument in B flat. A third type exists in the Austrian horn, which is still used by some players in Vienna. This instrument starts with a wider bore at the mouthpiece end, and the increase in width through the crook and mouthpiece is so slight that the bore at the valve-system is even narrower than on the French type ; the tube then expands considerably after leaving the valve-system, and ends in a bell which is approximately the same as on the German instrument. The old Vienna-valve is now generally replaced by the rotary valve on modern Austrian horns. At the time of

[1] French players generally use a horn with an ascending third valve.

writing (1938) it appears as if the German horn will in the course of time entirely replace the French instrument ; that even French players are now taking to the wide-bored horn is recent news which suggests that the impending doom of the older type is getting very near.

THE TRUMPET

(G.) Trompete.   (F.) Trompette.   (I.) Tromba.   Clarino.

THE earlier of the two periods into which the history of the trumpet divides itself came to an end during the first half of the 19th century, when the " natural " trumpet, unprovided with any devices for instantaneously increasing or decreasing its sounding length, began to be mechanised, and, by means of keys, slides or valves, was eventually transformed into the chromatic instrument which it is today.

Apart from the addition of lengthening or shortening apparatus, the trumpet in its later period has also been subjected to certain modifications which have combined to alter its tone-character to some extent, and have gradually brought it into closer kinship with its 19th-century rival, the cornet.   The earlier trumpet was based on a sounding-length which varied, according to the key in which it was pitched, from about 6 to 9 feet (F to low B flat), and covered a range of natural harmonics which reached as high as the 16th open note or even higher.   During the course of the 19th century a gradual shortening of the fundamental tube-length eventually reduced that dimension by half, so that the standard B flat trumpet of the present day has a tube-length which is only half as long as that of the (9 feet) B flat trumpet known to the classical composers, and consequently sounds its harmonic series an octave higher.   Similarly, the C trumpet, which formerly was an 8 feet tube, is now only 4 feet in length.   With the shortening of the sounding-length (while preserving the same bore), the range of available harmonics has necessarily been curtailed, and now rarely exceeds the 8th open note.   A change in the shape of the mouthpiece cup, which in the old type was shallow (hemispherical), and in the later type has become deeper and more conical, has also had its effect on the tone-quality of the trumpet, and again has brought the instrument a step nearer to the cornet. A more recent modification has had the same effect, and if carried much further will make the two instruments practically indistinguishable ; while the bore of the old trumpet remained cylindrical from the mouthpiece up to a point about 15 to 20 inches from the bell-mouth, the modern instrument is made to taper more or less towards that end of the mouthpipe where the mouthpiece is inserted.

Of the earliest stages in the story of the trumpet little can be said that is not rather vague or speculative. All the information that can be gleaned is necessarily based on representations of the instrument which occur in the pictures or carvings of the Middle Ages. These are neither accurate nor detailed enough to provide the enquirer with important information regarding the tube-length, bore and mouthpiece cup. The trumpet is at first represented as a straight tube up to about 4 or 5 feet in length, suggesting a range similar to that of a coach or posthorn, namely, up to the 6th or 8th harmonic. A desire to produce more of the higher harmonics no doubt led to an increase in the length of the tube, and when that became inconveniently long, it naturally followed that the tube began to be bent or folded in order to make it more compact, better balanced, and less liable to damage. Paintings of the 13th and 14th centuries already show instruments of a trumpet-like type folded in a wide zigzag or flattened S shape. A further flattening of the zigzags eventually brought three straight lengths of tube to within an inch or two of one another, lying in parallel formation, and united by two curved tubes or U-bends. These three tubes may conveniently be called the mouthpipe, the middlepipe and the bell-pipe. By turning the U-bend which connected the mouthpipe and the middlepipe in the opposite direction, the instrument was then made still more compact, and in spite of several unusual ways of folding or bending the tube which occur in contemporary illustrations, the twice-folded form, in which the mouthpipe and bellpipe lay about 1½ inches apart on the same level, seems to have become more or less standardised by the 16th century, and remained so till about the end of the 18th century. (See Fig. 39.)

Only very few trumpets made in the 16th century are in existence today, and any particulars given by writers of that time, excepting the rather fantastic *Modo per imparar a sonare di tromba* by an Italian named Fantini, are extremely meagre. 17th-century trumpets survive in fairly ample numbers, and can be seen in several collections on the continent. Moreover, Praetorius in the earlier years, and Speer at the end of that century, have left specific and useful information, and a number of parts written for the instrument are available to show what was expected of a trumpet player in that century. 18th-century trumpets are abundantly represented in most large collections, and there is no lack of contemporary parts written for them. All the evidence available, the actual instruments, contemporary writings, instructions and descriptions, together with the music specifically written for the trumpet, combine to show that, except in unessential details, the instrument underwent no important change during the 16th, 17th and the 18th centuries.

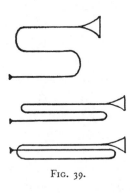

FIG. 39.

The old trumpets were commonly made of sheet brass, or more rarely of silver, hammered to the required tubular shape and joined by brazing the edges together. Of the three straight tubes, the mouthpipe and the middlepipe are cylindrical, with an inside diameter which varies slightly between $\frac{3}{8}$ and $\frac{7}{16}$ of an inch, or from about 9 to 11 millimeters. These three straight pieces are united by two U-bends, so as to make the whole one continuous tube which begins to expand only in the bellpipe, and reaches a width of about 4 inches at the extreme end of the bell. The joints are overlapped by short pieces of outer tubing or "sleeves", and a similar ferrule strengthens the end into which the mouthpiece is inserted ; the sleeves, and the " ball " which is situated about the middle of the bellpipe, also a broad band which encircles the outer edge of the bell, are generally decorated by engraved or embossed ornamental designs, and on the bell-band is usually inscribed the name of the maker, the name of the town where he worked, his trade sign, and not infrequently the year in which the instrument was made. Certain of the ornaments, notably a spiral design round the sleeves, and embossed cherubs or a shell-pattern on the bell-band, seem to have been traditional, and may be found on trumpets dating from the 16th up to the 19th century. A noticeable feature of the old trumpets, when in their original condition, is that the three main tubes are not soldered together or rigidly stayed like the later instruments ; the whole tube is really in a slightly flexible condition, and is made semi-rigid only by the presence of a piece of wood a few inches long fitted between the mouthpipe and the bellpipe, and wound round with either a cloth band or the cord which was attached to the instrument for the purpose of carrying it slung over the shoulder when not in use. This lack of rigidity was certainly not due to any inability to fix the pipes firmly together, but was probably based on the (mistaken ?) idea that the instrument would sound more freely if the tube was in a non-rigid condition, and quite free to vibrate. The same idea seems to underlie the loosely-fitted and removable stays found on the early trombones. The first U-bend, which often reaches to the rim of the bell, is generally attached to the latter only by a loop of wire ; this, again, points to some objection to fixing the pipes firmly together. Two rings, to which a banner might be tied, are generally found on old trumpets which were used for ceremonial purposes as well as for military duty and concert playing.

The standard trumpet was in D, with a sounding-length of rather over 7 feet ;[1] the actual length of the instrument was, of course, reduced to about 2 feet 3 inches by the two folds of the tube. A trumpet in 8 feet C also occurs at an early stage,

[1] This measurement varies by several inches on particular instruments owing to differences of pitch.

and from Praetorius we learn that by means of a tone-crook the C trumpet could be lowered to B flat, or the D trumpet to C. Shorter instruments in E flat and F occur more rarely in the 17th century, but become more common towards the end of the 18th century.

Most of the parts written for the instrument in the 17th and 18th centuries are for the D trumpet ; they also occur in C, and rather uncommonly for the low B flat, E flat and F instruments, although the latter became more common and were more frequently specified in the time of Haydn and Mozart ; by means of a semitone-crook the F instrument could be put into E natural. Tone and semitone crooks were in use from early in the 17th century, if not before then, and there seems to have been no objection to having two crooks on the instrument at the same time. The final adjustment (very necessary at a time when pitch varied considerably according to locality) was made by inserting small tuning bits (*setzstücke*) of various lengths. It is probable that one-and-half-tone and two-tone crooks were beginning to be used late in the 18th century. Early in the 19th century it became usual to make trumpets in F, and to supply them with a set of crooks for E, E flat, D and C. By combining two crooks, the lower keys of B flat and A were provided for.

It is difficult to find any evidence in support of the statement, made by Altenburg (1795) and a few other 18th-century writers, that a trumpet in G was used in this country and was known as the " English trumpet ". Old trumpets in any key higher than F are very rare, and composers up to Beethoven's time were obviously unwilling to write for them ; when a movement was in G major the classical composers employed a C trumpet, just as they specified a D trumpet for movements in A major. The mouthpieces found on old brass instruments are only too often unreliable guides as to the period of the instrument, but when it can be established that they were contemporary with the instrument, the old mouthpieces are usually heavy, shallow-cupped, with a sharp-edged outlet at the bottom of the cup, and have a broad rim.

Most of the old trumpets now preserved bear the names of German makers. Nürnberg was the centre where the craft flourished in the 16th, 17th and 18th centuries, and from there Europe was largely supplied with its brass instruments. Schnitzer, Neuschel (16th century), Schmied, Nagel, Hainlein, Kodisch, Veit, Haas (17th century), Ehe and Leichamschneider (18th century), are only a few amongst many names found on the old trumpets, horns or trombones now preserved in several collections ; most of these makers worked in Nürnberg, and handed on their craft from father to son, sometimes through several generations. A few Italian names occur, and instruments bearing the names Dudley, Bull (17th century), Winkings and Harris (18th century), show that the Nürnberg makers were not entirely without rivals in their specialised craft. Some of the instruments these old makers fashioned with their own hands, though now brittle and black with age, will still give forth the same sounds as they produced for the trumpeters who played the parts written for them by Monteverde and early Italian opera composers, by Purcell, by Lulli and his French contemporaries, by Handel, Bach, Haydn, Mozart and Beethoven. The trumpets made by Johann Wilhelm Haas near the end of the 17th century were said by Altenburg (at the end of the 18th century) to be still " the best ". (Plate XIX, A and B.)

The same trumpets, especially those in D or C, served equally well for the high *clarino* parts as for those lying in the medium or *principale* register. For the former the player had to command the 4th octave of the harmonic series, where the sounds lie scale-wise, but for the *principale* or medium register only from about the 3rd to the 9th open sounds were required. The two lowest sounds, namely the fundamental and its octave, although used in the 16th and 17th centuries,[1] began to be

---

[1] Originally each note or register had its name. These varied slightly according to different authorities. Speer (1687) names them as follows : Fundamental or No. 1=Flattergrob. No. 2=Grob. No. 3=Faul stim. No. 4=Mittel stim. Nos. 5 to 8=Principal. Nos. 8 to 16=Clarino I and II.

neglected on account of their rough quality early in the 18th century, and eventually the fundamental dropped out of use altogether, but the distinction between the *principale* and the *clarino* registers was maintained till the second half of that century, when clarino-playing languished, and finally died out. Much has been written about the high *clarino* parts on account of the difficulties which they offer to players who are not in a position to specialise in acquiring command over the harmonics of the 4th octave. It should be emphasized that for this purpose no special instrument was used by the old players, nor did they carry to their graves any lost secret which has never since been recovered. The sounds of the 4th octave, or even higher, are still there, and could be elicited by any player endowed with the right natural gifts, provided he used an instrument of sufficiently great sounding-length, and devoted himself specially to practise in the high register. Both Speer and Altenburg make it quite clear that *clarino*-playing was no easy matter ; it was hard work, and demanded a naturally suitable lip, good teeth and a flexible tongue, good breath control and endurance, bodily strength and, above all, assiduous practice. The modern trumpeter, who may be called upon to play parts written in any style from that of the late 17th century up to that of the present day, now plays the high *clarino* parts on an instrument which is pitched an octave higher (but in that part of the harmonic series which is an octave lower) than the trumpets which served the player of old ; he uses, of course, valve-produced sounds where open notes are not available. Some slight changes can be observed in the later 18th-century trumpets ; these include a tendency to make the instrument shorter and more compact by folding the tube four times, and to abandon the old wooden block and substitute stays or rigid connections between the outsides of the tubes.[1] A tuning-slide in one of the U-bends also makes its appearance near the end of the century. (Pl. XIX, c.) Trumpets with tuning-slides were made in the earlier part of last century, and usually stood in F without

[1] Koch (Lexikon) describes the wooden block as late as 1802.

a crook ; the four usual crooks lowered them to E, E flat, D and C, and by combining two crooks the lower keys B, B flat, A, and even low A flat, were reached. A trumpet in G makes its appearance in some French scores of Berlioz's time. Although at that time the valves were beginning to be adopted, especially in military bands, most composers of orchestral music still wrote for the natural instrument, or else made a compromise by including both natural and valved trumpets in their scores. The old trumpet died hard, and was not quite obsolete by the mid-century. It still survives, practically in its original form, in the state or fanfare trumpet of the present day, and in a more compact shape is now used as their signalling instrument by cavalry and artillery. (Pl. XXI.)

Keyed Trumpet

(G.) Klappentrompete.   (F.) Trompette à clefs.[1]   (I.) Tromba a chiavi.

Applied to lip-reed instruments, the shortening-hole system had been in use on the old cornetts and the serpent long before efforts were made in the second half of the 18th century to render brass instruments chromatic by the same means. Although it did not alter the principle, the substitution of keys for finger-tips had this advantage, that it became possible for the note-holes to be placed in better positions, and the diameter of the holes was no longer limited to such a size as could be covered by the fingers. Probably the first of these efforts dates from about 1760–1770, when one Kölbel of St. Petersburg constructed a horn of sorts with one or more keys. Altenburg clearly had some knowledge of keyed trumpets when he published his book in 1795, but it was not till 1801 that shortening-holes and keys were applied to the trumpet with any success. In that year a Viennese trumpeter named Anton Weidinger designed and introduced a keyed trumpet, made by Riedl of that city, and, for some forty years or so, such instruments enjoyed a limited success

---

[1] In France, in the early 19th century, the keyed bugle was often called *trompette à clefs*.

which, however, was more pronounced in military band circles than in the orchestra.

The keyed trumpets of the early 19th century were commonly made in the shortened form with four folds of the tube, to one of which a tuning-slide was fitted. The instrument was grasped by the R. hand, and was held " flatways ", so that the L. hand fingers lay over the ends of the key-shanks ; the latter were brought together in a group on the L. side of the instrument, so that they lay within reach of the fingers of the L. hand. The lowest note-hole was situated about 6 inches from the bell-mouth, and the remainder were pierced in the expanding part of the tube at such distances (a few inches apart) as would shorten the sounding-length, and consequently raise the pitch of the open notes by semitone stages when the keys were raised in successive order. The usual number of keys was five, but specimens with four or six keys also occur. Keyed trumpets were usually made in high keys, G and A flat being very general, and a set of crooks provided for the keys of F, E flat, D and C. As the distances between the note-holes always remained the same while the total sounding-length was altered with each change of crook, it followed that the use of the keys differed to some extent according to the crook which was on the instrument, as is shown in a fingering chart published in London about 1835. (See Fingering Chart, No. 8.) In the tutor from which the chart was extracted, it is stated that keyed trumpets were " of recent invention, and now in general use ".[1] (Pl. XX, A.)

The brighter tones of the trumpet probably suffered more by the opening of side-holes than did the duller sounds of its contemporary, the keyed bugle ; that was no doubt the reason why the instrument was ignored by orchestral composers, excepting a few who wrote for it in opera scores.

---

[1] In Harper's tutor for the slide trumpet (c. 1836) it is stated with some condescension that " the author is aware there are keyed trumpets, but as the trumpets written for in this work are capable of accomplishing in a Superior Style all that may be required, the scales of those with keys are omitted ".

Stopping Trumpet

(G.) Stopftrompete.   (F.) Trompette demilune.

Evidence of the existence of trumpets wound round in the circular form usually associated with the French horn, crops up at intervals from early in the 17th to early in the 19th century. Such an instrument is depicted by Praetorius (1619) ; it is provided with a crook, and is named *Jägertrummet*. A four-coiled trumpet of a similar type by Pfeifer of Leipzig, dated 1697, is preserved in the Heyer collection (No. 1819), and in a portrait of Bach's Leipzig trumpeter, Gottfried Reiche, that player holds in his hand a four-coiled instrument of a similar pattern, crooked in the manner of the Praetorius woodcut. Some specimens of 19th-century coiled trumpets occur in a few collections. (Pl. XXI, E.)

It may be that the *Italienische oder gewundene Trompeten* mentioned by a few 18th-century writers refer to the same sort of instrument. While it is possible that these trumpets were thus compactly coiled for the sake of handiness and portability, it is not by any means unlikely that they were so made in order that the player might be enabled to insert his R. hand into the mouth of the bell, and so modify the pitch of the open notes to the extent of a semitone or more. If that is so, these circular trumpets are an early form of another pattern which appeared late in the 18th century. These were made in the ordinary shortened trumpet-form, but the whole was bent round in such a way that the bell-mouth faced rather to one side, instead of pointing directly away from the player, thus making it feasible for the player to insert his R. hand in the bell. The stopping trumpets of the early 19th century were generally provided with a tuning-slide on a U-bend which projected across the general curve of the instrument, and were commonly made in either F or G, with the usual set of crooks for E, E♭, D and C.

Although stopping may have served to produce some chromatic sounds, and partially filled up some of the smaller gaps in the natural harmonic series, the characteristic clearness of trumpet-tone was largely lost when the instrument was thus muted by having the passage through the bell closed by the hand. Small wonder, then, that these instruments made little headway in face of the competition of keys, slides and valves.

SLIDE TRUMPET

(G.) Zugtrompete. (F.) Trompette à coulisse. (I.) Tromba da tirarsi.

The occurrence of the term *Tromba da tirarsi* in some of Bach's scores, and the nature of these parts, imply that some sort of slide trumpet was known in Germany in the first half of the 18th century. 16th- and 17th-century writers appear to have had no knowledge of such a thing, but towards the end of the 18th century the *zugtrompete* is mentioned by several authorities, and Altenburg describes it as being like a small alto trombone, with a slide by means of which the missing notes of the scale in the natural harmonic series could be sounded. He also states that it was used by " *Thürmer und Kunstpfeifer* " for the " *geistliche Lieder* ". It may be, then, that the *zugtrompete* or *tromba da tirarsi* was the treble trombone pitched a 4th or a 5th above the alto. Of these, a few 17th- and 18th-century specimens are preserved. They are ordinary trombones built on a small scale.

On the other hand, an instrument by Hans Veit, dated 1651, now shown in the Berlin collection (No. 639) is an ordinary trumpet in D provided, however, with a straight inner tube which can be made to slide in or out of the mouthpipe. This arrangement would require that the mouthpiece (which was attached to the inner tube) must be held steadily against the player's lips with one hand, while the body of the instrument is made to slide forwards or backwards by the other hand. The inner tube on this particular instrument measures about 22 inches, and allows the sounding-length of the trumpet to be increased to an extent which lowers the pitch by any interval up to a minor third. Although it is quite possible that it was for such an instrument that Bach wrote, it is at the same time unsafe to conclude that this solitary specimen represents a type which was ever in general use.

A later pattern, the English slide trumpet, generally said to have been invented by a trumpeter named John Hyde [1] in 1804, enjoyed considerable success in this country, and was used by the foremost English players during the greater part of last century. This instrument was made on the model of the ordinary natural trumpet, which it resembled both in tone and in appearance.[2] The U-bend connecting the middlepipe with the bellpipe was so contrived that the two arms of the U would slide inside the main tubes,[3] and could be drawn out (towards the player) by the 2nd and 3rd fingers of the R. hand; when released, the slide returned to the normal position by the action of a spring. The instrument was held " upside-down ", i.e. the bellpipe was lowermost instead of uppermost as on the ordinary trumpet. The slide served not only to correct the faulty intonation of the 11th and 13th sounds of the harmonic series, but could also be extended so far as to increase the sounding-length of the instrument sufficiently to lower the pitch of all open notes by a semitone, and to a limited extent, by a whole tone. In the tutor published c. 1836 by Thomas Harper (the elder) it is stated that " two or three whole tones may be obtained by the full length of the slide, but as they incline to be sharp they are generally used as passing notes ". In the younger Harper's tutor [4] (c. 1875) it is said that whole tones were not feasible when the instrument was crooked in any key lower than D.

English slide trumpets were made in (6 feet) F, and were provided with crooks for E, E flat, D and C; a few tuning bits,

[1] A specimen in the Galpin Coll. bears the inscription, " Woodham, Inventor and Maker, Exeter Court, Strand ".

[2] A shortened model occurs exceptionally.

[3] On some instruments one arm moved inside, and the other outside the fixed tubes.

[4] Thomas John Harper ; b. 1816, d. 1898.

sometimes slightly bent, completed the outfit. Crooks could be combined so as to put the instrument into D flat, low B, B flat, A, A flat and G, but as each increase in the sounding-length required a corresponding increase in the length to which the slide had to be drawn out, the tone-shift was limited to the higher keys.

On the earlier slide trumpets, the spring which pulled the slide back to its normal position was a clock spring enclosed in a drum around which a piece of catgut was wound and connected at one end to the slide ; thus, when the slide was drawn out, the clock spring was " wound up ", and on being released the spring unwound itself and drew the slide in again. The earlier specimens show two of these springs enclosed in cases, one for ordinary use, and the other in reserve in case of accident. On the later instruments the clock spring is discarded, and a piece of elastic, running through a thin tube situated between the two arms of the slide, was substituted. (Pl. XIX, D and E.)

Most of the English slide trumpets were made by either Köhler, Pace or Potter, although several other names occur which were probably those of sellers rather than actual makers. Harper's " Improved " model was made by Köhler. The two Harpers, father and son, were famous players on the slide trumpet ; on the instrument crooked in D they rendered the high *clarino* parts which occur in some of Handel's works, using the slide to correct the intonation of the 11th and 13th natural sounds. The absence of sharp bends in the tubing was distinctly advantageous to the tone of the slide trumpet ; the old-style hemispherical mouthpiece also served to keep the instrument true to the traditional tone and style of the natural trumpet. In France the slide was tried on trumpets with less success than in England, and more than one effort was made to combine the slide and valve on the same instrument. The last effort further to improve the slide trumpet dates from 1890, when W. Wyatt introduced an instrument with a four-times-folded or " double slide " ; the movements of the slide were thus shortened by half, but the weight of the instrument was considerably increased by some dummy tubing which was added (for the sake of appearance) to take the place of the cylindrical tubing now included in the slide. This instrument was exhibited at the Royal Aquarium Exhibition of 1892, but its advent was too late, for the day of the slide trumpet was practically over. (Pl. XIX, F.)

VALVE TRUMPET

(G.) Ventiltrompete. (F.) Trompette à pistons. (I.) Tromba cromatica.

The lengthening valve, invented by either Blühmel or Stölzel and patented by them in 1818, after remaining in the experimental stage for a few years, began to be introduced into Prussian military bands in the years 1825–1828. This was largely due to the exertions of Wilhelm Wieprecht, a young musician who settled at Berlin in 1824, where he became keenly interested in military bands and a strong advocate of the valve-system. Wieprecht was associated at first with the Berlin wind instrument makers Griessling and Schlott, and later with J. G. Moritz of the same city, both of whom made instruments fitted with piston valves. When entrusted with the reorganisation of the Prussian Guards' bands, Wieprecht specified, amongst other valve instruments, trumpets in E flat and in high B flat, with two and three valves. Before 1830 the piston valve was known in France, where the Paris makers Halary, Raoux, Labbaye, Guichard, and a little later Ad. Sax, Courtois and Besson busied themselves with improving its mechanism.[1] At the same time valve trumpets were already in use in Russian Guards' bands at St. Petersburg, and from there it is said they were introduced into England about 1831 [2]; soon after that, the London makers Köhler and Charles Pace began to make valved instruments. Pelitti at Milan, Müller at Mayence, Embach at Amsterdam and Uhlmann

---

[1] According to Catrufo (1832), Halary was the first to adapt valves to the trumpet in Paris.

[2] See Farmer, p. 103. In Harper's tutor (c. 1836) the instrument was named " The Russian valve trumpet ".

at Vienna, were also early in the field making valve trumpets which were readily adopted by military bands, if rather less eagerly, by opera and concert players. (Pl. XX, B, C and D.)

The earlier valve trumpets were generally made in F, or sometimes in G, and were provided with crooks for E, E flat, D and C, which could also be combined for the lower keys B flat, A and A flat. The earlier surviving specimens suggest that the slender " Stölzel " valve was the first to be generally adopted, but by the mid-century trumpets with the squat *Berliner-pumpen*, the double-tubed Vienna valve, and with the rotary mechanism, were being made and used all over Europe, each according to local custom or taste. After the mid-century all other types gradually disappeared and left the greatly improved piston and the rotary valves in possession of the field. Players then began to discard the lower crooks and, accustoming themselves to transpose at sight when necessary, preferred to play all their parts on one tube-length ; for this purpose they found the F or the E flat trumpets the most convenient, the former being the favourite for orchestral, and the latter for military band work. In the meantime composers continued to write for trumpets crooked in various keys till at length they discovered that their parts were being played without change of crook ; accordingly, towards the end of last century, the trumpet in F was generally specified in orchestral scores. (Pl. XX, F.) No sooner had composers accustomed themselves to writing for the F trumpet than they found that players were beginning to discard that instrument in favour of a shorter trumpet in high B flat or A.

The trumpet in high B flat (an octave above the old B flat instrument) made its appearance in the third decade of last century. In a price list issued in 1828 by Stölzel, who styled himself *Königl. Kammermusikus und Mechanikus*, a chromatic trumpet in B flat alto was offered at the price of 21 reichsthaler.[1] According to Constant Pierre, trumpets in high B flat were made as early as 1822 by Courtois, and by Chas. Sax in 1840. The

[1] See Sundelin.

short instrument, however, did not make much progress till the last quarter of last century, when it began to undermine the position occupied by the last survivors of the old long-tubed instruments, and eventually supplanted them altogether.

With the disappearance of the F and E flat trumpets early in the present century, the instrument lost caste to some extent, for not only was the sounding-length reduced to that of the cornet, but the mouthpiece-cup had been made deeper and more conical. The old mouthpiece, with its shallow cup and sharp edge at the lower outlet, was well suited to play the old parts in which every note was tongued, but was not so well adapted for slurring (*legato*) from note to note, as was frequently required in the newer parts. Added to these modifications of two characteristic features of the old trumpet, there followed the present tendency to taper the bore towards the mouthpiece. The trumpet of today is in B flat or A, in unison with the cornet. The former A shank is now replaced by an extra loop of tubing which can be embodied in the air-passage by a twist of a special rotary valve. This operation, however, does not provide for the lengthening of the valve-slides which should accompany any increase in the sounding-length of the main tube, so the " quick change " is not quite so quick as it might appear to be. In France a trumpet in high C (4 feet) has largely replaced the B flat instrument for orchestral work, and has been adopted by several players in this country.

The gradual shortening of the trumpet tube has resulted in a certain loss of character and dignity of tone, and for that reason the disappearance of the F trumpet may be regretted ; but it is not the players so much as the composers of the latter end of last century who are responsible for the loss. The trumpet parts written by such as Strauss, Elgar, Debussy, and many who followed their lead, demanded more of the instrument than could be accomplished without difficulty and uncertainty on the longer and more unmanageable tube of the older instrument ; their demands could only be met by using a shorter sounding-length, and the deeper mouthpiece of the modern instrument.

Increasing interest taken in the music of Bach, and more frequent performances of his works during the course of last century, brought into prominence the difficulty which had always to be faced by players when confronted with the old *clarino* parts for the trumpet. In 1884 a German player named Kosleck earned high praise for his rendering of the difficult Bach parts. After some experiments on an unfolded antique instrument, he had designed, and had made for him, a two-valved trumpet in A, of which the tube was quite straight except for the usual turns which had to be made when the air-passage was diverted through the valve-tubes. It was on this instrument, played, it is said, with a conical mouthpiece of the horn type, that Kosleck rendered the difficult parts with apparent ease and certainty ; this straightened valve-trumpet henceforth became known as the " Bach trumpet ", and was supposed by many to have been a replica of the instrument used in Bach's time for the special purpose of playing *clarino* parts. Other players then had similar instruments made for their own use, and for a long time it was considered almost improper to play the Bach *clarino* parts on anything but a straight trumpet. (Pl. XX, G.) A similar instrument in high D, also straightened out and provided with valves, was then constructed and used for the same purpose, and a yet smaller trumpet in high F followed,[1] being intended particularly for playing the high and very difficult part in Bach's Brandenburg concerto, No. 2 in F. It is now no longer considered necessary to employ straight trumpets for the purpose of playing *clarino* parts ; most of these parts are in D, and a folded valve trumpet in high D is generally used. On the rare occasions when the part in the Brandenburg concerto No. 2 is played as it was originally written, the instrument in high F is used.[2] Trumpets in high E flat (in unison with the sopranino cornet) have also been made, and a

---

[1] Besson's of Paris had already in 1885 made a straight trumpet in high G (Pierre, *La Facture*, pp. 115, 116).

[2] A full account of the so-called Bach trumpet by W. F. H. Blandford appeared in the *Monthly Musical Record* (London) in March-April, May and June 1935.

pigmy instrument in super-high B flat has been tried, but has not proved satisfactory.

At the other extreme lies the so-called Bass trumpet. This instrument has been made from time to time in various patterns and lengths without ever settling down to one particular type. Wagner's idea that a bass trumpet should be in the octave below 8 feet C was hardly a practicable proposition ; it has since been made, with a widened bore, in or near 8 feet C, and thus comes into such close relationship with the valve-trombone that it hardly seems worth while making a distinction between the two.

The trumpet has long ago shed its former noble associations. At one time a privileged instrument, reserved for the service of Church and State, for kings, princes and nobility, its players united in a protecting fraternity to which they were admitted only after a period of strict apprenticeship, it has, alas, recently been dragged down from the pedestal to the gutter. Towards the end of the 18th century the trumpet had lost some of its former exclusiveness, yet during the 19th century it remained the aristocrat, while the cornet was the plebeian, of the orchestra. The present century has seen the trumpet degraded to an extent which was never reached by the cornet even at its worst. Since it became the chosen instrument of the American dance bands whose " jazz " music swept like a plague over the whole world, the trumpet has been subject to the worst indignities that could possibly befall a musical instrument ; its throat has been stuffed up with all sorts of tone-distorting mutes ; it has been made to emit all manner of nasal whimpering sounds of the most drunken character, and *portamento* effects which are totally foreign to its nature have been forced upon it by players whose style is admirably described by their own word — " dirty ". The one-time noble instrument, the former associate of kings and princes, now splutters and hiccups in company with whining saxophones in the cosmetic-laden atmosphere of the modern dance hall.

THE CORNET

(G.) Kornett.   (F.) Cornet à pistons.   (I.) Cornetta.

THE modern cornet or, to give it its full name, the *cornet à pistons*, came into being in France during the third decade of last century. It is improbable that its advent can be placed earlier than 1826 or later than 1828.[1]   The new instrument was the outcome of adding piston-valves to a conical and circular-coiled small horn then known in France as the *cornet, cornet simple, cornet ordinaire, cornet de poste*, or *petite trompette aiguë*.[2]

In his *Cours d'Instrumentation* (1837)[3] Kastner distinguished between the valveless cornet and the *cornet à pistons* ; the former instrument is depicted by the same author in his *Manuel général de Musique Militaire* (1848)[4] as a small circular horn fitted with a tuning-slide.   The *cornet simple* is described by Caussinus (1846) and by Gevaert (1863) ; the latter states that it was used in some military bands, and Comettant includes a *cornet de poste* in his specification of a French cavalry band before the advent of the saxhorns.   The very existence of this little instrument is now almost completely forgotten.   It was made in 4 feet C, but could be lowered by means of coiled crooks to B, B flat, A and A flat. Its only sounds were the open notes ranging from No. 2 to No. 8 of its harmonic series.   (See Fig. 40.)

When valves were added to the *cornet simple*[5] it became the

[1] A cornet by Courtois Frères in the Paris coll. (No. 1141) is dated 1828 in the catalogue (1st Supp. 1894) ; the instrument, however, *bears no date*.

[2] A specimen in the author's collection is coiled in two complete circles ; the diameter of the outer circle is about 6 inches.

[3] P. 51.   [4] Pl. xv, No. 1. See also Andries, p. 29.

[5] The Paris maker Halary is sometimes given credit for having been the first to do so.

cornet à pistons,[1] and, although some of the early specimens retain the original circular form, a more convenient way of folding the tube was found to be that of a much shortened, but deeper, trumpet. The early cornets were provided with at first two, and later with three, long narrow valves of the Stölzel or *schubventil* pattern (Pl. XXII, A and B) ; before long, however, Paris makers began to improve on these, and in the course of time evolved the shorter and wider valves of the Périnet type.

The valved cornet soon became popular, and by the mid-century was being constructed in other countries, with all the varieties of valve-action current at that time. Till fairly late in last century the piston valves were placed to the left of the bellpipe ; on the modern cornet they lie to the right of the bellpipe, between it and the mouthpipe (Pl. XXII). Another peculiarity of the older cornets is that the valve-tube

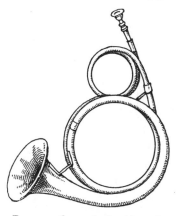

FIG. 40.—*Cornet simple* with crook.

belonging to the second valve projects towards the player instead of at right angles to the line of the instrument ; in consequence of this the second valve stood rather to the left and out of line with the first and third valves. The French cornet, when fully equipped, stood in C, and was provided with two shanks for the keys of B flat and A, and a set of coiled or oblong crooks for A flat, G, F, E, E flat and D. With the aid of short semitone shanks the instrument could also be put into B natural, F sharp or D flat. In his tutor of 1846, Caussinus described the tone of the cornet when crooked in its various keys as follows :

Low crooks : D flat, D, E flat, E—" mediocre and dull ".
Medium crooks : F, F sharp, G, A flat—" sonorous and pleasant ".
High crooks : A, B flat and B—" hard and bright ".

----

[1] Wieprecht gives " *Posthorn mit ventile* " as the German equivalent of *cornet à pistons*.

About the mid-century the low crooks were beginning to be discarded, and, although the medium crooks lingered on during the third quarter of the century, they also dropped out of use when players found that all their requirements were satisfied by the choice offered by the B flat and A shanks. In its earlier stage the cornet was regarded as a small horn rather than as a variety of trumpet [1]; the first French players of the instrument were not trumpeters, but horn-players.[2] The mouthpiece of the earlier cornets was indeed very similar to that of the French horn, lily-shaped and deeply conical. When the lower crooks were discarded and only the higher ones remained in use, the cornet lost something of its horn-like nature ; it was then that the instrument passed from the hands of horn-players into those of trumpeters, and the mouthpiece was made shallower and more cupped at the top of the bowl in order to emphasise the trumpet-like quality of its tone.

The present notation for the cornet seems to have been adopted in France at a fairly early stage, but in Germany and in England the old notation of the *cornet simple* (an octave lower) persisted for many years after the valved instrument had made its appearance in those countries. In Harper's tutor (*c.* 1836) the old notation is used, but the author states that " music is sometimes written for it (the cornet) an octave higher, the same as music for the bugle ".

It did not take long for the cornet to become known outside of France. It reached this country soon after 1830, and before long was being made in London after the French model by Köhler and by Charles Pace. Known as the cornopean, cornet, stop horn or small stop trumpet, the new instrument was welcomed by military and brass bands which up till then had been obliged to use the keyed bugle for melody-playing in the soprano register. English cornets of the period *c.* 1835 to 1850 were made in a

---

[1] " The cornet is to the horn what the piccolo is to the flute " (Catrufo, 1832, p. 33).

[2] Schlotmann, Forestier and Maury, for example, were French horn players who adopted the cornet as their instrument. (Lavignac-Laurencie.)

similar shape, and with the same narrow valves as the earlier
French instruments, and, in addition, were commonly fitted with
Macfarlane's clapper key. (Pl. XXII, A.) This was a closed
key controlling a hole bored about 12 inches from the bell-
mouth; it was worked by one of the fingers of the L. hand, and
was used to play shakes.[1] Köhler also made many cornets with
Shaw's disc-valves (pat. 1838), and for some twenty years or
so these were on their trial, but in the end were unable to com-
pete with the more reliable piston-valves. (Pl. XXII, c.) Made
in B flat when played with a short shank, and in A when a longer
shank was inserted, the early English cornets were usually provided with a set of crooks for A flat, G and F, and more rarely
for E.

Germany, Austria, Russia and the Netherlands had their
cornets early in the fourth decade of last century. By 1833 the
instrument had found its way to Germany, for in that year
Wieprecht introduced it to replace the keyed bugle in one of
the Prussian military bands at Berlin.[2] Belgian makers were
quick to copy the French models; these, no doubt, stimulated
the young man Ad. Sax (then working in his father's workshop
at Brussels) to design improvements of his own. Some instruments by Embach of Amsterdam, dating from round about 1830,
show ingenuity and enterprise in making unusual valve-actions.

Easily played, flexible and accommodating, by the mid-century
the cornet had won a place for itself in the music of practically
all European countries, particularly for use in military and brass
bands, but also in theatre and light opera orchestras. In Germany
and Austria, where it had to face some competition with the
new valved *flügelhorn*, the success of the cornet was not quite
so pronounced, but in France, Belgium and England it drove
the keyed bugle into retirement, and for some time seriously
threatened the status of the trumpet in concert and opera
orchestras. French composers, especially, made free use of the
cornet to supplement the brass ensemble in their orchestral scores.

---

[1] Keyed bugles were sometimes given similar shake-keys.
[2] Kalkbrenner.

Berlioz himself, although he was one of the first publicly to give the cornet a bad name,[1] nevertheless made willing use of it in his symphonic scores in order, as he said, " to complete the chords (harmony) of the trumpets ".

The instrument which had so quickly achieved popularity was, of course, subjected to the attention of many improvers and self-styled inventors. Amongst the cornets made round about the mid-century, there may be found specimens folded in many strange shapes. The bell may point in almost any direction, away from the player, upwards, over the player's head, over his shoulder, in fact, almost anywhere but directly in the player's face. The valves, too, are found to vary infinitely in detail and in type ; although the piston-valve was more or less standard in France, other types can also he found on cornets made in Paris during the period 1850–1860. Ad. Sax, for example, made some use of the short *Berliner-pumpen* (Pl. XXII, E) and cornets with rotary valves are extant bearing the name of Antoine Courtois. (Pl. XXII, H.) Some of these were exported and sold in this country, the former by Henry Distin, and the latter by Jullien and his successor Arthur Chappell who were the English agents for Courtois' instruments. English makers also endeavoured to capture the public fancy by inscribing their cornets with legends which included such words as " improved ", " patent " or " invented by ". Amongst these was Bayley's Improved Acoustic Cornet (1862), made in an unusually long shape by Köhler, and provided with short thick valves like the *Berliner-pumpen*. (Pl. XXII, F.) It seems that English makers never made the Vienna valve, and only rarely the rotary valve; but it is certain that imported cornets with rotary valves were sold in this country.

During the second half of last century, many French and some English makers and players were occupied in adding to the efficiency of the piston valve, and in inventing devices designed to rectify or to mitigate the inherent fault of the valve-

---

[1] " A phrase . . . would become poor and detestably vulgar if brought out by the snapping, noisy bold sound of the *cornet à pistons*. Berlioz (1848).

system. The following are some of those who contributed towards the improvement of the cornet between 1850 and 1890 : (France) Périnet, Ad. Sax, Antoine Courtois, Gustave Besson, Léon Cousin, Thibouville-Lamy, Arban, Koenig and Fontaine-Besson. (England) Henry Distin, William Brown, D. J. Blaikley (Boosey) and Joseph Higham (Manchester).

The cornet has not changed much during the last fifty or sixty years. Piston valves are almost universally used, and the shortened trumpet-form, neither so long and shallow as the trumpet, nor so short and deep as the original model, remains the standard shape. The straight mouthpipe turns at first into a wide U-bend, followed by a smaller U-bend which forms the tuning-slide ; yet another bend may be used to form a pitch-slide for either high or low pitch, and the tube then enters the third valve ; leaving by the first valve, the main tube soon begins to expand, and makes a wide bend which leads to the straight tube and terminates in the bell. The width and length of the passages which make up the tube of a cornet (in B flat) are approximately as follows :

Mouthpiece to tuning-slide : 17 inches ; conical bore $\frac{5}{16}$ to $\frac{7}{16}$ of an inch. Tuning-slide and valves : 18 inches, cylindrical bore $\frac{7}{16}$ of an inch. Valves to bellmouth : 20 inches, expanding from $\frac{7}{16}$ to 5 inches. Total length, about 4 feet 7 inches. (Pl. XXII, 1.)

Cornets in high E flat occur before 1850, and are still used to play the highest part in British brass band instrumentation.[1] Almost every writer on the subject of orchestration, or of wind instruments generally, seems to have considered it his duty to follow the lead of Berlioz in abusing and belittling the cornet.[2] Its tone has been described as being coarse, vulgar, common-place, trivial, toyish, and so on, whereas the trumpet was always

[1] A piccolo cornet in super-high B flat was made or designed by Hoffmann of Wiesbaden. (*Musical Opinion*, Sept. 1898.)

[2] " The cornet is a true bastard " (Mahan) ; " the *gamin de Paris* of the orchestra " (Lavignac) ; " thick and vulgar " (Widor) ; " coarse and vulgar " (Prout).

noble, lofty, majestic, or heroic. Compared with the old trumpets in F, E flat, D or C of Berlioz's time, then played, as they were, with a hemispherical mouthpiece, the tone of the early cornets, especially when crooked in the lower keys and played with a deep conical mouthpiece, may not have figured very favourably ; but compared with the short trumpet in B flat or A, played with the modern mouthpiece, the cornet in the same keys, also played with a cupped mouthpiece, can be made to produce a tone which differs so little from that of the trumpet that the two are difficult to distinguish when the hearer cannot *see* which is being played. A fair comparison can, of course, be made only when both instruments are equally well played, and in the same style. The cornet has been the victim of conditions and associations from which the trumpet of eighty or one hundred years ago was quite free. The former instrument was found to be easier to play ; it was more flexible and accommodating than the trumpet with a tube-length of from 6 to 8 feet ; hence the cornet was eagerly adopted and used for playing light music and dance tunes, or for rendering trivial, sentimental or ornate solos in open-air bands or at popular concerts ; in fact, it became associated with a type of music which may justly be called second-rate. Cornets have only too often been played (with excessive *vibrato*) in a style which is coarse, vulgar, over-sentimental and generally inartistic ; but it is not the instrument that deserves such epithets ; it is rather the type of music for which it has been used, and a bad style of playing, that has given the cornet its bad name. Now that only a 16th or a 32nd part of an inch in the taper of the tube and depth of the mouthpiece-cup separates the two instruments, the difference between the " vulgar " cornet and the " noble " trumpet has almost reached vanishing-point ; either or both may be played equally badly or equally well ; in fact, the dance bands of the present century have proved in a most convincing manner that the trumpet can be played in a style which is infinitely more vulgar and degrading than the very worst style of cornet-playing.

THE TROMBONE

(E.) Sackbut. Trombone. (G.) Posaune. (F.) Saqueboute. Trombone. (I.) Trombone.

THE history of the slide trombone extends over the last five or six hundred years ; during that period the instrument has remained practically unchanged except for unimportant details. The simple mechanism of the lengthening-slide is, indeed, so complete and perfect that it seems to be incapable of further improvement, and it is quite arguable that a trombone ceases to be one when the slide mechanism is replaced by any other device.

The trombone stands alone amongst the family of brass instruments in that it is by nature chromatic, and has never been anything else. Its tube is not limited to a fixed length, nor to certain fixed lengths calculated to sound semitones apart, but can be adjusted to all possible lengths within the limits of its shortest when the slide is drawn up, and its longest when it is fully extended. The cylindrical portion of its tube (over two-thirds of the whole) can be increased by almost imperceptible degrees to nearly double its original length, and is absolutely straight except for one U-bend. Its chromaticism is complete and its intonation can be perfect, whether measured by a tempered or by an untempered scale. Its only flaws are a slight but sudden change in the width of the bore at the points where the two parallel inner tubes end, and the impossibility of altering the sounding-length instantaneously. The latter, however, may possibly be regarded as a characteristic feature of the instrument rather than as an imperfection.

The principle of the slide can be traced back as far as the 15th century.[1] In the records of that century, the trombone

[1] Galpin, *Proceedings of the Musical Association* (London), 1906–1907.

(sackbut) is occasionally mentioned and depicted, and in the last quarter of the same century we hear of Hans Neuschel of Nürnberg, the first known maker (also player) of the instrument. In Doppelmayr's account of Neuschel[1] he is described as a skilled *posaunenmacher*, whose work had earned for him such a wide reputation that he received orders for instruments to be made for Royal Courts situated over several hundred miles distant from Nürnberg. For Pope Leo X he made some silver trombones, and visited Rome, where his playing was greatly admired and duly rewarded. Hans Neuschel died in 1533, and the craft was carried on by his successors, Hans and Jorg Neuschel.

Little can be learned about the trombone in the first half of the 16th century, except that which may be gleaned from pictorial representations of the instrument.[2] Virdung (1511) shows a rather crude woodcut of the *busaun*, apparently without one of the necessary stays ; Agricola (1528 and 1545) reproduces the same woodcut,[3] but, like Virdung, does not trust himself to give any informative details about an instrument which probably neither of them really understood.

If there is a suspicion of unreality about the early accounts and pictures of trombones, this uncertainty disappears when we come into touch with actual instruments made in the second half of the 16th century. Of these there are only a few still existing, but they are tangible things, real instruments which may even be played, and which at once dispel the vagueness which surrounds mere written or pictorial evidence. Dated trombones by Jorg Neuschel (1557),[4] Anton Schnitzer (1579),[5] Cunrat Linczer (1587),[6] all of Nürnberg, and one by Pierre Colbert (1593) of Rheims,[7] provide satisfying evidence that the instrument of some 350 or more years ago was in all its essentials a finished

---

[1] The name appears as Hanns Meuschel in Doppelmayr's book.

[2] The accuracy of the proportions and details may often be questioned.

[3] If these woodcuts could be trusted they would reveal the interesting fact that the trombone mouthpiece at that time was distinctly conical and horn-like ; unfortunately the trumpets depicted on the same page have similar conical mouthpieces.

[4] Galpin coll.   [5] Verona.   [6] Hamburg.   [7] Amsterdam.

product which did not admit of further improvement. Like
the trumpets of the same period, the trombones are made of
hammered brass, joined down the side by brazing. The various
pieces are held together by short sleeves overlapping the two
ends which they unite ; on the sleeves and on the band round
the end of the bell there is usually some engraved ornamentation,
and on the latter are also engraved the maker's name, his town,
and the year in which the instrument was made. The bells of
these old trombones are rather smaller and more funnel-shaped
than those of the modern instrument. The three necessary stays
are flat decorated strips of brass so contrived that they can be
detached from the instrument, and were evidently made so with
the intention of leaving the sounding-tubes in a non-rigid condition, and free to vibrate.[1]

The standard size of the trombone was then, as now, the
tenor in (9 feet) B flat. Smaller alto instruments were in E flat
or F, a fourth or a fifth above the tenor, and bass trombones
a fourth or a fifth below the tenor (*quart* or *quint*) were therefore
pitched an octave lower than the alto instruments.

A number of 17th-century trombones may be seen in the
principal German collections of old musical instruments.[2] Most
of these bear the names of the same Nürnberg makers which
are found on contemporary trumpets, and most of them are
dated. (Pl. XXIII, A.) They are in every respect similar to the
16th-century specimens, although a few cases do occur in which
fixed tubular stays replace the old flat stays on the slide.[3] There
are the same three sizes, the alto in E flat or F, the tenor in B flat,
and the *quart* or *quint* bass trombones in F or E flat. A contrabass or octave trombone, pitched an octave below the tenor,
is mentioned by Praetorius in 1619,[4] and towards the end of
the century a treble trombone, pitched a fourth or a fifth above

---

[1] The trumpets of the same period are also stayed in a non-rigid manner
by a piece of wood wrapped round by a cloth band or a cord.

[2] Nürnberg, Munich, Berlin, Salzburg, Heyer coll. (Leipzig), Frankfort.

[3] In such cases it is possible that the stays may have been altered at
some later date.

[4] An example in the Nürnberg coll. by Isaac Ehe is dated 1612.

the alto, makes its appearance. In the 17th century, or possibly
at an earlier date, folded or circular crooks were used to increase
the fundamental sounding-length of the trombone ; [1] these were
commonly inserted between the bellpipe and the slide,[2] or more
rarely between the slide and the mouthpiece. On the larger bass
instruments, the bellpipe was sometimes refolded in order to gain
length of tube without making the instrument unduly long, and
a hinged handle was attached to the stay of the movable slide
in order to enable the player to reach the lower positions. The
idea of halving the distance that the slide must be moved for
each shift by means of a refolded or double slide, appears to
have been thought of at a very early stage, for Jorg Neuschel
received an enquiry about such an instrument round about 1540–
1542.[3] A trombone so constructed by Jobst Schnitzer in 1612
is shown in the Heyer collection at Leipzig.[4]

Praetorius (1619) and Mersenne (1636) in the first half of
the 17th century, and Speer (1687) near the end of that century,
have left some information about the trombone as it was known
to them, and, if they add little to what can be learned from
a study of contemporary instruments, their contributions are
interesting as coming from musicians who were in touch with
the art of their day, and who actually handled or heard the sounds
of instruments which are now viewed as interesting antiquities.

Praetorius knew four sizes of trombone, as follows :

ALTO. *Alt* or *discant Posaun* (presumably) in F.
TENOR. *Gemeine Rechte Posaun*, in B flat.
BASS. *Quart and Quint Posaun*, respectively in F and E flat.
CONTRABASS. *Octav Posaun*, in BB flat.

Praetorius remarks that the contrabass instrument was uncommon at that time, and that two varieties were known ; the

[1] Praetorius depicts what are probably a tone crook and a semitone
shank as accessories to the tenor trombone. (Pl. VIII, No. 3.)

[2] The trombone depicted lying on the floor in Jan Brueghel's picture
" Hearing " (*c.* 1620) appears to have two crooks between the bell and the
slide sections.

[3] Galpin. (Proceedings.)   [4] No. 1908.

one, made by Hans Schreiber in 1614, was simply a double-sized
tenor, sounding an octave lower ; the other was not so large,
the low pitch being achieved by means of a crook (*Krum-Bügel*)
inserted between the slide and the bellpipe, and by an enlargement
of the bore. Praetorius' illustrations are excellent,[1] and show all
four instruments very clearly.

From Mersenne we learn that a crook was used in France
whereby the tenor was lowered in pitch by a fourth, thus becoming a bass trombone in F.

Speer's contribution is more technical, and reveals a better
understanding of the principle on which the slide-system is based.
He treats the trombone, however, as a diatonic rather than as a
chromatic instrument, and numbers the positions of the slide
as they occur in a diatonic scale ; thus, on the B flat or tenor
trombone the " first draw " (*Erster ʒug*) gives the harmonics of
A, and is therefore what would now be called the second position ;
the " second draw " (*Anderer ʒug*) gives the harmonics of G,
corresponding to the fourth position ; the " third draw " (*Dritte
ʒug*) again descends by a stage of a whole tone and gives the
harmonics of F, and the final or " fourth draw " (*Vierdte ʒug*)
corresponds to the seventh position :

..	= 1st pos. (B flat)
Erster ʒug	= 2nd pos. (A)
Anderer ʒug	= 4th pos. (G)
Dritte ʒug	= 6th pos. (F)
Vierdte ʒug	= 7th pos. (E)

The chromatic nature of the instrument, however, is recognised by Speer when he explains that for semitones or sharpened
notes, the slide must be drawn in for a distance which is described
as being about equal to the breadth of two fingers, while to
lower or flatten the notes, the slide requires to be pushed outwards
to the same extent.

The trombones of the 18th century show only a few unimportant changes. Nürnberg then began to lose its supremacy
as a centre for making brass instruments ; the more frequent

[1] *Theatrum Instrumentorum*, pls. vi and viii.

appearance of names of makers who worked in other German
towns show how the craft was gradually becoming decentralised.
On the earlier 18th-century instruments the old flat detachable
stays still steadied the bellpipe, but before the end of that century
the tubes of the trombone were held in the firmer grip of fixed
tubular stays ; the instrument was then beginning to find its
way into military bands, and a rather more robust construction
was called for. (Pl. XXIII, B.) The bell of the later 18th-century
trombone loses its former funnel-shaped appearance owing to a
more sudden expansion of the tube, and a slight increase in width at
the extreme end. Meanwhile the alto in F occurs less frequently,
leaving a group of three, namely, the alto in E flat, the tenor in B
flat, and the bass in either E flat or F, to form the standard instruments of the early 19th century. The custom of adding crooks to
trombones appears to have been gradually given up during the
course of the 18th century. Treble trombones were made at
that time, and it may be that these were the instruments which
were commonly known as *zugtrompeten* in Germany, and which
figure in some of Bach's scores under the name *tromba da tirarsi*.
(Pl. XXIII, C.) Until near the close of the 18th century the
trombone was hardly what we would now call an orchestral
instrument. It had hitherto been used largely in the service
of the Church, where, associated with the old cornett as the
soprano instrument, a group of trombones was used to support
the voices in the rendering of the Choral. Trombones were
also frequently included in the small groups of wind instruments
which were employed to provide the music on royal or civic
ceremonial occasions, for processions or banquets, and in France
even for dance music. Trombones had a place in the old German
town bands and, being free from the restrictions which sur-
rounded the use of trumpets, were allowed to take part in the
music of the people, the *bourgeoisie* and the commoner. But,
with the exception of a few isolated cases, parts for trombones are
not to be found in opera scores till late in the 18th century. At
about the same time, or possibly just a little later, the formation
and better organisation of regular military bands provided another

opening for the use of trombones. Hence, early in the 19th century there was a greatly increased demand for these instruments ; this is reflected in the fact that trombones of that period are extant bearing the names of many new makers who worked not only in Germany, but also in France, Belgium, Italy and Austria.

The alto in E flat, the tenor in B flat, and the bass in either E flat or F remained the standard sizes early in the 19th century, when the trombone was being freely used in military bands, for opera and oratorio, and when it was just beginning to find a place in symphony or concert orchestras. A smaller bass in G, which was destined to become the standard bass trombone in this country, makes a tentative appearance in the second quarter of last century.

Although a group of three (alto, tenor and bass) was nominally the standard trombone trio in the first half of last century, in actual practice the tenor was by far the most favoured instrument, and was frequently allowed to usurp the position of the alto and the bass. In Germany the bass in F or E flat held its own, but a wide-bored tenor in B flat (known as the *bassposaune*)[1] was sometimes used to play the lower part in orchestras in place of the real bass instrument. In French orchestras the alto was hardly known, and the bass trombone was practically unknown. In the meantime, the soprano was almost obsolete and, even if it lingered in Germany, was quite unknown in France. The increasing use of trombones in military bands brought about a few occasional changes in the outward appearance of the instrument ; some were made with the bell turned over the player's shoulder in order to project the sound backwards to troops marching in the rear of the band. In France and Belgium the bellpipe was sometimes bent in a curve, and ended in a fearsome dragon's head with a flapping tongue and bared teeth in place of the ordinary bell ; these heads were gaudily painted in red,

---

[1] In Nemetz's tutor the B flat trombone is named Bass, Tenor or Alto, each played with a different mouthpiece. The bass instrument in F was named *Quartposaune* by Nemetz (*c.* 1830).

green and gold, and this terrifying instrument was called a
buccin.[1] (Pl. XXIV.) The bass instruments were sometimes
made with double slides, and in 1817 Gottfried Weber designed
a complete set of trombones with double slides ; these (made
by Schott of Mayence) allowed nine positions of the slide, and
added two extra semitones to the downward compass of the
instrument.[2]

A tuning-slide on the U-bend of the bellpipe and a water-
key at the lower end of the slide are to be found on trombones
from about 1825–1830, and became very general and useful
accessories on 19th-century instruments.

Some time after the invention of the lengthening-valve, that
device began to be applied to trombones in place of the slide.
In a short notice which appeared in the *Allgemeine Musikalische
Zeitung* (Leipzig) of July 1818, it is stated that Stölzel and
Blühmel had invented two contrivances (two valves) by means
of which all the notes of the chromatic scale could be played
on the horn, trumpet and *trombone* without the use of either
crooks or stopping. The valves necessitated some additional
bends of the tube, and with their advent the trombone inherited
the weakness of all valve-systems, which becomes especially
pronounced when the instrument covers the bass register.
Although it was a handy instrument for marching or cavalry
bands, it seems to have been generally agreed in orchestral circles
that the trombone lost something when the characteristic slide
was replaced by valve-mechanism.[3] According to Nemetz,[4] the
first to apply the valve-system to the trombone was the Viennese
maker Riedl ; in or before 1830 Uhlmann of the same city
improved on Riedl's design, and made B flat and G trombones

---

[1] Choron (1813) names the bass instrument *Tuba curva*, and the tenor
Buccin. Catrufo (1832) heads his scanty description of the trombone
" *Le Trombone ou Buccin* ".

[2] Illustrations and scale in Gassner's *Partiturkenntniss* (1838), vol ii,
pp. 29-33. Also depicted by Kastner (*Manuel*) (1848), pl. xvii, No. 7.
Contrabass trombones with doubled slides occur towards the end of last
century.

[3] " Ihr Klang ist stumpf " (Gassner).   [4] *Neueste Posaun-Schule*, p. 20.

with the double Vienna valve.[1] Kastner depicts (in 1848) trombones with the early piston valve (*schubventil*), the Vienna valve,
the rotary valve,[2] and one by Ad Sax. with *Berliner-pumpen*,
folded in the form of a tuba with the bell pointing upwards.[3] In
the same year Berlioz wrote of the valve-trombone, that the pistons
gave it increased agility, but less " correctness of intonation ".

If it did, for some time round about the middle of last century,
threaten to supplant the slide instrument in military bands, the
valve-trombone never succeeded in gaining more than a rather
uncertain footing in concert and opera orchestras. From von
Gontershausen (1855) we learn that the best German players
were then getting rid of their valve-trombones, and were falling
back on the old slide instrument.

In the third quarter of last century continued efforts were
made to improve the instrument which steadily refused to be
improved. The players, indeed, seemed to be quite content
with the old slide trombone, which had remained practically
unchanged for over three hundred years, but makers insisted
that the imperfections of the slide must be remedied, and in
the end generally succeeded in creating some fresh fault or disadvantage in place of the one they had remedied. French makers
were particularly active in trying to cure a perfectly healthy and
uncomplaining instrument of ills which were really part of its
nature, and did not call out for remedial measures. Ad. Sax's
trombone with six *pistons à tubes indépendants* (1852) was perhaps the most drastic of these efforts ; the six shortening valves
each controlled six almost complete trombones combined in one
immense bundle surmounted by seven gaping bells.[4] Gustav
Besson's trombone with three *pistons dépendants* (1858) and a
registre (or fourth valve), was made in the shape of a tuba (in C),
and gave eight different sounding-lengths. The same maker's
instrument with a *registre* and *tubes indépendants* (c. 1860), and
his *trombone duplex* (1864), complete with slide and three valves,

---

[1] *Machin-Posaune* (B flat) ; *Machin-terz-Posaune* (G).
[2] *Manuel général*, pl. xvii.
[3] Pl. xxiv.   [4] Brussels Cat., vol. ii, No. 1288.

were further efforts which, like others of the same period, came and went without having any effect on the uneventful history of the trombone. The only addition of this period which came into general use was the pair of short metal outer tubes, called shoes or stockings, which were fixed over the ends of the inner tubes of the slide ; these facilitated the passage of the movable slide over the fixed tubes, if they rather accentuated the difference between the diameters of the inner and outer tubes. Trombones with double slides " invented " by Halary, Gott. Weber, Sax, Besson, Distin and Goodison, were only modified revivals of an idea almost as old as the trombone itself.

In the meantime the alto trombone in E flat [1] was beginning to lose its place in the orchestra (Pl. XXIII, D) ; even in Germany, where it had been used from the time when trombones first joined the orchestral family, the favourite tenor instrument now seemed to overlay and smother its smaller brother, and before the end of the century the alto was all but obsolete, its place in the orchestra being taken by another B flat tenor. In Germany the bass trombone in F held its own for some time, while the smaller bass in G grew more popular in this country and (when a real bass was used) in France. A contrabass in BB flat or CC, a revival of the old *octav posaun* of Praetorius' time, was called into life again mainly by Wagner's demand for such an instrument. At the beginning of the present century the instruments used in the principal orchestras for the two upper parts were ordinary slide trombones in B flat (non-transposing). The lower part was played on a bass in G in England, and to some extent in France where, however, three tenors had for long formed the standard trio. In Germany the bass in F (*quart posaune*) was being replaced by the so-called *tenorbass posaune* in B flat, provided with an extra loop of tubing controlled by a valve which, when it was operated by the L. hand, added enough to the normal tube-length to lower the pitch of the instrument by a fourth, and thus virtually turned it into a bass

---

[1] Also occasionally made in France in F, E and D flat. Pl. XXIII, E, shows a D flat trombone by Antoine Courtois.

trombone in F.[1] On such instruments the extent of the shifts, of course, increases proportionately when the tube is fundamentally lengthened, and a seventh position of the slide is hardly feasible. The compass (disregarding the pedal notes) reaches down to 8 feet C.

Valve-trombones, made with pistons in France and Belgium, and with the rotary action in Germany and Austria, have kept their places in some continental military bands, but have never been anything but aliens in this country.

The treble trombone, which had always been leading a rather precarious life ever since the late 17th century, has again been revived quite recently in the hope that dance bands would welcome it and make use of the gliding or *portamento* effect which is possible only on slide instruments ; it seems, however, as if this last effort to find a settled occupation for the treble trombone has been rather coldly received.

In spite of all the attentions it has received, the ordinary slide trombone of today remains very much as it was four or five hundred years ago. The few permanent modifications it has undergone are limited to such details as a slight change in the expansion of the bell, the addition of a tuning-slide, a water-key, and the shoes on the ends of the inner tubes of the slide ; even if it were now without these additions the instrument would not suffer much loss.

More than the instrument, it is the style of playing that has changed most. There is every reason to believe that the overwhelming *forte* or *fortissimo* of the trombones in a modern orchestra was a thing quite unknown before last century, and that if such sounds had been produced, they would have been condemned as intolerably coarse and inartistic. The mouthpieces found on old trombones (when there is no question that they belong to the same period as the instrument) [2] are conical and horn-like ; the gently contracting interior of the bowl is one

---

[1] Similar instruments had already been made in Paris by Ad. Sax, and later (1881) by Millereau.

[2] Old brass instruments are often found with mouthpieces of a much later period.

which has always been given to instruments from which a round and mellow tone is required. The shallow cup of the old trumpet mouthpiece was calculated to favour a strong, brilliant and penetrating tone ; but cupped mouthpieces belong only to the trombones of the 19th century, when the instruments found favour in military bands and opera orchestras, where a sharp-edged and powerful tone was expected of them. Mersenne, in 1636, insisted that the trombone should not be blown like a trumpet, but should rather be made to blend with the quality of human voices. Speer, in 1687, stated that trombone-playing did not require much bodily strength ; that a boy of eight, nine or ten years of age could well learn to play on it. The very fact that it was constantly used in conjunction with the old cornetts and with human voices in the performance of Church music, is in itself enough to prove that the trombone was played in such a way that its tone balanced, rather than overwhelmed, that of its associated instruments and voices. Anything like rapidity of execution was, of course, quite foreign to the old style of trombone-playing. The deliberate and steady tread of the chords in a choral suited its technique and its style ; it was expected to be dignified and solemn, but not warlike and aggressive. By the time of Berlioz, the trombone was already no longer only an instrument of solemn and dignified character ; its tone in *fortissimo* was " menacing and formidable " ; Berlioz allowed that trombones might " chant like a choir of priests ", but also that they might take part in the " wild clamour of the orgy ", or " break forth into frantic cries, or sound its dread flourish to awaken the dead or to doom the living ". Terrifying sounds such as these were surely not made by Hans Neuschel in the 16th century, nor would they have pleased Praetorius, Mersenne or Speer. Yet, if the old instruments could be rejuvenated, and were furnished with modern mouthpieces, they could no doubt be made to rend the air in the same way as do the most up-to-date trombones when their utmost is demanded by the composers and conductors of today ; for the playing has changed, but the instrument remains the same.

THE CORNETT, SERPENT, BASSHORN, KEYED BUGLE AND OPHICLEIDE

FROM a quite remote period, which goes back well beyond the limits of musical-historical research, the horns or tusks of various animals have been adapted for the purpose of making musical sounds or signals. These rudimentary lip-reed instruments were advanced a step when holes were bored in the side, and some additional sounds were made available by opening or closing the holes with the fingers.

By the later Middle Ages a type of musical instrument, made of wood or ivory more or less in the shape of a horn, had developed from such rude beginnings, and could boast a compass of about two octaves. The earliest of these, the medieval cornett, thus combined in itself the shortening-hole system of the pipe or flute, and the lip-reed method of sound-production which is common to the brass instruments. The 16th century added to the family of cornetts a bass instrument which, on account of its snake-like undulations, was called the serpent. Efforts, made at the end of the 18th century, to reshape the serpent, resulted in the bass-horn or Russian bassoon, which was made of either wood or metal, or both, but still depended largely on the opening or closing of finger-holes for its scale. Early in the 19th century, the small finger-holes were beginning to be abandoned in favour of larger note-holes controlled by key-work ; the all-metal keyed bugle and the keyed trumpet in the soprano register, and the ophicleide in the bass register, were the last of their type, and survived till the valved brass instruments drove them into permanent retirement round about the middle of last century.

(a) THE MEDIEVAL CORNETT

(E.) Cornet. Cornett. Mute cornet. Straight cornet.
(G.) Zink. Zinck. Krummer Zink. Stiller Zink. Gerader Zink.
(F.) Cornet. Cornet à bouquin. Cornet recourbé. Cornet droit.
(I.) Cornetto. Cornetto curvo. Cornetto muto. Cornetto diritto.

Although clearly recognisable representations of the cornett occur many centuries earlier, the old existing specimens do not appear to date from before the 16th century. At that time there were curved and straight cornetts; according to Praetorius (1619), the latter were made in two varieties, namely, the *cornetto diritto*, of which the mouthpiece was usually made of horn and was detachable, and the *cornetto muto*, on which the cup of the mouthpiece was hollowed out in the narrow end of the instrument. Praetorius' cornetts are classed as follows :

(a) The curved *cornettino* or *klein discant Zinck*, with a compass of two octaves from e' to e'''.

(b) The curved *cornetto curvo* or *Recht (gemeine) chor Zinck*, with a compass from a to a'', and a possible extension one tone downwards or several tones upwards when in the hands of specially skilled players. This was the ordinary " black " cornett.

(c) The straight *cornetto diritto* or *Gerader Zinck*, with a detachable mouthpiece, and a compass similar to (b).

(d) The straight *cornetto muto* or *Still Zinck*, a similar instrument, but without a detachable mouthpiece ; sometimes made a tone lower in g,[1] and provided with a little-finger-key which carried the compass down to f.

(e) The curved *cornetto torto*, *Cornon* or *Grosse tenor Zinck*, shaped like an S with a compass from d to d'', and an additional hole and open key for the little finger, extending the compass down to c.

Of these Praetorius describes (a) as sounding fairly sweetly (*nicht unlieblich*) ; the tone of (d) was quiet, soft and sweet, but (e) was rougher and more horn-like, and could best be replaced by a trombone.

---

[1] Theatrum Instrumentorum, pl. xiii, No 3.

A number of 16th- and 17th-century cornetts are preserved in several collections on the continent ; most of these are the ordinary curved soprano in *a*, the instrument which was commonly used to act as the highest voice in a quartet consisting of three trombones and a cornett. The smaller size is represented by only a few in *e'* (*quintzink*), but more generally by the *quartzink* in *d'*, a tone below Praetorius' *cornettino*. The usual group was apparently the three, respectively in *d*, *a* and *d'*, sounding a minor third below the contemporary recorders in *f*, *c'* and *f'*. The straight or mute cornetts, which are said to have been more difficult to play, seem to have dropped out of use before the curved variety. The ordinary curved cornetts were commonly made of wood, or more rarely of ivory, and are conical tubes about 2 feet long, with a bore of under $\frac{1}{2}$ an inch at the narrow end, increasing gradually to about 1 inch at the wide end. The wooden instruments were made from two transverse halves, hollowed out and then glued together again ; most of them are covered with leather. The exterior of the tube is octagonal in section, but between the uppermost finger-hole and the mouthpiece a series of indentations are cut, forming a sort of faceted ornamental pattern which was evidently a traditional design for these instruments. The ends of the tube are sometimes protected by a decorated ferrule of brass or silver. The gentle curve of the tube is generally to the right-hand side, but a pair made to match may be curved in opposite directions, so that they incline towards one another.

Six fairly large finger-holes pierce the upper side of the tube, and a seventh or thumb-hole penetrates the underside rather higher up than the uppermost finger-hole ; this arrangement is similar to that of the holes on the contemporary recorders, but there is not as a rule any little-finger-hole at the lower end, except on the larger tenor cornetts, and then the extra hole is usually controlled by an open key with the customary swallow-tail finger-plate and a protecting box. The fingering of the cornett is similar to that of the recorder, giving a diatonic succession of sounds which corresponds more or less to the major scale, but

which requires some adjustment of the intonation by either relaxing or compressing the lip pressure. Intermediate semitones
were produced by the usual forkfingerings, and there is little
doubt that the cornett players of old used the half-opened finger-
hole in the same way as did the players on the wood-wind
instruments of the same period. (Pl. XXV, B.)

Speer (1697) gave a fingering chart for the ordinary cornett
in A (see Fingering Chart, No. 9) ; this was repeated by Eisel
(1738), and by Majer (1741), who added a low *b* flat played with
all the finger-holes closed and the thumb-hole open.

When detachable, the cornett mouthpiece was made of horn
or of ivory in the form of a small shallow cup with a rather
sharp edge. It is almost useless to attempt to describe the tone-
quality of an instrument which has been out of use for about
two hundred years, without risk of doing it some injustice. The
lip-technique of the medieval cornett is quite unknown at the
present time, and any casual test made with surviving specimens
is likely to lead only to conclusions which are at best speculative
or unfairly based. Contemporary writers all insist that the tone
of the cornett was more like the human voice than that of any
other instrument. It is uncertain whether this should be inter-
preted as a compliment to the cornett playing, or as derogatory
to the voice production of the period ; neither can be reconstructed, therefore a standard is lacking. All the old writers,
however, agree that the cornett was a difficult instrument to
manage.

Virdung (1511) gives it scant attention, but Artusi (1600),
Praetorius (1619), Mersenne (1636) and Roger North (*c.* 1728)
had nice things to say about the instrument which writers in the
period of its decline were inclined to treat more and more un-
kindly. Artusi recommends the player to imitate the human
voice, and points out the importance of an adequate lip-technique;
Praetorius finds fault only with the tone of the tenor cornett,
but grants the smaller instruments a tone-quality characterised
by gentleness and sweetness. To Mersenne the tone of the
cornett suggested the brightness of a ray of sunshine, and towards

the close of the 17th century, Randle Holmes named it " a delicate pleasant wind musick if well played and humered ". Rather later, Roger North deplores that " it is seldom well sounded ", and suggests that this is because " the labour of the lips is too great ". Mattheson in 1713 was not so sure of the pleasant quality of the cornett tone ; he remarks that it was hard, and finds it rather like a raw and unpolished human voice. Walther's testimony is of less value, for he obviously took his information from Praetorius ; Eisel (1738) and Majer (1741) depended too much on Speer, Mattheson and Walther to be regarded as independent witnesses. The views of later 18th-century and early 19th-century writers are generally taken from earlier sources, and in any case are of little value, for to them the cornett was a mere relic of the past, an instrument hardly worth considering except as a historical curiosity.

Although the cornett is specified in some scores by Bach, Handel, Gluck and other 18th-century composers, it was an instrument which really belonged to a pre-orchestral period, when, with its contemporary shawms, pommers, krumhorns and sackbuts, small groups of wind instruments were played by musicians employed by the Church, royal and noble courts, and civic bodies. As the treble instrument in conjunction with a group of trombones, the cornett figures in the early stages of the development of the orchestra, and of opera and oratorio ; in that capacity it is to be found in the Church symphonies of Gabrielli and the operas of Monteverde, Rossi and Cesti ; but trombones were not one of the groups of instruments which formed the nucleus of the growing orchestra, and before they were called upon to amplify the orchestral choir their treble associate was already obsolete.

The decline of the cornett began towards the end of the 17th century, in a period which coincides with the advent of the jointed wood-wind instruments, the one-keyed flute, the two-keyed oboe, and the three-keyed bassoon ; before long the horns were invited to join the orchestral body, in which trumpets were already being treated as welcome guests ; thus, the beginnings of the wood-wind and the brass groups had each successfully attached themselves to the central backbone of bowed string instruments, but there was no place for a third type of wind instrument which was neither fish nor fowl, neither one of the wood-wind nor one of the brass family.

(b) THE SERPENT

(G.) Serpent.   (F.) Serpent.   (I.) Serpentone.

In the Abbé Lebeuf's *Mémoires concernant l'histoire ecclési- astique et civile d'Auxerre* (Paris, 1743) there appears an account of how, in or near the year 1590, a Canon of Auxerre named Edmé Guillaume found out how to make a large cornett in the shape of a serpent. This is the original source of the statement which has appeared in many books to the effect that the serpent was invented in 1590 by Canon Edmé Guillaume of Auxerre. A few surviving serpents, which are apparently of Italian origin, and are said to have been made prior to 1590, have been cited as evidence with which to controvert Lebeuf's story; if the date of these instruments can be established without any doubt, the appearance of the serpent must certainly be placed earlier than 1590. In any case the serpentine bass instrument of the cornett family cannot be traced further back than the 16th century, and even if of Italian origin, it is certain that France was the country in which it became naturalised in an ecclesiastical setting as a supporting instrument for the voices in Gregorian Chant.

The Frenchman Mersenne (1636), eulogised the serpent in glowing terms, and gave it credit for both strength and gentle- ness of voice; a little later, Kircher (1650) confirms the fact that France was the real home of the serpent; throughout the 18th century, the *serpent d'église* flourished in its original capacity in the Churches of France and Belgium. In Germany it appears to have been unknown during the 16th, 17th and the greater part of the 18th century; Virdung (1511), Agricola (1528-1545), Praetorius (1619) and Mattheson (1713) have nothing to say about it, and Walther (1732) just mentions it as an instrument well known in France. In the 18th century the serpent began to make itself at home in this country, and later on found a place in the English Church bands of the early 19th century.

Towards the close of the 18th century, when increased attention was being paid to the organisation of military bands in most countries, the serpent was enlisted and trained to serve as a martial bass voice, in which capacity it managed to hold its own, and to some extent to withstand even the competition of the bass-horn and ophicleide, till near the middle of last century, when the whole tribe of lip-reed instruments with side-holes began to be forced into retirement by the all-conquering progress of the valved brass instruments.

There can be no doubt that the peculiar shape of the serpent was the result of endeavouring to make a bass cornett in a form which would bring the finger-holes within convenient reach of the player, and would reduce the instrument to a reasonable size ; the length of the serpent, which would be about 8 feet if the tube were straight, was reduced to rather under 3 feet by making the tube undulate in a zigzag manner. The originator certainly selected a shape which was very troublesome to make and rather uncomfortable to play, whereas with less trouble he might have folded the tube once in the style of the bassoon. Near the end of the 18th century serpents were being made on lines of a bassoon, with two straight up and down tubes connected at the bottom, and were known as bass-horns or Russian bassoons ; this was no doubt because the instrument had by that time found favour in military bands, and the old form was ill-adapted for playing on the march. In spite of this, the old serpent survived in its original shape for a considerable time, for it was still made in zigzag undulations near the middle of last century.[1]

The serpent is usually a wooden, or more rarely a metal

[1] A man named Huggett, the last English maker of serpents, was said to be still living in 1894 (Rose). A wooden ophicleide by Huggett is shown in the Brussels coll., No. 2454.

tube, with a conical bore of about $\frac{7}{16}$ to $\frac{1}{2}$ an inch in diameter at the narrow end, increasing gradually to 4 or $4\frac{1}{2}$ inches at the wide end ; the total tube-length may be from about $7\frac{1}{2}$ to nearly 8 feet. A cupped mouthpiece, usually made of ivory, is inserted in the narrow end of a bent brass " crook " about 9 or 10 inches long, and this in turn fits into the wooden tube of which the inside at that point is about $\frac{3}{4}$ of an inch wide. The wooden tube then makes three U-shaped zigzag bends, and a final curl which ends abruptly without any extra expansion at the bell. The six finger-holes are in two groups of three, those for the L. hand being situated just before the third U-bend, and those for the R. hand almost at the top of the final curl. The finger-holes are about $\frac{1}{2}$ an inch in diameter, and lie about $1\frac{3}{4}$ inches apart from centre to centre. On the 19th-century serpents the finger-holes are often lined (or bushed) with ivory.

Considerable skill and patience must have been exercised in making such instruments, for the curved wooden tube could not be drilled through like a straight tube ; it was, therefore, made in transverse halves, each of which had to be hollowed out and made to match the other half with great exactitude, for the walls were not more than $\frac{1}{4}$ inch thick ; the two halves were then glued together, and the whole was generally bound round with leather, and sometimes further strengthened by metal bands and stays.

Originally the serpent was held vertically in front of the player, the lower end reaching a little above his knees ; when it became a regular constituent of the military band and was played on the march, a more convenient way of holding the instrument had to be found. The bends of the tube were compressed a little, and the lower end was then held rather to the player's right side, so that the instrument was out of the way of his legs. As held originally, the fingers of both hands lay on the upper side of the tube, but later on, when the instrument was held to one side, better support was secured by placing the R. hand under the tube, and in so doing the fingering for that hand was reversed. The rather precarious grip of the serpent was eased to some extent by hanging it on a ribbon or strap which was passed round the player's neck, or else attached to a button on his clothing.

When all the finger-holes were closed the serpent gave 8 feet C as its fundamental, and the harmonics proper to that tube-length up to the eighth sound of the natural series. By successively opening the finger-holes, starting with the one nearest the bell, something like a major scale with a flat seventh was produced, but not without some care in readjusting the intonation by means of lip compression or relaxation. The intermediate semitones were produced by varying the lip-compression (without changing the fingering), or by half-opening the finger-holes, and to a limited extent by forkfingering.

The first of these devices was an important and essential feature of serpent-playing, and was made use of to an extent which is unknown to the present-day players on lip-reed instruments. As a matter of fact, it is quite possible to raise or lower a sound approximately a semitone on such a wide-bored tube as that of the serpent by compressing or relaxing the pressure of the lips ; thus, two adjacent semitones were often played with precisely the same fingering. Some of the old fingering charts show that the downward compass could be extended three or four semitones below the fundamental simply by slackening the embouchure. The serpent, indeed, allowed room for considerable variety of fingering, and demanded a skilful use of the lips ; there is little doubt that each player would employ whatever device or combination of devices gave the best result on his own particular instrument. Forkfingering was used only in four or five places in the whole scale of the instrument. French fingering charts always show the open notes and natural scale of the serpent one tone higher than the real sounds, that is, in D instead of in C. Mahillon [1] explained that the customary pitch used in French Churches in the 18th century was a tone below normal, and that the notation was therefore a tone above the real sounds. This probably explains why Berlioz and others

[1] Brussels Cat., vol. i, p. 297.

state that the serpent is in B flat, meaning that it must be treated as
a transposing instrument sounding a tone below the written notes.

The fingering chart quoted here (see Fingering Chart, No. 10)
is taken from an early 19th-century French instruction book,
and is for a keyless serpent or *serpent ordinaire*. A comparison
with some other charts, most of which belong to the late 18th
or early 19th century, will show how much the details of the
fingering varied according to the instrument, the habit or the
skill of the player, and also the variability of the compass at both
ends of the scale. One French tutor carries the downward
compass four semitones below the fundamental, the five lowest
notes being produced with all finger-holes closed ; others allow
only two extra low notes, but all agree that no finger-hole was
to be opened till the scale rose to the next degree above the
fundamental. A number of shakes were possible ; these were
classified by Francœur-Choron (1772–1813) as (a) easy and
brilliant, (b) shakes made with the lips (difficult), and (c) those
which were just possible, but not effective ; apparently shakes
were not attempted in the lowest octave.

A few serpents which may have been made in the 16th
century now survive in company with many which are vaguely
labelled "17th-18th century". (Pl. XXVI, A.) Mersenne (1636)
states that they were made of nut-wood covered with leather,
and that the upper end was strengthened by a wrapping of ox-
sinew. When Laborde wrote in 1780, the French serpent was
apparently very much as it was in Mersenne's time ; the Church
required little of it beyond the capacity to play a limited number
of sustained sounds. Near the end of the 18th century, when
the serpent became a military instrument, some more attention
was given to improving it and trying to bring it into line with
other rapidly progressing wind instruments ; it was then that
the serpent was given a few keys, and was strengthened with
more brasswork. The usual additions were three closed keys
mounted in brass saddles ; these were commonly, a key for
B natural,[1] placed above the uppermost finger-hole on the front

---

[1] C sharp according to the French notation.

of the instrument, and worked by the first finger of the L. hand; a key for F sharp was situated between the two groups of finger-holes, and was controlled by the R. first finger, or by the little finger when the hand was placed underneath the tube ; a third key was for C sharp (also used for D sharp), and is sometimes found on the front, but more commonly on the back of the instrument. (Pl. XXVI, B.) A four-keyed serpent has usually separate keys for C sharp and D sharp. Most of the serpents now seen are three- or four-keyed instruments made during the first half of last century. Further additions of keys were some-times made, especially in France, Belgium and England ; seven-keyed serpents were planned so that the note-holes were more widely spread along the tube, and eventually, towards the middle of last century, when the ophicleide was in full bloom, and when the tuba was already beginning to threaten the life of the ophi-cleide, a few makers [1] covered all the holes of the serpent with as many as from twelve to fourteen keys. (Pl. XXVI, c.) It is said that George III suggested that the wide end should be turned slightly outwards as it usually is on the English serpents of that period.

Serpents made in the first half of last century show that some efforts were made to improve and strengthen the instru-ment which, in its original state, was anything but fitted to face the rigours of military life. The upper part of the tube was sometimes made entirely of brass, or the whole instrument might be made of copper. Some new ways of shaping the tube were tried from time to time in the early 19th century ; the whole instrument might be made in the shape of a tuba,[2] and some were given a brass expanding bell, or the latter might be shaped like a dragon's head.

The proper mouthpiece for the serpent is a true cup, like that of the old trumpet, but much larger, and with a rather sharp narrow rim at the lip and a small outlet at the throat ; most of the old mouthpieces are of ivory.

---

[1] Key of London, and Embach of Amsterdam.
[2] Amsterdam, Berlin, and Donaldson collections.

When it was purely a Church instrument it was not necessary to provide any tuning device for the serpent, as the voices could always take the pitch of the instrument; but when used in military bands or orchestras, some sort of tuning could be contrived by using a longer or a shorter crook.[1]

Although serpents do not appear to have been commonly made in different sizes, there have been exceptional cases of larger instruments; there is a record of a contrabass in E flat, by Jordan of Liverpool, which was exhibited at the Exhibition of 1851 in London.

It is hardly possible now to describe the tone of the serpent, partly because the instrument, adequately played, is no longer to be heard, and partly because there is no wind instrument now in use with which it may in fairness be compared. When anyone now picks up an old serpent, which has been out of use for perhaps a hundred years or more, which is dried up, brittle, and quite possibly in a leaky condition,[2] and blows into its dusty interior, the sounds issuing from it will most likely provoke either laughter or else amazement that such a contrivance could ever have been used for musical purposes; when the player is not used to the instrument, does not understand the necessary lip-technique, knows nothing about its tone-character, and perhaps expects it to sound like a tuba or a trombone, the serpent is all the less likely to do itself justice. A test under such conditions is quite useless and very unfair; any modern instrument, after having been neglected and out of use for a long period, if tried under the same conditions, would probably fare no better! In order to get a fair idea of the tone and the possibilities of the serpent, the instrument would have to be reconditioned and restored to its original condition, and the player would have to take as much trouble, and devote as much time to learning how to play it, as he would require to master any wind-instrument of the present day. A different lip-technique and a strange finger-technique would have to be

---

[1] Francœur-Choron, p. 70.
[2] Serpents, like old bassoons, are very liable to be worm-eaten.

acquired, and the ear would have to be readjusted to appreciate a shade of tone-colour which is neither that of any brass instrument nor of any wood-wind instrument now in use. As far as it is possible to judge, the tone-quality of the open notes of a serpent is quite pure, but it has a dry and somewhat choked quality which is without the metallic ring of brass-instrument-tone as we now know it.

After leaving the mouthpiece, the tube of the serpent expands immediately at a much greater rate than it does on any brass instrument ; there is no narrow or cylindrical portion at the beginning of the air-passage. At a distance of about 18 inches from the end of the mouthpiece the diameter of the tube is doubled ; at that distance along the tube the bore of the tuba has hardly yet begun to expand. At the half-way point the bore of the serpent has again doubled its diameter, and the expansion continues at the same rate till it reaches the lower end of the tube. The bore of the serpent is about $2\frac{1}{2}$ inches at the same point where a trombone is only about $\frac{1}{2}$ an inch wide. It is in the vastly different proportions of their respective tubes that the difference between serpent tone-quality and the usual brass-instrument tone-quality lies ; it is not its wooden body that gives the serpent its " woody " tone ; it is its capacious interior.

When the finger-holes of the serpent are opened, the tone-quality deteriorates, for the instrument has two acoustical faults ; the holes, which have to be closed by the fingers, are much too small, and, because they had to be placed within reach of the fingers, they are not situated far enough apart. The result of these flaws in its nature is reflected in the quality, the unevenness, and the uncertain intonation of the fingered sounds of the serpent. Of course, it was the business of the players to cover up these deficiencies as far as was possible, to smooth out the unevenness and adjust the intonation by a skilful use of the lips. When Berlioz remarked that three notes on the serpent, namely *d-a-d'*,[1] are more " powerful " than the others, he was picking out the 2nd, 3rd and 4th open notes of its harmonic

[1] The customary French notation ; in real sounds *c-g-c'*.

series, sounded with all the finger-holes closed ; the " startling inequalities of tone, which its players should apply themselves with all care to overcome as much as possible ", were certainly inherent faults of the serpent, but when Berlioz describes its "frigid and abominable blaring" and its "essentially barbarous" tone-quality, he was surely giving free play to an exaggerated eloquence which was as much part of his own nature as inequalities of tone were part of the nature of the serpent. Since Berlioz expatiated on the horrors of serpent-tone, most other writers on orchestration have indulged in uncomplimentary or facetious remarks [1] about an instrument which many of them can never have heard properly played, but which is specified in the scores of orchestral works, operas and oratorios written during the second quarter of last century by such composers as Berlioz (!), Mendelssohn and Wagner.

The serpent has to its credit a useful career of something like 300 years ; it should not be regarded as a poor imitation of a euphonium, a bass-tuba or a trombone ; it was a bass-cornett, and its tone-quality was its own, one which even the modern orchestra with all its wealth of resource and variety cannot now produce.

The serpent lingered after the middle of last century in remote parts of this country, and till more recent times in the country Churches of France and Belgium. Its voice no longer attracts the ear, but when displayed in a glass case with other relics of a bygone time, its strange black twisted form and red-painted interior never fails to attract the eye of the visitor.

(c) Bass-horn or Russian Bassoon

(F.) Basson Russe. Serpent droit. Serpent basson. Serpent Forveille. Serpent Anglais. Ophibaryton.

(G.) Basshorn. Englisches basshorn. Russisches fagott. Fagottserpent.

According to Gerber's Lexikon (1792), it was a musician of Lille named Régibo who was the first to design a serpent in

---

[1] " The whole instrument presented the appearance of a dishevelled drain-pipe which was suffering internally " (Forsyth).

bassoon-form, about the year 1780. From a later edition of the same Lexikon (1812) we learn that in 1800 Alexander Frichot, a French musician then living in London, designed a metal serpent in a similar shape, and that his idea was carried out by the London instrument-maker J. Astor.[1] Frichot named his instrument "bass-horn" and published a "complete scale and gamut" for it. During the first half of last century many such more or less straightened serpents were made in England, France, Belgium and Germany under various names which will here be included under the general term "bass-horn".

The object of straightening and doubling the tube of the serpent was evidently in order to make the instrument more convenient to hold and play while marching, and also to make it generally stronger and more compact, for the curved serpent was neither comfortable to handle, nor strong.

The bass-horns were largely used in military bands up to about the middle of last century, and were the successors of the serpent only in the sense that they were improved forms of that instrument, but they did not by any means displace the serpent altogether; for some time the two were contemporaries, which in their later days had to give way to the ophicleide. After a losing fight, which was carried on by the ophicleide for some time after the mid-century, all three instruments were finally displaced by the tubas, bombardons and other valved instruments which began to appear soon after 1830, and, in the course of thirty more years or so, drove the serpent and its improved fellows into the ranks of the unemployed.

A number of different models were made during the rather short period when bass-horns were in use, and the proportions of wood and metal used in making them varied considerably. Some were all-wood except the crook, while others were entirely of metal; on some the body is of wood, and the crook, bell and joints are of brass. Generally the instrument consists of two straight tubes lying more or less close together, and connected at the lower end by either a bassoon-like butt or a U-joint

[1] A specimen by Astor is preserved in the Paris coll., No. 1190.

of some sort. The wide tube is conical, and ends in an expanding bell much wider than the lower end of the serpent tube, and sometimes fashioned like a snake's or a dragon's head. The narrow end is always prolonged in a curved or coiled brass crook about 3 feet long, into the narrow end of which the mouthpiece is inserted. The bass-horns generally retain the six small finger-holes of the serpent, and these are situated in two groups, both on the narrower of the two straight tubes, the L. hand group being above the R. hand group. Most bass-horns were provided with three or four keys additional to the six finger-holes, but on some of the most advanced types every note-hole was controlled by a key.

As there was never any standard design, it is hardly feasible to describe fully every one of the various models of bass-horns turned out by a number of makers and " inventors " who worked during a period when so many wind instruments were being made more or less experimentally with the object of finding out the most practicable design. The bass-horns, however, may be roughly divided into two types, which may be distinguished as " English bass-horns " and " Russian bassoons ". On the former, the two straight tubes emerge like a narrow V from a small butt ; on the latter the two tubes lie close together in a parallel formation, and are either partially or wholly bored in the same piece of wood. Continental instruments were commonly fashioned of wood on the bassoon model, and English bass-horns are generally all-metal and V-shaped.

Most of the Russian bassoons have a regular bassoon-butt, in which the three lower holes for the R. hand are bored ; from this butt emerge a bell-joint, and a wing-joint which contains the three upper holes for the L. hand. (Pl. XXVII, A and C.) Others are not jointed, and the body of the instrument becomes practically one large butt. On another model, the *Serpent Forveille*, the narrower tube soon forsakes the wooden butt, and performs some metallic contortions of its own before settling down to join the crook. The English bass-horn model is not so variable ; it consists of a rather gracefully curved metal crook, a straight down-tube with six raised finger-holes, a very short butt, and a bell-tube with considerable expansion at the wide end. (Pl. XXVII, B.) This type was generally made of copper with brass fittings, but at least one of these bass-horns was made of wood, and was given a bulb-bell something like that of a *cor anglais*.[1]

Considering the short career of these instruments, it is surprising how many different shapes were tried, and surely never before had makers such a splendid opportunity of displaying their fancy as when designing fantastic bells for the Russian bassoons. The painted serpents' heads with bared teeth and flapping tongues were no doubt intended to add a certain frightfulness to the appearance of a military band, and may have been calculated to discourage an enemy even more than the sound of the band.[2] Bass-horns were commonly made, like the serpent, in 8 feet C; they are said to occur also in B flat, and exceptionally in low F or E. Some slightly smaller instruments, tunable by means of a slide in the crook into D or E flat, are also extant. (Pl. XXVII, C.)

The bore of the tube, although it would certainly be classed as wide, is not quite so wide as that of the serpent; the longer crook increases in width more gradually than the short crook of the serpent. The following are the approximate measurements of the bore on two particular specimens :

	(a) *A Belgian serpent.*	(b) *An English bass-horn*
At the 6th finger-hole —	$2\frac{1}{4}$ inches	$1\frac{1}{2}$ inches
One foot from the bell —	3 inches	$2\frac{1}{4}$ inches

The fingering is the same on the bass-horn as on the serpent, and the keys, although not necessarily operated by the same fingers, are those usually found on three- or four-keyed serpents :

B natural—situated above the uppermost finger-hole.

F sharp—situated between the two groups of finger-holes.

---

[1] Made by F. Pace. Photo, R.M.E. Cat., pl. vii, fig. c ; now in the Nettlefold coll.

[2] Several examples are shown by Kastner (*Manuel*), pl. xiii, but they are inaccurately described.

D sharp—on or near the butt.

C sharp—on the bell-tube.

The bass-horns inherited the acoustical weaknesses of the serpent, for the two were practically the same except for the straightened tube of the newer instrument. As on the serpent, the open notes are the purest and most resonant, but the quality deteriorates when the finger-holes are opened.

Although the particular form of the instrument designed by Régibo cannot be identified, some information is available regarding Frichot's bass-horn. It seems that Frichot left London, and was settled at Lisieux in France by 1806 ; in that year he presented his instrument in Paris under the name *Basse-cor*, and in 1810 it was patented as the *Basse-trompette*.[1] Choron, in 1813, gave some astounding particulars about Frichot's instrument, which by then seems to have been renamed *Tromba*. This all-metal bass-horn had six finger-holes and four keys, and was credited with a compass of four and a half octaves, fully chromatic, from A, to *d'''*. It could be used as a bass, a tenor, an alto or a treble instrument, and could combine all the advantages of a serpent, a trombone, a horn and a trumpet in its wonderful self. Choron, however, explains that no one player could be expected to cover all of that extended compass, and that for the low register a serpent mouthpiece, for the middle register an enlarged horn mouthpiece, and for the higher register a trumpet mouthpiece must be used.

Several other instruments which were half serpent and half ophicleide appeared from about 1820 to 1850. Streitwolf of Göttingen produced his *Chromatisches Basshorn* in 1820 ; this was made with two straight wooden tubes and metal bell, U-joint and crook ; the twelve note-holes were evenly distributed, and were controlled by ten or eleven keys. The *Serpent Forveille* (Paris, early 19th century) was half wood and half metal, with six finger-holes, and from two to five keys ; the three upper finger-holes were in the narrower tube, and the three lower in the butt of the larger wooden tube. Of the *Ophimonokleide* (1828)

[1] French patent No. 404, December 1810.

and the *Ophibaterion*, both French types, little is known, but the *Ophibariton, Serpent droit* and *Serpent basson* are known to have been of the bassoon-like type which was the most common form of bass-horn on the continent.

In an English tutor for the bass-horn (*c.* 1840) it is claimed that the " high notes are superior to the serpent ", and that the copper instrument has a " soft tone ". With a narrower bore the tone would probably gain some resonance, and lose some of the dry quality of the serpent, and the upper register would no doubt be more easily accessible and more amenable.

The bass-horn, however, was too much of a serpent to survive any longer than its progenitor; so when the ophicleide with its large and well-placed note-holes, its more resonant tone and more certain intonation presented itself as a rival bass voice, the two older types meekly retired hand in hand to the lumber room or the glass case.

Of course, Berlioz had not a good word to say for the Russian bassoon or bass-horn; in his opinion it "might be withdrawn from the family of wind instruments without the smallest injury to Art " ; and when he adds that D and E flat are the best notes of the Russian bassoon, and that " only detestable effects are to be obtained from shakes on this instrument ", what could it do but slink away into retirement to ponder over the uncertainty of life and fame. Only thirty-five years previously Choron had said that it possessed of all wind instruments " la plus grande intensité du son ".

Several composers of distinction had written parts for the serpent before it became obsolete, but the bass-horn was rarely allowed to join the orchestral family.[1] Perhaps this was because the serpent had a long record of respectability behind it ; for over two hundred years it had been a regular Church-goer, and only in its declining years did it join the army ; the bass-horn, on the other hand, never went to Church ; it spent its short life in the rougher society of army bandsmen ; or perhaps it was because composers were afraid that the bass-horn would

[1] Spohr's 9th symphony includes a part for the bass-horn.

turn up for the performance of a symphony or an oratorio with a fantastically coloured serpent's head.

(d) THE KEYED BUGLE

(G.) Klappenhorn. Klappenflügelhorn. Klapphorn.
(F.) Cor à clefs. Bugle à clefs. Trompette à clefs.
(I.) Cornetta a chiavi.

The first attempt to apply the shortening-hole system with keys to a brass lip-reed instrument appears to have been made about 1760 by one Kölbel of St. Petersburg, whose keyed horn was apparently a failure. In 1801, the Viennese trumpeter Weidinger made a similar experiment with the trumpet ; this instrument enjoyed only a limited success. Applied to the wider tube of a bugle, the shortening-hole system was much more successful, and from about 1810, till even after the middle of last century, the keyed-bugle, Kent bugle or Kent horn, was popular in smaller theatre orchestras, military and brass bands, and as an amateur's instrument.

The initiator of the keyed bugle was an Irish bandmaster named Joseph Halliday, who, in 1810, was granted a patent for " certain improvements in the Musical Instrument called the Bugle Horn ". Halliday's scheme consisted of five note-holes, each controlled by a closed key, cut in the tube of a bugle folded in the usual trumpet-form with two large U-bends. By opening the key-holes, the inventor claimed that he could sound "twenty-five separate tones ", namely, a complete chromatic succession from the second to the eighth open note of the 4 feet bugle tube. Two key-holes were pierced on the L. side of the wide bell-tube, and a third penetrated the upper side of the same tube. When the key-levers were depressed, the opened note-holes shortened the sounding-length of the instrument, and gave the first three semitones of the chromatic scale, namely, c' sharp, d' and d' sharp, also three or four of the harmonics of these notes. These three keys were operated, respectively, by the little finger, the first finger and the thumb of the R. hand, while the second finger lay over a brass tunnel or bridge which covered the middle of the d' key-lever. The two remaining holes were pierced just round the bend of the tube, and the keys controlling them were operated by the thumb and first finger of the L. hand. The fourth hole gave e' and its fifth (b'), and the fifth hole gave f' natural. The f' sharp was produced by opening the d' sharp and the f' holes. A chart accompanying Halliday's Patent [1] specification shows the fingering for the chromatic scale from c' to c'''.

It was, however, the six-keyed bugle that became the popular instrument in the first half of last century, and which must have been made in large numbers in England, France, Belgium and Germany. On the six-keyed instrument the additional hole was cut in the upper side of the bell-tube, about 4 or 5 inches from the end, and was controlled by an *open* key operated by the R. little finger; when the hole was closed by pressing down the key-lever, the pitch of the instrument was lowered a semitone, and the bugle then gave the harmonic series of B natural. The open key was provided with a screw-device [2] by means of which it could be fixed in the closed position if desired. A scale from an English tutor for the six-keyed bugle or Kent bugle [3] appears to date from between 1830 and 1845. (See Fingering Chart, No. 11.)

Most of the blackened and battered keyed bugles which are still to be found scattered about in this country, are six-keyed instruments made of copper, with brass keys and fittings. Instruments entirely of brass occur less commonly. These bugles are in 4 feet C, and were usually provided with a small circular crook which lowered the fundamental pitch to B flat. The keys are mounted in brass saddles, and have flat flaps and leathers, but some later instruments are found with more or less cupped keys filled with stuffed pads, and may be mounted in pillars standing on a footplate. A brass rim or " bush " was commonly soldered round the edge of the key-hole in order to

---

[1] No. 3334. May 5, 1810.   [2] (G.) *Stellschraube.*
[3] Named after the Duke of Kent ; also called Regent's Bugle.

accommodate the flat surface of the key-flap, but cases also occur in which the key-flap was slightly rounded to fit the curved surface of the tube. A white composite metal was sometimes used to make the keys and other fittings of the more recent instruments, and a single tuning-slide (sometimes fitted with a rack-and-pinion device) is found on some of the later and more expensive keyed bugles; otherwise the tuning was managed by means of short " bits " inserted between the mouthpiece and the crook. (Pl. XXVIII, A, B.)

The bore of the keyed bugle is about $\frac{7}{16}$ at its narrowest point, increasing steadily to about 1 inch in the middle of the last bend ; a further increase in width ends with a bell measuring about 6 inches across the mouth. The widest note-hole is nearest the bell, and the diameter of the holes decreases progressively from about $1\frac{1}{4}$ to $\frac{9}{16}$ inch, except that the second hole (counting from the bell) is about $\frac{1}{8}$ inch smaller than the third. The interior of the mouthpiece differs very little from that of the ordinary bugle of the present day ; the cup is rather deeper than on the old trumpets, and the diameter at the lip varies, very much as it does now, round about $\frac{5}{8}$ of an inch. The mouthpieces were commonly of cast brass, often with a silver rim round the lip ; occasionally they occur made entirely of ivory or bone.

A number of keyed bugles with seven keys are extant ; the extra key is often an additional e' flat key controlling a hole cut just a little further up the tube than the d'' sharp hole, and worked by the first finger of the L. hand ; [1] this key was also used to make certain shakes. Some eight-keyed bugles are provided with two shake-keys for the L. little finger, one of which was to be used when the instrument was in C, and the other when it was crooked in B flat. (Pl. XXVIII, C.) A few keyed bugles with one, two, nine and ten keys occur exceptionally, and an Italian instrument in the Heyer collection at Leipzig [2] is said to have no less than twelve keys.

[1] In his *Méthode de Bugle ou Trompette à clefs* (*Klapp-horn-schule*), Noblet provides a fingering chart for an instrument with separate E flat and D sharp keys. [2] No. 1744.

In addition to the ordinary soprano keyed bugles in C and B flat,[1] there were sopranino instruments in high E flat and F. Others in high D, D flat and in B natural are mentioned in various catalogues ; these may possibly have been constructed in those keys, or may be the ordinary instruments according to varying standards of pitch. If in sound condition, a keyed bugle will yield open notes of quite good quality, whether the large key near the bell is open or closed. When the keys are raised, the quality and intonation seems to deteriorate more or less progressively, and the tone becomes rather husky. However, as the instrument is now no longer played, it may be that any verdict which now condemns its tone-quality may be unfairly based. The following are views by contemporaneous writers who must have heard the keyed bugle properly played : Berlioz (1848) — " its quality does not differ from that of the simple bugle ". Von Gontershausen (1855)—"tender, woolly tone ". Gevaert (1863) — " son timbre est à la fois puissant et moëlleux ".

During its life of about fifty years the keyed bugle flourished as a useful melodist in military bands, and for some time as the only soprano melodist in brass bands. According to Berlioz it was used in some Italian orchestras,[2] and parts for it may be found in a few opera scores written during the first half of last century.[3] In Germany and Austria the *flügelhorn*, which was its successor in direct line, had largely replaced the keyed bugle before the mid-century, but it was the advent and progress of the valved cornet which gradually brought about the decline of the instrument in England and France, and not till some time after the middle of last century was the process complete. In respect of its powers of playing *legato*, its ready articulation and agility in execution, the keyed bugle is said to have at least equalled, if not surpassed, the contemporary valved instruments.

[1] There is evidence that it was also used in A.
[2] Berlioz may have been thinking of the keyed trumpet.
[3] Bishop's " Guy Mannering " (1816) ; Meyerbeer, " Robert le Diable " (1831).

(e) The Ophicleide

(G.) Ophikleïde.   Harmoniebass.   Klappenbass.
(F.) Ophicléide.   Contre-basse d'harmonie.   (I.) Oficleide.

In 1817 Jean-Hilaire Asté, a Paris brass instrument maker, better known as Halary, submitted to the French Académie des Beaux-Arts a group of conical, keyed brass instruments, which he eventually patented in 1821.[1]   The group comprised the following :

(a) *Clavitube.*—Keyed bugles [2] in high F or E flat, also in 4 feet C or B flat, made in trumpet-form.
(b) *Quinticlave.*— Alto ophicleides in 6 feet F or E flat, made in bassoon-form.
(c) *Ophicleide.*—Bass ophicleides in 8 feet C or B flat, also contrabass in F, made in bassoon-form.

Of these, the *clavitubes* or keyed bugles had already been known since 1810, and in the patent specification Halary remarked that the *quinticlaves* and ophicleides had already been submitted to the *Académie* in 1811 by M. Dumas under the names *basses et contrebasses guerrières.*[3]

The alto ophicleide enjoyed only a rather precarious existence, and retired as soon as its status was challenged by the valved tenor horns ; the bass ophicleide was almost immediately successful, and soon became popular in military and brass bands, also in some opera orchestras ; in Germany it gave way to the valved tubas or bombardons before the mid-century, but in France, Italy and England it managed to survive in competition with the tuba till well into the third quarter of last century.

The ophicleide was in every way the superior of the serpent and bass-horn. Because they were closed by keys instead of by

[1] French patent No. 1849, March 1821. (Description, diagrams and fingering charts.)   Catrufo (1832) states that Halary invented the keyed bugle, alto and bass ophicleides.

[2] These instruments, although described in the patent specification as *trompettes à clefs*, were keyed bugles with a wide conical bore.

[3] These are described as bass and contrabass clarinets in *Le Moniteur Universel* (April 19, 1811) and in the *Archives des Découvertes* (1810).

the fingers, it was possible to make the note-holes large and quite adequate for the width of the tube ; also, the holes could be placed evenly along the tube, instead of being situated close together within reach of the fingers. The tone of the ophicleide was therefore much freer, more even and more resonant than that of the serpent.

The bore of the ophicleide is strictly conical, and wide for its length; starting at about $\frac{7}{16}$ of an inch at the narrow end, the tube widens steadily without interruption and terminates in a bell measuring from $7\frac{1}{2}$ to $9\frac{1}{2}$ inches across the mouth. The mouthpiece fits into the narrow end of a detachable coiled or folded crook which is inserted in the top or narrower end of a straight and widening down-tube; this is united to the still widening up-tube by a U-bend at the bottom, so that the two main tubes lie in parallel formation about half an inch apart. The following are approximate and average measurements taken from a number of actual instruments :

	Length of Crook	Length of Main Tube	Bore at Wide End of Crook	Bore at U-bend	Width of Bell-Mouth
In 8 feet C	2 feet 6 ins.	5 feet 6 ins.			
In 9 „ B flat	3 „ 3 „	5 „ 9 „	$1\frac{1}{4}$ ins.	$2\frac{1}{16}$ ins.	8 ins.

The earliest ophicleides were provided with nine note-holes and keys, of which six were on the wider, and three on the narrower of the two parallel tubes. The levers of the keys were so contrived as to bring the fingerplates together in two groups, one for each hand ; the R. hand or lower group comprised five keys, and the L. hand or upper group consisted of four keys ; only the little finger of the L. hand was not used. The note-holes were all covered by closed keys, except the largest hole, which was situated about a foot from the bell-mouth ; this is an open key which, when closed, lowers the pitch of the harmonic series a semitone ; thus, an ophicleide in C will give about eight open notes of the fundamental (8 feet C) when none of the keys are touched, but when the large open key is closed, the instrument gives the corresponding series, based on the fundamental B,, a semitone lower. Starting from the bell, the keys were generally arranged as follows :

Ophicleide in C

No. 1. Open key, L. hand first finger $\begin{cases} \text{B, when closed} \\ \text{C when open} \end{cases}$

No. 2. Closed key, L. hand second finger, C sharp when open

No. 3. Closed key, L. hand thumb, D when open

No. 4. Closed key, L. hand third finger, D sharp when open

No. 5. Closed key, R. hand thumb, E when open

No. 6. Closed key, R. hand little finger, F when open

On the wider tube.

No. 7. Closed key, R. hand third finger, G when open

No. 8. Closed key, R. hand second finger, A when open

No. 9. Closed key, R. hand first finger, B flat when open

On the narrower tube.

Both thumb-keys are on the back of the instrument (nearest the player), that for the L. thumb being a cross-key. A screw is usually found in the first lever of the large open key by means of which this key may be fixed in the closed position ; this was evidently intended only to guard the key against damage when the instrument was not in use; it could not be used (like a crook) as a device for lowering the pitch of the instrument, for the key in question must be open when the other keys are used.[1] The keys shown in the above list provide for a series of ten fundamentals in chromatic succession, excepting the F sharp and G sharp ; these two notes, however, could be produced on nine-keyed ophicleides by playing the semitone above with the large open key closed. On the later and more complete instrument (1822), there are separate note-holes and keys for the F sharp and G sharp in the fundamental octave ; the hole for the former is situated on the U-bend, and the key is worked by the R. little finger ; the G sharp hole is placed in its appropriate position between the G and A holes, and the key is usually controlled by the R. third finger. On the more advanced instruments the levers of the F sharp and G sharp keys generally

---

[1] A similar device is found on the large open key of the keyed bugle.

act on the levers of the keys immediately below them, so that
the preceding note-hole is automatically opened when either key
is pressed down. (Pl. XXIX.)

The complete eleven-keyed ophicleide was therefore provided
with a series of twelve fundamentals in chromatic succession,
namely, every semitone from B, to B flat. On each of the
fundamentals the usual series of harmonics could be sounded,
but in actual practice only the harmonics of the lower fundamentals were used. The following shows the series of harmonics
or open notes which, with their fundamentals, gave the instrument a complete chromatic scale covering a compass of just over
three octaves (the seventh note of the harmonic series is not
included ; it is out of tune with the scale and, moreover, is quite
unnecessary) :

No keys, seven open notes of the series on C.
First key closed, seven open notes of the series on B.
Second key opened, six open notes of the series on C sharp.
Second and third keys opened, six open notes of the series on D.
Second, third and fourth keys opened, six open notes of the series on
    D sharp.
Fifth key opened, two open notes of the series on E.
Fifth and sixth keys opened, two open notes of the series on F.
F sharp key and sixth key opened, one note (fundamental) F sharp.
Seventh key opened, one note (fundamental) G.
G sharp key and seventh key opened, one note (fundamental)
    G sharp.
Eighth key opened, one note (fundamental) A.
Ninth key opened, one note (fundamental) B flat.

It will be noticed that when the 3rd, 4th and 6th keys are
opened, the keys just below each of them are also held open ;
similarly the F sharp and G sharp are sounded with the preceding note-holes open. In the upper register, where the harmonics lie fairly close together, several alternative fingerings
are available ; for example, the high F sharp could be taken as
the sixth open note of the fundamental B,, or as the fifth open
note of the fundamental D ; or the high D sharp might likewise
be a harmonic of either B, or D sharp. In this respect the

practice of individual players no doubt differed, and slight differences in fingering charts rather suggest that this was the case ;
it is also likely that some instruments would give a better note
with one particular fingering than with another. In general,
however, the best sounds are those produced as harmonics of
the fundamentals of the largest note-holes situated nearest to
the bell.

Many old ophicleides may now be seen displayed in various
collections, and more or less battered specimens can still be
picked up in unexpected places in this country. On the whole,
the surviving instruments differ from one another only in detail.
The shape of the crook, for example, may vary considerably ;
it may be once-coiled, twice-coiled, or it may be folded so as
to include a U-shaped tuning-slide. The end of the crook which
enters the straight down-tube may also be graduated for tuning,
and a tightening screw is then usually provided. Tuning " bits "
were also used. Two projections from the body of the instrument, placed so as to come between the thumb and first finger
of each hand, help to give support, and a ring is provided for a
cord or strap which is attached to the player, and takes some of
the weight off his hands or arms. The keys are usually mounted
on short pillars on footplates, and on some more recent instruments cupped keys with stuffed pads, rod-axles and needle
springs are to be found.

By far the most common are the ordinary bass ophicleides
in either C or B flat ;[1] altos in F or E flat,[2] and contrabasses
an octave lower, occur more rarely. A wonderful specimen
of the contrabass in E flat (*Ophicléide monstre*), with a gaping
serpent's head and the crook coiled round its throat, is depicted
in the catalogue of the Brussels collection (No. 1248). A few
wooden ophicleides are preserved,[3] but the large majority are
of sheet brass, strengthened at the joints by sleeves and stays.

---

[1] Berlioz mentions one in A flat.

[2] " *Timbre est généralement désagréable* " (Caussinus, *Méthode*, Paris,
c. 1840).

[3] Berlin, 3093 ; Paris, 1195 ; Brussels, 2454.

The ophicleide, for all its robust sound, was by no means a physically strong instrument ; the rather thin sheet brass is easily crushed, and the projecting key-work almost seems to invite damage.[1] The mouthpieces, usually of brass, but sometimes of ivory, measure round about 1 inch or a little more across the cup, and the latter is generally gently conical and horn-like, or slightly cupped. Caussinus gave exact measurements in millimetres for a rather funnel-shaped ophicleide mouthpiece in his *Méthode*, and recommended that two-thirds should be placed on the upper, and one third on the lower lip.

The tone of the ophicleide, when properly played, is full, resonant, and not unlike that of a euphonium ; the instrument is also capable of giving forth quite pleasant and gentle tones, and should not be supposed to be a roaring barbarous monster as is suggested by many who have described it after the period of its decline. Berlioz was (for him) not altogether uncomplimentary when describing the tone of the ophicleide, although it is true that he, or his translator (!) was perhaps being a little unkind when he stated that " the quality of these low sounds is rude ".[2] Some of the terms which have been applied to this and other obsolete types seem to be merely the outcome of an irresistible desire to be facetious at the expense of instruments which at the time of writing were reckoned out-of-date or " early Victorian " ; such epithets as " coarse ", " bellowing ", or the nickname " chromatic bullock ", could only be justified when the ophicleide was badly played, and could be applied with equal truthfulness to any roughly-played tuba or euphonium of the present day. Spontini (1819), Mendelssohn, Meyerbeer, Schumann, Berlioz, Wagner, Verdi and many other composers of note wrote parts for the ophicleide round about the middle of last century ; in some modern reprints of their full scores, " bass tuba " is substituted for " ophicleide ". The occurrence

---

[1] " These instruments (keyed bugles and ophicleides) do not suit an open air band. A few particles of dust (may) put them out of action " (Miller, *The Military Band*, 1912).

[2] See *Instrumentation*, first English translation, 1858.

of " ophicleide " in French scores of that period, however, did not necessarily indicate the keyed instrument. From as early as 1844, instruments made in the form of an ophicleide, but provided with piston-valve mechanism, were constructed in France, and still retained the old name ; [1] elsewhere these would have been called tubas or bombardons. Both Kastner and Caussinus describe the *Ophicléide à 3 pistons ou Bombardon* in their tutors published in Paris about 1840–1845, and a tutor for the ophicleide by Garnier (Paris, *c.* 1845) shows the instrument with three piston valves. The valved instrument was said by Caussinus to be " généralement moins juste que l'autre ".

[1] Raoux exhibited an ophicleide with three valves in 1844 (Pierre). In 1863 Gevaert made no distinction between *Saxhorn alto*, *Bugle alto* and *Ophicleide alto*.

FLÜGELHORNS, SAXHORNS, TUBAS AND KINDRED INSTRUMENTS

(a) The Flügelhorn

(G.) Flügelhorn. Bügelhorn. (F.) Grand bugle. Bugle-à-pistons. Saxhorn contralto. (I.) Flicornò soprano.

THE flügelhorn (sometimes written flugel horn) is well described as a valved bugle ; it is the successor of the keyed bugle, and differs from that instrument mainly in that it is provided with valve-mechanism instead of with note-holes and keys. The tone is better and more even on the valved instrument, for valve-produced notes are always superior to those produced by open side-holes. The tube of the flügelhorn is about $4\frac{1}{2}$ feet long ; it is therefore in B flat, in unison with the cornet and modern trumpet in the same key. The bore at the narrow end is about the same as that of a trumpet, namely, from $\frac{6}{16}$ to $\frac{7}{16}$ of an inch, but the gradual expansion of the bore is much more marked than on either the trumpet or the cornet ; at about 12 inches from the bell the tube of the flügelhorn has increased to rather over an inch, whereas the cornet or trumpet tubes are generally under $\frac{3}{4}$ of an inch at the corresponding point. In spite of the valves, the conical bore of the bugle is fairly well preserved in the flügelhorn, because the air-passage enters the valve-system only a few inches from the mouthpiece, leaving the greater part of the tube to expand steadily without interruption. The passage through the valves is more or less cylindrical (about $\frac{7}{16}$ inch) and the remaining portion of the tube, measuring about 3 feet 6 inches or more, then expands till it ends in a bell of about $5\frac{1}{2}$ to 6 inches across the mouth. The very considerable expansion of the bore from the last bend of the tube to the bell, is a feature of the keyed bugle which is not always preserved on the modern flügelhorn.

Unlike the cornet, the main tube of the flügelhorn enters the valve-system at the first valve and leaves it at the third valve. English and French instruments are made with piston mechanism, and those made in Germany are provided with rotary valves. (Pl. XXVIII, E.)

The proper mouthpiece for the flügelhorn is a rather deep cone, perhaps a shade wider and deeper, but otherwise not unlike the early cornet mouthpiece. Although a U-shaped tuning-slide has sometimes been incorporated in the main tube of the instrument, the more common form is a single-slide at the narrow end ; the end of this slide receives the mouthpiece, and the slide is held firmly in position by a screw which clamps the split end of the outer tube over the inner sliding-tube.

The open sounds used on the flügelhorn are from the second to the eighth note of the harmonic series. With a favourable mouthpiece the fundamental can easily be sounded, or even some valve-produced notes below the fundamental, but as they are hardly ever demanded, the flügelhorn is usually treated as having the same downward range as the cornet. Owing to its wider bore and deeper mouthpiece, the tone is not so bright as that of the cornet, but in spite of a greater mellowness it is nearer to cornet-quality than to French horn-quality.

The valved flügelhorn seems to have had its birth in Vienna, about 1830 or soon after. Kastner (1848) depicts some of the early types, and calls them *Flugelhorn de Vienne* or *Flugelhorn austrichien*. The earliest model was evidently in trumpet-form, rather shortened, with the bell pointing forwards, and the valve-mechanism was either the Vienna-valve or the rotary action. The first of these was gradually given up in the third quarter of last century in favour of the rotary type. In France the flügelhorn was practically recreated when the *saxhorn contralto* in B flat, the smallest but one of the family devised by Ad. Sax soon after 1840, made its appearance. Like all others of the group, Sax made his *contralto* at first in the upright tuba-form, with short thick valves, but later on the higher members of the group were also made in the more usual trumpet-form, with pistons, or (more rarely) with rotary valves. (Pl. XXVIII, D.)

The flügelhorn has been much used in continental military and brass bands; in Germany and Austria it has been assigned the parts which in English bands would be taken by the cornets. In this country the flügelhorn came as a very welcome addition to the brass band about the middle of last century, when the competitive festivals came into being, and it still holds a firmly established position in our brass bands.

In addition to the common instrument in B flat, there have been flügelhorns in C and in A, also a *saxhorn contralto* in A flat. In France a soprano saxhorn in high E flat, and in Germany a flügelhorn in the same key, has served the same purpose as the high E flat cornet has done in this country. (Pl. XXVIII, F.)

In Germany and Austria, the word *flügelhorn* (or *bügelhorn*) is sometimes used in a wider sense to denote not only the B flat instrument, but also the entire family of valved bugles or saxhorns, from the soprano down to the bass.

Another instrument, hardly distinguishable from the flügelhorn except in appearance, was the Koenighorn, "invented" by a well-known cornet-virtuoso named Koenig about 1855. The tubing is coiled in circular fashion like a small French horn, but the bell points directly downwards to the ground. The Koenighorn was made in 4 feet C with a short shank, and could be lowered to B flat or A by means of circular crooks. Starting at the narrow end of the crook or shank with a bore similar to that of the cornet, the bore quickly increases to a shade over $\frac{7}{16}$ of an inch at the point where the tube enters the third valve; remaining cylindrical through the valves, the bore then expands, as on the flügelhorn, to about 6 inches at the mouth of the bell. Tuning was managed by a single-slide at the end of the crook or shank. Koenighorns were made about 1890 with Boosey's compensating valves, and by the end of the century were more or less obsolete. (Pl. XXVIII, G.)

(b) TENOR HORN, E FLAT SAXHORN AND SIMILAR INSTRUMENTS

(G.) Althorn. Altkornett. Altsaxhorn.
(F.) Saxhorn alto. Bugle alto. Cor alto.
(I.) Flicorno contralto.

About 1820–1830, when the valve-system began to be known to makers and others concerned with brass instruments at the various European centres where these were made, it was not long before a crop of valved instruments came into being which were neither trumpets, French horns nor trombones. In general they were instruments of bugle or ophicleide proportions, with a bore wider than any of the older brass instruments, yet, unlike the flügelhorn which could look to the bugle as its parent, and the cornet which was the valved successor of the plain cornet, some of these lower-pitched types had no ancestor in direct line. The bass instruments, it is true, could look to the ophicleide as their prototype, but the intermediate size, the altos or tenors in E flat (a 5th below the cornet and flügelhorn), could produce no visible parent, unless it was the not very successful alto ophicleide, itself a mere upstart and unfit for parentage. Failing the alto ophicleide, they can only be regarded as parentless offspring which came into existence as one of the consequences of the invention of the lengthening valve-system.

At the time when these instruments began to appear, the only brass instruments pitched in that particular E flat were the old trumpets (when crooked in E flat) and the alto trombone. Both of these were mainly cylindrical and narrow-bored ; the new-comers were all largely conical and wide-bored. It was no doubt on account of their conical bore and deep mouthpieces that the word horn (or *cor*) was generally incorporated in the various names by which they were known. Otherwise the nomenclature of this class of instrument has always been, and still is, illogical and confusing. There is no agreement as to whether they are altos or tenors, nor whether they are horns, bugles or cornets. In Germany and France they are reckoned to be altos, in England they are tenors, and in Italy they are sometimes contraltos.

All these valved tenors (or altos) had important features in common; they all sounded, like the cornet and flügelhorn, from the second to the eighth note of their harmonic series, with, of course, an extension downwards by means of the valves to a diminished fifth below the second open note; the fundamental was within reach, but was not expected of them. Rather deep conical mouthpiece-cups, in some cases nearly approaching the depth of the French horn mouthpiece, were used, and gave a certain mellowness to the tone-quality. The valves were placed near to the narrow end of the tube, so that the expansion of the bore might be uninterrupted from the point where it left the third valve right down to the end of the bell. The width of the bore, it is true, varied a little, but all were proportionately wider than the trumpet, horn or trombone. They might be anything from large cornets to small tubas. The way the tube was folded, and the direction in which the bell was directed, has varied considerably; for some time they were made like small ophicleides, or in tuba-form with the bell pointing upwards; a little later in Germany and Austria they were coiled in an oval tuba-form with the bell directed slantingly upwards; others were in trumpet-form with the bell pointing forwards, and one type, which was specially intended to replace French horns in military bands, was coiled in horn-form with the bell turned downwards; on some less common varieties the bell has pointed at various angles, or even lay over the player's shoulder. Some of the tenor horns appeared singly under various names, while others were members of homogeneous groups or families ranging from sopranino to contrabass.

The earliest of these various alto or tenor instruments was probably the German *Althorn* or *Altkornett*, which appeared in Berlin round about 1830. According to Kalkbrenner, W. Wieprecht introduced the E flat *Altkornett* into Prussian military bands in 1833. Soon after 1835, the Berlin maker C. W. Moritz made similar instruments in an elongated tuba-form. From that time onwards, and till nearly the end of the century, several single or group-instruments were made on similar principles, and with the same range or compass, but differing more or less slightly in bore and tone-quality. The *clavicor alto* (Paris) dates from 1837 ; the *saxhorn alto* and *saxotromba alto* came into being soon after 1840, and were patented by Sax in 1845 ; the alto of a Viennese group, the bell-over-the-shoulder model, dates from 1838 (Pl. XXX, B) ; the *Néo alto* and *Néo cor* (Paris) are contemporaneous with Sax's two groups. Among later types were the *cor alto* and the *alto cor* or *tenor cor*, both circular-coiled in the manner of a French horn, but with only half the tube-length of a French horn in E flat. (Pl. XXX. E.) The *cornophone alto* (1880–1890) was another French contribution to an already ample number of instruments designed to play the inner harmony in military and brass bands.

By the end of the century many of the tenor horns had lost their individuality, and had become merged in the more or less common type which is now used in some military bands on the continent, and in brass bands all the world over. For use in mounted or marching bands they are no doubt more convenient than the French horn. The bore at the narrow end is about $\frac{3}{8}$ of an inch, increasing to a little over $\frac{7}{16}$ inch at the valves and tuning-slide ; a further expansion after the passage through the valve-system reaches a diameter of about $1\frac{1}{4}$ inches at about a foot from the bell-mouth, of which the final opening is about $6\frac{1}{2}$ to 7 inches wide. The upright or tuba-form is now very generally adopted, except in the case of the horn-like *tenor cor* or *alto cor*. All these instruments have a fairly mellow and rather neutral tone-quality which is bolder than that of the French horn, yet is not so bright and penetrating as those of the trumpet and trombone of the same tube-length.

Tenor horns have been made in F as well as in E flat ; the latter have sometimes been provided with a crook which lowers the fundamental pitch to D ; the instrument, however, has never found favour in orchestras, and for military and brass bands the E flat tuning has long been standard.

(c) The Euphonium and Baritone

(G.) Barytonhorn. Tenorhorn. Basstuba. Tenortuba. Bassflügel-
horn. Tenorflügelhorn. Barytonkornett.

(F.) Saxhorn basse. Saxhorn baryton. Saxhorn tenor. Basse-à-
pistons. Bugle basse. Bugle tenor. Tuba basse.

(I.) Flicorno basso. Flicorno baritono. Flicorno tenore.

The instruments now known in this country as the euphonium
and the baritone are 9 feet (or 8 feet) tubes, with a more or less
wide conical bore which is only interrupted near the narrower
end by a cylindrical portion where the air-passage passes through
the valve-system and tuning-slide ; they are therefore in B flat
(or C), and on account of their pitch and bore may claim to be
the successors of the bass ophicleides. In this country the
euphonium has a wider bore than the baritone, and is also distinguished by being very generally provided with a fourth valve
which carries the compass down to the fundamental, or even
lower. In Germany the *barytonhorn* is the wider-bored instrument of the two, while the *tenorhorn* corresponds to the English
baritone. The naming of these instruments has always been
inconsistent and confusing, but it may be said that on the continent generally, those which are described as being basses or
baritones are the equivalents of the English euphonium, and
that those named tenors are instruments of the narrower-bored
type with only three valves, which we in England call baritones.
In neither case does the bore expand so generously as on the
ophicleide, in fact, the expansion, which only begins in earnest
after the passage through the valves, is quite moderate till the
last bend of the tube is reached. Similar instruments in C or
B flat have also been called " althorns ", and on the continent
all such instruments with a tube-length of 8 feet or more are
sometimes included under the general family name of " tuba ".
However they are named, there is a clear distinction between the
wider and the narrower types ; the one may be regarded as a
double-sized bugle, and the other as a double-sized cornet.
Both are wider than the B flat or tenor trombone, and much

wider than the French horn is B flat alto, although all these are
9 feet tubes sounding the harmonic series of B, flat.

The earliest examples of this type appear to be the German
instruments which date from round about 1830. In Kalkbrenner's *Life of Wilhelm Wieprecht* (1802–1872) it is stated that
in the period 1825–1830, Wieprecht reorganised a Prussian
cavalry band, and included two *tenorhörner* in B flat, and one
tenorbass horn in B flat, all with three valves. This testimony
seems to confirm the German origin of these instruments, and
rather suggests that the wider- and narrower-bored types were
then already differentiated. Stölzel's price list in 1828 includes a
Chromatisches tenorhorn oder tenortrompete in B (priced at 40
Reichsthaler), and again points to Berlin as the birthplace of
instruments which in this country Ad. Sax has for long been
given the credit of " inventing ". The earliest instruments of
this class were made in ophicleide-form, or more rarely, in
trumpet-form. The instruments soon found their way into
military bands in most European countries, and before long the
two parallel tubes of the ophicleide-form were more widely
separated, and the broader but shorter tuba-model became more
and more general. This was the shape adopted at first by
Ad. Sax for the whole family of saxhorns. Later on, German
instruments were frequently made in the oval tuba-form, and
in the helicon-form which encircles the body of the player.
Another circular baritone, shaped like a French horn, but held
with the bell upwards, was sometimes made in England about
sixty years ago. (Pl. XXX, D.) In the end, the upright tuba-
form became the standard model for all instruments of this class,
although some in trumpet-form may still be found amongst the
German *tenorhörner*. B flat has long been the standard pitch for
both euphoniums and baritones, although the former are sometimes made in C. In due course, from about 1840, the basses,
baritones or tenors of the various family groups appeared, made
to match their larger and smaller fellows in accordance with
the group-plan ; thus, there were *clavicors* (Pl. XXX, A), saxhorns, saxotrombas and others in C or B flat, differing one

from the other slightly in bore, considerably in shape, not much in tone-colour, and not at all in range except that the wider four-valved instruments could descend more freely into the lowest octave.

The mouthpieces were generally of the rather deep-cupped and almost conical variety associated with the flügelhorn and early cornets. Even in the early stages of development, the wide-bored type was generally given a fourth valve, which provided additional tube-length equivalent to lowering the instrument to F, and the gap between the fundamental and the augmented 4th above it was chromatically filled up. Valves of every variety then in use are found on the instruments made between 1830 and 1860 ; of these only the piston and the rotary valve survived at the end of the century.

From their earliest days the euphonium and baritone were essentially military and brass band instruments ; although one or other of them have been specified in large orchestral scores from time to time, it was the similar but larger instrument, pitched a fourth lower (in F), which became the orchestral or bass tuba such as is now used in Germany and in this country.

Euphoniums are now generally provided with some sort of compensating device in order to supply sufficient tube-length for good intonation when the valves are used in combination. They are important solo instruments in both military and brass bands, but the baritone is now confined almost entirely to brass bands in this country. The distinction between the wider- and the narrower-bored instruments still holds good. The tone of the former is full-bodied, and some use is made of the fundamental or " pedal " sounds ; the latter is characterised by a lighter tone, and is treated as a tenor or alto melodist, rather than as a bass voice.

(d) The Tuba or Bombardon

(G.) Basstuba. Bombardon.
(F.) Contrebasse à pistons. Tuba contrebasse. Saxhorn contrebasse.
Bombardon contrebasse.
(I.) Tuba bassa. Bombardone.

If the bass tuba or bombardon of about 12 to 14 feet of tube-length, and therefore in either F or E flat, has any pedigree at all, it can hardly be traced farther back than to the contrabass ophicleide pitched a fifth below the ordinary bass ophicleide in C or B flat, an unwieldy monster which does not appear to have been much used at any time.

At the present time the difference between bass tuba and bombardon hardly exists, except in so far that the instrument used in orchestras is commonly called a tuba, whereas, when transferred to a military or brass band, it becomes a bombardon, or simply a " bass ". The British tuba, however, is usually made in F, while the military bombardon is in E flat. The term " tuba ", when used in France or Germany, may include 8 or 9 feet instruments of the euphonium class, also contrabasses pitched an octave lower, but the E flat size is a *basstuba* in Germany, and a *tuba contrebasse* in France. The term " bombardon " is generally reserved for the instruments in E flat or BB flat, and does not usually designate any instrument pitched higher than 12 feet F. In England and Germany the qualification " contrabass " is reserved for tubas or bombardons in 16 feet C or 18 feet B flat. Originally a distinction was made between the bass tuba and the bombardon ; the latter is said to have had a wider bore, but fewer valves, than the former. Berlioz described each instrument under a separate heading, and distinguished between the tone-quality of the tuba, which was " more noble ", and that of the merely " powerful " bombardon ; just about the same time (1848), Kastner did not make any clear distinction between the two, although the illustrations he provided show quite clearly a wider and a narrower-bored type.[1] Neither von

[1] *Manuel*, pl. xvi.

Gontershausen (1855) nor Gevaert (1863) suggest that there were two distinct instruments, with a wider and a narrower tube.

Stölzel's price list of 1828 (Berlin) includes a " *chromatisches Basshorn oder Basstrompete in F oder Es* " ; this is probably the first indication of the existence of a valved instrument in the bass tuba register, but nothing further is known about it.[1] The year 1835 marks the appearance of the bass tuba under that name ; in that year a patent was granted in Berlin to Wilhelm Wieprecht, in conjunction with the maker J. G. Moritz, for an instrument in F with five *Berliner-pumpen* valves, two of which were operated by the L. hand, and three by the R. hand. The use of the valves lowered the open notes of the instrument as follows :

1st valve — one tone.
2nd   ,,   — one semitone.
3rd   ,,   — two tones when combined with the first valve.
4th   ,,   — one and a half tones when combined with the first valve.
5th   ,,   — a perfect fifth.

These valves could be used singly or together in the eleven combinations necessary to produce a complete succession of semitones between the fundamental and the second note of the harmonic series.

Soon after 1835 a rather wider-bored instrument with three (or four) valves was devised by Wieprecht and Moritz, and to this was given the name " bombardon ".[2] Between 1840 and 1845 Ad. Sax produced his homogeneous group of saxhorns, and of these the lowest, named *saxhorn contrebasse*, was in E flat, one tone lower than the Wieprecht-Moritz tuba. The German tuba was immediately adopted by one of the Prussian Guards' bands, and by about 1840 was generally available when any such instrument was required in German opera orchestras ; in 1845 Sax's saxhorns were included in the newly reorganised French Army bands. From that time tubas or bombardons became the most important and useful instruments in the bass register

[1] It may have been such an instrument which was the " bombardon " introduced (according to Kalkbrenner) into the Prussian *Jäger* bands in 1831.
[2] Sachs, *Reallexikon*, art. Bombardon.

of all military bands, and began to take the place of the ophicleide in opera or concert orchestras.

The early tubas were made first in ophicleide-form, and soon after in the usual tuba-form ; by the mid-century they were also made for marching bands in the circular helicon-form. About that time (1835–1850), other makers in Berlin and Potsdam, also in Vienna, Prague and Paris began to construct tubas or bombardons in either F or E flat, with from three to six valves. The German instruments were given either Berliner-pumpen or Vienna-valves ; the latter variety is found on the Prague or Viennese instruments. Later on both of these types of valve-mechanism gave way to the rotary valve, which since then has been the standard valve on both German and Austrian tubas. In Paris and Brussels similar instruments were made by Sax, Gautrot and Bachmann, with piston valves. Soon after 1850 Ad. Sax introduced his new pistons indépendants to the E flat contrabasses of his saxhorn group ; this system required six shortening-valves, each of which could only be used separately. In spite of the theoretical perfection of this system, the idea was never generally favoured.

During the third quarter of last century nearly all makers of brass instruments constructed tubas or bombardons in F or E flat, in tuba- or helicon-form, with from three to six piston or rotary valves. The ophicleide [1] then finally retreated in favour of the newer and better instrument, which now became indispensable in military bands, and was also required in many of the larger opera orchestras. The tuba or bombardon found its way into this country shortly before or round about the middle of last century, [2] and was probably first made here between 1860 and 1870, either by Henry Distin, or by the Paris Bessons who established themselves in London in 1858.

The arrangement and exact purpose of the valves on the

[1] That is, the keyed ophicleide ; valved tubas and bombardons retained the name " ophicleide " for some time in France and Belgium.

[2] Probably imported instruments made by Sax or Besson. No less than 133 ophicleides, 155 E flat contrabasses and 2 B flat contrabasses were assembled for a performance by the combined bands at the first brass band contest held at the Crystal Palace in 1860. (Russell and Elliot.)

tubas made during the second half of last century has varied according to the plans of different makers and players. The simpler three-valve military instruments were given the usual 1, $\frac{1}{2}$ and 1$\frac{1}{2}$ tone valves ; a fourth valve added sufficient tube-length to lower the pitch 2$\frac{1}{2}$ tones, and a fifth or sixth valve might represent a perfect 5th of added tube-length, or might act as a compensation valve, the purpose of which was to adjust the intonation when other valve-combinations were employed. The third valve, has also been made to add tube-length equivalent to a major 3rd instead of the usual minor 3rd which could be effected by combining the tone and semitone valves. The addition of valves beyond the usual three was for the purpose of carrying the scale downwards to the fundamental, or even below it by means of valve-produced sounds, or to act as transposing or compensation valves.

The modern or 20th-century tuba is likewise far from being a standardised instrument. Various makers in different countries now construct tubas or bombardons which may differ slightly in width of bore, and considerably as regards the valve-scheme ; individual players even, especially in concert orchestras, some-times play on tubas made according to their own plans, and embodying valve-arrangements which demand particular systems of fingering.

In England the military bombardon, or " E flat bass ", with only three valves may still be found, but a more serviceable instru-ment with four valves is now generally used. The orchestral tuba in this country is made in F, and must be provided with at least four valves in order to be able to cope with the demands of composers who write down to four semitones below the fundamental. A fifth valve may be a " transposer " or " com-pensator ", or the whole scheme may be arranged according to the plan of some particular player. A wide bore is necessary in order to give sufficient resonance to the low notes, and, indeed, to enable the player to reach the extreme low register with any certainty. The large amount of comparatively narrow cylindrical tubing which comes into use when the fundamental is approached interferes considerably with the proportions and conicity of the tuba-bore, and this can be mitigated only to some extent by making the tubing attached to the fourth valve wider than that of the first three valves.

In Germany and Austria the concert tubas are also in F, and are of necessity provided with at least four valves. The following are two of the valve-schemes now used :

Valves	1st	2nd	3rd	4th	5th	
4-valve tuba . .	1	$\frac{1}{2}$	2	$2\frac{1}{2}$	—	tones
5-valve tuba . .	1	$\frac{1}{2}$	$1\frac{1}{2}$	2	$2\frac{1}{2}$	tones

A three- or four-valved tuba in E flat is used in German and Austrian military bands, and is called a *Helikon* when it is shaped in circular form. Both the orchestral and the military instruments are provided with rotary valve-mechanism.

In France the F tuba has never been a standard instrument. For the last sixty years or so an 8 feet instrument corresponding in tube-length to our euphonium in C, with from four to six valves, has been used to play the parts which in Germany and England have been played on the F tuba. Considerable use of valve-produced " pedal " notes, combined with a wide bore and a suitable mouthpiece, have made it possible for players to cover the downward compass required of them in the tuba parts written by Wagner and later composers. The following is the valve-scheme of a recent French orchestral tuba in C with six piston-valves :

1st valve — 1 tone.	4th valve — $2\frac{1}{2}$ tones.
2nd „ — $\frac{1}{2}$ „	5th „ — $\frac{1}{2}$ tone (a transposing valve).
3rd „ — 2 tones.	6th „ — $3\frac{1}{2}$ tones.

When the 5th valve is depressed the instrument is actually in B natural, and the fingering of rapid passages in sharp keys is considerably eased. This particular arrangement of the valves allows some alternative fingerings for each note, each produced with a slightly different tube-length, thus, by means of judiciously selected valve-combinations, faults of intonation may be readjusted.

The tubas used in other European countries would provide some further instances of diversity in pitch, bore and valve-schemes, and in America a cosmopolitan selection would be found.

(e) The Contrabass Tuba or Bombardon

The earliest contrabasses in 16 feet C or 18 feet B flat appear to date from about 1845 ; in 1855 Adolphe Sax exhibited some such monster basses at the Paris Exhibition of that year. Since then the B flat (sometimes called BB flat) bombardons, usually provided with three, or more rarely with four valves, have been played in military and brass bands, and a similar instrument in C has also been used to play the parts written for it in some of Wagner's works.

The English BB flat military bombardon is made in two varieties, one with a rather narrower, and the other with a wider bore, and as a rule with only three valves.

Still lower and larger tubas have been made. Sax's *saxhorn bourdon* in EE flat, an octave below the ordinary E flat bombardon, was probably the first of these sub-bass instruments. Other such giants have been and are still constructed, sometimes in fantastic shapes with exaggerated bells, under fancy names, for use in dance and show bands. These are designed to engage the eye as much as the ear, and become more and more unmanageable the larger they are. Although instruments of any size, and theoretically of any pitch, could be constructed, the capacity of the human player and the size of his mouth remain as before ; moreover, as the human ear refuses to distinguish between sounds produced by very slow rates of vibration, it seems as if the limit of usefulness has been reached with the 18 feet tube of the BB flat bombardon.

(f) Group-Instruments

Not long after the valve-system became known in Paris, and was being adopted by most of the makers of brass instruments in that city, certain groups of instruments began to appear which embodied the general idea that, while all members of the group should conform to a uniform standard of construction or shape, of fingering and mechanism, and of compass and tone-quality, each member should represent a different register in the choir of brass voices. The various groups had this in common, that all the instruments were so proportioned that their natural range extended from the second to the eighth note of the harmonic series, and might in some cases include the fundamental. The bore in all cases was not so narrow as those of the trumpet or horn, nor so wide as that of the ophicleide, and the resulting tone-quality had therefore neither the fine quality of the trumpet or horn, nor the robust quality of the ophicleide. The following are brief descriptions of most of these groups, covering a period of from about 1835 to the end of the century :

CLAVICORS, 1837–1844 (patent 1838). — The idea was due to a Paris maker named Danays, but the instruments were actually made by Guichard.[1] A considerable part of the tube is rather narrow and cylindrical, and remains so till after the passage through the valves, when it expands and terminates in a large bell. The bell points upwards in tuba-fashion, and the mouthpiece is inserted in a detachable curved crook which projects from the side of the instrument.[2] When being played, the main tubes of the *clavicor* are more or less vertical, and the valves lie horizontally at right angles to them. Three valves of the Stölzel type are provided ; the tone and semitone valves are placed close together in the lower part of the instrument, and are operated by the R. hand ; the third valve is situated by itself in the upper part, and is controlled by the L. hand (Pl. XXX, A). This arrangement appears to have been modified in 1839, when all three valves were placed in one group in the lower part of the instrument, and were operated in the usual

---

[1] Pierre. *Les facteurs*, p. 363.
[2] In the photograph in the catalogue of the Berlin coll. the crook is missing, and the mouthpiece is incorrectly inserted in the main tube. Pl. 23, No. 3111.

way by the R. hand. According to Lavoix, the *clavicor* was intended to replace the alto ophicleide, and it may be that it was first conceived as an alto or tenor instrument in E flat ; the full group, however, comprised five different sizes in 6 feet F, E flat, D flat, C and B flat. It seems that the *clavicors* were used for some time in French Army bands. The tone of the instrument in C is very similar to that of a baritone.

SAXHORNS, *c.* 1842–1845 (patent 1845). — A group designed and made by Adolphe Sax. The saxhorns can hardly be said to have been " invented ", for the Austrian *flügelhorn*, the German *Althorn, tenorhorn, basstuba,* and the French *clavicors* were already in existence before 1840. Sax's claim to have produced a group of new instruments was hotly contested by rival makers in Paris, including Raoux, Halary, Gautrot, Buffet and Besson ; these makers demanded that Sax's patent should be annulled, and he became involved in more than one law suit.[1] That he named his instruments after himself was regarded as an impertinence. Circulars issued by Besson and Halary [2] strenuously opposed Sax's claim, and disputed his right to call the instruments saxhorns. Wieprecht contemplated taking legal action against Sax, but after meeting him at Coblenz in 1845, decided that it would not be worth while invoking the law. When the Italian maker Pelitti was asked if he made Sax's instruments at Milan, he replied, " it is Sax who is making my instruments in Paris ". Sax, however, certainly did bring order and uniformity to a group of instruments each of which was developing independently without any ordered plan ; he also set up a standard of workmanship which undoubtedly contributed much to the progress of brass instrument-making in general.

The proportions of the saxhorn tube are very similar to those

---

[1] For full particulars, see Comettant.

[2] Halary, 1846 : " La commission nommée par M. le Ministre de la guerre afin d'améliorer et d'organiser les musiques militaires a jugé convenable d'adjoindre aux instruments en usage ceux qui lui furent nouvellement proposés. Ce sont les fugel-horns [*sic*] en différents tons, qu'un feuilletonist a nommés illégalement sax-horns, afin de leur donner une espèce de privilége qu'ils ne peuvent avoir, étant la propriété du domaine public."

of the bugle, namely, a wide conical bore with a considerable expansion in the last part which leads to the bell. The valves are situated near the narrow end of the tube, so that the cylindrical and narrow portion of the bore is limited ; this allows the remainder of the tube to expand without interruption.

A photograph of the Distin family, holding in their hands the set of saxhorns made for them by Adolphe Sax in 1844,[1] shows that these instruments were at first coiled in a circular form, but in the three groups of saxhorns depicted by Kastner in 1848 each instrument is in tuba-form, with the bell pointing upwards; in one of the groups, presumably the earliest,[2] the valve-tubes are apparently without tuning-slides. This group comprised five instruments, of which the two largest were in 9 feet B flat, and differed in width of bore much as do the present-day baritone and euphonium :

Saxhorns	German and Austrian Equivalent
Soprano in high E flat	..
Contralto in B flat	Flügelhorn
Alto or tenor in E flat	Althorn
Bass or baritone in B flat with 3 pistons	Tenorhorn
Bass in B flat with 4 pistons (wide bore)	Barytonhorn

The other two groups depicted by Kastner (Pls. XX and XXIII) suggest that some additions and improvements were made before 1848 : a contrabass in E flat was added, with either three or four valves ; another contralto was in A flat ; all valve-tubes were given tuning-slides ; the contralto in B flat could be crooked in A, and the contrabass might be crooked in either F or E flat.

Some time after 1850 a still lower contrabass in BB flat was added, carrying the scale yet further downwards, and a sopranino in super-high B flat was less successful in extending the range upwards. The monster sub-bass or *Bourdon* in EE flat is said to have been exhibited at the Paris exhibition of 1855.

[1] See Kastner (Manuel), p. 248 ; Comettant, p. 53 ; *Musical Opinion*, July 1896. The Distin brass quintet toured Europe from 1838 to 1849.
[2] *Manuel*, pl. xxii.

Although the earliest saxhorns were shaped at first in circular and then in tuba-form, the high soprano in E flat, the contralto in B flat and the tenor in E flat were also made later on by Sax himself in trumpet-form (Pl. XXVIII, D and Pl. XXX, c). For all except the soprano and the contralto, the tuba-form eventually became the standard pattern.

Sax's first valves were the short wide *Berliner-pumpen*,[1] but at a later period he made them after the more slender Périnet

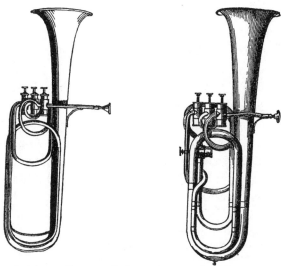

Fig. 41.—Saxhorns (from Kastner).

model; existing instruments prove that Sax also made some saxhorns with rotary valves.[2] Soon after 1850 Sax applied his system of *pistons indépendants* to the whole group, apparently without success, for the six shortening-valves appear never to have been generally adopted.

In France the term " saxhorn " is still used, and in England only the E flat tenor is sometimes called by the family name.

---

[1] According to Wieprecht (1845) Sax had previously purchased a bass-tuba and some cornets from the instrument-maker Moritz in Berlin (Kalk-brenner, p. 93.)

[2] An E flat tenor in the author's coll., made by Sax for the Distin family, is in trumpet-form with rotary valves. (Pl. XXX, c.)

Very generally these instruments, which by now have practically lost their identity, and have become merged in the more universal flügelhorns, tenorhorns, baritones, euphoniums and tubas or bombardons as we now know them, are named either by local names, or by their key or register.

SAXOTROMBA, *c.* 1842–1845 (patent 1845). — Another group devised by Sax, and made in the same form and keys as the saxhorns. The family characteristic was a rather narrower bore which was intended to give the instruments a tone-quality more akin to that of the trumpet or trombone, and it was especially with the hope that they would prove suitable for playing on horseback that Sax gave them the upright bell. Kastner states that the E flat tenor was used in French army bands about 1845.

SAXTUBA, 1852. — Another similarly organised group made by Sax for a stage production ; they were coiled in a very wide circular form in imitation of the Roman *buccina.*

NÉO ALTO AND BOMBARDON, 1844–1845. — A group very like the saxhorns, made in Paris about the same time :

Néo alto in (6 feet) F with 3 (Stölzel) vertical valves.
Néo alto in E flat   „   „   „   „
Néo alto in C   „   „   „   „
Bombardon in B flat with 3 or 4 valves.
Bombardon contrebasse in E flat with 3 or 4 valves.

All the instruments were in tuba-form and, with the *clavicors,* were the subject of litigation between Rivet and Sax.

NÉO COR, 1837–1844. — Patented by Guichard, the maker of the *clavicors.* This was a single instrument, practically a tenor cornet in F, with seven shanks or crooks. The tubing was folded into something like the shape of a cornet, but the bell stood erect or was tilted to one side. There were three vertical Stölzel-valves.[1]

CORNOPHONES (patent 1890). — Made by Fontaine Besson. A group of instruments with wide conical bore and deeply conical mouthpieces, intended to sound something like French horns. The tubing is looped downwards like a tuba, but the

---

[1] A *néo cor* with a tilted bell is in the Berlin coll., No. 3102.

bell faces forwards in line with the mouthpiece tube. These instruments have been used in Paris in place of Wagner tubas. Sachs [1] informs us that the bass *cornophone* is used in English Churches to accompany choral singing ! The complete group is as follows :

> Soprano in B flat
> Alto in F or E flat
> Tenor in C or B flat
> Bass in C or B flat
> Contrabass in F or E flat

SUDREPHONES (patent 1892.) — Invented by the Paris maker F. Sudre. These were of saxhorn type and were made in ophicleide-form. Their peculiar feature was a contrivance fixed to the bell which enabled the player to produce a novel tone-quality at will. This device consisted of a cylinder fixed outside, but communicating with the inside of the instrument through an opening in the side of the bell. An opening in the side of the cylinder was covered with a skin or membrane which vibrated in sympathy with the air-column of the instrument when the passage leading to it was opened. When in operation the vibrating membrane was said to impart a reedy or string-like quality to the tone.

WAGNER TUBAS (Horn-tubas). — Two pairs of special tubas, in addition to a contrabass tuba in C, were specified by Wagner in the score of *Der Ring des Nibelungen*. The two pairs were to be instruments with a conical bore more slender than that of the tuba, yet not so narrow as that of the French horn, and the tone-quality was intended to combine some of the weightiness of the tuba-tone with the mellowness of the horn ; the tube-lengths were to correspond, respectively, with those of the horn in B flat alto and in F, and the instruments were to be played by horn-players using horn mouthpieces. The range was to reach up to the 12th sound of the harmonic series on the tenor, and rather less on the bass instruments. As originally constructed according to the composer's design, these tubas were

[1] *Real-lexikon.*

made in oval tuba-form with the bell cocked to one side and, as they were meant to be played by horn-players, the valves were placed so that they had to be operated by the L. hand. Each instrument was provided with four rotary valves ; those of the tenor in B flat lowered the open notes a semitone, a whole tone, one-and-a-half tones and two tones, and those of the bass in F, a semitone, a whole tone, two tones and three tones. Wagner's notation in the score was the same as for French horns ; at first he wrote as if for horns in B flat alto and in F, but later on he changed his mind and wrote as if for horns in E flat and B flat basso ; in both cases he adhered to the traditional custom of writing an octave too low when the bass clef was used.

Sets of these tubas, made more or less in conformity with Wagner's plan,[1] have been used in various opera-houses where the " Ring " has been staged, but it has sometimes been found more convenient to have them played by tuba- or trombone-players instead of by horn-players. In some places, where it has not been feasible to provide special instruments, the parts have been played on other instruments and by any players who could cover the compass demanded in the score. In Paris, Fontaine Besson's cornophones have been used, and until recently in this country a set of tubas, specially made for the purpose by Mahillon of Brussels, have been played by trombone-players. The modern Wagner tubas, as now made and used in Germany, are in 9 feet B flat and 12 feet F, and are provided with ordinary horn mouthpieces, and four L. hand valves ; the bore at the narrow end is therefore practically the same as on the modern horn. The tube then expands gradually for a length of about 5 feet till the valve-system is reached, at which point the inside diameter is about half an inch ; a further expansion of the tube then leads to a bell measuring between 9 and 10 inches across the mouth.

" BELL-OVER-THE-SHOULDER " GROUP, 1838–1854. (Pl. XXX, B.) — Before the middle of last century some group-

[1] The original set was made in Munich.

instruments of the saxhorn type, but shaped so that the bell projected backwards over the player's shoulder, were made in Vienna for use in American military bands. Folded like a tuba, but held horizontally, the mouth-tube was in line with the main tube and parallel to the bell-tube, instead of projecting at right angles as on the ordinary tuba model ; thus, the bell-joint lay over the player's left shoulder, facing the troops marching in the rear of the band. These instruments were made in the usual keys, alternately in B flat and E flat, and were provided with three rotary valves and a tuning-slide. This model was patented in the U.S.A. in the name of Dodsworth in 1838.[1]

No doubt other instruments, all in varying degree akin to the cornet, bugle or ophicleide, could be found if the records, catalogues and patent files of last century were searched and the museums ransacked. The collection of varied types could be enlarged by including some solitary instruments made only in one size and named according to register, kinship to type, or perhaps with the idea of perpetuating the name of some optimistic inventor. Most of these would probably fail to establish a claim to any individual existence, for the field is limited, and there is not room for any great variety between the tone-quality of the cornet and that of the bugle, whether large or small ; nor does the admixture of trumpet-, horn- or trombone-bore, and their characteristic mouthpieces, supply sufficient variety to provide very many new and clearly different tone-qualities. Many claimants to a separate existence within this restricted field have had to give up their pretended individuality and throw in their lot with the common types which are in use to-day. The flügelhorns and contralto saxhorns, the tenorhorns and baritones, the tubas and bombardons may be differently named in each country, or may even be differently named in the same country, but their nomenclature is always more varied than their tone-qualities. Different widths of bore and diversity of mouth-

---

[1] A complete set is shown in the Met. Museum, New York ; other specimens occur in the Vienna, Berlin and the author's collections.

piece-cup will give variety of tone-quality within a certain radius, but that radius is limited in extent. In the highest register, the field of the brass instruments in high E flat, it matters little to the hearer whether the instrument be a trumpet, cornet, saxhorn or flügelhorn. In the contralto or B flat register, there is room enough for the cornet and the flügelhorn, but hardly for anything in between the two. So it is also in the tenor or E flat register, the baritone and the bass registers ; we can admit instruments which are large-sized cornets or large-sized bugles, but anything between these two makes the distinction too fine for ordinary ears, and therefore too fine for practical use. The fact that such as clavicors, saxhorns, saxotrombas, néo altos or any other such types do not now enjoy independent existences proves well enough that there is not, and never was, room for them all. The tone-qualities of such brass instruments in any one register have too much in common to admit of their being split up into infinitely varied shades. Anyone may now tinker with the bore or the mouthpiece of a large or a small valved instrument of the bugle type, be it flügelhorn, tenorhorn or tuba, but he who endeavours to invent a new lip-reed instrument with a bore wider than the trumpet, horn or trombone, will surely find that his instrument has already been invented over and over again.

BIBLIOGRAPHY

(A) BOOKS, ETC., MENTIONED IN THE TEXT

[Anonymous tutors are entered under the name of the instrument, and catalogues
of collections, etc., under the name of town where they are situated.]

Agricola. Musica Instrumentalis deudsch. Wittemberg, 1528–32–42–45.
Reprint, Liepzig, 1896.
Allgemeine Musikalische Zeitung. Leipzig, 1815, 1816, 1818.
Almenräder. Abhandlung über die Verbesserung des Fagotts. Mayence,
c. 1820. Fagottschule. Mayence, 1841.
Altenburg, J. E. Versuch einer Anleitung . . . Trompeter und Pauker-kunst.
Halle, 1795. Reprint, Dresden, 1911.
Altenburg, W. Die Klarinette. Heilbronn, 1904.
Andries. Aperçu théorique de tous les instruments de musique. Ghent, 1856.
Antolini. La Retta Maniera di scrivere per il Clarinetto. Milan, 1813.
Archives des Découvertes. 1810.
Artusi. Delle imperfettione della moderna Musica. 1600–1603.

Backofen. Anweisung zur Klarinette. Leipzig, 1803, 1824.
Bainbridge and Wood. The Preceptor, or a key to the Double-Flageolet.
London, 1820.
Banister. The most Pleasant Companion. (Recorder). London, 1681.
Basel. Cat. Historisches Museum. (Nef.) Basel, 1906.
Berlin. Cat. Staatlichen Hochschule für Musik. (Sachs.) Berlin, 1922.
Berlioz. Instrumentation. Paris, 1848. London, 1858.
Memoirs. Paris, 1870. London, 1884.
Berlioz-Strauss. Instrumentation. Leipzig, 1904.
Bierdimpfl. See Munich.
Blandford. Monthly Musical Record. March-April, May, June. London,
1935.
Boehm. An Essay on the construction of Flutes. (Trans.) London, 1882.
Boehm-Miller. The Flute and Flute-playing. Cleveland, 1908, 1922.
Breslau. Cat. Schlesisches Museum. (Epstein-Scheyer.) Breslau, 1932.
Brussels. Cat. Musée Instrumental-Conservatoire. (Mahillon.) (4 vols.).
2nd ed. Ghent, 1893–1912.
Burney. A General History of Music. London, 1776. Reprint, London, 1935.
The Present State of Music in Germany and the Netherlands (2). 2nd ed.
London, 1775.
The Present State of Music in France and Italy. London, 1773.

Busby. Concert room and Orchestra Anecdotes (3). London, 1825.

Catrufo. Traité des Voix et des Instruments. Paris, 1832.
Caussinus. Solfège-méthode . . . de cornet-à-pistons. Paris, 1846.
   Solfège-méthode pour l'ophicléide-basse. Paris, *c*. 1840.
Choron. See Francœur.
Clarinet. Anonymous tutors.
   Compleat Instructions for the Clarinet. London, 1798–1804.
   Clarinet Preceptor. (Metzler.) London, *c*. 1820.
Comettant. Histoire d'un inventeur. (Ad. Sax.) Paris, 1860.
Copenhagen. Cat. Musikhistorische Museum. (Hammerich.) Copenhagen,
   1911
Corrette. Méthode pour apprendre aisément à jouer de la Flûte Traversière.
   Paris, *c*. 1730.

Day. See London.
Devienne. Nouvelle Méthode Théorique et Pratique pour la Flûte. Paris,
   c. 1795.
Diderot et D'Alembert. Encyclopédie. Paris, 1767. Supp. 1776.
Doppelmayr. Historische Nachricht von den Nürnbergischen Mathe-
   maticis und Künstlern. Nürnberg, 1730.

Eisel. Musikus Autodidaktos. Erfurt, 1738.

Fantini. Modo per imparar a sonare di tromba. Frankfurt, 1638.
Farmer. Rise and development of Military Music. London, 1912.
Fitzgibbon. The Story of the Flute. London, 1914.
Flute. Anonymous tutors.
   The Compleat Tutor for the German Flute. (Several.) London, 1750–
   1800.
   New Instructions for the German Flute. (Several.) London, 1780–1810.
Forsyth. Orchestration. London, 1914, 1922.
Francœur. Diapason Général . . . des instruments à vent. Paris, 1772.
Francœur-Choron. Traité Général . . . des instruments d'orchestre.
   Paris, 1813.
Frankfurt. Cat. Historisches Museum. (Epstein.) Frankfurt, 1927.
Freillon-Poncein. La véritable manière . . . jouer . . . hautbois. Paris,
   1700 ?
Frichot. A complete scale and gamut of the Bass-horn. London, 1800.
Fröhlich. Vollständige theor.-pract. Musiklehre . . . Orchester. Bonn, 1811.
   Clarinet-schule. Bonn.
   Allgemeine Musikalische Zeitung. Leipzig, 1817.
Fürstenau. Zur Geschichte der Musik am Hofe der Kurfürsten von Sachsen,
   Dresden. Dresden, 1861–1862.

Galpin. Old English Instruments of Music. London, 1910, 1911, 1932.
European Musical Instruments. London, 1937.
Proceedings of the Musical Association. London, 1906–1907.
Garnier. Méthode pour l'ophicléide (à pistons). Paris, *c.* 1850.
Gassner. Universal-Lexikon der Tonkunst. Stuttgart, 1849.
Partiturkenntniss (2). Karlsruhe, 1838.
Gehot. A treatise on the theory and practice of music. London, 1784 ?
The complete instructor for every instrument. London, 1790 ?
Gerber. Hist. Biog. Lexikon der Tonkünstler. Leipzig, 1792.
Gevaert. Traité général d'Instrumentation. Ghent, 1863.
Gontershausen, von. Neu eröffnetes Magazin Musikalischer Tonwerkzeuge. Frankfurt, 1855.
Granom. Plain and Easy Instructions for playing on the German Flute. London, 1766.
Grassineau. A Musical Dictionary. London, 1740.
Greeting. The Pleasant Companion or New Lessons for the Flagelet. London, 1661.
Grove. A Dictionary of Music and Musicians (5). 3rd ed. London, 1927.
Gunn. The Art of Playing the German-Flute. London, 1793.
The School of the German-Flute. London, 1794.

Hamburg. Cat. Museum für Hamburgische Geschichte (Schröder.) Hamburg, 1930.
Harper. Instructions for the Trumpet. London, 1835–1837.
Hawkins. General History of Music (5). London, 1776.
Heckel. Der Fagott. Leipzig, 1899, 1931.
Hermenge. Méthode élémentaire de Serpent ordinaire et a clé. Paris, *c.* 1820.
Heron. A treatise on the German Flute. London, 1771.
History of Music in Pictures, A. (Kinsky.) Leipzig, 1929.
Holmes. (*Randle.*) Academy of Armory. (MS.) *c.* 1688.
Hotteterre. Principes de la Flute Traversiere. Paris, 1707, 1710.

Innsbruck. Cat. Museum Ferdinandeum. Innsbruck.

Junker. Musikalischer Almanach. 1782.

Kalkbrenner. Wilhelm Wieprecht. Berlin, 1882.
Kastner. Manuel Général de Musique Militaire. Paris, 1848.
Cours d'Instrumentation. Paris, 1837.
Méthode élémentaire d'ophicléide. Paris, *c.* 1840.
Kircher. Musurgia universalis. 1650.
Klosé. Méthode . . . de la clarinette. Paris, 1844.
Koch. Musikalisches Lexikon. Frankfurt, 1802.
Koch-Dommer. Musikalisches Lexikon. Heidelberg, 1865.

Laborde. Essai sur la Musique (4). Paris, 1780. Supp., 1781.

Lavignac-Laurencie. Encyclopédie de la Musique. Paris, 1927.

Lavoix. Histoire de l'instrumentation. Paris, 1878.

Lebeuf. Mémoires concernant l'histoire ecclésiastique et civile d'Auxerre. Paris, 1743.

Lefèvre. Méthode de Clarinette. Paris, 1802.

Leipzig. (Heyer coll.) Cat. Musikhistorisches Museum. (Kinsky.) Leipzig, 1913.

London. Cat. Royal Military Exhibition. (Day.) London, 1891.

Luscinius. Musurgia. Strassburg, 1536.

Mahaut. Nieuwe Manier om binnen korten tyd op de Dwarsfluit te leeren speelen. Amsterdam, 1759.

Mahillon. See Brussels.

Majer. Neu eröffneter Musik-Saal. 2nd ed. Nürnberg, 1741.

Mattheson. Das neu-eröffnete Orchester. 1713.

Meifred. Méthode pour le cor chromatique, à pistons ou à cylindres. Paris, 1840.

Mersenne. Harmonie Universelle. Paris, 1636.

Miller, G. The Military Band. London, 1912.

Miller, D. C. See Boehm-Miller.

Minguet Y Yrol. Reglas, y Advertencias Generales que ensenan el modo de taner todos los instrumentos mejores, etc. Madrid, 1754, 1774.

Modern Musick Master. (Prelleur). London, 1731.

Moniteur Universel. 1811.

Muller. Chromatic scale for the Bass-horn. London, *c.* 1830–1840.

Munich. Cat. Baierischen National Museum. (Bierdimpfl.) Munich, 1883.

Muses' Delight, The. Liverpool, 1754.

Nemetz. Neueste Posaun-schule. Vienna, *c.* 1830.

Noblet. Nouvelle Méthode de Bugle ou Trompette à clefs. (Klapp-Horn-Schule.) Bonn, *c.* 1820–1830.

North (Roger.) Memoirs of Musick. (MS.) 1728.

Oboe. Anonymous tutors.
  The Compleat tutor for the Hautboy. London, *c.* 1750.
  The Compleat tutor for the Hautboy. London, *c.* 1808.
  New and Complete Instructions for the Hautboy. London, 1790.
  New and Complete Instructions for the Hautboy. London, *c.* 1800.

Paris. Cat. Musée du Conservatoire National. (Chouquet). Paris, 1875. Supp., 1894, 1899, 1903.

Parke. Musical Memoirs. London, 1830.

Pierre. Les facteurs d'instruments de Musique. Paris, 1893.
  La facture instrumentale à l'exposition . . . de 1889. Paris, 1890.

Praetorius. Syntagma Musicum. Wolffenbüttel, 1619. Reprint, Kassel, 1929.
Prelleur. See Modern Musick Master.
Prout. Instrumentation. London.

Quantz. Versuch einer Anweisung die Flöte traversiere zu spielen. Berlin, 1752, 1780, 1789. Partial reprint, Leipzig, 1906.

Recorder. Anonymous tutors :
  The Compleat Flute-Master. London, *c.* 1690.
  The Compleat Flute-Master. London, *c.* 1750.
  Compleat Instructions for the Common Flute. London, 1779–1798.
  The Delightful Companion. London, 1684.
  Lessons for the Rechorder. London, 1679.
Reynvaan. Muzijkaal Konst-Woordenboek. Amsterdam, 1789, 1795.
Riemann. Musik-Lexikon. Leipzig, Berlin, 1882–1922.
Rockstro. The Flute. London, 1890, 1928.
Rode. Zeitschrift für Musik, 1858, 1859. Leipzig.
  Neue Berliner Musikzeitung, 1860, 1877. Berlin.
Rose. Talks with Bandsmen. London, *c.* 1894.
Roxas. Leben . . . Frantz Anton, Grafen von Sporck. Amsterdam, 1715.
Roy and Muller. Tutor for the keyed trumpet. London, *c.* 1830–1840.
Rühlmann. Neue Zeitschrift für Musik. 1870.
Russell and Elliot. The Brass Band Movement. London, 1936.

Sachs. See Berlin.
  Real-Lexikon der Musikinstrumente. Berlin, 1913.
  Handbuch der Musikinstrumentenkunde. 2nd ed. Leipzig, 1930.
Salter. The Genteel Companion (Recorder.) London, 1683.
Salzburg. Cat. Museum Carolino Augusteum. (Geiringer.) Leipzig, 1932.
Schickhard. Principes de la Flûte. Amsterdam, 1730.
Schlosser. See Vienna.
Schneider. Historisch-Technische Beschreibung der Musikalischen Instrumente. Leipzig, 1834.
Sellner. Oboeschule. Vienna, 1825.
Simiot. Tableau explicatif . . . à la clarinette. Lyons, 1808.
Speer. Grund-richtiger Unterricht der Musikalischen Kunst. Ulm, 1687, 1697.
Stockholm. Cat. Musikhistoriska Museet. (Svanberg.) Stockholm, 1902.
Sundelin. Die Instrumentirung . . . Militär Musik-Chöre. Berlin, 1828.
  Die Instrumentirung für das Orchester. Berlin, 1828.

Terry. Bach's Orchestra. London, 1932.
Tromlitz. Kurze Abhandlung vom Flötenspielen. Leipzig, 1786.
  Ausführlicher . . . Unterricht die Flöte zu spielen. Leipzig, 1791.
  Ueber die Flöten mit mehrern Klappen. Leipzig, 1800.

Vanderhagen. Nouvelle méthode de clarinette. Paris, 1780–1782.
Vienna. Cat. Kunsthistorisches Museum. (Schlosser.) Vienna, 1920.
   Cat. Gesellschaft der Musikfreunde. (Mandyczewski.) Vienna, 1912.
Virdung. Musica Getutscht. Basel, 1511. Reprint, Kassel, 1931.

Walther. Musikalisches Lexikon. Leipzig, 1732.
Wasielewski. Geschichte der Instrumentalmusik im 16. Jahrhundert.
   Berlin, 1878.
Weber. Versuch einer . . . akustik der Blasinstrumente. All. Mus. Zeitung,
   Leipzig, 1816.
Weigel. Abbildungen derer gemeinnützigen Hauptstände. Regensburg,
   1698.
Welch. Six Lectures on the Recorder. London, 1911.
   History of the Boehm Flute. London, 1883, 1892, 1896.
Widor. The modern orchestra. (Trans.) London, 1905.
Wieprecht. Letters in Berliner Musikalische Zeitung, 1845. Berlin.
Wood. Complete instructions for the Alto Fagotto. London, 1830.

Zacconi. Prattica di Musica. Venice, 1596.

(B) BOOKS NOT MENTIONED IN THE TEXT

Bechler-Rahm. Die Oboe. Liepzig, 1914.
Brancour. Histoire des Instruments de Musique. Paris, 1921.
Buhle. Die Musikalischen Instrumente in den Miniaturen des frühen Mittel-
   alters. Leipzig, 1903.
Busby. A Dictionary of Music. London, 1786, 1813.

Carse. The History of Orchestration. London, 1925.
Clappé. The Wind-band and its instruments. London, 1912.
Clodomir. Traité . . . de l'organisation . . . harmonies et fanfares.
   Paris, 1873.

Daubeny. Orchestral wind instruments. London, 1920.
Dörfel. Geschichte der Gewandhausconcerte zu Leipzig. Leipzig, 1884.

Eichborn. Die Trompete in alter und neuer Zeit. Leipzig, 1881.
   Zur Geschichte der Instrumental-Musik. Leipzig, 1885.
   Das Clarinblasen auf Trompeten. Leipzig, 1894.
   Die Dämpfung beim Horn. Leipzig, 1897.
Eisenach. Cat. Bach-haus zu Eisenach. (Buhle-Sachs.) Leipzig, 1913,
   1918.
Elsenaar. De Clarinet. Hilversum, 1927.

Engel. Musical Instruments. London, 1875.
See London.
English Music. Loan Exhibition, 1904. London, 1911.
Euting. Zur Geschichte der Blasinstrumente im 16. und 17. Jahrhundert.
Berlin, 1899.

Hanslick. Geschichte des Concertwesens in Wien. Vienna, 1869.
Hind. The Brass Band. London, 1934.
Hipkins. Musical Instruments. London, 1888, 1921.

Jahn. Die Nürnberger Trompeten und Posaunenmacher im 16. Jahrhundert. (Archiv für Musikwissenschaft, vii, 1925.)

Kappey. Short History of Military Music. London, *c.* 1890.
Kastner. Traité général de l'Instrumentation. Paris, 1837, 1844.
Koch. Abriss der Instrumentenkunde. Kempten, 1912.

London. Descriptive Cat. of the Musical Instruments in the S. Kensington
Museum. (Engel.) London, 1874.
Cat. Exhibition . . . Crystal Palace, 1900. London, 1900.
List of Wind instruments in the private coll. of Adam Carse. London,
1934.
Lotter. Der sich selbst informirende Musikus. Augsburg, 1762.

Mahillon. Les Éléments d'acoustique musicale et instrumentale. 1874.
Meifred. Notice sur la fabrication des instruments de musique en cuivre.
Paris, 1851.
Menke. History of the trumpet of Bach and Handel. London, 1934.
Milan. Cat. Museo del Conservatorio. Milan, 1908.
Miller. Bibliography of the Flute. Cleveland, U.S.A., 1935.
The Science of Musical sounds. New York, 1926.
Musical Instruments in Pictures. Königstein, 1922.

Piersig. Die Einführung des Hornes in die Kunstmusik. Halle, 1927.

Ribock. Bemerkungen über die Flöte. Stendal, 1782.
Richardson. Cantor Lectures on Wind Instruments. London, 1929.

Siccama. Theory of the New Patent Diatonic Flute. London, 1847.
Straeten, Van der. La Musique aux Pays-Bas. Brussels, 1867.

Taut. Die Anfänge der Jagdmusik. Leipzig, 1928.
Teuchert & Haupt. Musik-instrumentenkunde in Wort und Bild. Leipzig,
1911.
Turpin. Some observations on the manipulation of modern wind instruments. London, 1883.

Vandenbroeck.   Traité général de tous les instruments à vent. . . . Paris, c. 1800.

Volbach.   Das moderne Orchester.   Leipzig, 1910.
    Die Instrumente des Orchesters.   Leipzig, 1913.

Wetzger.   Die Flöte.   Heilbronn, c. 1897.

Zeitschrift für Instrumentenbau.   Leipzig, from 1880.

INSTRUMENTS SHOWN IN THE PHOTOGRAPHIC PLATES

PLATE I. TRANSVERSE FLUTES

A. *Stanesby, jun., London.* 1 key (D sharp). 1734–1754.

B. *Lawson, London.* 1 key. *c.* 1800.

C. *Potter, sen., London.* 1 key. 1785–1806.

D. *Wafford, London.* 4 keys. *c.* 1800.

E. *Laurent, Paris.* Glass flute with 4 keys. Dated 1826.

F. *Potter, sen., London.* 6 keys (2 foot-keys). Dated 1777.

G. *Hale, London.* 6 keys, *c.* 1800.

H. *Wood, London.* Ebony. 7 keys (no long F). Patent 1814.

I. *Prowse, London.* Nicholson's Improved. 8 keys. *c.* 1820.

J. *Monʒani, London.* 8 keys with extra B flat lever. *c.* 1820–1830.

K. *Boehm, München.* Conical 1832 Boehm flute. Open G sharp. 1832–1840.

L. *Walpot, Brussels.* Cylindrical metal Boehm flute. Modern.

PLATE II. FLUTES, PICCOLOS, ETC.

A. —— Alto flute in A (so-called). No foot-keys. Early 19th century.

B. *Brickel, London.* F flute (so-called). 1 key. *c.* 1800.

C. *Hill, late Monʒani, London.* F flute. 5 keys. *c.* 1836.

D. *Potter (W. H.), London.* E flat flute (so-called). 4 keys. Dated 1823.

E. *Muss, Wien.* 9 keys, with low B. *c.* 1850.

F. *Rudall & Rose, London.* 10 keys, to low B flat. 1845–1847.

G. *Siccama, London.* " Diatonic flute." 11 keys. Patent 1847.

H. *Wallis, London.* Giorgi flute. 1 key. 1888.

I. *Astor, London.* Flute in (high) B flat (so-called). 1 key. *c.* 1780–1800.

J. —— *London, Improved.* Flute in (high) B flat (so-called). 1 key. *c.* 1800.

K. *Bilton, London.* Flute in (high) B flat (so-called). 5 keys. *c.* 1825–1850.

L. *Parker, London.* Piccolo in D (so-called). 1 key. *c.* 1800.

M. *Hawes, London.* Piccolo in D (so called). 4 keys. Early 19th century.

N. *Dawkins, London.* E flat Piccolo (so-called in F). 6 keys. 2nd half 19th century.

O. —— Piccolo. 6 keys. Late 19th century.

P. *Thibouville, Paris.* D flat Piccolo, Boehm system. Late 19th century.

Q. *Townsend, Manchester.* B flat Fife. 1 key. Early 19th century.

PLATE III.   WHISTLE-FLUTES

A. Flûte-à-bec (Recorder) in A.   French.   18th century.
B. Ivory Blockflöte (Recorder) in F by *Heitz, Berlin. c.* 1724.
C. Double Flageolet in B flat by *Simpson, London. c.* 1835–1850.
D. Double Flageolet in B flat by *Bainbridge, London.*   Patents 1807, 1819.
E. English Flageolet by *Simpson, London. c.* 1835.
F. English Flageolet by *Keith Prowse, London. c.* 1850.
G. French Flageolet in A.   Late 19th century.

PLATE IV.   OBOES

A. *T. Stanesby, London.*   3 keys (duplicate D sharp).   Before 1734.
B. *F. Lehner.*   3 keys.   1st half 18th century.
C. *Richters (Netherlands ?).*   3 keys.   1st half 18th century.
D. *C. Delusse, Paris.*   2 keys (no duplicate D sharp).   2nd half 18th century.
E. *Goulding, Wood & Co., London.*   2 keys.   *c.* 1800.
F. *Milhouse, Newark.*   2 keys.   Late 18th century.
G. *D'Almaine, London.*   5 keys.   *c.* 1835.
H. *Power, London.*   6 keys, to low B flat.   Early 19th century.
I. *Goodlad, London.*   9 keys.   *c.* 1825.

PLATE V.   OBOES

J. *Cotton, London.*   2 original keys, 6 added later.   *c.* 1800–1830.
K. *Golde, Dresden.*   13 keys (Sellner's).   *c.* 1840.
L. *Rönnberg, New York.*   11 keys.   *c.* 1840–1850.
M. *Triebert, Paris.*   10 keys.   *c.* 1830–1840.
N. *Triebert, Paris.*   11 keys, 3 rings, 2 octave keys.   *c.* 1840–1850.
O. *Triebert, Paris.*   17 keys.   Cocus.   2nd half 19th century.
P. *Triebert, Paris.*   Low B flat, Barret-action, thumbplate.   2nd half 19th century.
Q. *Zimmermann, Leipzig.*   German pattern.   2nd half 19th century.
R. *Lorée, Paris.*   Conservatoire model.   Modern.

PLATE VI.   COR ANGLAIS

A. *Riedlocker, Paris* (?).   Basset-Oboe.   5 keys.   Late 18th century.
B. *Bertani, Modena.*   Cor Anglais with 2 keys.   *c.* 1760–1800.
C. *Triebert, Paris.*   Cor Anglais with 10 keys.   *c.* 1840–1850.
D. *Rivet, Lyons.*   Cor Anglais with 7 keys.   *c.* 1840–1850.
E. *Morton, London.*   Cor Anglais.   Barret-action and thumbplate.   Late 19th century.

PLATE VII. CLARINETS

A. *I. S. W.* (*Johann Stefan Walsh?*). (B flat) 4 keys. *c.* 1750–1760.
B. *Goulding, London.* (B flat) 5 keys. *c.* 1800.
C. *Metzler, London.* (C) 6 keys. Shake-key. *c.* 1800.
D. *Baumann, Paris.* (B flat) 6 keys. C sharp. Early 19th century.
E. —— (High F) 6 keys. Early 19th century.
F. *D'Almaine, London.* (B flat) 8 keys. Wood's patents, 1814 and 1819.
G. *Ulrich, Leipzig.* (B flat) 11 keys. *c.* 1820–1830.
H. *Bilton, London.* (E flat) 8 keys. *c.* 1825.
I. *Key, London.* (B flat) 13 keys. *c.* 1825–1850.
J. *Clementi, London.* (B flat) Ebony. 13 keys. *c.* 1840.
K. *Sax, Brussels.* (B flat) 13 keys. *c.* 1840.

PLATE VIII. CLARINETS

L. *Goulding & D'Almaine, London.* (C) 13 keys. 1835–1850.
M. *Metzler, London.* (A) 13 keys. *c.* 1840–1860.
N. *Martin, Paris.* (B flat) 13 keys. *c.* 1840–1860.
O. —— (E flat) 13 keys and 2 rings. *c.* 1840–1860.
P. *Meyer, Hanover.* (B flat) Metal. 13 keys and 2 rings. *c.* 1860–1870.
Q. *Distin, London* (*Ad. Sax, Paris?*). (E flat) Metal. 13 keys and 2 rings. *c.* 1850–1860.
R. *Boosé, London.* (E flat) Metal. 13 keys and 2 rings. *c.* 1870.
S. —— (B flat) 13 keys, R. H. rings. Cocus. *c.* 1870–1880.
T. —— (B flat) 13 keys and " Patent C sharp ". Modern.
U. *Aug. Buffet, Paris.* (B flat) Klosé-Boehm system. 1843–1850.
V. *Buffet Crampon, Paris.* (E flat) Klosé-Boehm system. Late 19th century.

PLATE IX. ALTO CLARINETS, ETC.

A. *Griessling & Schlott, Berlin.* Basset-horn. 12 keys. *c.* 1820.
B. *Higham, Manchester.* E flat Alto Clarinet. 13 keys and 4 rings. *c.* 1860.
C. —— E flat Alto Clarinet. Ebonite. 13-keyed system. Late 19th century.
D. *Ad. Sax, Paris.* B flat soprano saxophone. 15 keys and octave key. *c.* 1850–1860.
E. —— (*Adler, Markneukirchen?*). Octavin in B flat. Invented 1890.
F. *Thibouville-Lamy.* Tárogató, modern.

PLATE X. CONTRABASS CLARINET

A. *Besson, Paris.* Contrabass Clarinet in B flat. 13-keyed system. 1890.
B. Same as Pl. VII, E.

PLATE XI. BASSOONS, FRONT

A. ——— 4 keys. *c.* 1750.
B. *Caleb Gedney, London.* 4 keys. *c.* 1760.
C. *Goulding, London.* 6 keys. *c.* 1800.
D. *Tuerlinckx, Malines.* 7 keys. One wing key. Early 19th century.
E. *H. Grenser, Dresden.* 7 ivory keys. No F sharp. 1796–1806.
F. *Astor, London.* 8 keys. *c.* 1800–1815.
G. *Milhouse, London.* 8 keys. Brass bell. Early 19th century.

PLATE XII. BASSOONS, BACK

The same instruments as in Plate XI

PLATE XIII. BASSOONS, FRONT

H. *H. Grenser, Dresden.* 9 keys. C sharp. 1806–1813.
I. *D'Almaine, London.* 9 cupped keys. *c.* 1835.
J. *Savary, jun., Paris.* 11 keys. Dated 1829.
K. *Schott fils, Mayence.* 16 keys. Almenräder's system. 1825–1828.
L. *Schaufler, Stuttgart.* 14 keys. Neukirchner's system. *c.* 1845.
M. *Key, London.* 16 keys and crook key. *c.* 1850–1856.
N. *Heckel, Biebrich.* 17 keys. *c.* 1870.

PLATE XIV. BASSOONS, BACK

The same instruments as in Plate XIII

PLATE XV. SARRUSOPHONES

A. ——— Contrabass in E flat. *c.* 1870.
B. *Gautrot, Paris.* Soprano in B flat. 1856–1884.

PLATE XVI. HORNS

A. *Fürst, Elwangen.* Jagdhorn in high E. Dated 1770.
B. *Gautrot, Paris.* Cor de Chasse in D. *c.* 1850.
C. *Gautrot, Paris.* Cor de Chasse in D. *c.* 1850.
D. *Potter, London.* French horn in E flat. 19th century.

PLATE XVII. HAND HORN

Hand horn with 9 crooks. French. Early 19th century

PLATE XVIII. HORNS

A. ——— Hand horn. *c.* 1800.
B. *Key, London.* Horn with 2 valves. *c.* 1840–1850.
C. ——— Valve horn. French model. 2nd half 19th century.

PLATE XIX. TRUMPETS

A. *Haas, Nürnberg.* Trumpet in D. Late 17th century.
B. *I. G. U.* Trumpet in E flat. Dated 1794.
C. —— Trumpet in E flat. Early 19th century.
D. *Pace, London.* Slide trumpet (F to C). Clockspring. *c.* 1830–1840.
E. *Köhler, London.* Slide trumpet (F to C). Elastic spring. 1862–1870.
F. —— Wyatt's double slide trumpet. 1890.

PLATE XX. TRUMPETS

A. —— Keyed trumpet. *c.* 1800–1830.
B. *Sandbach & Wyatt, London.* Two-valved trumpet. *c.* 1840–1850.
C. *Pace, London.* Two-valved trumpet (F to C). *c.* 1840.
D. *Pace, London.* Three-valved trumpet. *c.* 1840–1850.
E. —— Trumpet in C. Rotary valves. 2nd half 19th century.
F. *Mahillon, Brussels.* Valve trumpet in F. Late 19th century.
G. *Hawkes, London.* Straight (so-called " Bach ") trumpet in B flat. Late 19th century.

PLATE XXI. TRUMPETS

A. —— Cavalry trumpet in E flat. 1st half 19th century.
B. *Hawkes, London.* Fanfare or State trumpet in E flat. Late 19th century.
C. —— Fanfare trumpet in E flat. French. *c.* 1850.
D. —— Fanfare trumpet in E flat. High Sheriff of Cardiganshire. 1874.
E. —— Coiled trumpet in E. 19th century.

PLATE XXII. CORNETS

A. *Köhler, London.* " Cornopean " with clapper-key. *c.* 1830–1850.
B. *Guichard, Paris.* Cornet à pistons. 7 crooks. 1830–1845.
C. *Köhler, London.* Cornet with Shaw's disc-valves. 1838–1850.
D. *Courtois, Paris.* Cornet à pistons. *c.* 1850.
E. *Distin, London (Ad. Sax, Paris ?).* Cornet. *c.* 1850–1860.
F. *Köhler, London.* Bayley's Improved Acoustic cornet. 1862.
G. *Pask & Koenig, London.* Cornet. 2nd half 19th century.
H. *Courtois, Paris.* Cornet with three upright rotary valves. 2nd half 19th century.
I. *Besson, London.* " Prototype " cornet. Late 19th century.

PLATE XXIII. SLIDE TROMBONES

A. *Nagel, Nürnberg.*   Alto in E flat.   Dated 1663.
B. ——— Tenor in B flat.   German.   *c.* 1800.
C. *Keat, London.*   Treble in B flat.   19th century.
D. *Besson, Paris.*   Alto in E flat.   2nd half 19th century.
E. *Courtois, Paris.*   Alto in D flat.   *c.* 1850.

PLATE XXIV. TROMBONE

Ricchi, Rome.   Buccin.   Early 19th century.

PLATE XXV. TROMBONE AND CORNETT

A. Same as Plate XXIII, A.
B. Cornett in A.   17th century.

PLATE XXVI. SERPENTS

A. ——— No keys.   18th century.
B. *Baudouin (Netherlands ?).*   3 keys.   Early 19th century.
C. *Key, London.*   13 keys.   *c.* 1840–1850.

PLATE XXVII. BASS-HORNS

A. *Tabard, Lyons.*   " Russian bassoon ", 3 keys.   1st half 19th century.
B. ——— English Bass-horn, 4 keys.   *c.* 1840.
C. *Jeantet, Lyons.*   " Russian bassoon ", 3 keys.   1st half 19th century.

PLATE XXVIII. KEYED BUGLES, FLÜGELHORNS, ETC.

A. *Metzler, London.*   Keyed bugle, 6 keys.   1810–1850.
B. *Holles, Dublin.*   Keyed bugle, 7 keys.   1810–1850.
C. *Fentum, London.*   Keyed bugle, 8 keys.   1810–1850.
D. *Distin, London (Sax, Paris ?).*   Sop. saxhorn in B flat, rotary valves.
    c. 1850–1860.
E. ——— German flügelhorn, rotary valves.   2nd half 19th century.
F. *Gautrot aîné, Paris.*   Saxhorn in high E flat.   Dated 1860.
G. *Boosey, London.*   Koenighorn in C, B flat or A.   1890.

PLATE XXIX. OPHICLEIDES

A. *Cottrell, Birmingham.* Ophicleide in C. 11 keys. 1820–1870.
B. *Metzler, London.* Ophicleide in B flat. 11 keys. 1820–1870.
C. —— Ophicleide in B flat. 11 keys. 1820–1870.
D. *Gautrot aîné, Paris.* Ophicleide in C. 11 keys. 1820–1870.

PLATE XXX. TENORHORNS, ETC.

A. *Guichard, Paris.* Clavicor in C. 1838.
B. —— Tenorhorn in E flat. " Bell-over-the-shoulder." Rotary valves. 1838.
C. *Sax, Paris.* Tenor saxhorn in E flat. Rotary valves. *c.* 1845–1848.
D. —— Circular Baritone in B flat. Pistons. 2nd half 19th century.
E. *Distin, London.* Tenor-cor in F or E flat. 1850–1868.

FINGERING CHARTS

I. FLUTE. HOTTETERRE (1707)

2. RECORDER. VIRDUNG (1511)

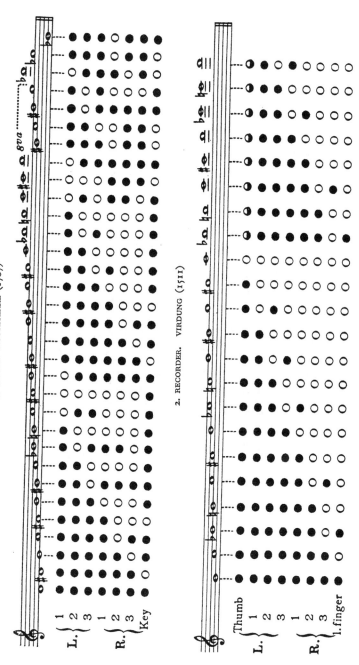

3. OBOE.   THE COMPLEAT TUTOR (c. 1750–1800)

4. CHALUMEAU.   REYNVAAN (1795)

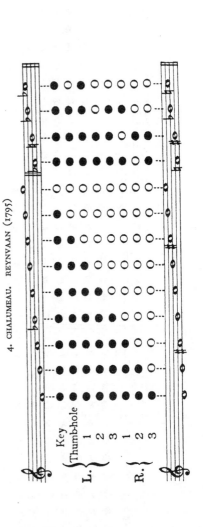

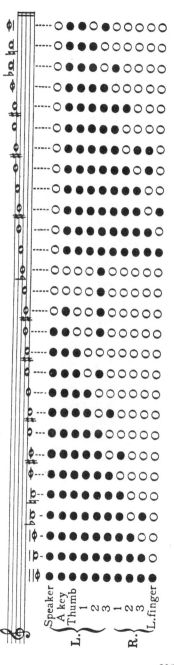

5. CLARINET. EISEL, MUSICUS AUTODIDAKTOS (1738)

6. BASSOON. SPEER (1697)

335

7. BASSOON. EISEL (1738)

8. SCALE FOR A KEYED TRUMPET WITH FIVE KEYS

Keys are numbered, counting from the bell.

336

9. ZINCK ODER CORNET. SPEER (1697)

337

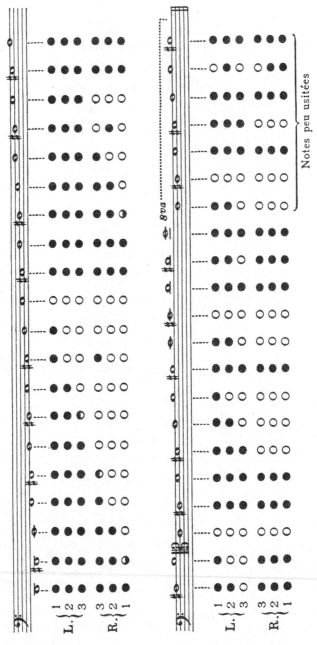

10. SERPENT. HERMENGE, TABLATURE GÉNÉRALE DU SERPENT ORDINAIRE (c. 1816)

338

11. TULLY'S TUTOR FOR THE KENT BUGLE (c. 1835)

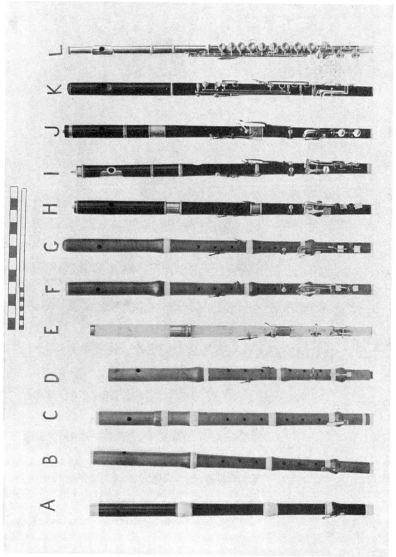

PLATE I

341

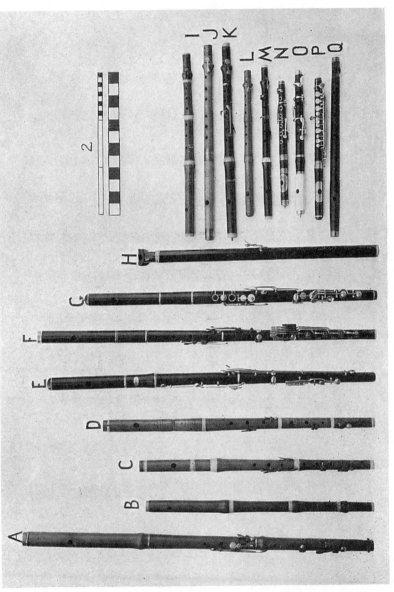

PLATE II

342

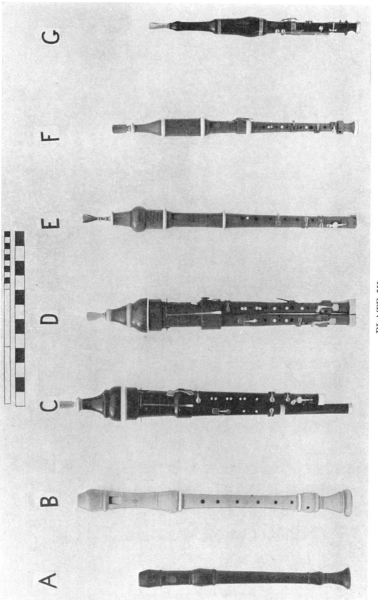

PLATE III

343

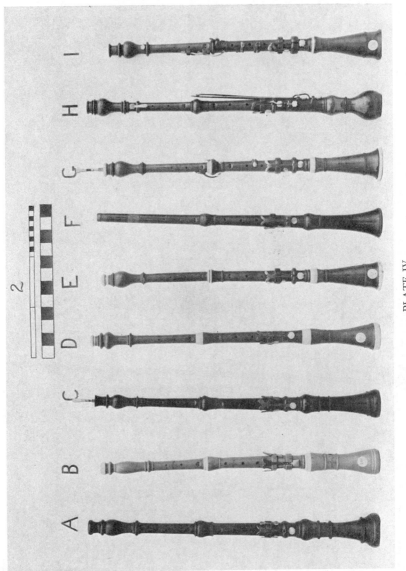

PLATE IV

344

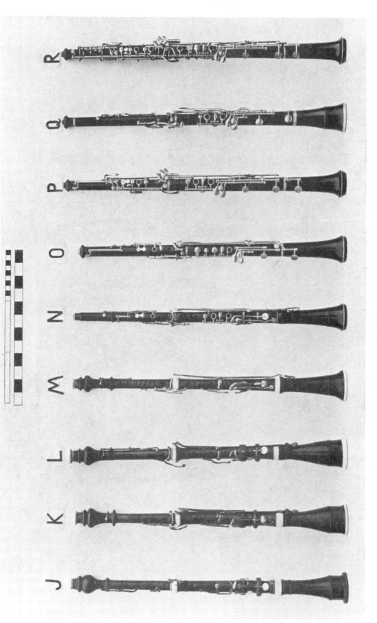

PLATE V

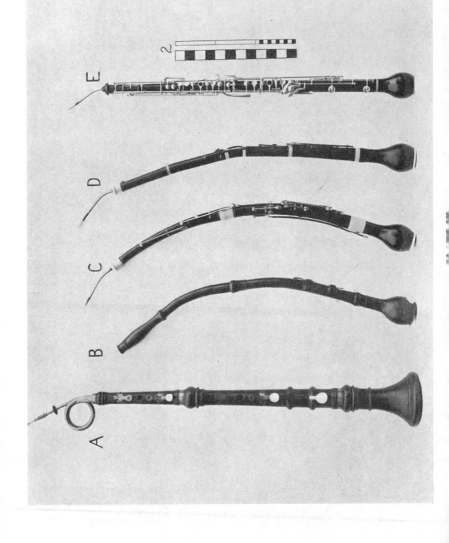

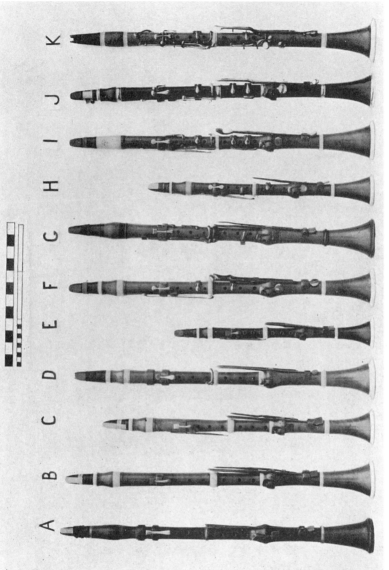

PLATE VII

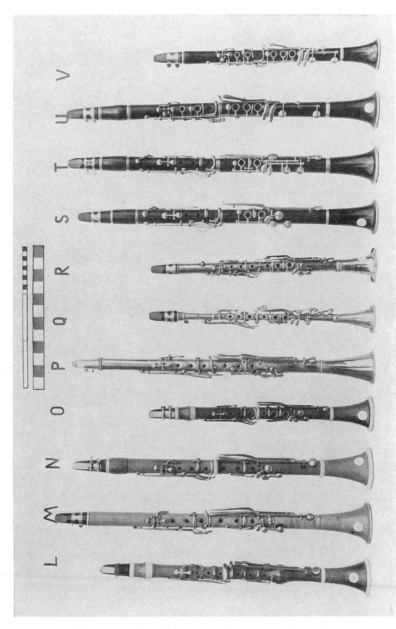

PLATE VIII

348

PLATE IX

349

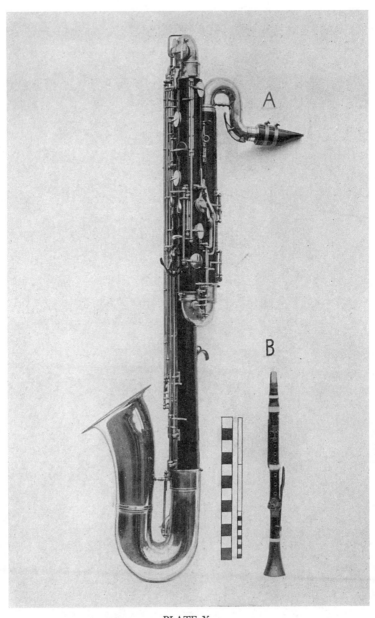

PLATE X

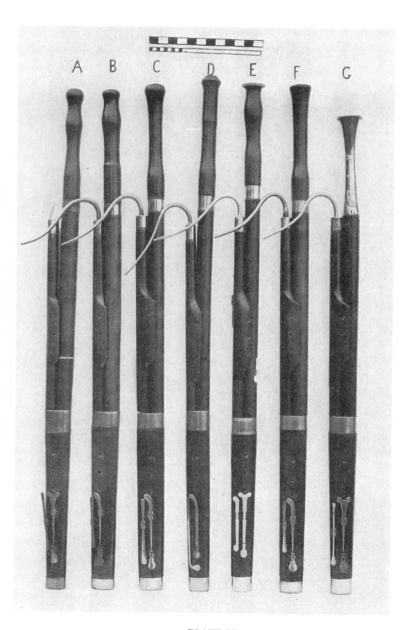

PLATE XI

351

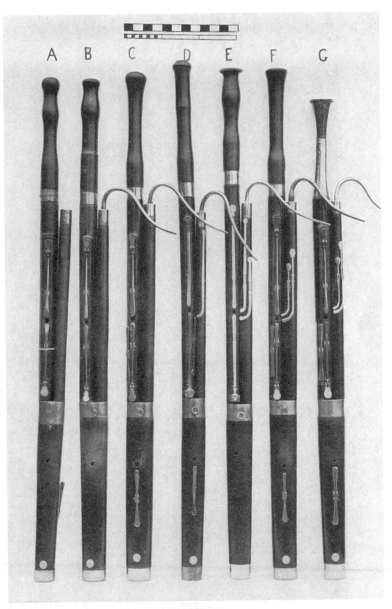

PLATE XII

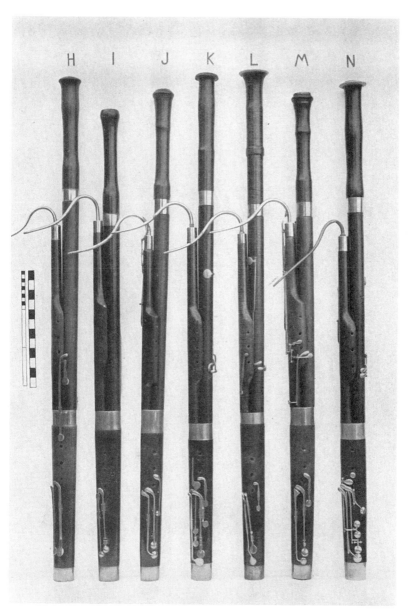

H I J K L M N

PLATE XIII

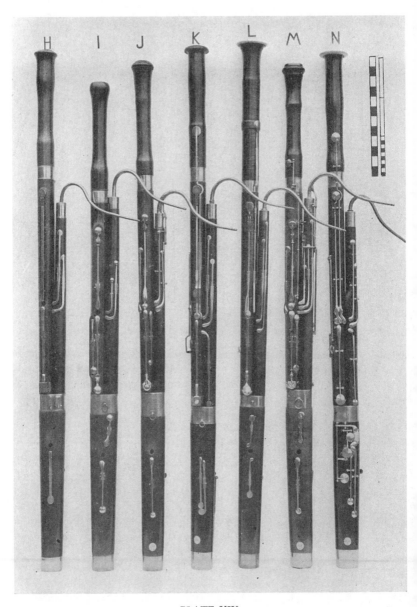

PLATE XIV

354

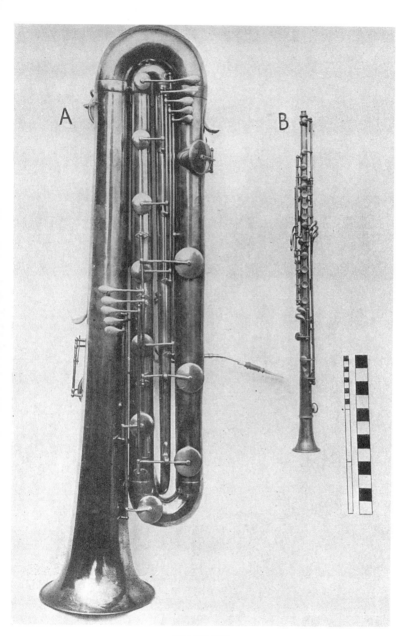

PLATE XV

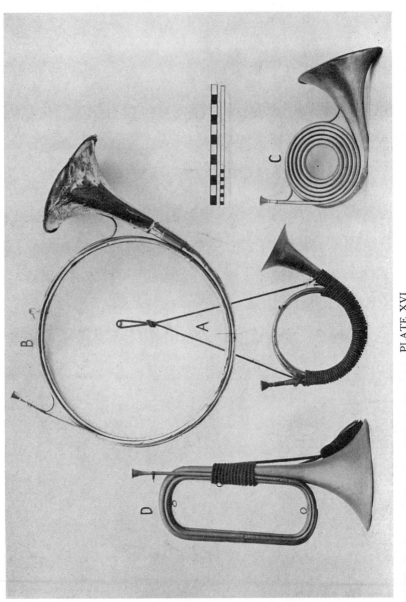

PLATE XVI

356

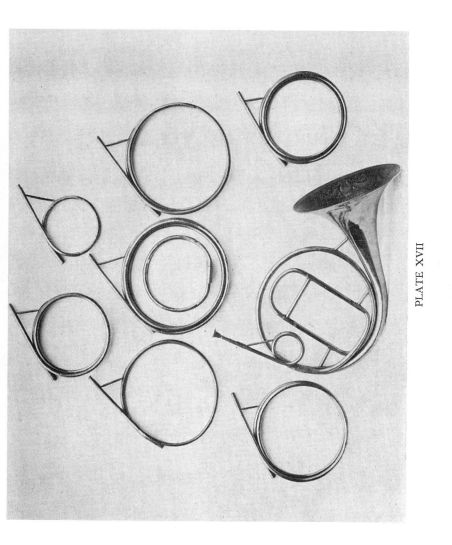

PLATE XVII

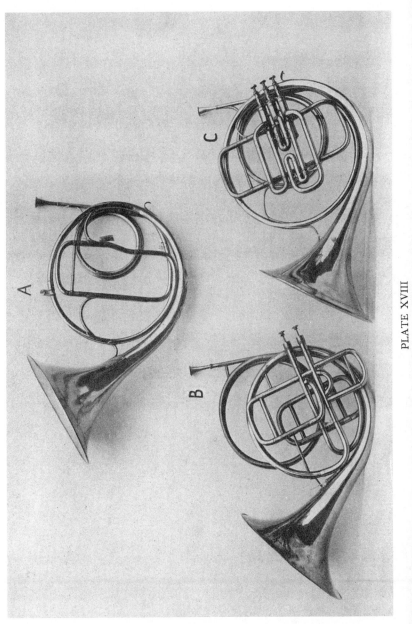

PLATE XVIII

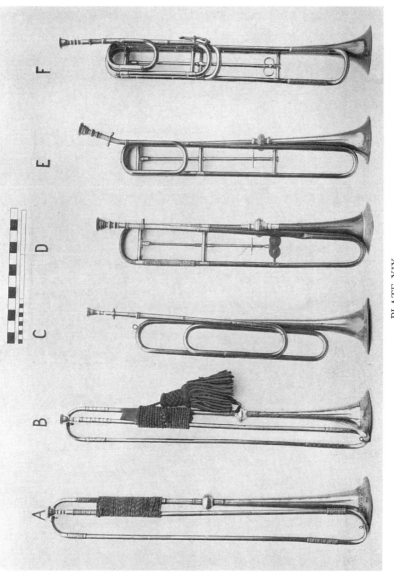

PLATE XIX

359

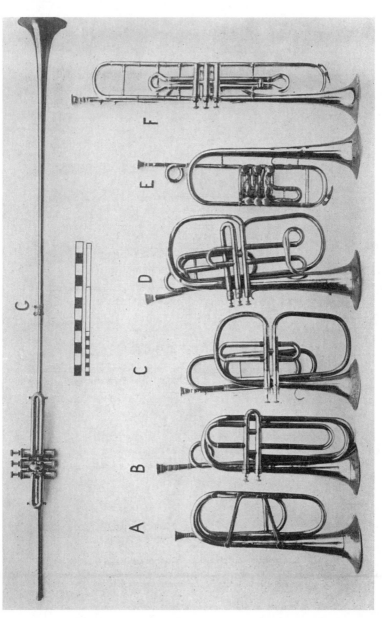

PLATE XX

360

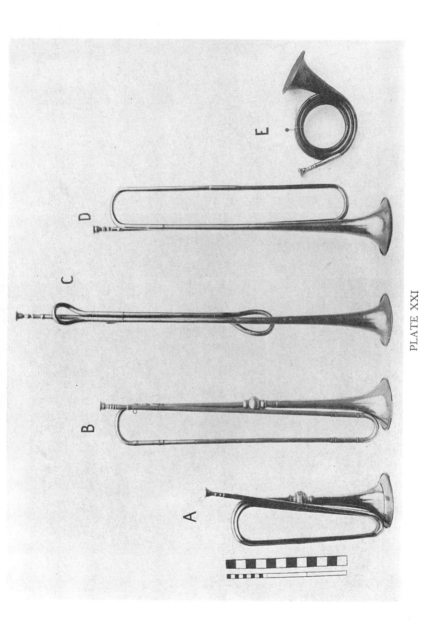

PLATE XXI

361

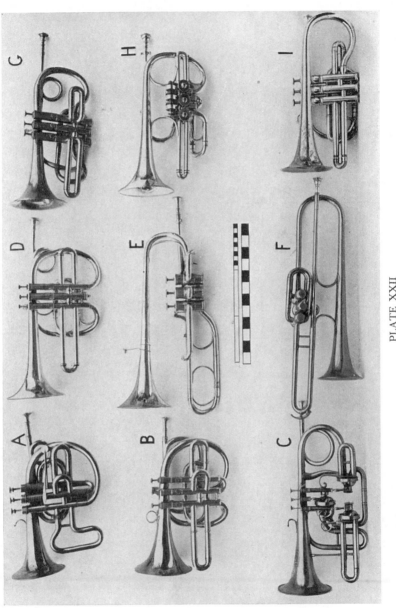

PLATE XXII

362

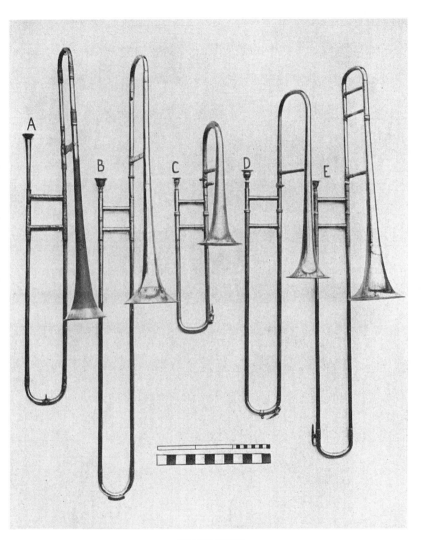

PLATE XXIII

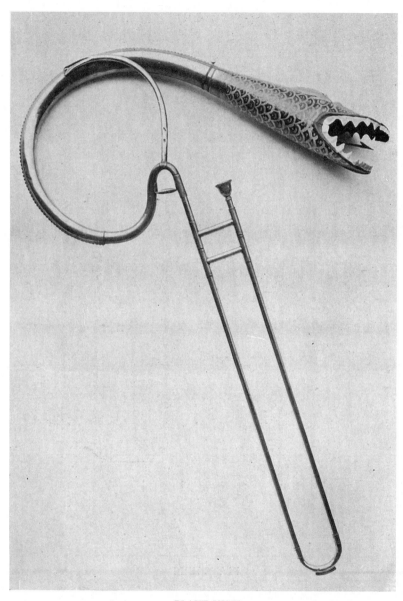

PLATE XXIV

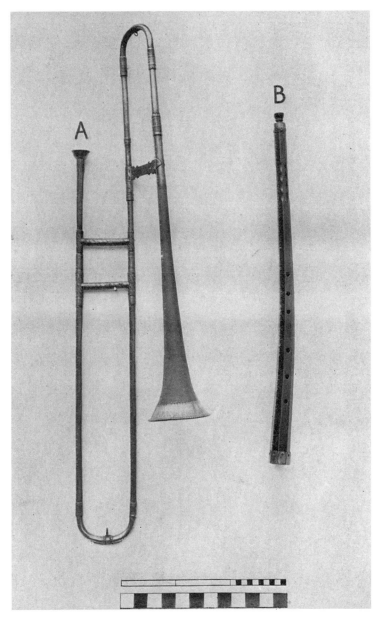

PLATE XXV

365

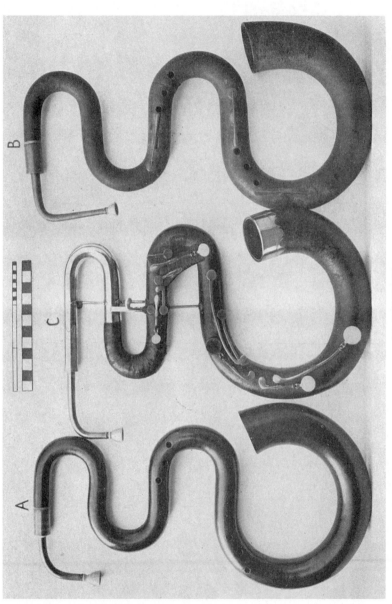

PLATE XXVI

366

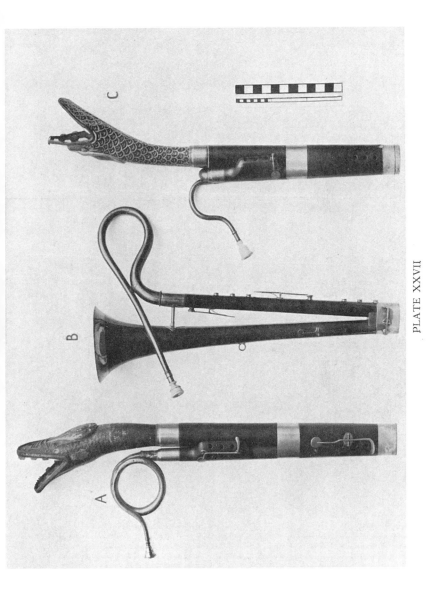

PLATE XXVII

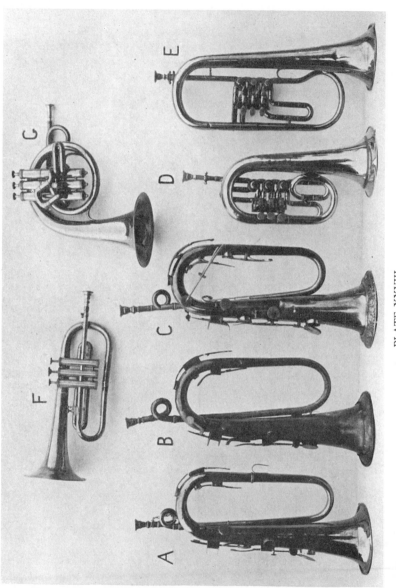

PLATE XXVIII

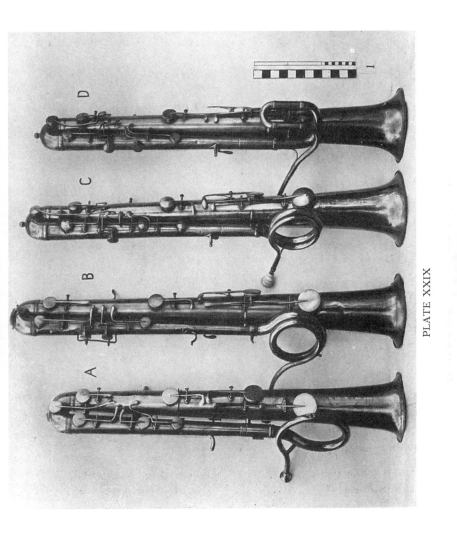

PLATE XXIX

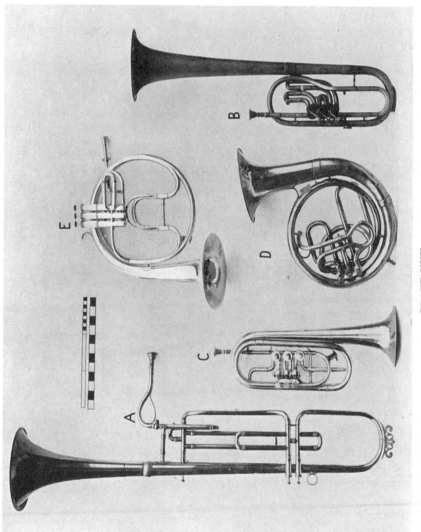

PLATE XXX

370

INDEX

A CATALOG OF SELECTED
DOVER BOOKS
IN ALL FIELDS OF INTEREST

A CATALOG OF SELECTED DOVER
BOOKS IN ALL FIELDS OF INTEREST

CONCERNING THE SPIRITUAL IN ART, Wassily Kandinsky. Pioneering work by father of abstract art. Thoughts on color theory, nature of art. Analysis of earlier masters. 12 illustrations. 80pp. of text. 5⅜ x 8½.   23411-8

ANIMALS: 1,419 Copyright-Free Illustrations of Mammals, Birds, Fish, Insects, etc., Jim Harter (ed.). Clear wood engravings present, in extremely lifelike poses, over 1,000 species of animals. One of the most extensive pictorial sourcebooks of its kind. Captions. Index. 284pp. 9 x 12.   23766-4

CELTIC ART: The Methods of Construction, George Bain. Simple geometric techniques for making Celtic interlacements, spirals, Kells-type initials, animals, humans, etc. Over 500 illustrations. 160pp. 9 x 12. (Available in U.S. only.)   22923-8

AN ATLAS OF ANATOMY FOR ARTISTS, Fritz Schider. Most thorough reference work on art anatomy in the world. Hundreds of illustrations, including selections from works by Vesalius, Leonardo, Goya, Ingres, Michelangelo, others. 593 illustrations. 192pp. 7⅛ x 10¼.   20241-0

CELTIC HAND STROKE-BY-STROKE (Irish Half-Uncial from "The Book of Kells"): An Arthur Baker Calligraphy Manual, Arthur Baker. Complete guide to creating each letter of the alphabet in distinctive Celtic manner. Covers hand position, strokes, pens, inks, paper, more. Illustrated. 48pp. 8¼ x 11.   24336-2

EASY ORIGAMI, John Montroll. Charming collection of 32 projects (hat, cup, pelican, piano, swan, many more) specially designed for the novice origami hobbyist. Clearly illustrated easy-to-follow instructions insure that even beginning papercrafters will achieve successful results. 48pp. 8¼ x 11.   27298-2

THE COMPLETE BOOK OF BIRDHOUSE CONSTRUCTION FOR WOODWORKERS, Scott D. Campbell. Detailed instructions, illustrations, tables. Also data on bird habitat and instinct patterns. Bibliography. 3 tables. 63 illustrations in 15 figures. 48pp. 5¼ x 8½.   24407-5

BLOOMINGDALE'S ILLUSTRATED 1886 CATALOG: Fashions, Dry Goods and Housewares, Bloomingdale Brothers. Famed merchants' extremely rare catalog depicting about 1,700 products: clothing, housewares, firearms, dry goods, jewelry, more. Invaluable for dating, identifying vintage items. Also, copyright-free graphics for artists, designers. Co-published with Henry Ford Museum & Greenfield Village. 160pp. 8¼ x 11.   25780-0

HISTORIC COSTUME IN PICTURES, Braun & Schneider. Over 1,450 costumed figures in clearly detailed engravings—from dawn of civilization to end of 19th century. Captions. Many folk costumes. 256pp. 8⅜ x 11¾.   23150-X

STICKLEY CRAFTSMAN FURNITURE CATALOGS, Gustav Stickley and L. & J. G. Stickley. Beautiful, functional furniture in two authentic catalogs from 1910. 594 illustrations, including 277 photos, show settles, rockers, armchairs, reclining chairs, bookcases, desks, tables. 183pp. 6½ x 9¼. 23838-5

AMERICAN LOCOMOTIVES IN HISTORIC PHOTOGRAPHS: 1858 to 1949, Ron Ziel (ed.). A rare collection of 126 meticulously detailed official photographs, called "builder portraits," of American locomotives that majestically chronicle the rise of steam locomotive power in America. Introduction. Detailed captions. xi+ 129pp. 9 x 12. 27393-8

AMERICA'S LIGHTHOUSES: An Illustrated History, Francis Ross Holland, Jr. Delightfully written, profusely illustrated fact-filled survey of over 200 American light-houses since 1716. History, anecdotes, technological advances, more. 240pp. 8 x 10¾. 25576-X

TOWARDS A NEW ARCHITECTURE, Le Corbusier. Pioneering manifesto by founder of "International School." Technical and aesthetic theories, views of industry, eco-nomics, relation of form to function, "mass-production split" and much more. Profusely illustrated. 320pp. 6⅛ x 9¼. (Available in U.S. only.) 25023-7

HOW THE OTHER HALF LIVES, Jacob Riis. Famous journalistic record, expos-ing poverty and degradation of New York slums around 1900, by major social reformer. 100 striking and influential photographs. 233pp. 10 x 7⅞. 22012-5

FRUIT KEY AND TWIG KEY TO TREES AND SHRUBS, William M. Harlow. One of the handiest and most widely used identification aids. Fruit key covers 120 deciduous and evergreen species; twig key 160 deciduous species. Easily used. Over 300 photographs. 126pp. 5⅜ x 8½. 20511-8

COMMON BIRD SONGS, Dr. Donald J. Borror. Songs of 60 most common U.S. birds: robins, sparrows, cardinals, bluejays, finches, more—arranged in order of increasing complexity. Up to 9 variations of songs of each species.
Cassette and manual 99911-4

ORCHIDS AS HOUSE PLANTS, Rebecca Tyson Northen. Grow cattleyas and many other kinds of orchids—in a window, in a case, or under artificial light. 63 illus-trations. 148pp. 5⅜ x 8½. 23261-1

MONSTER MAZES, Dave Phillips. Masterful mazes at four levels of difficulty. Avoid deadly perils and evil creatures to find magical treasures. Solutions for all 32 exciting illustrated puzzles. 48pp. 8¼ x 11. 26005-4

MOZART'S DON GIOVANNI (DOVER OPERA LIBRETTO SERIES), Wolfgang Amadeus Mozart. Introduced and translated by Ellen H. Bleiler. Standard Italian libretto, with complete English translation. Convenient and thoroughly portable—an ideal companion for reading along with a recording or the performance itself. Introduction. List of characters. Plot summary. 121pp. 5¼ x 8½. 24944-1

TECHNICAL MANUAL AND DICTIONARY OF CLASSICAL BALLET, Gail Grant. Defines, explains, comments on steps, movements, poses and concepts. 15-page pictorial section. Basic book for student, viewer. 127pp. 5⅜ x 8½. 21843-0

THE CLARINET AND CLARINET PLAYING, David Pino. Lively, comprehensive work features suggestions about technique, musicianship, and musical interpretation, as well as guidelines for teaching, making your own reeds, and preparing for public performance. Includes an intriguing look at clarinet history. "A godsend," *The Clarinet,* Journal of the International Clarinet Society. Appendixes. 7 illus. 320pp. 5⅜ x 8½. 40270-3

HOLLYWOOD GLAMOR PORTRAITS, John Kobal (ed.). 145 photos from 1926-49. Harlow, Gable, Bogart, Bacall; 94 stars in all. Full background on photographers, technical aspects. 160pp. 8⅜ x 11¼. 23352-9

THE ANNOTATED CASEY AT THE BAT: A Collection of Ballads about the Mighty Casey/Third, Revised Edition, Martin Gardner (ed.). Amusing sequels and parodies of one of America's best-loved poems: Casey's Revenge, Why Casey Whiffed, Casey's Sister at the Bat, others. 256pp. 5⅜ x 8½. 28598-7

THE RAVEN AND OTHER FAVORITE POEMS, Edgar Allan Poe. Over 40 of the author's most memorable poems: "The Bells," "Ulalume," "Israfel," "To Helen," "The Conqueror Worm," "Eldorado," "Annabel Lee," many more. Alphabetic lists of titles and first lines. 64pp. 5³⁄₁₆ x 8¼. 26685-0

PERSONAL MEMOIRS OF U. S. GRANT, Ulysses Simpson Grant. Intelligent, deeply moving firsthand account of Civil War campaigns, considered by many the finest military memoirs ever written. Includes letters, historic photographs, maps and more. 528pp. 6⅛ x 9¼. 28587-1

ANCIENT EGYPTIAN MATERIALS AND INDUSTRIES, A. Lucas and J. Harris. Fascinating, comprehensive, thoroughly documented text describes this ancient civilization's vast resources and the processes that incorporated them in daily life, including the use of animal products, building materials, cosmetics, perfumes and incense, fibers, glazed ware, glass and its manufacture, materials used in the mummification process, and much more. 544pp. 6¹⁄₈ x 9¹⁄₄. (Available in U.S. only.) 40446-3

RUSSIAN STORIES/RUSSKIE RASSKAZY: A Dual-Language Book, edited by Gleb Struve. Twelve tales by such masters as Chekhov, Tolstoy, Dostoevsky, Pushkin, others. Excellent word-for-word English translations on facing pages, plus teaching and study aids, Russian/English vocabulary, biographical/critical introductions, more. 416pp. 5⅜ x 8½. 26244-8

PHILADELPHIA THEN AND NOW: 60 Sites Photographed in the Past and Present, Kenneth Finkel and Susan Oyama. Rare photographs of City Hall, Logan Square, Independence Hall, Betsy Ross House, other landmarks juxtaposed with contemporary views. Captures changing face of historic city. Introduction. Captions. 128pp. 8¼ x 11. 25790-8

AIA ARCHITECTURAL GUIDE TO NASSAU AND SUFFOLK COUNTIES, LONG ISLAND, The American Institute of Architects, Long Island Chapter, and the Society for the Preservation of Long Island Antiquities. Comprehensive, well-researched and generously illustrated volume brings to life over three centuries of Long Island's great architectural heritage. More than 240 photographs with authoritative, extensively detailed captions. 176pp. 8¼ x 11. 26946-9

NORTH AMERICAN INDIAN LIFE: Customs and Traditions of 23 Tribes, Elsie Clews Parsons (ed.). 27 fictionalized essays by noted anthropologists examine religion, customs, government, additional facets of life among the Winnebago, Crow, Zuni, Eskimo, other tribes. 480pp. 6⅛ x 9¼. 27377-6

FRANK LLOYD WRIGHT'S DANA HOUSE, Donald Hoffmann. Pictorial essay of residential masterpiece with over 160 interior and exterior photos, plans, elevations, sketches and studies. 128pp. 9¼ x 10¾.   29120-0

THE MALE AND FEMALE FIGURE IN MOTION: 60 Classic Photographic Sequences, Eadweard Muybridge. 60 true-action photographs of men and women walking, running, climbing, bending, turning, etc., reproduced from rare 19th-century masterpiece. vi + 121pp. 9 x 12.   24745-7

1001 QUESTIONS ANSWERED ABOUT THE SEASHORE, N. J. Berrill and Jacquelyn Berrill. Queries answered about dolphins, sea snails, sponges, starfish, fishes, shore birds, many others. Covers appearance, breeding, growth, feeding, much more. 305pp. 5¼ x 8¼.   23366-9

ATTRACTING BIRDS TO YOUR YARD, William J. Weber. Easy-to-follow guide offers advice on how to attract the greatest diversity of birds: birdhouses, feeders, water and waterers, much more. 96pp. 5³⁄₁₆ x 8¼.   28927-3

MEDICINAL AND OTHER USES OF NORTH AMERICAN PLANTS: A Historical Survey with Special Reference to the Eastern Indian Tribes, Charlotte Erichsen-Brown. Chronological historical citations document 500 years of usage of plants, trees, shrubs native to eastern Canada, northeastern U.S. Also complete identifying information. 343 illustrations. 544pp. 6½ x 9¼.   25951-X

STORYBOOK MAZES, Dave Phillips. 23 stories and mazes on two-page spreads: Wizard of Oz, Treasure Island, Robin Hood, etc. Solutions. 64pp. 8¼ x 11. 23628-5

AMERICAN NEGRO SONGS: 230 Folk Songs and Spirituals, Religious and Secular, John W. Work. This authoritative study traces the African influences of songs sung and played by black Americans at work, in church, and as entertainment. The author discusses the lyric significance of such songs as "Swing Low, Sweet Chariot," "John Henry," and others and offers the words and music for 230 songs. Bibliography. Index of Song Titles. 272pp. 6½ x 9¼.   40271-1

MOVIE-STAR PORTRAITS OF THE FORTIES, John Kobal (ed.). 163 glamor, studio photos of 106 stars of the 1940s: Rita Hayworth, Ava Gardner, Marlon Brando, Clark Gable, many more. 176pp. 8⅜ x 11¼.   23546-7

BENCHLEY LOST AND FOUND, Robert Benchley. Finest humor from early 30s, about pet peeves, child psychologists, post office and others. Mostly unavailable elsewhere. 73 illustrations by Peter Arno and others. 183pp. 5⅜ x 8½.   22410-4

YEKL and THE IMPORTED BRIDEGROOM AND OTHER STORIES OF YIDDISH NEW YORK, Abraham Cahan. Film Hester Street based on *Yekl* (1896). Novel, other stories among first about Jewish immigrants on N.Y.'s East Side. 240pp. 5⅜ x 8½.   22427-9

SELECTED POEMS, Walt Whitman. Generous sampling from *Leaves of Grass*. Twenty-four poems include "I Hear America Singing," "Song of the Open Road," "I Sing the Body Electric," "When Lilacs Last in the Dooryard Bloom'd," "O Captain! My Captain!"–all reprinted from an authoritative edition. Lists of titles and first lines. 128pp. 5³⁄₁₆ x 8¼.   26878-0

THE BEST TALES OF HOFFMANN, E. T. A. Hoffmann. 10 of Hoffmann's most important stories: "Nutcracker and the King of Mice," "The Golden Flowerpot," etc. 458pp. 5⅜ x 8½. 21793-0

FROM FETISH TO GOD IN ANCIENT EGYPT, E. A. Wallis Budge. Rich detailed survey of Egyptian conception of "God" and gods, magic, cult of animals, Osiris, more. Also, superb English translations of hymns and legends. 240 illustrations. 545pp. 5⅜ x 8½. 25803-3

FRENCH STORIES/CONTES FRANÇAIS: A Dual-Language Book, Wallace Fowlie. Ten stories by French masters, Voltaire to Camus: "Micromegas" by Voltaire; "The Atheist's Mass" by Balzac; "Minuet" by de Maupassant; "The Guest" by Camus, six more. Excellent English translations on facing pages. Also French-English vocabulary list, exercises, more. 352pp. 5⅜ x 8½. 26443-2

CHICAGO AT THE TURN OF THE CENTURY IN PHOTOGRAPHS: 122 Historic Views from the Collections of the Chicago Historical Society, Larry A. Viskochil. Rare large-format prints offer detailed views of City Hall, State Street, the Loop, Hull House, Union Station, many other landmarks, circa 1904-1913. Introduction. Captions. Maps. 144pp. 9⅜ x 12¼. 24656-6

OLD BROOKLYN IN EARLY PHOTOGRAPHS, 1865-1929, William Lee Younger. Luna Park, Gravesend race track, construction of Grand Army Plaza, moving of Hotel Brighton, etc. 157 previously unpublished photographs. 165pp. 8⅞ x 11¾. 23587-4

THE MYTHS OF THE NORTH AMERICAN INDIANS, Lewis Spence. Rich anthology of the myths and legends of the Algonquins, Iroquois, Pawnees and Sioux, prefaced by an extensive historical and ethnological commentary. 36 illustrations. 480pp. 5⅜ x 8½. 25967-6

AN ENCYCLOPEDIA OF BATTLES: Accounts of Over 1,560 Battles from 1479 B.C. to the Present, David Eggenberger. Essential details of every major battle in recorded history from the first battle of Megiddo in 1479 B.C. to Grenada in 1984. List of Battle Maps. New Appendix covering the years 1967-1984. Index. 99 illustrations. 544pp. 6½ x 9¼. 24913-1

SAILING ALONE AROUND THE WORLD, Captain Joshua Slocum. First man to sail around the world, alone, in small boat. One of great feats of seamanship told in delightful manner. 67 illustrations. 294pp. 5⅜ x 8½. 20326-3

ANARCHISM AND OTHER ESSAYS, Emma Goldman. Powerful, penetrating, prophetic essays on direct action, role of minorities, prison reform, puritan hypocrisy, violence, etc. 271pp. 5⅜ x 8½. 22484-8

MYTHS OF THE HINDUS AND BUDDHISTS, Ananda K. Coomaraswamy and Sister Nivedita. Great stories of the epics; deeds of Krishna, Shiva, taken from puranas, Vedas, folk tales; etc. 32 illustrations. 400pp. 5⅜ x 8½. 21759-0

THE TRAUMA OF BIRTH, Otto Rank. Rank's controversial thesis that anxiety neurosis is caused by profound psychological trauma which occurs at birth. 256pp. 5⅜ x 8½. 27974-X

A THEOLOGICO-POLITICAL TREATISE, Benedict Spinoza. Also contains unfinished Political Treatise. Great classic on religious liberty, theory of government on common consent. R. Elwes translation. Total of 421pp. 5⅜ x 8½. 20249-6

MY BONDAGE AND MY FREEDOM, Frederick Douglass. Born a slave, Douglass became outspoken force in antislavery movement. The best of Douglass' autobiographies. Graphic description of slave life. 464pp. 5⅜ x 8½. 22457-0

FOLLOWING THE EQUATOR: A Journey Around the World, Mark Twain. Fascinating humorous account of 1897 voyage to Hawaii, Australia, India, New Zealand, etc. Ironic, bemused reports on peoples, customs, climate, flora and fauna, politics, much more. 197 illustrations. 720pp. 5⅜ x 8½. 26113-1

THE PEOPLE CALLED SHAKERS, Edward D. Andrews. Definitive study of Shakers: origins, beliefs, practices, dances, social organization, furniture and crafts, etc. 33 illustrations. 351pp. 5⅜ x 8½. 21081-2

THE MYTHS OF GREECE AND ROME, H. A. Guerber. A classic of mythology, generously illustrated, long prized for its simple, graphic, accurate retelling of the principal myths of Greece and Rome, and for its commentary on their origins and significance. With 64 illustrations by Michelangelo, Raphael, Titian, Rubens, Canova, Bernini and others. 480pp. 5⅜ x 8½. 27584-1

PSYCHOLOGY OF MUSIC, Carl E. Seashore. Classic work discusses music as a medium from psychological viewpoint. Clear treatment of physical acoustics, auditory apparatus, sound perception, development of musical skills, nature of musical feeling, host of other topics. 88 figures. 408pp. 5⅜ x 8½. 21851-1

THE PHILOSOPHY OF HISTORY, Georg W. Hegel. Great classic of Western thought develops concept that history is not chance but rational process, the evolution of freedom. 457pp. 5⅜ x 8½. 20112-0

THE BOOK OF TEA, Kakuzo Okakura. Minor classic of the Orient: entertaining, charming explanation, interpretation of traditional Japanese culture in terms of tea ceremony. 94pp. 5⅜ x 8½. 20070-1

LIFE IN ANCIENT EGYPT, Adolf Erman. Fullest, most thorough, detailed older account with much not in more recent books, domestic life, religion, magic, medicine, commerce, much more. Many illustrations reproduce tomb paintings, carvings, hieroglyphs, etc. 597pp. 5⅜ x 8½. 22632-8

SUNDIALS, Their Theory and Construction, Albert Waugh. Far and away the best, most thorough coverage of ideas, mathematics concerned, types, construction, adjusting anywhere. Simple, nontechnical treatment allows even children to build several of these dials. Over 100 illustrations. 230pp. 5⅜ x 8½. 22947-5

THEORETICAL HYDRODYNAMICS, L. M. Milne-Thomson. Classic exposition of the mathematical theory of fluid motion, applicable to both hydrodynamics and aerodynamics. Over 600 exercises. 768pp. 6⅛ x 9¼. 68970-0

SONGS OF EXPERIENCE: Facsimile Reproduction with 26 Plates in Full Color, William Blake. 26 full-color plates from a rare 1826 edition. Includes "The Tyger," "London," "Holy Thursday," and other poems. Printed text of poems. 48pp. 5¼ x 7. 24636-1

OLD-TIME VIGNETTES IN FULL COLOR, Carol Belanger Grafton (ed.). Over 390 charming, often sentimental illustrations, selected from archives of Victorian graphics—pretty women posing, children playing, food, flowers, kittens and puppies, smiling cherubs, birds and butterflies, much more. All copyright-free. 48pp. 9¼ x 12¼. 27269-9

PERSPECTIVE FOR ARTISTS, Rex Vicat Cole. Depth, perspective of sky and sea, shadows, much more, not usually covered. 391 diagrams, 81 reproductions of drawings and paintings. 279pp. 5⅜ x 8½.   22487-2

DRAWING THE LIVING FIGURE, Joseph Sheppard. Innovative approach to artistic anatomy focuses on specifics of surface anatomy, rather than muscles and bones. Over 170 drawings of live models in front, back and side views, and in widely varying poses. Accompanying diagrams. 177 illustrations. Introduction. Index. 144pp. 8⅜ x11¼.   26723-7

GOTHIC AND OLD ENGLISH ALPHABETS: 100 Complete Fonts, Dan X. Solo. Add power, elegance to posters, signs, other graphics with 100 stunning copyright-free alphabets: Blackstone, Dolbey, Germania, 97 more–including many lower-case, numerals, punctuation marks. 104pp. 8⅛ x 11.   24695-7

HOW TO DO BEADWORK, Mary White. Fundamental book on craft from simple projects to five-bead chains and woven works. 106 illustrations. 142pp. 5⅜ x 8.

20697-1

THE BOOK OF WOOD CARVING, Charles Marshall Sayers. Finest book for beginners discusses fundamentals and offers 34 designs. "Absolutely first rate . . . well thought out and well executed."–E. J. Tangerman. 118pp. 7¾ x 10⅝.   23654-4

ILLUSTRATED CATALOG OF CIVIL WAR MILITARY GOODS: Union Army Weapons, Insignia, Uniform Accessories, and Other Equipment, Schuyler, Hartley, and Graham. Rare, profusely illustrated 1846 catalog includes Union Army uniform and dress regulations, arms and ammunition, coats, insignia, flags, swords, rifles, etc. 226 illustrations. 160pp. 9 x 12.   24939-5

WOMEN'S FASHIONS OF THE EARLY 1900s: An Unabridged Republication of "New York Fashions, 1909," National Cloak & Suit Co. Rare catalog of mail-order fashions documents women's and children's clothing styles shortly after the turn of the century. Captions offer full descriptions, prices. Invaluable resource for fashion, costume historians. Approximately 725 illustrations. 128pp. 8⅜ x 11¼.   27276-1

THE 1912 AND 1915 GUSTAV STICKLEY FURNITURE CATALOGS, Gustav Stickley. With over 200 detailed illustrations and descriptions, these two catalogs are essential reading and reference materials and identification guides for Stickley furniture. Captions cite materials, dimensions and prices. 112pp. 6½ x 9¼.   26676-1

EARLY AMERICAN LOCOMOTIVES, John H. White, Jr. Finest locomotive engravings from early 19th century: historical (1804–74), main-line (after 1870), special, foreign, etc. 147 plates. 142pp. 11⅜ x 8¼.   22772-3

THE TALL SHIPS OF TODAY IN PHOTOGRAPHS, Frank O. Braynard. Lavishly illustrated tribute to nearly 100 majestic contemporary sailing vessels: Amerigo Vespucci, Clearwater, Constitution, Eagle, Mayflower, Sea Cloud, Victory, many more. Authoritative captions provide statistics, background on each ship. 190 black-and-white photographs and illustrations. Introduction. 128pp. 8⅞ x 11¾.

27163-3

LITTLE BOOK OF EARLY AMERICAN CRAFTS AND TRADES, Peter Stockham (ed.). 1807 children's book explains crafts and trades: baker, hatter, cooper, potter, and many others. 23 copperplate illustrations. 140pp. 4⅝ x 6. 23336-7

VICTORIAN FASHIONS AND COSTUMES FROM HARPER'S BAZAR, 1867–1898, Stella Blum (ed.). Day costumes, evening wear, sports clothes, shoes, hats, other accessories in over 1,000 detailed engravings. 320pp. 9⅜ x 12¼. 22990-4

GUSTAV STICKLEY, THE CRAFTSMAN, Mary Ann Smith. Superb study surveys broad scope of Stickley's achievement, especially in architecture. Design philosophy, rise and fall of the Craftsman empire, descriptions and floor plans for many Craftsman houses, more. 86 black-and-white halftones. 31 line illustrations. Introduction 208pp. 6½ x 9¼. 27210-9

THE LONG ISLAND RAIL ROAD IN EARLY PHOTOGRAPHS, Ron Ziel. Over 220 rare photos, informative text document origin (1844) and development of rail service on Long Island. Vintage views of early trains, locomotives, stations, passengers, crews, much more. Captions. 8⅞ x 11¾. 26301-0

VOYAGE OF THE LIBERDADE, Joshua Slocum. Great 19th-century mariner's thrilling, first-hand account of the wreck of his ship off South America, the 35-foot boat he built from the wreckage, and its remarkable voyage home. 128pp. 5⅜ x 8½.
40022-0

TEN BOOKS ON ARCHITECTURE, Vitruvius. The most important book ever written on architecture. Early Roman aesthetics, technology, classical orders, site selection, all other aspects. Morgan translation. 331pp. 5⅜ x 8½. 20645-9

THE HUMAN FIGURE IN MOTION, Eadweard Muybridge. More than 4,500 stopped-action photos, in action series, showing undraped men, women, children jumping, lying down, throwing, sitting, wrestling, carrying, etc. 390pp. 7⅞ x 10⅝.
20204-6 Clothbd.

TREES OF THE EASTERN AND CENTRAL UNITED STATES AND CANADA, William M. Harlow. Best one-volume guide to 140 trees. Full descriptions, woodlore, range, etc. Over 600 illustrations. Handy size. 288pp. 4½ x 6⅜. 20395-6

SONGS OF WESTERN BIRDS, Dr. Donald J. Borror. Complete song and call repertoire of 60 western species, including flycatchers, juncoes, cactus wrens, many more–includes fully illustrated booklet. Cassette and manual 99913-0

GROWING AND USING HERBS AND SPICES, Milo Miloradovich. Versatile handbook provides all the information needed for cultivation and use of all the herbs and spices available in North America. 4 illustrations. Index. Glossary. 236pp. 5⅜ x 8½.
25058-X

BIG BOOK OF MAZES AND LABYRINTHS, Walter Shepherd. 50 mazes and labyrinths in all–classical, solid, ripple, and more–in one great volume. Perfect inexpensive puzzler for clever youngsters. Full solutions. 112pp. 8⅛ x 11. 22951-3

PIANO TUNING, J. Cree Fischer. Clearest, best book for beginner, amateur. Simple repairs, raising dropped notes, tuning by easy method of flattened fifths. No previous skills needed. 4 illustrations. 201pp. 5$\frac{3}{8}$ x 8$\frac{1}{2}$. 23267-0

HINTS TO SINGERS, Lillian Nordica. Selecting the right teacher, developing confidence, overcoming stage fright, and many other important skills receive thoughtful discussion in this indispensible guide, written by a world-famous diva of four decades' experience. 96pp. 5$\frac{3}{8}$ x 8$\frac{1}{2}$. 40094-8

THE COMPLETE NONSENSE OF EDWARD LEAR, Edward Lear. All nonsense limericks, zany alphabets, Owl and Pussycat, songs, nonsense botany, etc., illustrated by Lear. Total of 320pp. 5$\frac{3}{8}$ x 8$\frac{1}{2}$. (Available in U.S. only.) 20167-8

VICTORIAN PARLOUR POETRY: An Annotated Anthology, Michael R. Turner. 117 gems by Longfellow, Tennyson, Browning, many lesser-known poets. "The Village Blacksmith," "Curfew Must Not Ring Tonight," "Only a Baby Small," dozens more, often difficult to find elsewhere. Index of poets, titles, first lines. xxiii + 325pp. 5$\frac{3}{8}$ x 8$\frac{1}{4}$. 27044-0

DUBLINERS, James Joyce. Fifteen stories offer vivid, tightly focused observations of the lives of Dublin's poorer classes. At least one, "The Dead," is considered a masterpiece. Reprinted complete and unabridged from standard edition. 160pp. 5$\frac{3}{16}$ x 8$\frac{1}{4}$. 26870-5

GREAT WEIRD TALES: 14 Stories by Lovecraft, Blackwood, Machen and Others, S. T. Joshi (ed.). 14 spellbinding tales, including "The Sin Eater," by Fiona McLeod, "The Eye Above the Mantel," by Frank Belknap Long, as well as renowned works by R. H. Barlow, Lord Dunsany, Arthur Machen, W. C. Morrow and eight other masters of the genre. 256pp. 5$\frac{3}{8}$ x 8$\frac{1}{2}$. (Available in U.S. only.) 40436-6

THE BOOK OF THE SACRED MAGIC OF ABRAMELIN THE MAGE, translated by S. MacGregor Mathers. Medieval manuscript of ceremonial magic. Basic document in Aleister Crowley, Golden Dawn groups. 268pp. 5$\frac{3}{8}$ x 8$\frac{1}{2}$. 23211-5

NEW RUSSIAN-ENGLISH AND ENGLISH-RUSSIAN DICTIONARY, M. A. O'Brien. This is a remarkably handy Russian dictionary, containing a surprising amount of information, including over 70,000 entries. 366pp. 4$\frac{1}{2}$ x 6$\frac{1}{8}$. 20208-9

HISTORIC HOMES OF THE AMERICAN PRESIDENTS, Second, Revised Edition, Irvin Haas. A traveler's guide to American Presidential homes, most open to the public, depicting and describing homes occupied by every American President from George Washington to George Bush. With visiting hours, admission charges, travel routes. 175 photographs. Index. 160pp. 8$\frac{1}{4}$ x 11. 26751-2

NEW YORK IN THE FORTIES, Andreas Feininger. 162 brilliant photographs by the well-known photographer, formerly with *Life* magazine. Commuters, shoppers, Times Square at night, much else from city at its peak. Captions by John von Hartz. 181pp. 9$\frac{1}{4}$ x 10$\frac{3}{4}$. 23585-8

INDIAN SIGN LANGUAGE, William Tomkins. Over 525 signs developed by Sioux and other tribes. Written instructions and diagrams. Also 290 pictographs. 111pp. 6$\frac{1}{8}$ x 9$\frac{1}{4}$. 22029-X

ANATOMY: A Complete Guide for Artists, Joseph Sheppard. A master of figure drawing shows artists how to render human anatomy convincingly. Over 460 illustrations. 224pp. 8⅜ x 11¼. 27279-6

MEDIEVAL CALLIGRAPHY: Its History and Technique, Marc Drogin. Spirited history, comprehensive instruction manual covers 13 styles (ca. 4th century through 15th). Excellent photographs; directions for duplicating medieval techniques with modern tools. 224pp. 8⅜ x 11¼. 26142-5

DRIED FLOWERS: How to Prepare Them, Sarah Whitlock and Martha Rankin. Complete instructions on how to use silica gel, meal and borax, perlite aggregate, sand and borax, glycerine and water to create attractive permanent flower arrangements. 12 illustrations. 32pp. 5⅜ x 8½. 21802-3

EASY-TO-MAKE BIRD FEEDERS FOR WOODWORKERS, Scott D. Campbell. Detailed, simple-to-use guide for designing, constructing, caring for and using feeders. Text, illustrations for 12 classic and contemporary designs. 96pp. 5⅜ x 8½. 25847-5

SCOTTISH WONDER TALES FROM MYTH AND LEGEND, Donald A. Mackenzie. 16 lively tales tell of giants rumbling down mountainsides, of a magic wand that turns stone pillars into warriors, of gods and goddesses, evil hags, powerful forces and more. 240pp. 5⅜ x 8½. 29677-6

THE HISTORY OF UNDERCLOTHES, C. Willett Cunnington and Phyllis Cunnington. Fascinating, well-documented survey covering six centuries of English undergarments, enhanced with over 100 illustrations: 12th-century laced-up bodice, footed long drawers (1795), 19th-century bustles, 19th-century corsets for men, Victorian "bust improvers," much more. 272pp. 5⅝ x 8¼. 27124-2

ARTS AND CRAFTS FURNITURE: The Complete Brooks Catalog of 1912, Brooks Manufacturing Co. Photos and detailed descriptions of more than 150 now very collectible furniture designs from the Arts and Crafts movement depict davenports, settees, buffets, desks, tables, chairs, bedsteads, dressers and more, all built of solid, quarter-sawed oak. Invaluable for students and enthusiasts of antiques, Americana and the decorative arts. 80pp. 6½ x 9¼. 27471-3

WILBUR AND ORVILLE: A Biography of the Wright Brothers, Fred Howard. Definitive, crisply written study tells the full story of the brothers' lives and work. A vividly written biography, unparalleled in scope and color, that also captures the spirit of an extraordinary era. 560pp. 6⅛ x 9¼. 40297-5

THE ARTS OF THE SAILOR: Knotting, Splicing and Ropework, Hervey Garrett Smith. Indispensable shipboard reference covers tools, basic knots and useful hitches; handsewing and canvas work, more. Over 100 illustrations. Delightful reading for sea lovers. 256pp. 5⅜ x 8½. 26440-8

FRANK LLOYD WRIGHT'S FALLINGWATER: The House and Its History, Second, Revised Edition, Donald Hoffmann. A total revision–both in text and illustrations–of the standard document on Fallingwater, the boldest, most personal architectural statement of Wright's mature years, updated with valuable new material from the recently opened Frank Lloyd Wright Archives. "Fascinating"–*The New York Times*. 116 illustrations. 128pp. 9¼ x 10¾. 27430-6

PHOTOGRAPHIC SKETCHBOOK OF THE CIVIL WAR, Alexander Gardner. 100 photos taken on field during the Civil War. Famous shots of Manassas Harper's Ferry, Lincoln, Richmond, slave pens, etc. 244pp. 10⅝ x 8¼. 22731-6

FIVE ACRES AND INDEPENDENCE, Maurice G. Kains. Great back-to-the-land classic explains basics of self-sufficient farming. The one book to get. 95 illustrations. 397pp. 5⅜ x 8½. 20974-1

SONGS OF EASTERN BIRDS, Dr. Donald J. Borror. Songs and calls of 60 species most common to eastern U.S.: warblers, woodpeckers, flycatchers, thrushes, larks, many more in high-quality recording. Cassette and manual 99912-2

A MODERN HERBAL, Margaret Grieve. Much the fullest, most exact, most useful compilation of herbal material. Gigantic alphabetical encyclopedia, from aconite to zedoary, gives botanical information, medical properties, folklore, economic uses, much else. Indispensable to serious reader. 161 illustrations. 888pp. 6½ x 9¼. 2-vol. set. (Available in U.S. only.) Vol. I: 22798-7
Vol. II: 22799-5

HIDDEN TREASURE MAZE BOOK, Dave Phillips. Solve 34 challenging mazes accompanied by heroic tales of adventure. Evil dragons, people-eating plants, blood-thirsty giants, many more dangerous adversaries lurk at every twist and turn. 34 mazes, stories, solutions. 48pp. 8¼ x 11. 24566-7

LETTERS OF W. A. MOZART, Wolfgang A. Mozart. Remarkable letters show bawdy wit, humor, imagination, musical insights, contemporary musical world; includes some letters from Leopold Mozart. 276pp. 5⅜ x 8½. 22859-2

BASIC PRINCIPLES OF CLASSICAL BALLET, Agrippina Vaganova. Great Russian theoretician, teacher explains methods for teaching classical ballet. 118 illustrations. 175pp. 5⅜ x 8½. 22036-2

THE JUMPING FROG, Mark Twain. Revenge edition. The original story of The Celebrated Jumping Frog of Calaveras County, a hapless French translation, and Twain's hilarious "retranslation" from the French. 12 illustrations. 66pp. 5⅜ x 8½. 22686-7

BEST REMEMBERED POEMS, Martin Gardner (ed.). The 126 poems in this superb collection of 19th- and 20th-century British and American verse range from Shelley's "To a Skylark" to the impassioned "Renascence" of Edna St. Vincent Millay and to Edward Lear's whimsical "The Owl and the Pussycat." 224pp. 5⅜ x 8½. 27165-X

COMPLETE SONNETS, William Shakespeare. Over 150 exquisite poems deal with love, friendship, the tyranny of time, beauty's evanescence, death and other themes in language of remarkable power, precision and beauty. Glossary of archaic terms. 80pp. 5$\frac{3}{16}$ x 8¼. 26686-9

THE BATTLES THAT CHANGED HISTORY, Fletcher Pratt. Eminent historian profiles 16 crucial conflicts, ancient to modern, that changed the course of civilization. 352pp. 5⅜ x 8½. 41129-X

THE WIT AND HUMOR OF OSCAR WILDE, Alvin Redman (ed.). More than 1,000 ripostes, paradoxes, wisecracks: Work is the curse of the drinking classes; I can resist everything except temptation; etc. 258pp. 5⅜ x 8½.   20602-5

SHAKESPEARE LEXICON AND QUOTATION DICTIONARY, Alexander Schmidt. Full definitions, locations, shades of meaning in every word in plays and poems. More than 50,000 exact quotations. 1,485pp. 6½ x 9¼. 2-vol. set.
Vol. 1: 22726-X
Vol. 2: 22727-8

SELECTED POEMS, Emily Dickinson. Over 100 best-known, best-loved poems by one of America's foremost poets, reprinted from authoritative early editions. No comparable edition at this price. Index of first lines. 64pp. 5³⁄₁₆ x 8¼.   26466-1

THE INSIDIOUS DR. FU-MANCHU, Sax Rohmer. The first of the popular mystery series introduces a pair of English detectives to their archnemesis, the diabolical Dr. Fu-Manchu. Flavorful atmosphere, fast-paced action, and colorful characters enliven this classic of the genre. 208pp. 5³⁄₁₆ x 8¼.   29898-1

THE MALLEUS MALEFICARUM OF KRAMER AND SPRENGER, translated by Montague Summers. Full text of most important witchhunter's "bible," used by both Catholics and Protestants. 278pp. 6⅝ x 10.   22802-9

SPANISH STORIES/CUENTOS ESPAÑOLES: A Dual-Language Book, Angel Flores (ed.). Unique format offers 13 great stories in Spanish by Cervantes, Borges, others. Faithful English translations on facing pages. 352pp. 5⅜ x 8½.   25399-6

GARDEN CITY, LONG ISLAND, IN EARLY PHOTOGRAPHS, 1869–1919, Mildred H. Smith. Handsome treasury of 118 vintage pictures, accompanied by carefully researched captions, document the Garden City Hotel fire (1899), the Vanderbilt Cup Race (1908), the first airmail flight departing from the Nassau Boulevard Aerodrome (1911), and much more. 96pp. 8⅞ x 11¾.   40669-5

OLD QUEENS, N.Y., IN EARLY PHOTOGRAPHS, Vincent F. Seyfried and William Asadorian. Over 160 rare photographs of Maspeth, Jamaica, Jackson Heights, and other areas. Vintage views of DeWitt Clinton mansion, 1939 World's Fair and more. Captions. 192pp. 8⅞ x 11.   26358-4

CAPTURED BY THE INDIANS: 15 Firsthand Accounts, 1750-1870, Frederick Drimmer. Astounding true historical accounts of grisly torture, bloody conflicts, relentless pursuits, miraculous escapes and more, by people who lived to tell the tale. 384pp. 5⅜ x 8½.   24901-8

THE WORLD'S GREAT SPEECHES (Fourth Enlarged Edition), Lewis Copeland, Lawrence W. Lamm, and Stephen J. McKenna. Nearly 300 speeches provide public speakers with a wealth of updated quotes and inspiration–from Pericles' funeral oration and William Jennings Bryan's "Cross of Gold Speech" to Malcolm X's powerful words on the Black Revolution and Earl of Spenser's tribute to his sister, Diana, Princess of Wales. 944pp. 5⅜ x 8⅜.   40903-1

THE BOOK OF THE SWORD, Sir Richard F. Burton. Great Victorian scholar/adventurer's eloquent, erudite history of the "queen of weapons"–from prehistory to early Roman Empire. Evolution and development of early swords, variations (sabre, broadsword, cutlass, scimitar, etc.), much more. 336pp. 6⅛ x 9¼.
25434-8

CATALOG OF DOVER BOOKS

AUTOBIOGRAPHY: The Story of My Experiments with Truth, Mohandas K. Gandhi. Boyhood, legal studies, purification, the growth of the Satyagraha (nonviolent protest) movement. Critical, inspiring work of the man responsible for the freedom of India. 480pp. 5⅜ x 8½. (Available in U.S. only.) 24593-4

CELTIC MYTHS AND LEGENDS, T. W. Rolleston. Masterful retelling of Irish and Welsh stories and tales. Cuchulain, King Arthur, Deirdre, the Grail, many more. First paperback edition. 58 full-page illustrations. 512pp. 5⅜ x 8½. 26507-2

THE PRINCIPLES OF PSYCHOLOGY, William James. Famous long course complete, unabridged. Stream of thought, time perception, memory, experimental methods; great work decades ahead of its time. 94 figures. 1,391pp. 5⅜ x 8½. 2-vol. set.
Vol. I: 20381-6   Vol. II: 20382-4

THE WORLD AS WILL AND REPRESENTATION, Arthur Schopenhauer. Definitive English translation of Schopenhauer's life work, correcting more than 1,000 errors, omissions in earlier translations. Translated by E. F. J. Payne. Total of 1,269pp. 5⅜ x 8½. 2-vol. set.
Vol. 1: 21761-2   Vol. 2: 21762-0

MAGIC AND MYSTERY IN TIBET, Madame Alexandra David-Neel. Experiences among lamas, magicians, sages, sorcerers, Bonpa wizards. A true psychic discovery. 32 illustrations. 321pp. 5⅜ x 8½. (Available in U.S. only.) 22682-4

THE EGYPTIAN BOOK OF THE DEAD, E. A. Wallis Budge. Complete reproduction of Ani's papyrus, finest ever found. Full hieroglyphic text, interlinear transliteration, word-for-word translation, smooth translation. 533pp. 6½ x 9¼. 21866-X

MATHEMATICS FOR THE NONMATHEMATICIAN, Morris Kline. Detailed, college-level treatment of mathematics in cultural and historical context, with numerous exercises. Recommended Reading Lists. Tables. Numerous figures. 641pp. 5⅜ x 8½. 24823-2

PROBABILISTIC METHODS IN THE THEORY OF STRUCTURES, Isaac Elishakoff. Well-written introduction covers the elements of the theory of probability from two or more random variables, the reliability of such multivariable structures, the theory of random function, Monte Carlo methods of treating problems incapable of exact solution, and more. Examples. 502pp. 5⅜ x 8½. 40691-1

THE RIME OF THE ANCIENT MARINER, Gustave Doré, S. T. Coleridge. Doré's finest work; 34 plates capture moods, subtleties of poem. Flawless full-size reproductions printed on facing pages with authoritative text of poem. "Beautiful. Simply beautiful."–Publisher's Weekly. 77pp. 9¼ x 12. 22305-1

NORTH AMERICAN INDIAN DESIGNS FOR ARTISTS AND CRAFTSPEOPLE, Eva Wilson. Over 360 authentic copyright-free designs adapted from Navajo blankets, Hopi pottery, Sioux buffalo hides, more. Geometrics, symbolic figures, plant and animal motifs, etc. 128pp. 8⅜ x 11. (Not for sale in the United Kingdom.) 25341-4

SCULPTURE: Principles and Practice, Louis Slobodkin. Step-by-step approach to clay, plaster, metals, stone; classical and modern. 253 drawings, photos. 255pp. 8⅛ x 11. 22960-2

THE INFLUENCE OF SEA POWER UPON HISTORY, 1660–1783, A. T. Mahan. Influential classic of naval history and tactics still used as text in war colleges. First paperback edition. 4 maps. 24 battle plans. 640pp. 5⅜ x 8½. 25509-3

CATALOG OF DOVER BOOKS

THE STORY OF THE TITANIC AS TOLD BY ITS SURVIVORS, Jack Winocour (ed.). What it was really like. Panic, despair, shocking inefficiency, and a little heroism. More thrilling than any fictional account. 26 illustrations. 320pp. 5⅜ x 8½.
20610-6

FAIRY AND FOLK TALES OF THE IRISH PEASANTRY, William Butler Yeats (ed.). Treasury of 64 tales from the twilight world of Celtic myth and legend: "The Soul Cages," "The Kildare Pooka," "King O'Toole and his Goose," many more. Introduction and Notes by W. B. Yeats. 352pp. 5⅜ x 8½.
26941-8

BUDDHIST MAHAYANA TEXTS, E. B. Cowell and others (eds.). Superb, accurate translations of basic documents in Mahayana Buddhism, highly important in history of religions. The Buddha-karita of Asvaghosha, Larger Sukhavativyuha, more. 448pp. 5⅜ x 8½.
25552-2

ONE TWO THREE . . . INFINITY: Facts and Speculations of Science, George Gamow. Great physicist's fascinating, readable overview of contemporary science: number theory, relativity, fourth dimension, entropy, genes, atomic structure, much more. 128 illustrations. Index. 352pp. 5⅜ x 8½.
25664-2

EXPERIMENTATION AND MEASUREMENT, W. J. Youden. Introductory manual explains laws of measurement in simple terms and offers tips for achieving accuracy and minimizing errors. Mathematics of measurement, use of instruments, experimenting with machines. 1994 edition. Foreword. Preface. Introduction. Epilogue. Selected Readings. Glossary. Index. Tables and figures. 128pp. 5⅜ x 8½.
40451-X

DALÍ ON MODERN ART: The Cuckolds of Antiquated Modern Art, Salvador Dalí. Influential painter skewers modern art and its practitioners. Outrageous evaluations of Picasso, Cézanne, Turner, more. 15 renderings of paintings discussed. 44 calligraphic decorations by Dalí. 96pp. 5⅜ x 8½. (Available in U.S. only.)
29220-7

ANTIQUE PLAYING CARDS: A Pictorial History, Henry René D'Allemagne. Over 900 elaborate, decorative images from rare playing cards (14th–20th centuries): Bacchus, death, dancing dogs, hunting scenes, royal coats of arms, players cheating, much more. 96pp. 9¼ x 12¼.
29265-7

MAKING FURNITURE MASTERPIECES: 30 Projects with Measured Drawings, Franklin H. Gottshall. Step-by-step instructions, illustrations for constructing handsome, useful pieces, among them a Sheraton desk, Chippendale chair, Spanish desk, Queen Anne table and a William and Mary dressing mirror. 224pp. 8⅛ x 11¼.
29338-6

THE FOSSIL BOOK: A Record of Prehistoric Life, Patricia V. Rich et al. Profusely illustrated definitive guide covers everything from single-celled organisms and dinosaurs to birds and mammals and the interplay between climate and man. Over 1,500 illustrations. 760pp. 7½ x 10⅛.
29371-8